A Happy Life

Non nobis solum sed toti mundo nati

by Peter Gripton

A Happy Life

First Edition 2008 by Las Atalayas Publishing

Author and Editor Peter Gripton
Copyright © Peter Gripton 2008

ISBN 978-0-9556753-7-9

Design and Typesetting by kenandglen.com

Dedication

I dedicate this book to my Mum, who started the ball rolling – and in particular to my wife Joyce, who has put up with my incessant tapping at the keyboard for so long!

Pete Gripton, March 2008

'Yours truly'

Contents

The Gripton boys

Introduction

The original inspiration for this family history came sometime between 1983 and 1985, but in fact it shouldn't have been me writing it at all! My Mum, Ruth, had recently returned to England after an all too short period of living in Perth, out in Western Australia, 'the most isolated capital city in the world'! She had gone to live there with her second husband, Jack Whitley, but Jack died only a few months later so Mum 'came home'. Returning to her Liverpool roots, she bought a splendid upstairs flat in Cambridge Road, Crosby, with both of her daughters, my sisters Elisabeth Susan and Pamela Helen, then living nearby. On one occasion, my wife Joyce, along with her sister Eileen, went up north to visit Mum, who regaled them with vivid and interesting stories about her childhood and early days.

Both Eileen and Joyce said then that she ought to write down her memories, in order to pass them on some day. Mum never did, which was a bit sad, and in 1985 returned to Australia as Mrs Joseph 'Bill' Walker. Over the next few years, Mum and Bill made quite a number of visits to 'Blighty', once hiring a variety of accommodation in the Cotswolds in 1990. In 1994 (and again in 1997) they exchanged houses with a couple that hailed from the pleasant town of Nailsea, near the Bristol Channel coast in Somerset. It was here, during one of our weekend visits, that Joyce and I encouraged Mum to at least start putting together a 'family tree' of her side of the family, which naturally has been a great help in starting me off on this history.

Sometime early in 2002, I had been working away for quite some time on the research and writing of two separate books. One was an attempt to detail the history of my local Parish, Greatham in Hampshire; the second detailed the history of the Army Apprentices' School (later College) at Arborfield, Berkshire, where I had been an apprentice tradesman between 1956 and 1959. Having been 'bitten' by the writing bug, I decided to start putting my own personal story down on paper – well, computer to start with! I have since been greatly assisted, with the aid of the modern e-mail system and the international post, by Mum, sisters Sue and Pam, and my brother Geoff. They have read and digested what I had written, coming up with many corrections, reminders and ideas, with which I have been able to, hopefully, make a correct record. Thus it is not just *my* history, but rather a combined effort, but I know that my co-conspirators will not mind if I claim first title!

The book is split into chapters, but they are not intended to be in any chronological order. I just put down thoughts as they came back to me – and readers will have to forgive me where I have repeated things. Any mistakes made are down to me, but hopefully I have not made too many. I certainly don't expect this to be a best seller! But I do hope that it gives some pleasure to those family members who may possibly read it in the future, both on the Gripton side and on Joyce's Jones side.

Memories of a happy life

Born at an early age!

For me, it all started on August 24th 1940 in the maternity ward of Walton Hospital, Liverpool, where my mother Ruth, only just turned twenty the week previously, gave birth to the first (Peter Douglas – that's me!) of her eventual seven children. *(I understand that the Germans bombed London that night for the first time, but hope it had nothing to do with my arrival!)* Ruth's second son, my brother Clifford Robert, came along almost three years later, on July 31st 1943, an event that must have passed me by with no childhood recollection, I guess I was just too young for it to have made an impression on me. However, the birth of yet another boy, Geoffrey John, on June 16th 1945, must have taken place at home, at number 5 Milton Road, Walton, Liverpool 4 (that was the postal district identification). Although I am equally sure, from my own child-like memories, that he actually arrived 'ready-cooked' in a large wickerwork basket, carried on the front handlebars of Nurse Gibson's bicycle! *(And, for the life of me, I can't remember how he got the nickname 'Geoffrey Grunter'!)*

Nurse Gibson was the local or district midwife, who lived in a 'pre-fab' at the bottom of Stuart Road, just as you turned right into Hale Road. Pre-fabs were widespread in Liverpool after the war; they were pre-fabricated single-storey buildings that could be very quickly erected on a bombed site to alleviate the severe housing shortage caused by what was commonly called *'The Blitz'*. Liverpool had been very badly damaged by German *Luftwaffe* bombing during the early years of war, due to its then reputation as a major seaport and its docking availability to the brave Atlantic convoys bringing much needed supplies from America and from the free lands of the British Empire. Although those pre-fabs were meant to serve only as a temporary measure, I seem to remember them living on in Liverpool for many years, long after the war had ended in 1945.

(It's incredible to think that the effects of that bombing were still being felt in 2006! But on May 16th of that year, the Royal Navy minesweeper 'HMS Atherton', on a routine patrol up the Mersey, located a 'monster' seven-foot 1,000-pound bomb lying

3

on the riverbed, just a short distance from the waterfront at Birkenhead. The bomb must have been lying there below the surface for longer than sixty years; experts believe it was dropped in 1940 or 1941. It must have been buried in mud, but then exposed following dredging work near Twelve Quays ferry terminal – and caused quite a lot of disruption to ferry services for some 24 hours! It also caused the 60,000 vehicles-a-day Wallasey Tunnel to be closed for a period, until the bomb was finally towed out to sea and blown up.)

My grandmother (or 'Nin', as we called her) used to clean for Nurse Gibson in later years, as I remember going into the place – in effect a bungalow - with her when I was but a young lad. Despite its pre-fabricated construction, my own memories recall that it was a veritable palace, very clean, spacious and modern, it must even have had its own bathroom – and an inside toilet! Another memory that comes back to me is associated with the material used to make those pre-fabs. The local teenagers (although I don't know if that term was then in vogue!) used to shape staple-firing guns out of the material, along with a strong elastic band, which could be pretty deadly when fired. Homemade catapults were also very much in fashion, made from the forked branch of the nearest stout hedge!

My father was Joseph – or Joe – Gripton, himself one of five boys and a sister, and he worked as a wages clerk at *Blackledges*, a local firm of bakers and confectioners, which had shops all around the Liverpool area. Their main competitor in those days was another such firm, called *Sayers*. *Blackledges* was based down at Derby Road, Bootle (where the bugs wore clogs!), and I can remember Dad taking me, and possibly the other boys, down to the bakery on the occasional Sunday morning. I suppose it was my first glimpse of an automated system, as the loaves were carried along on rollers from place to place. Some of the roller mechanisms even went up and down from one height to another – quite an eye-opener for young eyes.

Home life

Our house at No.5 was only rented, with just two rooms and a small vestibule (or lobby) downstairs and two upstairs bedrooms, served by a central staircase. I can still remember 'the snake' that, for many years, lay alongside the bottom of the vestibule door in order to keep the draughts out! Household decorations that spring to mind include a brass plaque that featured a sailing ship on one wall – they were all the rage then – and a largish brass cartridge case, complete with metal nose-cone, that sat on the fireplace. I guess that it was a souvenir of the wartime environment in which we then lived. Next to that was the brush-and-pan (or companion?) set, accompanied by the coal-scuttle. Once the family had expanded, with the arrival of we three boys, a

4

set of bunk beds was purchased for the back bedroom, where the three of us had to make the most of the small space available. At one time in my early life, I must have had a nightmare, in which I can vividly remember being on a bike and being chased by a pack of dogs, which were jumping up at me as I rode along. I obviously had to hold my legs up away from the pedals, to avoid being bitten. For absolutely years afterwards, in bed I always had to bend my knees and draw my legs up towards my chest before going to sleep – just in case those dogs ever came back!

As I recall, we didn't have the convenience of electricity when I was a toddler or, if we did, then it wasn't the prime source of power. The front room – the lounge, or living room I guess you'd call it – had a coal fire and a gas lamp for lighting. The gas element (or mantle?) appeared to be very fragile and was constantly breaking. I was probably too young to remember 'the range', which was replaced by what was termed a 'modern' fireplace, with a tiled surround, probably sometime after the end of the war. If memory serves me right, Nin's house hung onto its range well into the 1950s; it was a huge black thing, which was kept well polished (with black-lead), and had an oven at one side that was used for cooking. A kettle would sit on the hob, always hot for a pot of tea, either *'Golden Stream'* or *'Brooke Bond Dividend'*, if I remember rightly! Plus, the old fashioned smoothing iron would be warmed up on the hob too, when this was needed. Oh – and it made great toast, holding a slice of *Mother's Pride* on a long fork in front of the open fire! *(We all know the saying "The best thing since sliced bread" - but what I want to know is, what was the best thing* before *sliced bread?)*

Just thinking about a cuppa there brings another of those 'pop-up' memories to mind. There was no such thing as teabags in those days, so tea was made in the pot with loose-leaf tea. This inevitably left a residue of tea leaves in the bottom of the cup and, with me being so fussy, I would never drink down to the bottom of the cup, preferring to leave those tea leaves to be washed down the sink. To this day, I still tend to leave some dregs in the bottom of a cup, of either tea or coffee, despite the fact that there are no dregs in the coffee and no leaves in the tea! Just one of those unbreakable habits I guess!

Back at No.5, the toilet – or lavatory, as it was more commonly known, or even shortened to 'the lav' - was located in splendid isolation at the bottom of a small backyard. It was freezing cold down there in winter, with torn up newspaper, either the *'News of the World'* or *'The People'*, hanging from a nail as the only comfort! A galvanised tin bath hung on another nail in the yard, while a hand-driven mangle, with huge rubber rollers, provided the main means of drying out the washing. I can

5

still remember operating this old-fashioned machine myself; adjusting large screws at either side to alter the pressure. From there, the washing would be brought inside and hung on a clotheshorse in the 'kitchen', raised on a pulley and rope system to the ceiling. No doubt the smell of damp flannelette sheets lives on in those houses that still stand there!

In later years, we 'got modern', when a small 'kitchenette' was added in the backyard, allowing the back room to be used just for dining. *(That extension was put up by Jack Whitley, of whom more will appear later! I also remember that I later helped him to build a similar extension down in Bootle – I think it was for a woman that Mum worked with, in a Sayer's shop down at Marsh Lane.)* I can still picture myself sat at the table at a Saturday dinnertime, waiting to go to 'the match', whilst listening to the *Jack Jackson Show* on the wireless. A popular song that springs to mind from those moments is *'Memories are made of this'*, sung by Dean Martin. At the bottom of the yard, the waste-bin was located in the wall so that, when the bin-men came to collect, they didn't need access to the yard, they could lift the oblong-shaped bin directly out of its slot in the back alley – or 'entry', as we knew it.

Milton Road and its surrounds

Milton Road was the top road on the right if you went 'up' Stuart Road from the County Road end. (Although named as a 'road', I suppose that we always really used to refer to it as 'our street'.) Anyway, it contained some sixteen terraced houses, eight each side, and was easily recognisable by the bombsite on the corner; we had a lot of

The Milton Road gang. Donny Kelly, Geoff, Harry Hayes and me (at rear); Georgie Elliot, Alex Hurley and Cliff (at front)

bombsites in Liverpool in those days! Across the other side of Stuart Road was 'the rezzy', well that's what we kids always called it. It was actually a reservoir belonging to 'the Corporation', consisting of what seemed to us a large park-like area on top of a grassy hill. In the centre was a rather grand looking hut, from where the 'cocky-watchman' would supervise the area, chasing troublemakers off by waving his stick. Also on top of the rezzy was a water-pump – well remembered by my Mum, as I believe one day the other kids sat me down under the pump and gave me a good soaking! The rezzy was surrounded by a barrier of cast-iron railings, with its entrance up a double set of quite imposing steps, complete with cast-iron gates, no doubt Victorian, located around the corner in Breeze Hill. Needless

Milton Road kids again - Donny Kelly, Harold Hayes, me and John Cowan (rear). Cliff, Geoff, Marjorie Cowan, Rita Hayes and Georgie Elliot (front)

to say, we kids from Milton Road hardly ever used the steps, preferring to make our illegal entries and exits via the walls of an electrical sub-station just across the road from Alec Hurley's house, which butted onto the bombsite on the corner.

Exactly where the water was stored – well, it **was** called a reservoir – has always remained a mystery to me! After all, we have visited many a 'reservoir' over the years, usually consisting of a large man-made lake, such as those up near Bolton where Lorraine used to live and the one outside Leicester, Calum and Tom's favourite (?), where we have enjoyed walking. Plus the largest one of all, Kilder Water up in Northumberland – all of these have been located in areas of natural beauty. But all I can remember of 'our rezzy' is that there was a 'working' entrance to the Corporation yard in Stuart Road, where lorries and workmen would make their entrances and exits past some offices, and I think they had a weigh-bridge there too. The yard itself was always full of long lengths of water pipes. Some of these were quite narrow, but a lot of them were big enough for a youngster to hide in – and of course sometimes we did! This despite the fact that the yard was 'off limits', which gave an added excitement to the venture!

Friends and neighbours

One fact that stands out in my mind, which set Alec Hurley's house apart from those in Milton Road, is that it had its own coal cellar. This was located underneath the main hallway, with the coal being tipped down into it through a metal cover, which was positioned in the flagstones just outside the front door of the house. This meant of course that their coal was always dry, whereas we used to keep ours under an old tarpaulin sheet in the backyard. Alec was just one of many youngsters in the group of us who used to play together, in a mostly friendly fashion, in Milton Road. The bombsite was a natural play area, providing an improvised cricket pitch in summer and soccer field in winter. The 'wicket' or 'goal' was always chalked on the side wall of May Beckett's house, the corner one as you turned left down Stuart Road. The sound of a ball hitting her side wall must have driven May mad at times. Sometimes she gathered the courage to chase us off, but mostly she put up with us, we were only snotty-nosed kids! I think she had a son herself, but he was only a toddler, still in his pushchair as far as I remember.

You'll notice that I used the phrase 'mostly friendly' just now! That certainly wasn't the case on one occasion, when Alec threw a half-brick at our Cliff, which caught him a right old whack on the back of his head. A few years later, Cliff was diagnosed as being epileptic; he used to have frequent blackouts and had to start taking tablets, which he probably still uses to this day. It has been assumed all along that this came about from that childhood incident, I don't suppose Alec intended any serious injury, but that's certainly what he caused. No.1 Milton Road was home to Missus Hoare – I don't know if that's spelled correctly, but she was a forbidding old harridan, who always had it in for us kids whatever we did, especially me! Climbing up on the backyard wall, and then walking along the top in a sort of balancing act, was a childhood challenge – especially when you got past Ruby Kelly's as far as Mrs Hoare's! Once I went on to attend Grammar School, at the age of eleven, she would come out with such statements as *"Can't yer learn to speak proper, College puddin'?"* and always referred to my Mum as *'The Duchess'*!

Not that 'Old Ma Hoare' was a master of elocution! We did play her up, of course. One of our tricks was to tie up the door handle of the backyard door, then knock loudly and run off as she struggled to open it! And near November 5th, when penny bangers were being thrown around, quite a few would find their way over her backyard wall. I can't ever remember a 'Mr Hoare', but there was certainly an older boy living there, I think he went by the name Cyril Davison, and he may well have been adopted.

The 'kids' started with us three Griptons and the aforementioned Alec Hurley. Then there was Donny Kelly from No.3, joined some years later by his younger brother Paul. Their mother, Ruby, was a friendly enough soul, but must have had quite a hard time. I believe her husband, Don, had served in the Royal Air Force, but then spent a lot of time in a mental asylum, so she was left to bring up the two boys mainly on her own. I can remember Don Kelly being at home only occasionally, there was certainly a time when he went round the district selling lolly ices from a cold-box, mounted on the front of a bicycle. Those ices were red and triangular in shape and we had fun in sucking the colour out until they were just white ice! Our other next-door neighbours were a couple by the name of Crosier – or it could have been Crozier? - but they had no children and kept themselves to themselves. John Cowan lived further up at No.9, along with his younger sister Marjorie; a real tomboy was Marjorie! She was proud of the fact that she had to squat down to pee in the back-yard drain, boldly showing us boys how it was done! Of course, we wondered why she didn't do it standing up like we did! Perhaps that was our first experience of that age-old children's game, 'Doctors and Nurses', without even knowing we were playing it!

John seemed to suffer from a perpetual cold, in that he always had a streak of 'candle wax' on his upper lip, which he would occasionally lick into his mouth – very tasty! He used to be a bit of a nuisance to the rest of us, forever jumping on us, piggyback style, and demanding a lift down the street! John and Marjorie's mother was 'Aunty' Madge, who was a bit on the large side, while Mr Cowan was called Jim and was rather frail. He had been in the Merchant Navy during the war and I seem to remember being told that his ship had been torpedoed. Anyway, he ended up with only one lung, and didn't survive for very long. *(Marjorie went on to have a certain claim to fame, in that her eldest son, Gary Barlow, became part of a boy band in the 1990s – the well known 'Take That'.)* Up at the top of the street lived Derek Fuller, he was a bit older than the rest of us and had a sister called Sylvia. I can remember that their Dad was called Ben, but cannot remember their Mum's name. Quite out of the blue, I bumped into Derek on two occasions in later years, once whilst shopping in *Marks and Spencer* in Southport and another time at the bottom of steps leading up into Wembley Stadium. I think it was a game when Everton and Liverpool were contesting the Charity Shield, the opening game of the season, with lovely August sunshine.

Harold - or Harry - Hayes and his younger sister, Rita, lived opposite at No.8, with their mother, May, and father Joe. For some reason or other, May always seemed a few steps ahead of the rest of us. I guess they must have had a few bob stashed away, as they were the first in the street to get a new-fangled television, and Harry was the proud owner of a bright shiny bike! I can't remember ever having a bike of my own, but I think I must have learned to ride on Harry's! The Hayes's later left Milton Road to move to Milman Road, just off City Road near Goodison Park, even though Harry was always a Liverpool supporter. I think I am right in recalling that Harry was a Roman Catholic and attended St Francis Xavier's school in Hale Road. But his Mum 'converted' him so that he could go to the same school as us other boys in later years!

Both Harry and Rita are now long-since settled in Australia, around the Sydney area, though Harry and his wife Angela once lived in Adelaide for about sixteen years. I think it was our Geoff who made contact with them when he was working for *Goodyear* and covering both West and South Australia as 'his patch'. Anyway, my wife Joyce and I stayed with them for a week in 1992 and we still keep in touch – occasionally – through the magic of e-mail. At one time they lived in either Lydiate or Maghull (was it called Coronation Avenue?) and we dropped in on them there a couple of times while their two girls, Lisa and Rachael, and our two were of similar age. At the time, Harry worked for either *Cadburys* or *Rowntrees*, I think – and both Lorraine and Michelle will still recall the 'chocolate pieces' they were presented with!

A lad by the name of Georgie Elliott often used to join our gang, though he actually lived elsewhere, over in Anfield I think. He used to visit his aunt's house, around the corner in one of the 'big houses' on Breeze Hill. Whenever he was there, which seemed pretty much like always, he would be only too pleased to join in any games being played. Another boy, probably about my age or just a bit older, lived across the street, Neil Gaynor, but he hardly ever seemed to join in with the rest of us. His mother was called Dolly and the father was Bill. I think Neil had a cousin (Norman Galley?) living a couple of streets away. More often or not, we would be making ourselves up into 'gangs', I think I was always the one to organise them, writing down members names in a little notebook and trying to take a weekly subscription! If we ever did put any money together, I haven't a clue as to what ever happened to it! I know that at one time we called ourselves the *'Milton Skid Kids'*, probably due to the game where we played 'hoopla' with a stick and old bicycle wheels, most times down to their metal rims, but sometimes there was the luxury of a solid rubber tyre.

Other occupants, those with no children, tend to be less vivid in the memory. There was a Mr Graham opposite, who kept himself to himself, apart from his nightly walks down to the pub. In common with most men of his era, he wouldn't be seen out in the road without wearing his trilby. Old Mrs Johnston lived across at No.10, I can remember once that she gave me a collection of *'Flags of the World'*, printed on silk and which had been issued in packets of *Kensitas* cigarettes. No doubt these were eventually swapped or lost, but if I'd held on to them they would possibly be worth a lot of money today.

Those families with children had some sort of natural affinity and their houses were mostly 'open house' for all other children in the street. Mothers and fathers became surrogate 'aunties and uncles' to the rest of the children. There was little or no crime then, as far as can be remembered, so doors were left unlocked all day long. One thing that springs to mind is the pride taken in the outside appearance of those little houses, with window-sills and doorsteps washed and 'red-raddled' on almost a daily basis.

Games and adventures

Apart from the rezzy, the whole of Walton district used to form our playground, nowhere seemed out of bounds. Games were played with the street itself as the 'den', but most games were of the 'hide and seek' variety - and the seeking took a lot of time and effort! The games went by the names of *'Reallio'*, *'Kick-the-can'* and *'Stroke-the bunny'*, but each usually involved one poor soul having to seek out the rest of us. In those days, every house seemed to be open to all of us; we were just like one big family, always 'playing out', as there were few indoor distractions such as television. A knock on the door would inevitably mean the appearance of another lad, asking if we could 'come out to play?' Just outside our own house was a street-lamp, originally lit by gas, as were the houses themselves. I can remember sitting in the front room with the lights off, being illuminated by the lamplight alone. Dad would then use his hands to form shadows on the wall – you know the sort of thing, a dove or an angel or maybe even an elephant? As this lamp-post provided not only a climbing-frame, but also our only source of light on dark winter afternoons, it was the natural place for everyone to congregate, as well as home to our hopscotch area, laid out on the paving slabs and numbered with chalk from 1 - 10. If I remember rightly, Georgie Elliot used to swing on the lamp's bar, just like a monkey!

There was a great feeling of 'belonging', as we always used to hang around together. Days out would sometimes take place down in Walton Hall Park, where we would consume our jam butties and drink our 'pop', made up of a bottle of tap water mixed with fizzy lemonade powder. Summer holidays from school seemed to stretch away endlessly and the weather was always warm and sunny – or so the memory tells me! The other thing that comes back to me is that we always felt totally safe in those days, quite free to wander the district and, in the summer, 'play out' until it was almost pitch dark.

As already mentioned, there was a bombsite – 'the bommie' - at the bottom of the street, on which we played many games, such as marbles – not that we called them marbles, to us they were always 'ollies'. The green ones were 'snotballs', there were red ones that looked like bloodshot eyes, and of course the 'steelies'. These were actually ball-bearings, the bigger the better, as not only could you knock a lot of ollies out of the ring or hole with a steely, but you could probably smash a few too! Another game that you don't see today's children playing is 'whip and top'. It took a certain amount of skill to wind the string around the top, then pull it away fast enough to get the top spinning on its own. Then you'd keep on 'whipping' it to keep it going as long as possible – simple but effective, a long cry from the play stations and computer games that seem to fill the void nowadays!

Milton Road itself was a *cul-de-sac*, and at the 'dead end' top of it was a narrow strip of ground that contained a few struggling laurel bushes, none of the individual houses had gardens. Down Stuart Road, the houses had the 'luxury' of a raised wall at the front, with some houses also boasting a hedge – good hiding places for childhood 'chase and catch' games! During the war years and for some time afterwards, there were two bomb shelters down the centre of the street, huge brick-built blocks with thick reinforced concrete roofs. They obviously served their purpose when the bombs were falling but, when we used to go inside them after the war, they were dark, damp, smelly and forbidding places. The smell no doubt came from their being used as emergency toilets at times! I remember the huge tracked cranes that came along after the war, using heavy steel balls to eventually knock down the shelters.

I doubt very much that any of the infamous V1 'doodle-bugs' or V2 rockets ever made it as far as Liverpool, we were probably well beyond their range, which must have centred upon London and the south-eastern counties. But certainly, during the early part of the war, the city suffered badly from the bombing attacks, being a vital port to be kept open during the Battle of the Atlantic, when the American convoys were assisting to bring supplies to our shores. Dad never joined the Forces, but he did act as an ARP (Air Raid Precautions) warden and I remember him telling us of once spotting a deadly landmine, still hanging by its parachute cords, from a chimney somewhere on Morval Crescent.

I honestly cannot remember a direct raid myself, I was fortunately too young for that. But I do recall one warm summer's day, it must have been during the latter days of the war, or perhaps even after the end of hostilities. A gang of us was playing out in the street as usual when the air-raid sirens went off – this had been a familiar and frightening warning during the darker days earlier in the war. Mum dashed out and hustled us inside the house, where we were put into the under-stairs cupboard until the 'all clear' sounded. Even if we kids saw a high-flying aircraft leaving an innocent vapour trail across the blue sky, we'd probably dash indoors, frightened of an air raid. In fact, come to think of it, we often used to imagine that they were rocket ships on their way to another world!

When November 5th came round in those days, rather than being associated with the Guy Fawkes plot, we kids – I'm sure with parental approval – instead made it part of the wartime story. Our 'Guys' were made up in the image of Hitler, along with the sign of the swastika, while on the evening itself, the bonfire somehow became the 'bombfire' and November 5th was always known as *'Bombfire Night'*! I remember that for weeks prior to the event, we would trawl around the district, going into bombed-out buildings to strip out floorboards and doors for use as tinder on the fire. Looking back, this was a precarious and dangerous pastime, as we'd often be walking across 'floors' that consisted only of cross-joists! Certainly no parental approval for those exploits! The fire would be built on the bombsite, it always seemed a huge affair, and was more often than not still spitting and smouldering the following morning. Other streets had their fires in the road, so that the tarmac suffered quite a lot of damage!

I remember one year when our 'guy' looked really professional, in that one of the mothers (I guess?) had actually knitted a head, then stuffed it with rag and even made a face to look quite realistic. If memory serves me correctly, we would push the guy around the district on some sort of 'vehicle', begging passers by with the plea *"Penny for the guy!"* These pennies would of course be spent on 'penny bangers' – I can't recall any ban on selling them to us youngsters in those days. That 'vehicle' just mentioned brings to mind the racing cars that we used to make. These would consist of an old set of wheels, from a pram undercarriage, onto which would be lashed planks of wood for the chassis and seating – all steered along by a length of rope connected to the front axle. The 'engine' would be supplied by the poor kid who was designated to push you along at high speed!

As I've already mentioned, the top end of the street ended at a few poorly tended poplar hedges trees. Behind them ran a brick wall that formed a ten-foot drop on one side of the back entry behind Makin Street, which ran down from Breeze Hill down to County Road. Across the entry were the backyard toilets of the houses in Makin Street, and as we kids got older and more daring, we would jump across from the wall in Milton Road, onto the toilet roofs opposite – hoping that they weren't occupied!

With the benefit of hindsight, we must have been mad, particularly when the roofs were wet with rain, but it seemed like fun at the time. Jumping back in the reverse direction was called 'belly flopping' – quite a challenge at the first attempt! Once mastered, of course, this exercise made a good impression on the younger kids!

Further afield

Milton Road was the street usually referred to as being 'at the top' of Stuart Road. Stuart Road ran up from County Road, crossed at an intersection with Bedford Road, and then continued across Breeze Hill, where the district changed from Walton (Liverpool 4 was our 'post code') into Bootle (which was Liverpool 20). If you looked down Bedford Road, from its junction with Stuart Road, you'd be confronted in the distance by the splendid sight of Walton Church, which is where many of us were christened and married – unless you were Roman Catholic (RC) of course. *(I'm sure I can remember RCs being called 'roman candles' by some of the other kids!)* Halfway between Bedford Road and the bottom of Stuart Road, the kids living in the houses along Stuart Road always seemed to be a tough lot, there was one boy who we thought had the surname of 'Hitler', probably incorrect, but he certainly frightened the life out of us! It took a brave lad to walk all the way down Stuart Road unaccompanied when we were young; more generally we would walk as a group, or even take the short cut down the back alleys behind the houses. That was definitely the 'approved route' that led from Milton Road to the *Bedford* cinema!

Just across Breeze Hill, on the opposite side of the road, was a large building, *Bootle Grammar School for Girls*, I believe. It was surrounded by a fairly high brick wall, but not so high that we couldn't climb up on top of it. The top was fairly wide, so you could sit there quite comfortably and the reason we'd be there was to collect caterpillars, stashing them away in jam-jars with a few leaves for their lunch. Whether or not any lived long enough to survive to the butterfly stage, I don't know – but I doubt it! On that wall was a street sign that read *'Breeze Hill, City of Liverpool'*, but for some reason, our Cliff misread this and would ask, *"Who's this Kitty, of Liverpool?"* True or not, it's always been good for a laugh.

On Sunday mornings, it wasn't unusual for a whole bunch of us kids, carrying our 'cossies' wrapped in towels, to make our way down to the public swimming baths down at Queen's Drive. This was usually before breakfast, so a good appetite was built up. I never ever did learn to swim properly myself, but then the greatest sport was 'dive-bombing' the other kids and making a huge splash – we were all pretty good at that! No doubt we all went home afterwards reeking of chlorine. Sunday afternoons would see us all sent off to Sunday school at the Presbyterian Church round on Breeze

Hill. As we got older – and wiser? – we used to by-pass the church and head straight down to Mr Morris's hobbies and toy-shop down towards Rice Lane, where we would try to buy small bits and pieces with our collection money! Either that, or we would go round towards Walton Church, where the *'Herb Shop'* (or 'Herbie') sold bottles of refreshments in all colours – white lemonade, yellow lemonade, orangeade, cherryade, white cream soda, green cream soda, sarsaparilla, dandelion & burdock, *Tizer*, *Vimto* – you name it, they sold it!

All those drinks in those days came in real glass bottles – not the throwaway plastic ones you get nowadays. Each bottle came with a black, sort of hardened-rubber, stopper that screwed into the top of the bottle. The bottles themselves were bought with a 'deposit paid', so that when you took it back, you got your money back. It was quite an occasion if you came across a discarded bottle to boost your pocket money! Although I never came across the pastime at the *Bedford*, I do believe that certain cinemas in Liverpool would accept so many clean and empty jam-jars as the entrance fee – what you may nowadays call 'recycling', well ahead of its time!

Looking back, there were many 'treats' that we had as children that wouldn't see the light of day now! Remember the 'sherbet dip', sold in small cones? Then there were 'liquorice sticks', they looked just like twigs of wood – and tasted as bad! Aniseed balls, gob-stoppers, sherbet lemons, pear and acid drops, dolly mixtures, bubble-gum – I'm sure they all live on in our memories!

'The Park'

A favourite play area in Walton was (and still is maybe?) 'Wally Hall Park', probably no more than half-a-mile away down Breeze Hill, then across Rice Lane and a little way along Queen's Drive. Not far away, as I've said, but it could have been the other side of the world to us kids in those days. Never the prettiest of places as I remember it, but no doubt it had been a 'proper' park in earlier days, with laid-out flower beds and a mass of trees and shrubs. My memory may be a bit light here, but even in those 'more innocent' days, I think we were all warned about going into the park's public toilets! Graffiti and 'loiterers' are not just a modern-day occurrence.

Just before arriving at the park entrance, there was a large building that served as the local children's clinic. I think you took your coupons down there, exchanging them for bottles of orange juice, cartons of baby's milk powder and possibly tins of powdered egg. Also in the building was the schools' dentist, I used to hate it when I had an appointment there. Of course, in those days, the only available cure for toothache seemed to be that the offending molar was extracted. The only anaesthetic available at the time was gas, administered through a large rubber mask. Prior to the mask being fitted, a large metal clamp was placed between your teeth for you to bite upon and, once you smelled that horrible gas, you knew that a few seconds later you would be fast asleep.

I always came round crying my eyes out! And it always seemed to follow the same dream, where I would be outside in the street playing, but dressed only in a vest, which I would be desperately trying to tug down for reasons of modesty, only to find it was too short. No doubt Professor Freud could tell me what it meant, but to me it always meant that I'd lost another tooth! However, some compensation was at hand, because after an extraction, you'd always go home to 'pobs'! This was literally only pieces of bread in hot sweetened milk, but it always tasted wonderful.   That brings another thought to mind – if you had a toothache or an earache in those days – a not uncommon experience – the cure-all for both symptoms was to have a sweaty sock wrapped around your face! 'Old wives' tale' perhaps and whether or not it used to be an effective deterrent, I don't remember, but it was certainly used quite a lot in our house!

Perhaps I'm wrong about this, but there also seemed to be a lot of other extractions around in Liverpool in those days - those of tonsils and adenoids! These organic lumps of tissue were always prone to infection – there are rumours around that say the Scouse accent derives from those infections, which forced *Liverpudlians* (and *Evertonians* of course!) to 'talk through dere noses'! Whatever, children suffering from tonsillitis and the like were swiftly taken into hospital and, at the drop of a hat, the offending organs were removed. I don't think I actually had the operation, but I do remember being either in the doctor's or some hospital waiting room, with some tuning fork-like prongs of wire stuck forcibly up my nostrils! What that was in aid of, I can't remember, but I can still feel the pain!

Back to happier memories. I can remember going down to the park during those seemingly endless summer holidays, well provided for with jam butties, bottles of water and fizzy lemonade powder, from which we would make up our own drinks – pretty horrible stuff when measured against today's products! The park was on the large side, with a driveway that ran down through its middle, ending up in Walton Hall Drive at the far end. Somewhere in the middle was a boating-lake, I can actually remember it being used as such, though we never ever used it ourselves – either too young or lack of cash! Alongside that was a sort of concert-stage, where occasionally a band would be seen and heard, playing in front of a scattered crowd sat out on either deck chairs or those folding wooden chairs.

At one corner of the park there were a number of streets named after famous ocean-going liners of the *Cunard* line, such as *Lusitania*, *Mauretania* and *Saxonia*. A memory comes back to me of being in that area one summer, when a thunder and lightning storm broke out and we all dashed for shelter – hope it wasn't under a tree! One of Mum's friends must have had a house down there, it could even have been a prefab, but I can remember going there to visit. One feature that has always stuck in my memory was the amount of brass in the house, it appeared to be everywhere, from a small dinner gong sat on a hall-table to one of those large plaques hanging on the wall, displaying an old galleon. They were quite popular then, I've already mentioned that we had one at home ourselves.

On the other side of Breeze Hill to the clinic and the park was a municipal bowling green and, behind that, a small children's playground with swings and a metal maypole, around which swung metal chains on which we would hang. I'm pretty sure we often had a few casualties after playing down there, today's Health and Safety Executive has no doubt closed it down by now! Alongside this was a large school, I don't know if I'm going to spell this correctly, but I think it was called *'Allsops'*. *(I'm pretty sure too that we used to call the kids that went there 'All Slops'!)* At the back of this area ran the lane called Walton Village, which ran along from the rear of Walton Church.

Growing up

Most of the boys in the district used to have their hair cut at *Tom Williams'* barbershop, located on the corner of Euston Street, along County Road towards Walton Church. Tom and his brother Joe would have to put a board across the sides of the high barber's chair when we first attended, so that we were sat at 'cuttable height'! The order of the day was a military-style 'short back and sides', which always caused the back of the neck to feel rather cold. This was followed by a liberal application of some pale mauve 'hair-cream' which subsequently set into a hard shiny layer, which your Mum would then have to wash off. The whole event would conclude with either Tom or Joe 'spitting' on his hand, then slapping the back of your head to the saying, *"First wet"*.

Eventually of course, as we grew older, we would like to look a little more human or stylish, so we started going up to City Road. Here, a much younger barber by the name of Mark had just set up his business, following a tour on one of the *Cunard* liners. He was much more up-to-date, with all the latest American styles based on the 'Tony Curtis', side-burns, the 'Boston' and the 'DA', which didn't stand for District Attorney, but 'duck's arse'! These styles were much in demand once the 'Teddy

Boy' mode of dress began to be fashionable. If I remember it correctly, the first fully blown 'Ted' to adorn the streets of Walton was a lad named Monks. I think he lived somewhere up Morval Crescent or Brimstage Road – he certainly looked very strange at first sight, with his long Edwardian jacket with velvet collar, fancy waistcoat, drainpipe trousers and 'brothel creeper' crepe-soled shoes. There's no doubt that we lads tried to mimic this style somewhat, but of course being 'without any visible means of support', keeping up with fashion proved difficult.

However, I've leapt ahead a few years there! Childhood memories mainly consist of the good times, I suppose, but there was one occasion when I went down with 'scarlet fever', and had to be isolated in a hospital somewhere in the Everton Brow area – it could have been Netherfield Road. I can remember being taken there in a green ambulance, especially reserved for such 'isolation' cases and thinking I was something special! The sight of any ambulance would quickly bring out the response of *"Touch yer toes, touch yer nose, never go in one of those"*. I suppose I still say it mentally today, without going through the actual motions!

At the end of the war in 1945, victory was celebrated by street parties, held on the occasions of 'VE Day' and 'VJ Day'. I don't have strong recollections of these, but seem to remember being sat at a long set of trestle-tables along Stuart Road, in the area of the chip-shop, so I guess it was for one or maybe both of the above. The 'Coronation Party' that was held in 1953 is much more vivid in my memory. I, along with Cliff and Geoff, attended the one that was held in Romley Street and I still have some photographs of that memorable event. *(I can't remember having such a party in Milton Road itself, perhaps there just weren't enough of us to make it worth while?)* Looking back at such photos, one can see the style of dress of the women then, most of the 'housewives' of the day favoured the 'pinny' or apron, and their hair always seemed to be 'in curlers', wrapped round with a head-scarf. In fact it was fashionable for even young girls to have their hair like that, particularly if they were at work all day, perhaps in a factory. That way, then as soon as they had eaten their evening meal after work, out would come the curlers, a quick comb or brush and they'd be ready for the evening's entertainment!

Childhood pastimes

Hobbies and pastimes were probably few and far between, but I do remember collecting both tram and bus tickets, then making them up into long concertina-style chains. Then there were cigarette cards, mainly of favourite film stars, cricketers or footballers. 'Ciggies' could then be purchased in paper packets of five or ten, I suppose twenties were too expensive. We even used to collect what we called 'fag

Romley Street Coronation Party, 1953

packets' – *Woodbines, Park Drive, Robin, Turf, Player's Navy Cut, Capstan Full Strength*, even the exotic sounding *Passing Cloud* still springs to mind. Then there was the *'Lucy'* – or that's how it sounded! It was actually a 'loosie' and what you would ask for if you wanted just one 'loose' cigarette - and they were definitely sold like that too, a sure sign that it wasn't an affluent age!

Another 'craze', which wouldn't count for much in today's 'street cred' stakes, was a sort of knitting! A wooden cotton-reel would have four small nails hammered into it, and lengths of wool, of all different colours, would be woven around these nails and passed down through the hole in the reel, coming out as a multi-coloured sausage-shaped roll, about the diameter of a pencil. This could then be made up into place mats or something similar, but we'd probably leave that to our Mums, as by that stage we'd have become fed up! Milk bottles in those days were fitted with a pressed-in waxed cardboard disc. This had a circular part in the middle, which you could press through with your finger, enabling you to then lift the disc out of the bottle's neck. The remaining discs, with their perfectly circular holes in the middle, made an ideal basis for yet another little hobby! Using the disc as a frame, you would wind some wool all around the circular frame, the wool building up into a ball, which could then be used as the 'bobble' on top of a hat or beret!

Other bottles – and here I'm lost as to their contents, but it could well have been light ale – came with the corrugated metal top, that was pressed on. It could only be opened either by a proper opener, or by holding the top against a sharp corner and then hitting the top firmly with the heel of your palm. This either brought the top off in one clean movement – and made you an instant hero to your mates – or just left you nursing a very sore hand! The top itself was 'treasure', as it contained a cork seal insert, which could be prised gently out. The top could then be 'mounted' on the outside of your pullover, with the cork seal pressed in from 'inside' to hold it in place – an instant shiny coloured badge!

Another source of endless fascination to us kids was the collecting of car numbers! Yes, we'd sit on the corner of Stuart Road and Breeze Hill, with notebooks and pencils, just writing down the number plates of any cars that occasionally passed by – imagine doing that today, you'd never be quick enough to catch many! The big event would be when a *'BRS'* lorry (that stood for *British Road Services*) went by, they were 'special' because you'd also look for the town in which the vehicle was based, which would be printed somewhere on the side. All this information would be diligently written down in a notebook, a veritable treasure trove! *(The modern equivalent would, I suppose, be the collection of the names printed on the Eddie Stobart lorries.)*

One more thing that comes to mind used to take place during what always seemed to be cold winters in those days, and that was the construction of 'Winter warmers'! Take one old tin can, a fairly large one if available. Using a hammer and nail, make one hole either side of the top opening and tie a length of wire through the holes to make a fairly longish handle. Hammer further holes around the tin in some sort of pattern (if artistically minded) – or at random – which was the normal way! Pack some dry paper into the bottom of the can and then fill with small twigs or wooden lolly handles - and if possible, some small pieces of coal or coke. Set fire to the paper, wait until it gets going, then grasp the handle and whirl the 'Winter warmer' around your head until the whole contents of the can are ablaze. Then warm your hands!

I think I've mentioned catapults elsewhere, but we also used to try our hand at making bows and arrows. Nothing fancy of course, just made by stripping branches from trees and then begging some strong twine from somewhere. The arrows would be fashioned from a piece of cane and the 'point' would actually be quite blunt, probably because we were warned of the dangers of a sharp arrowhead. To fashion these blunt tips, we'd make use of a 'tar bubble'. These games were usually a summer fad, so the hot weather would inevitable lead to bubbles of tar in the street surface. We'd dip the arrowhead into the tar and then roll it into a nice soft ball, to cushion around the tip. And then there was that other summer craze – kites! In those days, of course, you'd make your own, out of a diamond-shaped construction of canes, stuck over with brown wrapping-paper. The tail would be a long piece of string, tied around a succession of pieces of old rag. I doubt very much that they ever flew, they were too heavy for that – but the fun was in trying!

Looking back at those long-gone but happy days, it seemed that we kids spent most of our time 'playing out', a pastime that nowadays is out of fashion, as kids tend to stay indoors with their videos and play-stations. Crimes against children must have been committed then, I'm sure, but it certainly seems more prevalent nowadays and parents have become very much more protective. I can remember once, when Joyce and I were visiting Liverpool – we were walking up Arnot Street at the time. Two young lads were 'playing out' and we overheard one of them saying, to the other, *"I know, you think I'm dead – but I'm not really!"*

The year 1948 brought the first post-war Olympic Games to London and with it a set of stamps, specially issued for the occasion. This was probably the first time that I'd become interested in stamp collecting, but I hardly set the fashion, sticking the stamps in an album with some form of sticky tape which was red in colour! There was a young lad living just round the corner in Stuart Road, I can't remember his name, maybe it was Alan Woolstenholme or something like that. Anyway, he had a great stamp collection, no doubt handed down to him by his parents or relations. Poor Alan – I seem to remember that he came to the door in a wheelchair, possibly a victim of the 'polio' that was prevalent in those days. Anyway, his Mum was glad that at least someone came around to talk to him occasionally. I'm pretty sure that I somehow managed to become the owner of a lot of his stamps, whether by accident or design now escapes me. But I still get an occasional guilty twinge from time to time!

At one point in my life, along with John Cowan and Harry Hayes, I joined the *'Lifeboys'*, which was run, if I remember correctly, by a chap named Mr Knowles. (Somewhere on the horizon too, though I can't remember where he fitted in, was a guy called Mr Poley. We used to snigger behind his back, with the phrase *"Holy Moly, Mr Poley!"*, based on the saying of *Captain Marvel*.) *Lifeboys* was a once-a-week thing at the local church around in Breeze Hill, which I think belonged to the Scottish Presbyterians. I was probably baptised as Church of England, but this church was close by so I guess that's why we went – or were sent - there! Exactly what we did each week is a bit vague in my memory, but I do recall that we were encouraged to join the *Temperance Society* and thus not give in to the evils of drink! I think it was called 'taking the pledge'. We also had to attend church services on Sunday mornings, parading in our dark blue uniforms. This was a precursor to our joining the *'Boys' Brigade'*, which the three of us eventually did, but this was located down at (probably) the school in Evered Avenue, and we soon became disillusioned with the whole thing.

I passed my eleven-plus exam in 1951 and started at the Liverpool Institute, which will be the subject of another chapter. It must have been during my first year there that I developed a nasty dose of double pneumonia. This laid me up for a number of weeks and I remember having to be sat up all the time, propped by pillows, as it was too painful to lie down. With both Mum and Dad out at work, I was left on my own a lot and used to listen to the wireless. I recall that there was a daily serial being broadcast on *'Woman's Hour'* at the time, with the theme music bringing a cold shiver down my spine. It was years later that I found out that the music was Ravel's *'Bolero'*, a really haunting piece.

Footnote

Coming now to the present times *(I was writing this part in August 2005)*, it is quite amazing that I have, over the past couple of years, made contact with Marjorie Barlow – or Cowan as she used to be! I'm not too sure as to how this contact was first made, but I think it started when Mum and Bill went to visit Madge Cowan at her home in Frodsham, Cheshire, probably during their last visit to England in 1997. Since then, both Madge and Bill have sadly passed on and Mum now lives up in Culcheth – as told elsewhere. Now Marjorie lives at a village called Cuddington, which is not too far away from Culcheth – down the A49 from Warrington towards Northwich. So, on a few occasions, when we have visited Mum, we have taken the opportunity to meet up with Marjorie and her husband Colin, who originates from Frodsham.

It is only a few days since our last visit, when we – that's myself, Mum and Joyce – took the Barlows to lunch at the *Willington Hall Hotel*, which had been a favourite spot of Marjorie's Mum, Madge. When we got back to their place we began reminiscing and Marjorie came up with the name of a shop in Stuart Road, called *'Mushets'*. She thought it was on one of the corners where Stuart and Bedford Roads cross, but once I'd heard the name, I placed it – correctly – as down at the bottom of Stuart Road, on the left as you approach County Road. I asked our Geoff if he recalled the name and he e-mailed back that he did, adding the phrase *"'Ere y'are lad, stick that under yer coat"*, which probably says it all!

22

The Gripton Boys

As a final note to this chapter, I must add that Marjorie and Colin have moved back to Frodsham, since I wrote the above. Their place at Cuddington was on a large estate that included homes for their two sons and respective families. As mentioned before, it just happens that one of the sons is none other than Gary Barlow, who is a leading songwriter and part of the *'Take That'* group. Gary was living at what once must have been the old 'manor house' on the estate but, when the group started enjoying a renaissance, sometime during 2006 if I remember correctly, he decided to sell up the estate and move to London. So Marjorie and Colin are now established in another farmhouse, where we last visited around the time of Mum's 87th birthday in August 2007.

Entertainment, transport and services

Going to the flicks!

All the local roads or streets in Walton had back alleys – or 'entries' as we called them. They were there to provide access to back yards and for refuse collection, but they would also provide short cuts all across the district, especially on Saturday afternoons, when we would nip down all the entries that led down to the *'Bedford'*. This was 'our' nearest local cinema, located in Bedford Road, next door to *Abraham and Mitchell's,* which was a furniture removals firm and had a yard full of ancient lorries. At those Saturday afternoon film shows, we would spend a couple of fantasy hours in another world, for the price of a tanner (sixpence), watching *The Three Stooges, The Dead End Kids, The Bowery Boys, Laurel and Hardy, Abbott and Costello, George Formby, Old Ma Riley* and the like. I guess that even the old Bing Crosby and Bob Hope 'Road' films were also part of our film watching at the time. George Formby became pretty much a cult figure in his time and was famous for his double entendre songs, like *'With my little ukulele in my hand'* – though we were probably too young to pick up on them at the time. His films usually ended with his catch-phrase – *'Turned out nice again!'*

Each afternoon performance would be preceded by this guy with an accordion, who stood up on the stage and would attempt to have us all singing along to the popular songs of those days. I recall such tunes as *'I've got a lovely bunch of coconuts', 'Don't fence me in', 'Give me five minutes more', 'Now is the hour', 'Cruising down the river'* and *'Goodnight Irene'.* It all sounds a bit corny when you look back, but it was just the way things were back then. On the way back home, we would have our navy-blue gabardine macs trailing over our shoulders, buttoned around the neck to act as a cloak, as we acted out our cowboy fantasies. It was easy to pretend that we were the *Lone Ranger, Hopalong Cassidy, Roy Rogers* or *Gene Autrey,* slapping our own backsides in imitation of making our horse go faster! Or maybe it was a more futuristic hero, like *Flash Gordon, Zorro* or *Captain Marvel. Shazam!* The *'Bedford'* (in Bedford Road, of course) was the closest cinema to Milton Road, so was the one most often used. In those days, cinemas were dotted across the landscape of Liverpool like a dose of measles and 'going to the flicks' was a national, not just local, pastime. If you picked up a copy of the *Liverpool Echo*, the daily evening newspaper, for instance, its front page was just one long list of cinemas and the current films being shown.

There were no multi-screen palaces then, just auditoriums with downstairs stalls and an upstairs balcony. It wasn't unusual for a film to suddenly stop mid-reel and, as the projectionist frantically tried to get it going again, the hall would echo to cries of *"Put a shilling in the meter!"* Those who were unfortunate enough to sit in the stalls would be bombarded with bits of rubbish from the balcony above, while the air would be full of silver flashes, as pieces of orange peel soared through the projected beam of light onto the screen. In later years of course, when we had grown up enough to attend an 'adult' show, you'd be looking at the screen through a barrier of ciggie smoke – there were no health and safety regulations in those days! There would usually be two films per showing. First would come a cartoon or public interest film, then what was termed the 'B' movie, followed by *Pathe News* and finally the main feature. And who could forget the *Edgar Lustgarten* murder mysteries? Most cinemas would have an afternoon matinee and an evening performance. This programme would differ from the children's Saturday show, which would have cartoons, a 'cliff-hanger' serial, which went on over a number of weeks, and the main feature – usually a 'Western', starring one of our cowboy heroes and a whole bunch of whooping Red Indians.

I suppose 'Westerns' were always one of the most popular films, although we tended to call them 'Cowboys and Indians'. There were lots of scenes where one lot of guys on horseback chased after another lot, with lots of shooting and falling off horses! The 'goodies' always seemed to have on white Stetsons, while the 'baddies' wore black! Anyone who had been shot would clutch his chest and gradually subside to the ground like a dying swan, with none of the blood and guts that are such a feature of the modern movie. And all accompanied by lots of cheering and booing from the assembled audience of course! Just occasionally on TV, there is a showing of one of those old-style films, and it always reminds me of Saturday afternoons at 'the flicks'!

I recall one occasion very well from those afternoons in the *Bedford*, one that started in absolute terror but ended with me as the somewhat unwilling hero! As usual, there were probably half a dozen of us from Milton Road, we normally all went to the flicks together. We found that these kids in the row behind us were a rough lot – most of them were, in Walton, in those days! They insisted on deliberately putting their knees or feet up on the backs of our seats and then pushing as hard as they could, meaning that we were subjected to the indignity and discomfort that this obviously caused. Now I was hardly a violent type and found this treatment not only annoying - but also pretty terrifying. But, having suffered this treatment for a while, it got just a bit tedious and I turned round to glare at the perpetrator behind me. He started getting mouthy and it was clear that he wasn't prepared to stop his actions. I must have had a rush of blood to the head, because I ended up giving him a right hard slap across the face! My heart must have been beating like a sledgehammer and I feared the direst of retribution. But thank goodness, it worked, and we were left in peace for the rest of the film.

Other local cinemas that we occasionally visited included the *'Princess'*, at the Kirkdale end of Hale Road, and the *'Coliseum'*, located on City Road – this later became the Everton Supporters Club. One visit to the *Princess* stands out in my mind was when Mum took me there to see the film of Queen Elizabeth's Coronation in 1953, it was titled *'A Queen is crowned'*. What was quite memorable about that film was that it was in colour, whereas most of the films we used to see as kids were still in the old black and white format – innovations like *'Technicolor'* and *'Cinemascope'* were still only just beginning to make their mark on our entertainment. There were countless other picture houses of course but, as children, we didn't have to venture too far to find something suitable to watch. I recall one Saturday afternoon when we got as far as the front entrance to the *Bedford*, only to find that our Cliff had managed to swallow his entrance money of a 'tanner'! *(I seem to remember that the chamber pot got used for a while until the tanner appeared – you couldn't afford to lose such a large sum in those days!)*

One film that definitely stands out in my mind, although it wasn't exactly a children's classic, was *'High Noon'*, that famous Western starring Gary Cooper and Grace Kelly. That must have come out around 1950 and its theme song had become very popular on the radio in those days – *"Do not forsake me, oh my darling"*. I think the movie version was by one of the 'singing cowboys' of the day, Tex Ritter, although another excellent version came out by Frankie Laine. Anyway, I was desperate to see the film and, as you had to be accompanied by an adult, I actually persuaded my Nin to take me one weekday afternoon. I'm pretty sure we must have caught a bus down to the *'Astoria'*, which was located down Walton Road near Everton Valley.

Another film that made a big impression on me, at some time during the Fifties I think it must have been, was *'The Cruel Sea'*. It starred Jack Hawkins as the captain of a Liverpool based ship, the *Compass Rose*, which sailed across the Atlantic on those convoys during the war. It was based upon the book of the same title, written by a chap called Nicholas Monserrat, who I believe came from Liverpool. Then there was another film, whose title I can't remember, but it may well have been *'Wages of fear'*. It was French with subtitles and I went to see it by myself, so I must have been around fifteen at the time, at a cinema (was it the *'Curzon'*?) in Crosby. It told the tale of a couple of lorry drivers who were delivering nitroglycerine to a mine in the jungle somewhere, very tense and nail biting. It actually featured a scene where a coloured lady is shown naked in the shower – pretty *avant garde* in those days and a severe shock to this particular young lad!

Apart from the pictures, another source of entertainment was the weekly comic. We no doubt started off with the 'cartoon style' characters that adorned the pages of *'Dandy'* and *'Beano'*. If memory serves me right, the fronts of those comics featured *'Corky the Cat'* and *'Desperate Dan'* when I first started reading them. I'm pretty sure that there were other comics issued, based upon characters from the wireless and cinema, and then there would be those comics more likely to amuse a 'boy's own' readership, such as *'Wizard'* and *'Adventure'*. A large-format comic became an instant best-seller when introduced – that was *'Eagle'*, featuring *'Dan Dare – Pilot of the future'* and the bumbling detective, *'Harris Tweed'*. I seem to recall that it was actually printed in Liverpool, by the firm *'Bemrose'* – or something like that. Just going back to the *Liverpool Echo* – and this must be classed as 'entertainment' I suppose, it used to run a daily cartoon for children, much along the lines of *'Rupert the Bear'* as featured in the *Daily Express*, the national daily. Our more parochial offering was *'Curly Wee and Gussy Goose'*, still fondly remembered!

The 'wireless'

In my earliest days, the wireless (now termed radio) formed the main part of any entertainment, apart from the games we sometimes played. Our wireless was a huge affair, powered not only from the electrical mains, but also by a large glass-encased lead-acid battery, which would require frequent charging. To have it charged, it would be carried up to a charging shop on City Road, not far from Everton's football ground and, boy, wasn't it heavy when you were 'volunteered' for the job! Thinking back, you probably didn't bring the same battery back with you, it would need a few hours 'on charge'. So you would no doubt bring one of the same type back on the return trip. No matter, it was carried by a wire handle, which had just about cut your fingers off by the time you got home!

I can remember the grown-ups chortling to the antics of *'Itma'*, which stood for *'It's that man again'*, and starred a Liverpool comic, one Tommy Handley. They always said that if you came from Liverpool, you were a born comic and, certainly, it has proved so, with the likes of Arthur Askey, Rob Wilton, Ken Dodd, Jimmy

Tarbuck, Stan Boardman and Freddie Starr – the list seems endless. That show was very popular during the war years and featured a host of characters, some of whom I can still vaguely remember. There was Mrs Mop, who would utter the phrase *"Can I do you now, Sir?"* A crusty old Colonel – I think he was called Chinstrap - would always chip in with *"I don't mind if I do, Sir!"* I'm probably getting mixed up here, please forgive me, but either on *'Itma'* or the *'Charlie Chester Show'* were a couple of 'spivs' called Tish and Tosh, who could always provide a pair of black-market nylon stockings on request! I'm pretty sure that it was the latter show that featured the jingle that went:

"Down in the jungle looking for a tent,
Better than a pre-fab – no rent!"

Other programmes which spring to mind include *'Henry Hall's Guest Night'*, a sort of musical variety show that was broadcast on Sunday evenings. The gentleman himself would introduce it with words that went along the lines of, *"This is Henry Hall speaking and tonight is my guest night"*. Then there was the lunchtime edition of *'Workers' Playtime'*, which always came from a factory somewhere, with workers being interviewed and choosing their favourite pieces of music. An evening programme went by the name of *'Variety Bandbox'*, and was basically a version of one of those theatrical shows that toured the provinces. Wilfred Pickles had a sort of quiz show, and was accompanied on the piano, I think by Violet Carson, who later went on to star as Ena Sharples in television's *Coronation Street*. The catch phrase of the show involved the handing over of the cash prize to the words *"Give him the money, Barney"*. Al Read was another popular radio comedian, with his famous remark, *"That's the wife from t' kitchen"*. *'Mrs Dale's Diary'* was on every afternoon, very easy to listen to, it always seemed to start with Mrs Dale, the doctor's wife, uttering those famous words *"I'm worried about Jim"*. Another daily serial which was avidly followed was *'Dick Barton, Special Agent'* – who can forget Dick, with his two colleagues, Snowy and Jock? And isn't it hard to believe that one of the top shows on the wireless was *'Educating Archie'* – which actually featured a ventriloquist's dummy as its star?

I can't remember the name of the singer, it must have been an American guy, who used to have a song that made us laugh during the hotter summer days. The words went something like:

"I open the door and the flies swarm in,
I close the door and I'm sweating again,
Life gets tedious, don't it?"

Whilst on the subject of 'words', I must relate a few lines from another song that, to me, always seemed to have a strong Liverpool connection when I first heard it. I quote:

'Mersey dotes and dozy dotes
But little lamsy tivey'

It wasn't until much later in life that I found out that the true words actually came out as:

'Mares eat oats and does eat oats
But little lambs eat ivy'

These were pretty meaningless words, to say the least; they may well have been sung by Bing Crosby, but somehow I think I prefer my originally misunderstood version!

One thing about listening to the wireless, it gave your imagination the chance to run riot. In those days, it wasn't all endless pop music and inane presenters who 'gob off' for what seems like hours on end. One serial that certainly gained a lot of popularity, although I think it was restricted to a weekly presentation, was *'Paul Temple Investigates'* – rather in similar mould to Dick Barton, but more intelligently written I guess. The theme music played its part too – was it something to do with *'The Flying Scotsman'*? And who could predict that *'Journey into Space'* would ever be the pre-cursor for the real investigation of outer space that followed some years later?

The subject of 'imagination' brings to mind an episode mentioned elsewhere, which still brings the hairs up on the back of my neck if I dwell upon it! It was that *'Woman's Hour'* serial, which I was following daily while laid up in bed during my bout of pneumonia. The story was about a house and was quite a spooky tale. As I was lying in bed in an otherwise empty house, it was easy to let the wireless story become reality – which it did when I heard footsteps creaking their way upstairs to the bedroom! Convinced that someone was sneaking their way up to do me all kinds of harm, I even got to talking out loud, asking my would-be attacker to hurry up and make himself known to me! It's pretty amazing how normal house noises can magnify and become the steps of a vicious murderer – thankfully I lived to tell the tale.

Other later programmes that come to mind are quite varied, though remembered with a lot of pleasure. Who can forget the *'Billy Cotton Band Show'*, with Billy's opening raucous cry of *"Wakey, wakey!"* Then there was *'Down your way'*, which paid a visit to some small village, town or suburb every week, playing musical requests and interviewing local people. One very popular feature was presented around lunchtime on a Sunday, that was *'Family Favourites'*, which played requests and passed messages on between families in Britain and their relatives serving overseas with the Forces. One song that really epitomised the programme was *'I'll be home'*, sung by Pat Boone.

I don't think that music on the wireless really made a huge impression on me while still living at Milton Road. It only caught on with me after we'd moved away to Cherry Lane – and I'll mention this in the appropriate chapter! But I do remember that John Cowan must have been 'ahead of his time', because he'd effortlessly trot out the names of some singers that I was still to catch up with – like Tony Bennett, Johnny Ray, Guy Mitchell and Al Martino. The popular female chanteuses of the day included Rosemary Clooney and Dinah Shore. I know I've mentioned this elsewhere in my narrative, but Uncle John (Hodgson) was a great wireless fan, his 'Bush' set always tuned in to some concert of classical music, which used to go 'right over my head' in those days.

Television makes its debut

It wasn't until I was about eight years old that the first television sets, in wobbly black and white, began to appear in homes. Not that we got one at the time – I'm pretty sure that May and Joe Hayes were the first proud owners in Milton Road. I seem to think the first programme I ever saw on the 'telly', provided you could manage to master the vertical and horizontal 'hold' buttons on the back of the set, was *'Muffin the Mule'*. Another favourite of the times was *'The Interlude'* – a sort of 'in-filler' that was used to fill the screen when there wasn't a programme being broadcast! Looking at some of the present-day programmes, I say 'bring back the interlude!' However, things began to look up when we three Gripton boys used to get 'invited' each year to go and watch the Cup Final on TV, this would be at Mr Slater's house on Southport Road. I recall the first such game that I saw on TV was around 1948, and I can definitely recall the famous Stanley Matthews' display for Blackpool in the 1953 Final. Mr Slater used to come round collecting the rent money and he must have taken pity on us poor neglected football fans! Richard 'Dick' Slater worked for the *Royal Liver* and was commonly known as a 'knocker man', as this was how he collected his monies – knocking on doors!

Further pastimes

Walking was hardly the most popular pastime for kids, but occasionally Dad would take us out, most likely on a Sunday morning. He was hardly an advertisement for good health himself, what with his ulcers and everything, but while we were striding along – usually in the Bootle direction, at least he would encourage us to *"breathe in through the nose, then out through the mouth"*. I don't suppose there were that many walks really, but the one that's sticks in the memory would be the traditional one that took place during the afternoon of Christmas Day. This was from Romley Street, as we accompanied Uncle John on a stroll. This would take us down into Wally Hall Park, usually all the way through from one end to the other. We'd get back to wake the adults from their after-dinner slumbers and it was probably at this point that the cards came out, along with the port and lemon!

I suppose the cheapest form of entertainment I can remember would be the occasions when some local man would appear on the sidewalk carrying a basket of racing pigeons! I think I'm right in saying that they were also known as 'homing' pigeons, as this was were they would hopefully return. Anyway, somehow the 'jungle grapevine' would quickly pass the message around and there would soon be a posse of youngsters begging the question *"Can we watch mister?"* – or even possibly *"Can we let one go mister?"* Probably the best vantagepoint for releasing these racing birds would be from the top of the rezzy, which was high enough to give a fairly commanding view of the surrounding area. Certainly, for the birds, it must have provided a head start on their flight back to their back-yard coops in various parts of the city. I'm not too sure as to the popularity of this pastime in present-day Liverpool, but I've hardly seen any sign of this once-popular 'sport' down here in Hampshire over the past thirty-five years. *(Amazingly, in early May of 2006, driving back into the village one day, I actually spotted a guy letting some pigeons free near the church, so the sport does still go on!)*

An occasional visitor to Milton Road used to be the 'spoons' man. He would turn up in the street with just a couple of old spoons and begin playing a tune, by banging those spoons on different parts of his body – head, elbows, knees etc. Basically, I suppose he was just a beggar on the lookout for a few coppers, but to us kids he was 'entertainment'. Another occasional public show was the escape artist who used to operate on the bombed site at the bottom of Arnot Street. He would try to emulate the most famous escapologist of all – Harry Houdini – as he worked his way out of assorted shackles and chains and a large hessian sack. While he was wriggling his way to freedom, an accomplice would be going round with the hat for appearance money, before the local bobbies could move in and shoo them away!

Transport

As far as I remember, most transportation in my early childhood days, particularly just after the war, was still horse-drawn, with cars a very rare sight. Certainly, the local coal-man delivered from a horse-drawn trailer, while the rag-and-bone man

31

made a weekly visit with his horse and cart, shouting out his cry of *"Any old rags?"* *Hanson's Dairy*, located on Carisbrooke Road, down near the tram sheds, was the local milk supplier. Deliveries were made on what seemed a 'chariot', again pulled by the faithful cart-horse, and loaded with huge metal milk churns, from which the milk was dispensed into your own jug or jar, to be taken into the house. *(Years later, when on holiday down at Padstow in Cornwall, I remember walking through the village of Saint Issey and having a look round what was then an antique shop on the corner. It was quite a pleasant surprise to come across one of those old milk churns, all nicely copper plated – and bearing the name Hanson's!)* Another 'fetch your own' type of service was provided by the local pub at the bottom of Stuart Road, *'The County'*, where an off-licence door was used to dispense a jug full of beer to it's customers.

Stuart Road was a well-used route for the horse-drawn trailers, particularly those of *Hanson's Dairy* and *Taylor's Bakery*. Those lucky people with small gardens or allotments would soon be outside with brush and shovel, once a horse had been heard trotting past! The bakery carts were large slow-moving things, across the back of which ran a huge wooden axle. Coming out of Arnot Street School, should a *Taylor's* cart be heading your way up Stuart Road, on its way back to the bakery in Buchanan Road, it was convenient to nip under the rear of the cart. Then you could drape yourself over the wooden axle-rod - and let the poor old horse pull you along. As well as the horses, motor-driven vehicles started making their re-appearance after the war-time fuel rationing, and we kids used to sit for hours on the corner of Stuart Road and Breeze Hill, taking down the numbers of passing cars for our collections. Then came the *'BRS'* *(British Road Service)* lorries, which always had the town or district name on the side – writing down these names was another hobby which lasted for the odd day here and there! We kept a special eye out for those lorries carrying hessian sacks of brown sugar – we called it 'togo' - from the docks. The hobby of 'racker catching' became popular, which meant jumping on the back of such lorries, using a knife to split the sacks, then grabbing handfuls of lovely dark brown sweetness – remember, food rationing went on for many years, even after the war ended. Where the terms 'racker' and 'togo' came from, I don't know!

Shops and pubs

Shopping used to be mainly a local affair, with shops located on most street corners in Walton, with whole rows of them along County Road, the main shopping thoroughfare that ran from Rice Lane in the north to Spellow Lane in the south – a couple of miles I would think. If I remember correctly, there was a greengrocer's shop located just around in Breeze Hill, I think it was called *Atherton's*. I can recall a sort of joke from those days, which I always associate with *Atherton's:* Mother to son: *"No of course not, Jimmy, you haven't got a big head. Now just pop around to the greengrocer's with your school cap and get me five pounds of potatoes!"*

Halfway up Stuart Road, where Bedford Road crossed it, the corners were occupied by four different outlets. *'The Stuart'* public house was one, with Byrne's chip-shop lying directly opposite. Then there was Charlie MacDougal's little grocery shop, where everything used to be on display in cube-shaped metal containers and you used to buy everything by 'the quarter' (quarter pound). Tea, sugar, biscuits etc would be served in little conical wrappers, with the top turned over and tucked in. Wonder where this story started? A little kid pops his head into the grocery shop and shouts, *"Got any broken biscuits, Mister?"* When the grocer says he has, the kid responds, *"Well get some glue and stick 'em back together!"* Finally, on the last corner was one of *Taylor's* bread shops. There, you could buy what seemed an enormous 'parkin', a type of gingerbread cake, for only a farthing - hard now to believe that a quarter of an 'old' penny was legal tender in those days! The bread shop eventually gave way to a newspaper and sweet shop, run by a guy called Jim Thompson. One of the treats from 'the chippy' would be a bag of all the little bits of batter that had been discarded and stored up on the hotplate – no doubt for those cheeky enough to ask!

(Note on Byrne's chip shop: In 2004, whilst watching a news item on TV about a hostage situation in Iraq, an interview was held in Bedford Road, where the hostage, a guy by the name of Ken Bigley, used to live – you could see Walton Church in the background. Then the scene shifted to the interior of 'Byrne's Sandwich Bar'. Yes, it was still the same shop, though with a somewhat healthier output! Sadly for Ken's family, his captors eventually murdered him – not a great advert for the world we live in today.)

It must have been many years later that I finally found what lay behind the doors of *'The Stuart'*! Dad used to frequent that pub of course, it being 'the local' as far as Milton Road residents were concerned. I was astonished to find that he never used to sit down in there. He would take his pint (or two or three) whilst standing in what used to be called 'the vestibule' or 'the lobby', ordering his liquid refreshment through a side window at the end of the main public bar.

Going into town

Sometimes a treat would be when you caught the tram into 'town' – the city centre. Electrically-driven trams were a feature of city life in those days, great green beasts of burden, clanging their way along the bustling streets on their metal tracks (or rails), with the pick-up wheel sparking against the overhead electric cable. They were eventually replaced by buses, of course, but this may now seem to have been an unnecessary step, when you think of the pollution put out by what are now mainly diesel-engine driven vehicles. One thing I do remember is the huge amount of trams that used to be kept waiting at the back of Goodison Park, ready to whisk away the crowds after football matches. They were very efficient at it too, they must have had a larger capacity than the later buses. There was one particular stopping-place on the route into town, whose name still sticks in my mind. I think at one time it must have been a theatre of sorts, but it was called 'The Rotunda' and had one of those high-domed roofs. It was located just on the junction where Kirkdale Road ran into Scotland – or 'Scotty' – Road, and may even still be there to this day. *(Mum later told me that 'Nana', my great grandmother, performed on the stage there when she was young.)*

The top deck of the tram was my favourite, from there you could see everything going on below. But one of my own personal experiences of 'the tram' was when I once went upstairs on one, and caught my finger in the door at the top of the stairs – pretty painful! However, the top deck was still a great vantagepoint, especially along bustling Scotland Road, where there must have been a pub on every street corner. Here the men played a game of 'toss' against the wall of their pub, no doubt using pennies and half-pennies, and the 'shawlies' carried their loads of washing high on their heads to and from the nearest wash-house. No washing machines in those days! Not many bathrooms either – it was either the tin bathtub in front of a fire or a trip to the public baths, such as the one at Norris Green that we were later to utilise when living at Cherry Lane.

The main destination for trams, otherwise known as the Terminus, seemed to be the Pier Head, down at Liverpool waterfront. Here, the trams would congregate before making their return journeys to all corners of the city. The driver would sit in his cab with a cigarette or pipe, while the conductor would change the pick-up arm over, to allow the tram to take the reverse direction. Then off they would go into the depot for a well-deserved cuppa, while the tram filled up with passengers. The Pier Head has always been a centre of attraction in Liverpool. When I was a boy, the ferries would be bustling backwards and forwards across the river, between Liverpool and the opposite bank, to Woodside (Birkenhead), Wallasey, Seacombe, Egremont and New Brighton. To embark on a ferry, one had to walk down a sort of gangplank onto the floating landing stage, a real source of wonder to impressionable children of all ages. From one's vantagepoint on the ferry, you could see the famous waterfront, with its symbolic trio of the *Royal Liver Building*, the *Cunard Building* and the offices of

34

the *Mersey Docks and Harbour Board* – sometimes called 'The Holy Trinity'. And behind all that, the shadow of the Anglican Cathedral looming over the city skyline from its home high on St James' Mount. *(Reading back through these memoirs, I remember seeing quite recently that the famous Liverpool waterfront skyline is changing tremendously, with the addition of some high-rise buildings – but that's progress for you!)* Just north of the landing stages was another ferry terminal, from where sailed the Isle of Man ferries on their four-hour journeys to that famous little island in the middle of the Irish Sea; home to the Tourist Trophy motor-cycle race and the fairies! We must have spent a few holidays on the Isle of Man, but I cannot remember looking forward to the trip, I was usually seasick!

It's not such a strong memory for me personally now, because I never actually used it, but I can still remember the overhead railway that ran along the front of the docks and was known to the locals as 'the dockers' umbrella', for obvious reasons. The docks and warehouses extended for some fair distance, and the railway ran all the way along, from Seaforth Sands in the north to Dingle in the south. It had been constructed between 1888 and 1893, serving an eventual total of seventeen stations along the waterfront, with magnificent views of the docks and all the huge ships that used to dock in Liverpool. The railway was hit by German bombers during the blitz, which caused some very serious damage, but it never completely closed down. However, its metal construction was under continuous attack by the salt air, causing it to eventually corrode so badly that it finally closed down at the end of December 1956, shortly after I'd gone off to join the Army.

Bicycles were used for all sorts of purposes, not just for fitness and pleasure, as is the case today. Ice-cream men began to appear on the streets after the war, selling their wares from containers mounted on bicycles, they must have used dry ice to keep the ice cream at the required low temperature. I've no doubt mentioned it elsewhere, but Mr Kelly from No.3 Milton Road did this sort of business on occasion. Another fairly regular service was supplied by the knife and scissors sharpener, whose grindstone must have been linked somehow by chain-drive to the bike gears, in order for him to ply his trade.

Services

Early on in my tale, I went on about the storage of coal – either indoors or outdoors. Well, of course, that coal also had to be delivered, and that was the task of the coal-man. The coal arrived on the back of a horse-drawn trailer, until these were later replaced by new-fangled lorries. But in both cases, the coal was stacked up in hessian sacks, which the coal-man and his assistant would have to haul up onto their shoulders

Mum with Cliff and me

and carry them into the storage area. Weighing in at a 'hundredweight' a time, this must have proved quite tiring after a long day's work. Eventually, as I seem to remember, the coal was replaced by coke, which was probably an attempt to reduce the amount of smoke pumped into the atmosphere. Another term I recall is 'nutty slack', which seemed to be a cheap form of coal and would 'spit' sparks from the fireplace, so that you would always need some form of fireguard in front of the fireplace to prevent hot sparks from landing on the linoleum! That term is short for linoleum, which is what everybody seemed to have as a floor covering in those days. What luxury it must have been, to be able to afford a wall-to-wall carpet - that's when you knew you 'had arrived'!

With those old coal fires, there were always huge amounts of smoke being drawn up the chimney, which led to an accumulation of soot. If this was left to build up, a chimney fire was a sure result. Thus it was that, periodically, one called on the talents of the local chimneysweep. Due to the obvious dirty work involved, the sweep would look pretty dirty too, and would usually be attired in a cloth cap and with a fag stuck behind his ear – well, that's the impression that sticks in my mind! Old sheets would be used to cover the furniture as the sweep began assembling his chimney-brush on the end of his pole. The pole would then be extended by the addition of extra sections, until the brush cleared the top of the chimney-stack, sending soot showering down the roof. Any soot that fell back down the chimney would be collected in sacks and often 'sold back' to the householder if he had a garden or allotment, as the soot apparently made a good addition to the soil.

Football – the stuff of life!

True Blues

Before our trips to the Saturday afternoon pictures, during the football season, we boys would stand at the corner of the street, watching the crowds making their way down Stuart Road, heading for either Goodison Park or Anfield, depending on which team was at home that day, Everton or Liverpool. There were no in-betweens, you either supported the Blues or Reds. With Dad being a Liverpool supporter, it was inevitable that we three brothers all became 'True Blues'! By the time that both the pictures and the football matches had finished, we would be back from the *Bedford*, standing outside May Beckett's house on the corner, hopefully trying to cadge a programme off one of the returning fans, first asking them *"What was the score, mister?"*

If Everton had managed to win, there would then be the excitement of waiting for the *Liverpool Echo* football edition to reach the shops, around six o'clock. *(Those were the days when **all** soccer matches kicked off at 3 o'clock Saturday afternoon, before games all began to be controlled by the vagaries of the TV scheduling.)* If I remember correctly, the paper shop that I used to dash to was down Breeze Hill, towards Rice Lane, where the paper would arrive, still warm from the printing. This would then be read from cover to cover, it was full of football news on a Saturday evening – in fact it was known as the *'Football Echo'* that day. Pictures and stories about our heroes would be diligently cut out and pasted into large scrapbooks, full of brown paper pages, to be read over and over again in the months ahead – I wonder what happened to them all? One of the highlights of the football reports in those days was the inevitable cartoon drawn by the famous George Green. Very simple in style and content, but with witty and honest comments, they were always a delight to read.

(During the summer months, if we fancied a change from 'playing out', we would sometimes head down to Wadham Road in Bootle, where Bootle Cricket Club played their home matches, I'm pretty sure they had a couple of guest West Indian players on their books at one time. I seem to remember that there was a concrete 'grandstand' at

one end of the ground, uncovered it's true, but it afforded an excellent view of events. Then there was a great big lolloping man called Ben, whose job it was to keep us boys from straying onto the playing area. Poor Ben was obviously simple and, in the way that boys do, we made fun of him and ragged him mercilessly, but I don't recall there being any malice, it was just a game to us then.)

But it was football that played a large part in the lives of most boys in Liverpool. I can remember that the first game I ever saw at Goodison was a pre-season friendly between Everton and an Irish side, Shamrock Rovers, which Everton – 'The Blues' – won by a whopping 7 – 1. Most of the first games I went to see were when 'the reserves' played on alternate Saturdays, these were cheaper than watching the first team and Ben Fuller, Derek and Sylvia's dad, would often give us a couple of spare tickets in the stands – a dream come true! I still remember most of the names of my heroes of those days, such as Ted Sagar, TG 'Tommy' Jones, Peter Farrell, Tommy Eglington, Cyril Lello, Ted Buckle, Dave Hickson, and John Willie Parker, to name just a few. Of course, at that time, there were no real 'foreign' players in the Football League, apart from the Irish, Scots and Welsh lads. Most of the Everton squad seemed quite old to us lads, and usually sported the slicked-down shiny hairstyles of the day. I guess Dave Hickson bucked the trend, with his unruly blonde hair a touch longer than was the fashion. He was certainly a 'boyhood hero' to me, and was referred to by the local soccer reporters as 'the stormy petrel'.

Centre-halves in those days were uncompromising in their play, and it was no surprise to see attacking forwards 'gently nudged' off the ball – to such an extent that they sometimes ended up over the concrete and into the crowd! So Dave always had his work cut out, trying to emulate his Goodison predecessors like Dixie Dean and Tommy Lawton. What he may have lacked in skill, he certainly made up for in the 'guts' department, able to give out as good as he got. I once saw him play against big Jack Chisholm – was he then with Plymouth Argyle? – and the two literally kicked each other all over the park. But there was no resentment, just a desire to get on with the game – and a handshake at the end said it all. Another I recall who came from the same mould was Malcolm Barrass, I think he was with Bolton Wanderers. In those days, the First Division seemed to be mainly made up from Lancashire sides such as Bolton Wanderers, Blackburn Rovers, Blackpool, Preston North End and the like. *(Good to see that a few have returned in recent years!)*

As we got older, we boys then used to go to the first-team games, paying ninepence to take up our places in the 'boys' pen'. This was in one corner of the ground, tucked under the stand at the Gwladys Street end, where we were literally penned in by railings, so I guess the view wasn't all that great. But the main thing is that we were there! As the games got towards the end, some fifteen minutes before the final whistle, all the ground gates would be opened to let out those spectators who wished to get away early. This was also the signal for loads of youngsters, who couldn't afford the entrance fee, to dash into the ground and get a brief glimpse of their heroes before the end of the match.

The Goodison goal machine!

I can recall one season, probably when I was about thirteen, when Everton scored twenty goals in three games, two sixes and an eight. This was when Everton were pushing for promotion back to the First Division, as it was then - they'd been relegated for some three seasons at the time. *(George Green's cartoon showed an 'Everton tank' firing footballs from its barrel – either into an empty net or knocking the goalie over on their way in.)* While on that subject, I was actually at the game, the last of the season in 1954, when Everton did get their promotion – and they have managed (but only just!) to retain their senior status ever since. The match was at Oldham, who were skippered then by George Hardwick, an ex-England international. Oldham's goalie was George Burnett, who had previously played for Everton, and he seemed to do the Blues a few favours that evening, dropping the ball at Parker's feet on a couple of occasions. Everton won 4 – 0, and went up as runners-up to Leicester City and have managed to 'stay up' in the higher echelon right up until the current season.

How well I remember the thrill of that day. I caught the bus home from school, dropping off at Walton Church, and being picked up by Jack Whitley and a couple of his mates in a *'Standard Vanguard'*. The game had an evening kick-off and the East Lancs Road seemed thronged with traffic, every single Evertonian must have been going there. When we arrived at Boundary Park, the Oldham ground, the low walls surrounding the terraces had been coated with fresh tar, but this still didn't stop hundreds of fans from 'bunking in'! We had tickets, bought legally I suppose, so we actually went through the turnstiles – but we were probably in the minority that evening! One disappointment was buying 'a programme' for the game, only to find out that it was a bootleg copy, run off by some enterprising local and not worth the paper it was printed on – what a rip-off!

A Cup Final to savour

Many years later, in 1966, the same season that England won the World Cup, I was fortunate enough to attend my first ever Cup Final at Wembley Stadium. I'd actually been able to see the Blues in action in the third round that season, when they

Victorious

came down to play non-league Bedford Town, a game which they won fairly comfortably by three goals to nil. By then, Jack Whitley had become an established Insurance broker, having a lot of both Everton and Liverpool players on his books. This meant that tickets to big occasions, previously like the proverbial gold dust to obtain, started to become readily available. I was still in the Army and living at Bordon at the time, so I made my own way up to London from Farnham on the train. Then it was the hustle and bustle of 'the Tube' up to Wembley, followed by that magical walk up Wembley Way towards the famous old stadium, with its twin towers. *(The 'new' Wembley, minus those towers, is currently under construction – and about a year behind schedule!)* Not so magical was the fact that Sheffield Wednesday moved into a 2-0 lead, with only around twenty minutes left to play!

Our regular centre-forward at the time was a lad called Fred Pickering, who had signed from Blackburn, but manager Harry Catterick had dropped him that day, in favour of an unknown youngster, Cornishman Mike Trebilcock – that name must have taken a lot of living up to on Merseyside! Anyway, it is now history how Mike scored two famous goals to bring the game level, leaving outside left Derek Temple to streak away and hammer the winner past the Wednesday and England goalie, Ron Springett. From tears of sorrow to tears of delirious joy in the space of a few minutes, I could have floated my way home, but actually did it conventionally, by train and bus!

The first game of the following season was away at Craven Cottage, in west London, against Fulham. Everton had just signed England's World Cup star Alan Ball from Blackpool and he scored what was the only goal of the game. I recall that it was a hot summer's day and, whilst standing on the terraces, I heard a voice behind me that I recognised. It turned out to belong to Geoff Getty, whose parents had owned the butcher's shop just along County Road from Romley Street. Hadn't seen him for a few years – and never since! A couple of years later, Everton were back at Wembley to play West Bromwich Albion. This time I met both Cliff and Geoff at some hotel in north London, and all three of us made our way to Wembley – I actually had a slimy blue monkey (honestly!) hanging around my neck for luck. But surely we didn't need luck with lots of new exciting players like Joe Royle, Jimmy Husband, Alan Ball and the like? Sadly, they never lived up to expectations that day, missing a hat-full of chances and eventually losing to the only goal of the game, scored after a lucky rebound by the current England centre-forward, Jeff Astle.

April 1970 saw the Blues win the League Championship, cementing Harry Catterick's position as one of the most successful managers in Everton's history. The midfield trio of Harvey, Ball and Kendall was no doubt one of the finest in football at the time. Sadly however, the rest of the Seventies proved a barren spell, with only a couple of long unbeaten spells (22 in 1977 and 19 in 1978) to their credit. Managers during that period were Billy Bingham and Gordon Lee. It wasn't until Howard Kendall returned to Goodison as manager in 1981, that a new era dawned.

Another three Finals

It was to be many years before the Blues got their chance of another FA Cup Final at Wembley. That was 1984 in fact, but it was the beginning of a 'purple spell' in Everton's history. By that year, younger daughter Michelle had become very interested in football and we began to attend quite a number of games, particularly if they took place within travelling range – the London clubs of course, plus such places as Southampton, Oxford, Swindon and Watford. Everton reached the semi-final and I took Michelle up to Highbury to see the game against Southampton. Adrian 'Inchy' Heath scored the only goal and it was *'Wembley, Wembley, here we come!'* We played Watford in the final, I remember the Everton fans singing *'Elton John's a homosexual'* before the game, as the singer was chairman of Watford at the time. Graeme Sharp and Andy Gray scored the goals that won us the Cup that year. Andy's clincher was a typically old-fashioned centre-forward goal. He went up with the Watford goalkeeper and virtually headed the ball out of his hands! The next two seasons followed a similar pattern, with both semi-finals taking place at Villa Park, Birmingham, and both leading on to another Final appearance beneath the twin towers. *(I think I'm right in saying that Joyce made one of those trips with me. I dropped her off at Birmingham's shopping-centre, 'The Bullring', and she whiled away a few hours while I went to the match!)* But Manchester United beat us 1-0 after extra-time in 1985's Final and next year it was Liverpool's turn by a margin of 3-1. These were obviously disappointing results, but it had proved a memorable three years, especially after the lads had gone on to win the European Cup Winners' Cup in 1985. 1989 brought another all-Merseyside Final, but once again the Reds got the better of us with a 3-2 victory.

Close to relegation

Things haven't quite lived up to some high hopes since then, I'm afraid; in fact the Blues have drifted far too close to relegation in recent years. In 1994, they had to win their last game of the season in order not to go down. Sue and Geoff were over visiting from Australia at the time and, in fact, we were all down in Devon together for a weekend at Colyton. We were actually in Sidmouth on the Saturday afternoon; I seem to recall it was a bit drizzly. We were walking around the town under brollies, while I had a 'tranny' (transistor radio) up against my ear.

Most depressing, as with about twenty minutes to go, the Blues were 0-2 down, at home against Wimbledon. *(Sounds familiar? Check out the 1966 Cup Final!)* Game over, season over, my interest in football definitely over! Then, incredibly, they began to claw their way back and it ended up with Graham Stuart mishitting the softest, jammiest goal you could imagine. But they all count and Everton lived to fight another day – and they're still fighting! The natives of Sidmouth must have thought there were a couple of loonies on the loose, as Geoff and I danced through the rain in celebration!

After that earlier series of Cup Finals, things turned quiet again for a few years. But, in 1995, with another 'old Blue', Joe Royle, back at Goodison as manager, the team returned to Wembley again. They were up against Manchester United and few neutral observers gave them much of a chance, but a Paul Rideout goal gained a surprise victory. Also starring in that side was a Nigerian player, I think he was called Daniel Amakachi, or something similar. On Merseyside he was referred to as 'The Black Cab' – from the Scouse wit version of Daniel 'I'm a taxi'! I had to make do with watching that game on the telly, but it was very exciting, nonetheless. I didn't get to Wembley for the game, I watched it on TV at home, with Michelle and James, who were visiting for the weekend. Sadly, I won't get to see Wembley's twin towers again, as they've now pulled them down!

By the way, the reader will notice a Latin connection in my chapter referring to my schooldays at the Liverpool Institute. Well, Everton's motto is in Latin too! *'Nil satis nisi optimum'* – literally 'not enough, unless the best'. A more contemporary translation comes out as *'Only the best is good enough'*. Again, a high aiming point I suppose, but hardly one that has been reached since 1995! Ah well, one can only live in hope and expectation – perhaps next season! *(As I sit browsing back through this chapter, early in 2005, the Blues have miraculously been going great guns this season, and are presently in fourth position in the Premier League – what used to called the First Division. This coming weekend they are drawn to play down at Plymouth in the FA Cup – bringing back memories of exactly thirty years ago when I made the trip down there for another 3ʳᵈ-round tie.)*

Just bringing things up to date at the end of the 2006 season, the Blues managed to hang on to fourth place in 2005 and qualified to represent the English Premier League in European football. Sadly, that didn't last further than the first qualifying round and probably led to the poor League performance that followed. Heading towards the end of the year, you'd have bet on them being relegated. But a fairly successful run of games, mid-season, finally saw them end in mid-table. I'm afraid you've got to have millions of pounds nowadays to be a successful club – and the 'Merseyside Millionaires' of earlier days have long since disappeared. But we still live in hope!

Footnote

It was quite an amazing coincidence that two of Everton's most famous heroes both died whilst later attending football matches at Goodison. Dixie Dean was the first, in March 1980, followed by Harry Catterick in March 1985. More recently, another two favourites died at early ages – Brian Labone in April 2006, aged 66, and Alan Ball in April 2007, he was only 61 years of age.

Uncle John and my Dad (Joe)

School days

My first (primary) school was the one in Arnot Street, Walton, just across the railway line from the back of Romley Street. It was many years later that I found out that my Dad and all his siblings had attended the same school, as did myself, followed by Cliff, and lastly Geoff. Although I cannot even picture her now, I'll always remember that my first teacher was a 'Miss Rimmer', who taught us to shine our shoes with *"a little bit of polish and a big, big rub"*. Another memory is of the young girl who shared my desk in the back row of that first classroom – by the name of Irene Niblock. Another name that springs to mind is that of Billy Culshaw, his hands were covered in warts and no one wanted to hold his hand during 'ring-a-roses'.

Apparently when I got home after my first day, Mum asked what I'd eaten for dinner and my reply came out as *"maroons and selomina"* – I think she eventually worked out that I'd had prunes and semolina! Anyway, that was nothing compared to the time I was sent down to Mr Byrne's, the local chippy, and actually asked for *"corn plasters"*, instead of Cornish pasties! Those little mistakes aside, I must have enjoyed Arnot Street School and got on quite well, as I eventually ended up at the Liverpool Institute High School for Boys. This was a grammar school, located in the city centre, under the shadow of the Anglican Cathedral – a most impressive looking building which has always been an outstanding feature of the city's skyline.

Arnot Street

Arnot Street seemed such a huge place; it took up the whole length of the street, if memory serves me correctly. I used to go in through a huge door, like the gateway to a castle, into the schoolyard at the County Road end. Just behind the yard ran the 'LMS' *(London Midland Scottish)* railway and, if a train went past, smoke and steam would billow up into the air and fill the yard. On the right-hand side were some iron stairs that ran up to an iron bridge, which you would have to cross if you were in one of the class-rooms located on the other side. It's likely that those rooms were for the senior class, as I recall going over the bridge only in my last year, when I was in Mr Tom Hulse's class. Amazingly, I can't remember any of the Arnot Street teachers between my first one and my last!

The schoolyard served, of course, as the playground, with all sorts of games going on at break time and during the lunch-break – conkers, 'ollies' (marbles), yo-yo, all depending on the season. Mind you, it was difficult playing 'footie' in the yard, while the girls were also there with their skipping ropes *("salt, mustard, cayenne pepper")* and other groups would be playing hopscotch! But we managed, honing our skills by kicking around an old tennis ball – and kicking out the toes of our shoes in the process. The arrival of snow in the winter would give us an added attraction – that of 'the slide'. By the time a few of us had slid our way across the length of the yard, the slide would become like a shiny mirror and you'd be able to go faster and further with each go. This would leave the toes of our shoes intact, but of course the soles must have worn through pretty quickly! We must have cost our parents a packet. The answer, of course, was to put us into 'wellies', those black shiny rubber ones from *Dunlop* that always ended up so smelly! Trouble was, your socks would always end up under your feet, while the back of each welly would rub your leg red raw on the back. The trick was to turn down the tops of the wellies, then pull your socks right up and turn them down over the tops of the boots too. While playing in the snow, however, you'd inevitably get snow pushed down your wellies by the 'bullies', ending up with wet, cold feet and a few chilblains (or did we call them 'chaps'?) to take home and toast in front of the fire! Wonderful times!

Going to school generally meant that you would also attend school dinners. You would pay your 'dinner money' on a Monday morning and be given your five tickets, one for each day of the week that followed. Anyone remember what happened if you lost a ticket? I can't say for certain what those meals were like in those days, but memories of pale green cabbage, boiled to destruction, come to mind, followed by watery yellow custard! No, I'm sure they weren't that bad, at least Mum swore by them – she has always said that school dinners changed me completely! Apparently, I had, up to then, been a very fussy eater. So fussy that, if given a slice of bread and jam, I would only hold it if the slice had been left clear of either marge or jam down one edge, so that I didn't get my fingers sticky! Anyway, I suppose that going to school dinners meant that you either ate or went without and I must have made up my mind to eat! From those days on, I've eaten just about anything that has been placed before me and I don't mind trying something new at any time.

Arnot Street had no 'sports ground' as such, but if an open space was required for football or cricket, we would be taken down to 'Wally Hall Park', going through what was always known as Walton Village. *(I'm sure I read somewhere that Walton-on-the-Hill was there long before Liverpool itself came into being.)* The 'goal' would be marked by a couple of articles of someone's clothing, laid down on the floor to indicate the goalposts. Another pastime that was encouraged was swimming, though I can't honestly remember any formal swimming lessons. Again, each class would be marched down to the swimming baths on Queen's Drive, with your 'cossie' wrapped up in a towel and tucked under one arm. Remember those navy blue woollen cossies? One encounter with the water and they would stretch and hang down almost to your ankles!

Those early school days must have gone by in a blur, it is difficult to pick out any defining moments. I do recall being sent to school in what was called a 'lumber jacket', a sort of *blouson* affair with buttoned sleeves and a buttoned-up front. It was in a dark shade of green and had a lighter green diamond-shaped piece of material on the back. For some reason, this got me the nickname *'Greenie'* by at least a couple of boys and I recall having to fight back after being picked on by a lad (name of Wiseman?) who lived down Breeze Hill. I remember bashing his head on the metal stairs in the playground and being told off quite sternly over it.

Bullying at school is not a new thing, I'm pretty sure every generation has seen it in some shape or form. One poor lad who came under its influence at Arnot Street had the surname 'Cam', I believe his Dad ran a hairdressers' salon near Inman Street on County Road. Young Cam, for some reason that I don't know, had crapped himself in the schoolyard and I remember a whole gang of kids being gathered around him, taking the mickey and calling him all sorts of unsavoury names, and remarking upon how smelly he was. It was hardly the occasion to go to his rescue, as he did niff a bit!

Having attended Arnot Street from the age of five, secondary education then beckoned. I must have done reasonably well up to then, because I was entered for the *'Margaret Bryce'* scholarship, not really knowing what that meant. But it did mean that I was given my own ruler and geometry set, and no doubt a propelling pencil, which meant that it was something 'top drawer'! I also know that I had first one 'recall', followed by a second, though I never actually passed this prestigious examination. However, I had managed to gain my '11-plus' qualification and consequently went on to enter the famous Liverpool Institute High School for Boys, located in Mount Street, just north of the city centre.

The 'Inny'

The school building was very imposing, with huge gothic looking columns rising towards the sky outside of the front entrance. The school had been founded ever since 1825 and was long renowned as a centre of excellence in educational circles.

It is no longer a school in the original sense, it finally closed as such in 1985 and the building was well on its way to becoming derelict. In recent years, however', it has been resurrected to become the Liverpool Institute for the Performing Arts (LIPA), following a lot of effort and publicity from one of its famous ex-pupils, Sir Paul McCartney, he of *'Beatles'* fame, who attended a couple of years behind me. Another of that famous band was George Harrison, who was also an 'Inny' boy, probably a year after McCartney. I cannot claim to have known either of them at school, but Cliff and Geoff would have been there at approximately the same time. *(This doesn't prevent me from doing a spot of name dropping when the occasion arises!)*

Going to grammar school meant having to wear school uniform. This consisted of a black blazer and grey flannel trousers, adorned by the school badge, school tie and school cap, all in a mixture of black and green. All the masters – and Miss Inkley! (but you can call me 'Sir') – wore flowing black gowns and mortar-board hats, a tradition handed down from the 'public school' way of life and which certainly added a spice of interest to those of us who had never encountered this mode of dress before. By the time I was due to leave 'the Inny', I had started to rebel against the uniform and started wearing a brown-check sports jacket along with drainpipe style trousers, copying the then *in vogue* 'Teddy boys' of the mid-Fifties. In fact the lads in my last form all actually called me 'Ted', a nickname that has stuck to this day with those who remember me!

Another change, for me personally, was the need to get to school by bus. This would first involve what seemed a long a walk down Stuart Road, then along County Road (past Arnot Street of course) to Spellow Lane, where the No.3 bus to its Dingle destination would be waiting outside *'Burtons the Tailors'* shop at the end of Barlow Lane. My bus journey would end by my jumping off outside of Lime Street station, from where I would walk up Mount Pleasant, then along Rodney Street, to the school. When I say 'jumping off', that was in the literal sense, as it was regarded as 'dead cissy' to wait until the bus had stopped before alighting! Another Walton boy, Billy Edwards, lived just a couple of streets away from me, in Cromwell Road. As he was also a pupil at 'the Inny', I would usually knock on his door on the way past, to see if he was ready. But, more often than not, he was late, despite his mother making frantic calls into the house, and eventually I gave up waiting for him as a lost cause! As hinted at previously, both of my brothers, Cliff and Geoff, eventually followed in my footsteps by attending at the same school – although I can't for the life of me ever remember travelling to school with either of them!

One thing that has remained with me for the rest of my life is the school motto, in Latin, which went *"Non nobis solum, sed toti mundo nati"*. The meaning of this, literally, is *"Born not for ourselves alone, but for the whole world"*. Quite something to live up to really! At the end of each academic year, the whole school would assemble in the Liverpool Philharmonic Hall, at the other end of Hope Street. Here we would listen to the speeches, particularly that made by the Head Boy – again in Latin, which I'm sure not that many understood, but it sure sounded impressive! The headmaster was a stern looking chap by the name of Mr Edwards – or 'the Baz', as he was universally known. J R Edwards had been headmaster since 1935 and went on right through until 1961.

At first I seemed to sail through 'the Inny' quite well, even with the new subjects thrust at me. I took Latin with Danny Willot and German with Danny Booth, my first form-master. Chemistry was taught by Nicky Naylor, who hobbled round with an iron frame on his leg and seemed to wheeze a lot, poor chap; and Physics was with B L Jones – or 'Bilge' as he was called, whose gown front always seemed to be littered with cigarette ash! But then I went down with double pneumonia and was off school for a long period of time. When I returned, the 'powers that be' decided that, due to my previous success, I would probably soon catch up but sadly, this didn't turn out to be the case! Being in the 'science stream' was hard enough, but having that long break meant that I never did do that well afterwards and I ended up in Form RA – the 'Removes', which inevitably became the last year of school – no sixth form and certainly no going on to University. I finally ended up with just the two O-levels, one in Maths and the other in English, both of which had always been my favourite subjects and remain so until today.

Not that being in RA seemed like a disaster, I don't think I've enjoyed a year like it! Everything seemed to be going past in a whirl, growing up fast and learning all the dodges, rather than any useful schoolwork! Wednesday afternoons would be a time when we'd bunk off early and go down to the *Palais de Luxe* (pronounced of course as 'Pally de Loo'!) cinema in town. Here we would watch some dreadful old black and white horror film, like *'The Bride of Frankenstein'* or *'Dracula meets the Werewolf'* – and we'd probably sneak in for free via a side-door! Those were the days when Lon Chaney and Bela Lugosi were the stars of horror, long before the British *'Hammer Films'* versions of later years. Lunch breaks would give us the chance to nip down to one of the 'record shops' to listen to the latest offerings. I'd usually go with a lad called Verd Moore – I think the 'Verd' was short for Verdun, which had been one of the battles during the First World War. We'd usually end up in the record shop

48

in Manchester Street (it may have been one of *Epstein's*), just above the entrance to the Mersey Tunnel. I remember once 'nicking' that old skiffle favourite *'Rock Island Line'* by Lonnie Donegan, only to find that our radiogram at home would only play 78's, and not those new-fangled 45's!

This sporting life!

Just like Arnot Street before it, 'the Inny' did its best to encourage a sporting tradition, owning its own sports grounds down at Mersey Road, alongside the river in Aigburth. However, the schoolyard still represented the epitome of most boys' sporting achievements at footie and cricket. Within the 'lower yard' were a couple of courts, where the game of 'fives' was carried out. This was very similar to what I now know as squash, though it was played without a racquet. Instead, a leather glove would be used to protect the hand, and it was the five fingers of the hand that smashed the ball around – hence the term 'fives' I suppose! Swimming also continued, I think we probably attended the one session every week. This would be to the salt-water baths in Cornwallis Street, down towards the waterfront, where the water always had a greenish hue. It was here, when we were undressing to put on our cossies, that we found out where red-headed and bespectacled Lionel Fullwood got his nickname 'Lash' from – and it certainly wasn't from the old cowboy film-star Lash Larue! Another boy with a certain claim to fame in that department was Alastair Graves, who was well known for hanging it through the gates in the 'upper yard', where the local factory girls could cop a free feel as they went past!

I had always enjoyed a game of cricket – well, the sort you played against the wall at the end of Milton Road! A similar game was played in the schoolyard at the Inny, the ball used was actually of the 'tennis' variety, so was reasonably easy to hit. One year there was some sort of 'trial' in the yard and young Gripton was noted down as a 'slogger'. This actually got me into some sort of white apparel and an appearance on the cricket pitch down at Mersey Road. I came up against one of the schoolmasters, Les 'Squinty' Morgan, nicknamed for two obvious reasons, both of which looked in different directions! *"This is going to be easy, he's old and slow and I'm a slogger"* – well, that was how the script was supposed to read! Unfortunately, Squinty's eyes weren't the only things going in all directions – so did the ball. With the benefit of a seam on the ball and his knowledge of spin bowling, Squinty tore up the script and managed to make me look a complete fool. I never got near one ball of my single over, thus my short trial as a *bona fide* cricketer ended very quickly indeed! *(I did manage to revive my cricket career in the Seventies – but that's for another chapter!)*

I didn't have too glorious a career at soccer either! It's strange just how good you can play, using an old tennis ball, either in the street or in the schoolyard – but just try converting this skill onto a pitch of muddy grass with a leather ball that gets heavier and heavier as it soaks up the water! I do remember one glorious and shining moment in the schoolyard, when I actually managed to dribble the ball, not once, not twice, but three times, past a struggling J J Gurney, and then lash the ball through the metal posts of the bike-shed that stood in for goalposts! I had a very lucky escape one year – nothing to do with football directly, but my feet were certainly involved! It may have come about through wearing second-hand shoes that were a bit too small, Mum has always professed her guilt over this, but it was hardly her fault, there wasn't too much money about in those days! But somehow, I began to suffer in-growing toenails. Now, I know that sounds funny, in fact many a comedian (and there were plenty in Liverpool, believe me!) has used this complaint as a ready-made laugh generator. But, believe me, it was no joke when the big toes on both my feet became inflamed with gangrene, it could have led to the loss of both limbs or even death!

Fortunately, having suffered from painful toes for some time, they got so bad that I was ushered into Walton Hospital for a check. The next thing I know is that I'm coming around from the anaesthetic, having had an operation on both feet, where the whole root of the nail on each big toe was removed, it was pretty painful at the time, I can tell you! The stupid thing is that, soon after being released from hospital, I played football in the schoolyard once again. It wasn't until I got home that I found I couldn't take my shoes off. The stitches had burst and profuse bleeding had led to a sticky situation. Thankfully, there were no dire consequences, but it was to be quite a while before I dared kick a ball again.

Nicknames that will never fade

Returning to the educational side of life once again, it is amazing how the names of the schoolmasters can stay so long in the memory – particularly those who had an accompanying nickname. Even today, when I attend a reunion dinner, generally at Anfield on the first Friday in March each year, all the talk is about 'old so-and-so'. In no particular order, I'll try to recall as many of those masters as I can, besides those already mentioned:

Slimy Reece – he was the 'VP' or Vice-Principal, Fanny Bentliff, Prolly Peters, Pinhead Preece, Whiffy Edge, Jolly Rogers, Alfie Hosker, Dickie Moore, Doc Wallace, Tudor Jones, Stan Reed, Danny Booth, Danny Willot *et al*. The list is seemingly endless and each single name immediately brings his face to mind too, they must have made quite an impression. Certainly, it was 'Pinhead' who gave me my love of the English language; I've always prided myself on spelling and pronunciation and endeavoured to use the language in the way that I was taught all those years ago. I hope that this particular 'history' proves the point!

W F Edge – hence the 'Whiffy' – also went by the name of 'Cliff', again for a patently obvious reason! He used to take us for history and was a particular victim of schoolboy pranks, due to his usually easy-going nature. Our classrooms were heated by these huge cast-iron radiators, which were connected to pipes of an enormous circumference. In those days too, we were still issued with a daily bottle of milk at morning break. Once the milk had been drunk, at a given cue the empty bottles would be dropped onto the metal pipes, where they would either shatter or at least make a terrible racket!

I've already mentioned the gowns that the masters wore. When Whiffy was writing on the blackboard, someone from a front desk would sneak up and pin a notice on the back of his gown, usually with either *'Kick Me'* written on it, or *'Whiffy Stinks'*! Poor Cliff, he must have had his leg pulled by his colleagues when he went back to the masters' common room bearing such messages on his back. On one occasion, Fatty Norris crept up behind Whiffy's back while he was in his usual chalking mode, and set fire to the paper in the wastebasket. When Whiffy turned round and spotted the flames leaping up, he put his foot firmly into the basket in order to put out the fire. Trouble is, his foot got stuck in the basket and he was last seen tearing hotfoot down the corridor!

I'd taken Latin as a subject during my early days at the Inny, not that I was particularly enthusiastic about it, but it probably put into one's mind the 'structure' of language, to say the least. It also gave rise to the occasional 'double entendre', such as the 'verse' that follows!

'Caesar et sum iam forte,
Marcus et erat.
Caesar sic in omnibus,
Marcus sic in at!'

If one 'interprets' the first line as *'Caesar ate some jam for tea'*, then the final three lines make an odd sort of sense too! A proper Latin phrase that has always stuck in my mind is *'festina lente'*, literally translated as 'hasten slowly'. When one expands that into 'more haste, less speed', it is quite a good philosophy on life!

As already mentioned, my last year was spent in 'the Removes', under the stern eye of Jake Edwards our form master – the same name as the headmaster. He took us for geography and did his best to instill some sort of discipline in us, but it must have

Brig. Tom, Burf, Perce, Jake, Quine, Tay, Snakey, Ken, Hitch, Marlon.
Doc, Geoff, Baldy, M.o, Verd, Bill, Lionel.
Chas, Eddie, Me, Rick, Kate, Hoppy, Phil, Col.

FORM RA. 1955-6.

proved very difficult. By then, all our thoughts had turned to the future and what we'd do when we left school. (Personally, I still didn't have a clue!) I do still have in my possession a photograph that features most of the lads in that class, and caught up with one of them, Richard 'Dickie' Quirk, at a reunion held at the old school itself in the summer of 2001. This should have been held the previous year, which was the 175th anniversary of the school's founding, but what's a year between friends?

One particular day stays in my memory, I think we all stayed in the same classroom all day long, before being allowed to go home early that afternoon. This was due to the fact that King George the Sixth had just died, it was in February 1952, and across the schoolyard from us, the bells of the Liverpool Anglican Cathedral rang their mournful tones continually, once the sad news had been officially announced. If I remember correctly, it was Whiffy's classroom that we were ensconced in on that fateful day.

At some period prior to leaving school, I was asked whether I'd like to apply for 'WOSB' (War Office Selection Board), which could lead to entry into the military services. This idea I put firmly to one side – I mean, who wanted to join the Army? – so it is pretty strange that only a few short months later I had actually joined the Army as an apprentice tradesman!

52

Reunions and Liobians

I mentioned 'reunions' a couple of paragraphs ago. This came about when my sister Sue contacted me around 1996, to say that she'd heard about the LIPA organising an 'open day' for ex-pupils from the 'Inny'. Along with Colin Drasutis, who lives in Hampshire not too far away from me, I duly went to attend this open day, as well as Sue, who had herself attended Blackburne House, the associated 'sister' school to the Institute. Having enjoyed a film and a presentation, we were all sat there chatting, when I happened to hear the term *'Liobians'* mentioned, by a couple of 'old' guys just along the bench from us. Now the *Liobians* had always been famous as a soccer team when I was a lad, I think they played in one of the local leagues – was it the *Zingari*? I questioned one of those older guys, called Bill Thomas, whether this was still the case. It wasn't, but the name lived on as a 'cover' for ex-Inny boys who gathered together each year for a 'Reunion Dinner'. It turned out that Bill was (and still is) the Secretary, so our names were added to his list of ex-pupils. This set Colin and myself off on a journey of pure nostalgia and we've been attending these annual get-togethers (at Anfield) as often as possible over quite a few years now.

In 2001, I had a letter inviting me to attend the Inny once again, this time at a celebration evening for the school's 175th anniversary – as already mentioned, this should actually have been in 2000, but it got delayed! I went along by myself to that function, and was delighted to meet up with three guys from my own school year, in the shape of Dickie Quirk, Mo Scholl and Harry Fynn. The following year, Dickie and Mo made it to the Anfield dinner, but for reasons best known to the organisers, we were on separate tables! I'm making sure that we sit together in 2003! At that 2002 dinner/reunion, I spoke with Dr Iain Taylor, another old boy of the School who has been commissioned to write up the history of the old place from 1935 – 1985. It was only then that I realised that there was already a history written – by a guy whose name was Herbert Tiffen – from the founding of the School in 1825, up until 1935. I mentioned this to Sue and her husband Des, and was delighted when Des actually went into Liverpool just a day or so later and found an old copy and posted it on to me. Amazingly, the Headmaster in 1935 was J R Edwards – still there when I made my entrance in 1951 and going strong as I left in 1956.

A few years back, Colin Drasutis loaned me a CD, which I then tape-recorded, on cassette of course, called *'Liverpool Oratorio'*, written by Paul McCartney. It is operatic in theme and based on Macca's early life story, most of it with his years at the Liverpool Institute as the backdrop. If anyone reading this, especially those with Scouse blood or an Inny education, hasn't heard this musical piece, I'd certainly

53

encourage you to do so. In closing this chapter, I'm sure that Paul McCartney won't mind me quoting the words of one of the *Beatles'* songs, which just seems so appropriate for the spirit of what I am hoping to instill from this written account:

"There are places I'll remember all my life,
Though some have changed.
Some forever, not for better,
Some have gone and some remain.
All these places had their moments,
With lovers and friends I still can recall.
Some are dead and some are living,
In my life I've loved them all."

Postscript

I didn't really think I'd have anything further to add to this chapter, but bear with me! Early in 2006, I contacted Dicky Quirk regarding trying to get in touch with any old members of RA 1955/56. He subsequently posted an advert in the *Liverpool Echo* and results from that are still awaited. Knowing my own previous difficulties in raising contacts for my 56B Army pals, the whole effort may prove negative. However, Dicky happened upon an e-mail address for Verd Moore and passed it on to me. Happy to say that I posted off an e-mail and got an instant reply from Verd! Hopefully we shall keep in touch again after all those years – fifty of them, even with my Inny maths background! And then another contact arrived, courtesy of *Friends Reunited*, in the shape of Ken Lawson, now living down in Devon. Having missed out at Anfield in 2005, I managed to miss the Liobian Reunion again in 2006 – snowed in at Culcheth! – but hopefully I shall make it 'third time lucky' in 2007.

Another 'last word'! I did make it to the 2007 reunion and was pleased to sit at the same table as Dicky once more, as well as Ken Lawson, who had made it for the first time. Many old memories surfaced, as you can imagine, including the remembrance that Ken had been known as 'Kate' when in RA – due to his initials, KT – Katey? But what's in a name? My last glance at this before committing it for publication is during February 2008 – only three weeks to the next reunion!

Memories of holidays

The early days

As I recall them, from the foggy shrouds of nostalgia, childhood summer holidays, away from school at last, seemed to go on forever. *(I suppose they did really, seeing that they were something like eight weeks at a time!)* They were great days for us kids in Milton Road and, as already mentioned, the street itself provided our major environment and playground. However, on special occasions, one or two of our 'aunties' would gather a few of us together and take us round by the 'rezzy' steps in Breeze Hill, where we would catch the big green double-decker No.60 bus down to Bootle railway station. Here we would jump on an electric train and head up the coastal line – Seaforth, Litherland, Crosby, Blundell Sands, Formby, Ainsdale, and Birkdale. These were all stops on the line between Liverpool's Central Station and Southport, and, once outside the city boundary, offered a little seaside spot where we kids could run around and play to our hearts' content.

I was pretty skinny as a kid (more skinny than pretty did I hear you say?) and I'm sure that Mum must have despaired of me ever putting on weight. If we went to the seaside for the day, we didn't have all the fancy designer shorts and t-shirts that the present-day children wear, we'd just have to make do with our everyday short trousers, the same ones that we wore to school. The trouble was that I had no hips on which they would rest, so even if I occasionally took my shirt off, I would still need to wear a pair of braces to hold up the trousers! Nor did we have the wetsuits and surfboards, or goggles and snorkels, of these modern days, so activities tended to be restricted to the odd game of hide-and-seek and a paddle in the briny. I can hear the shouts to this day – *"Don't you dare get your trousers wet, they've got to last another fortnight!"* There was one occasion when I managed to get myself caught in some 'sinking sand' and had to pulled out by John Cowan and Harry Hayes – no wonder they remained my mates for years afterwards!

During the early war years, when I was still but a toddler, Mum and I were both evacuated, away from German efforts to destroy the Liverpool docks, down to a small town called Wellington, deep in rural Shropshire. *(Wellington has now been mainly*

Myself as a baby, with Rex on Aunty Annie's Shropshire farm

subsumed into the 'new town' of Telford.) Dad's own father, another Joe Gripton, had originally come from that area, having been born in Shifnal I believe. *(I've promised myself many times that I will pay a visit there one day!)* This family connection meant that he had an 'Aunty Annie' down there, who lived on a farm called Wheatley Grange. I remember it had its own water-well and pump just outside the door, an orchard full of fruit trees out back somewhere and an external two-seater wooden toilet! I'm told that Annie refused to go there unless accompanied by one of her sons! I still have a photo at home of myself, a happy smiling little fair-haired lad then, sitting in the orchard alongside Rex, the farm's collie dog.

Some years later, along with younger brothers Cliff and Geoff by then, Mum took us down to the farm one year for a summer holiday. What a thrill that journey turned out to be! Firstly we must have taken the tram down to the Pier Head, then caught a ferry across the Mersey, then finally a 'real' train i.e. steam engined, down from Birkenhead, via Chester, to Shrewsbury. I'm sure that we sat on the train at one stage for what seemed an eternity, stationary and isolated on the line in the middle of the countryside. Eventually, a ride on a *'Midland Red'* bus took us down to our final destination, I suppose it would have taken us most of the day to get there. Thinking back, my main memories of the farm, and its inhabitants, must have come from that era, as my earlier visits took place when I was too young to make much sense of everything.

Anyway, it must have seemed like a wonderland to three city kids, being out in the countryside, surrounded by green fields, rivers and canals. One of Annie's sons took me fishing one day, I can remember sitting alongside a canal where the road ran across it by a bridge. I can also recall that, as you came downstairs in the farmhouse, there was a huge overhead shelf, piled high with jars of goose-grease, which I think was Annie's eternal remedy to every symptom imaginable! The three of us boys slept in the same huge bed, constantly ducking our heads under the covers as we were bombarded by what must have been 'daddy long legs' and moths. No doubt they seemed more like German dive-bombers to us at that age! Another memory is of Mum taking just me to the picture house in Wellington, we saw an American musical called *'Under the sheltering palms'*, or some such title.

(Many years later, while visiting old Army pal Dave Howlett when he was stationed at Donnington, we looked up the old Wheatley Grange, which by then had been converted into a private dwelling. Remarkably however, it was still fairly recognisable to me, particularly the old cowshed facing onto the road, but now converted into a smart barn. Unfortunately, there was nobody in the house at the time, but to cut a long story short, I actually caught up with 'Cousin Bill', still living in the area then at Oakengates, but now sadly passed on. What really pleased me – and caused the hairs on the back of my neck to stand up! - was that when he opened his door in response to my knock, he said *"Well I'll be blowed, if it isn't our Pete"!*)

Going out from Walton on the occasional coach – or charabanc -trip springs to mind, these were very much local ones, probably run as 'day trips' by one of the neighbours. Mainly we would go to some seaside town on the North Wales coast, such as Rhyl, Colwyn Bay or Prestatyn. I recall one such trip where we went into the local *Woolworth's* and competed with each other as to how many *Dinky* toys we could walk off with, without paying! The return trips during the evening inevitably ended up in a singsong, with someone playing the banjo or ukulele – just hope it wasn't the driver! The 'pop star' (and, indeed, film star) of the day was George Formby – and everybody used to try and emulate his 'cheeky' songs such as *'I'm leaning on the lamppost'*, *'When I'm cleaning windows'* and *'With my little ukulele in my hand'*! And at the end of each of his films, George would utter his eternal phrase – *"Turned out nice again!"*

I can remember once staying at a 'camp' in North Wales for a couple of weeks, it may have been a school trip, or perhaps it was as a member of the *'Lifeboys'*. Anyway, it was at a place called Dyserth, and parents were allowed to visit during the middle weekend. As we were sleeping in wooden huts, on straw-filled palliasses and bunk beds, goodness knows what impression our parents got – I seem to remember my Mum visited, probably with Ruby Kelly from next door, and went away crying!

It's amazing how some things stick with you, and that trip gave rise to a singalong rhyme that I still recall:

"There is a prison camp down Dyserth way
Where you get bread and jam three times a day,
Eggs and bacon you don't see,

Bloody great beetles in your tea,
Down Dyserth way."

I also seem to remember that we made a couple of trips to a place called Cartmel – or was it Carnforth? What we did at either of the two, I don't know, both are located at the edge of the Lake District, around the Morcambe/Grange-over-sands area. It may have been on one such trip that we first passed a large country-style pub on the old East Lancs Road, I think it may have been called the *'Rose and Crown'*. As far as I recall, it was run by Albert Pierrepoint, who at that time had a second occupation – that of public hangman! Is it my imagination, or did the coach always speed up a little as it went past? *(Our Geoff later reckoned that the pub in question was on the Preston Road, near a place called Penwortham.)*

The Isle of Man

It's hard to remember on how many occasions we went to the Isle of Man, or even to know if we went for one week or two at any one time. Recalling Dad's low wages, I suspect it was just for the one week, but there must have been sufficient trips for the place to remain firmly in my memory. The start and finish would always be that ferry trip across the Irish Sea from Prince's Dock, it could be pretty daunting at times, when rough weather would cause the boat to toss up and down like a cork in the water. I can certainly remember being as sick as a dog on at least one occasion and the cure for it seemed to be to go out on deck and let the cold spray off the Irish Sea whip into your face. I think it worked too! But there was always the magical thrill of looking out for the first sight of land, either approaching the island or returning 'across the bar' into the mouth of the Mersey, to be confronted by that fascinating collection of waterfront buildings. The ferries were operated by the *Isle of Man Steam Packet Company*. They all had names that were associated with the island, like *'Mona's Queen'*, *'Snaefell'*, *'Tynwald'* and *'Lady of Mann'* – no doubt my memories aren't too accurate on that score! (Geoff again adds his two penn'orth with *'Manxman'*, *'Mona's Isle'* and *'Ben-my-chree'*.)

Postcard of Ronaldsway Airport, Isle of Man, 1962

We used to stay at what must have been a small guesthouse, which was located in a street somewhere behind the *'Crescent'* cinema in the centre of Douglas Bay, and run by a woman named Mrs Quayle – with that name, she could well have been of Irish descent. It was a bit like one of those old seaside postcard jobs – yes, there was a 'sea view' all right, provided you popped your head up through the skylight in the roof! Perhaps it was there that I tasted my very first kipper! These smoked herrings were one of the delicacies that could be described as an 'acquired taste'. But certainly, Manx kippers have some claim to fame and can be posted off all over the world from their smoking houses alongside Peel harbour, if I remember correctly.

Douglas was the capital of the island, a bustling place in those days soon after the war, with horse-drawn trams (usually referred to as 'toast-racks') running the length of the promenade, from Douglas Head at one end to Onchan Head at the other. The ferry harbour was at the Douglas Head end, and there was a small island located in the bay, with a little castle built upon it. Behind the harbour on Douglas Head was a man who operated some weighing scales. You would actually sit on one side and he would put big brass weights on the other side until the scales balanced. Going on from Onchan Head, an electric train line would take you on day-trips along the coast, where we would drop off at such places as Groudle Glen and Garwick Glen – I don't know if I've spelled them correctly, it's a long time ago! Along the sea front was a theatre called the *Villa Marina*, which always featured those holiday-style evening variety shows that proved so popular for many years. I have always associated the *'VM'* with Ivy Benson and her All-girl Band; they must have been on a regular retainer to appear each season. Top of the bill would always be a comedian, such as Norman Evans (*'Over the garden wall'*) or Arthur 'Big Hearted' Askey, with inevitable support from the dancing girls, magicians, jugglers, acrobats and such like. Behind the theatre was a 'pitch and putt' miniature golf course, around which we would dutifully traipse each summer, before setting off for a walk round Noble's Park – if I've remembered the name correctly.

One of the pleasures of a visit to the island was definitely the ice cream. You could get it in a cornet of course, but 'wafers' were very popular at the time, they seem to have gone completely out of fashion today. One wafer would go into the bottom of a rectangular box, ice cream would then be piled into the box with a wooden ladle, before being smoothed down for the application of the other wafer. A 'magic' button then popped the whole wafer out, ready for consumption! The local supplier was named *'Felice's'*, and their brand of ice cream tasted so good after the local *'Fusco's'* brand that was on sale at a parlour along County Road, though again I guess some biased childhood memories come into the equation!

'The Osborne' waitresses, Isle of Man, 1956

Just before I joined the Army in 1956, I returned on holiday to Douglas, just with Dad, as by then Mum had split up with him and we were all living elsewhere. Anyway, we stayed at a hotel on the sea front called *'The Osborne'*, which had a quotient of Irish girls there, working as maids for the summer season. By this age, I was becoming quite interested in girls, though not yet brave enough to pursue the subject! Though I did think that Mary Houlihan was very pretty – I still have a small photograph taken of three of these girls, taken in those days of innocence. I remember going to the pictures at *'The Strand'* cinema, located, strangely enough on a street by the same name; it was one of those old American gangster movies, starring George Raft and John Garfield. Ah, those were the days!

The next time I went to Douglas was with my 'blushing bride'! That was in 1962, Joyce and I had just got married and went back to *The Osborne* on our honeymoon, flying to Ronaldsway airport all the way from the West London air terminal, which of course has now grown into Heathrow, the busiest airport in the world. Then, of course, you still walked across the tarmac to board your plane! As a holiday, it was absolutely fine, but the hotel itself was hardly the most romantic of places, because the walls were as thin as cardboard and there was a young toddler in the next room who seemed to cry a lot! It couldn't have done us too much harm though, as Joyce has put up with me now for more than forty-five years – I think the term I'm looking for is 'long suffering'! Another cinema visit from that holiday was to the *Crescent* cinema, when we went to see that fabulous musical, *'West Side Story'* – still as fresh and vibrant today as it was back in 1962.

The highlight of the holiday was, as it probably always had been, the 'round-the-island' tour by charabanc (coach), stopping at such seaside places as Port Erin and Port St Mary. I think I'm right in saying that the seashore at Port St Mary had the most wonderful collection of tiny little shells, in all the colours of the rainbow, but of a delicate pastel shade. Then there was Peel, with its castle, harbour and world-famous kipper smoking huts. Rushen Abbey was memorable for its peaches and ice-cream. Laxey and its famous water-wheel, always well worth climbing the stairs to the viewing balcony. The Calf of Man was, and still is, a small islet off the southernmost tip and Point of Ayre is the most northerly part of the island. Finally, Ramsey is a large holiday resort to the north of Douglas. Going out of Douglas, the bus would cross the Fairy Bridge – woe betides anyone who failed to say *'Hello fairies'*, it would bring bad luck

Another holiday with Mum

to all! The tallest part of the island was the mountain called Snaefell, and the bus would groan its way up towards the summit, especially of interest was the so-called 'magnetic mountain'. Here, the lie of the land meant that whereas you thought you were going uphill, the driver would switch off the engine and let off the hand brake. But instead of the bus running backwards, it would in fact roll gently forwards – uphill in everyone's eyes.

Further holidays

Since then, of course, holidays have become a little more varied and adventurous. When Lorraine and Michelle were small, even a trip up to Mum's new house at Ainsdale was a challenge, looking back at some of the old cars I had in those days! Most of our journeys in those days would be via the A40 from Oxford across to Cheltenham, then up the M5 and M6, not the route we'd take nowadays. I remember one occasion, I think it was 1975, when we actually visited Dad and Cliff in Milton Road – probably my first time back there since leaving in 1954. We also persuaded my Dad to join us on a trip to the Lake District and stayed overnight at a 'B&B',

located in a little village soon after we left the M6 motorway. It was to be a few more years before we were up that way again.

That must have been 1987, I guess it was at 'Whitsun', when we stopped for a week at a site in Ambleside, accompanied by Eileen & Mike, as well as Jan & Roy. The accommodation was in a series of buildings that must once have been cottages, with the addition of a block of toilet and washing facilities. I recall that there was a 'beck' running alongside the site, which provided a wonderful soothing noise during the night. We had a few good trips out, including a walk along 'Striding Edge' and up to the summit of Helvelyan, but a favourite walk was the one that went up from Ambleside to Grasmere, very pretty indeed. That trip would also have included a visit to Mike's sister, Ros, who lived in Dalston, a small place just outside of Carlisle. I recall the drive back during the evening, across lots of high moorland, it was like being on another planet. The following year we were at Ambleside again, this time with Lorraine & Steve, this must have been after they had married and were living then in Hoddlesden, a nice little village nestling on the Lancashire side of the Pennines.

Going back to when the two girls were young, we would often join the rest of the 'Reading clan' on holiday, all the cousins got on so well and it was nice for them to be all together for a couple of weeks. Probably the first such occasion was 1973, when we stayed at a camp at Brighstone on the Isle of Wight, stopping in self-catering chalets. There was a 'club house' on the site, where the kids could all go in the evening for a bit of entertainment. We also used to love walking up to the village each morning for freshly baked scones and a coffee, sitting outside what was basically a lady's house. I think we asked her for the scone recipe, but she wouldn't part with it!

The following year we stayed at an old farmhouse at Braunton, not too far from Barnstaple in North Devon. We'd had the place recommended to us by Pam and John Teasdale and the food was absolutely fabulous. The lady who ran the place actually baby-sat for us one night, while Joyce and I went into Barnstaple to see *'The Sting'*, starring Robert Redford and Paul Newman. Another place not too far away was Ilfracombe, which was a nice spot to visit in the evening for a stroll around the harbour. That holiday took place just a short time after Joyce's Dad, Stan Jones, had died from a heart attack. It may have been purely coincidental that June, Wack and children were on a tent-site just a few miles away, I honestly cannot remember the circumstances of their being in close proximity to us. What stands out is that we were being fed like royalty every night, with mounds of steaming fresh food and giant puddings, while the Davis family was repairing to their tent for much more modest fare! Other place names that spring to mind are Croyde Bay and Saunton Sands.

That reminds me of another previous Isle of Wight holiday, when we had shared a caravan at Sandown, along with Mum and Dad (June and Stan) Jones, Joyce's parents. We didn't know it at the time, but Mum was suffering from cancer and naturally not in the best of moods, so sharing with us must have been quite a strain for her. That was in 1969 and it was only another eighteen months later that she died – and not at an advanced age either, which was a terrible blow to Joyce and her sisters. That year of 1971, after June's death in March, we had a week's holiday down at Swanage, in a flat just behind the *Mowlem Building* in the centre of the town near the seafront. I remember that, when we first walked into the place, it smelled as if the previous tenant – or tenants – had been sick in it, and Joyce spent ages in cleaning and sterilizing the place! It was only one room as I recall, with the girls sleeping behind a screen in one corner - with the smell of a chip-shop just below and the noise of bikers congregated on the promenade just outside the window! Apart from that, I'm sure we must have enjoyed it – I have the feeling that Eileen, Janet and families were located somewhere up the other end of town.

Bitten by the Barmouth bug

It was the year after Stan's death in 1974 that we made our first visit to Barmouth, up on the coast of Wales at the southern edge of the Snowdonia National Park. Eileen and Janet had been up to North Wales for maybe one or two years previously, and invited us to join them that year. We remember pulling in under the railway-bridge, near the harbour, it was drizzling heavily and everywhere looked so grey and miserable! And, after what seemed like an interminable journey, *"Why have we come here?"* was the question on our lips! That first year, Joyce and I, plus Lorraine and Michelle, stayed at a bed and breakfast place in the street alongside the railway, adjacent to the footbridge. I think the family we stayed with was called Griffiths – I do recall that the husband worked for the Post Office.

After that, for a few following years, we all shared a huge house on the promenade, called the *'Red Dragon'*. It was a vast cavern of a place, self-catering, and any heating at all was provided by a two-bar electric fire, in the main living room. Washing was achieved at a small washbasin in the toilet, as the so-called shower leaked all over the place! We also had to make sure we were well equipped with hot water bottles to make sure the beds were 'aired' before their first use - and then kept warm each evening prior to bedtime. Yes, it was 'rough and ready' to say the least, but all the kids really enjoyed each other's company, and were happy to go off with a few pennies in their pockets to the 'fun fair' just along the sea-front near the railway station – remember the *'Slippery Dip'*? Despite that rather dismal introduction that we had the first time in 1975, Barmouth certainly must have had something though – some of us have been going back there almost every Easter, ever since!

Most of those early holidays with all the children were spent on walking and, despite all protests, the kids always managed to make it. But how many times did we hear Mike saying, *"It's just around the next bend"* or *"Just one more hill to climb"*? It was always Mike that would plan the trip, assisted by Roy, as they pored over their OS maps each morning to the accompanying groans of the assembled children. We may have got slightly misplaced on occasion, but never lost! If memory serves me correctly, we also seemed to get wet quite often! This meant trying to dry out clothes and wellies in front of that electric fire previously mentioned - no mean feat! As time progressed and the kids grew up, the older ones gradually found other pastimes, until it was only the six adults (Griptons, Gillards and Rocketts) left for the annual pilgrimage. I must add though that, on a couple of occasions, we also had June and Wack there too, along with Kevin and Karen at least once, so it was always a 'family affair'. I remember climbing up the hillside towards Cadair Idris, with Karen going at a hell of a pace, like a mountain goat!

It's always been Barmouth at Easter, except for a couple of rare occasions. In 1982, it was decided to 'have a change', and all of us, including the Davis family, descended upon a set of wooden chalets in the town of Llanwryst, up in the Conway Valley. It was back to Barmouth the next year, but by then the 'charm' of the *Red Dragon* had worn off and, in 1984, we started using a flat on the Quay, where we have been fairly comfortable for over twenty years now. *(Just underneath the flat is a small café called the 'Isis'. It appears to have been run by the same family for a number of years now – they seemed like 'hippies' when we first came across them. But they provide a pretty good pizza, which Joyce and Eileen have enjoyed on occasion. Mike tends to go for the spaghetti Bolognaise, while I quite like the chicken curry served with a stack of chips!)*

There was just one other break in that time. One year the flat had been sold and the new owners were in the thralls of re-decorating etc. By this time, ranks had been reduced to just Joyce and myself, along with Eileen and Mike. We stayed in a static caravan-style place just up the coast from Barmouth at Tal-y-bont, which was in 1991. Since then, the four of us have been returning to Barmouth at Easter each year, it is always the first holiday of the year and eagerly anticipated. The present owner, at the time of writing, is a Mancunian called Marcus – and very difficult to contact! We're always getting twitchy by the time he rings to confirm our booking,

Over the last few years, we've managed to visit just about all the local towns and resorts in the area, most times incorporating a walk around the local area too. Harlech, Porthmadog, Criccieth, Pwlleli and Abersoch come to mind as you sweep around the Lleyn Peninsular; then there are Fairborne, Tywyn and Aberdyfi on the coast run to the south; while Dolgellau and Macynllethh usually provide a more mountainous environment. We've also ventured up into Snowdonia – Beddgelert, Betys-y-Coed, Capel Curig and even as far as Caernarfon, Conwy and Llandudno on various occasions.

As already mentioned, we have mainly had Ei & Mike for company for nigh on thirty years. In earlier days there were Jan & Roy and, on just a couple of times we were accompanied by June & Wack, along with their respective families. We even had guests in those early years! I know that Lorraine brought along Catherine, a school friend – while Mark had mates Steve and Paul with him on separate occasions. Our journey used to incorporate a stop at a large pub on the outskirts of Shrewsbury, usually coinciding with lunchtime opening. Mind you, I think we always had our own sandwiches to hand, so the pub only had to provide soft drinks!

We just occasionally had other visitors while staying at Barmouth - our Pam came down one year and Sue, Des and Tom also made the trip down from Merseyside. Michelle & James came just the once I think, while Lorraine & Steve came a couple of times, along with Jake! We even had our Geoff with us one year, it was while he was over here from Australia by himself – that was in 1990. During one of our more recent Barmouth holidays, in 2004, Lorraine & Phil came and stayed at a farmhouse just outside the town for a couple of nights, where we joined them for a lovely meal. Talking of meals, being in the flat means that we mainly cook for ourselves. But we do get out for a meal occasionally – and not just downstairs at the *Isis*! One of the nicest places was *'The Angry Cheese'*, located just up the road going out of the town towards Dolgellau. Sadly, after a couple of really nice meals there, the place closed down – a symptom of quite a few Barmouth businesses.

Just opposite 'our' flat is a pub called *'The Last Inn'* – we tried that once – just the once, say no more! The year that Geoff came, we had quite a nice meal in *'The Inglenook'*, a fish restaurant just under the railway bridge – don't know why we haven't tried that place again! We've even ventured further afield, heading up to Harlech a couple of times, but usually we are quite happy with the frozen dinners, pre-cooked by the girls at home! I don't think I need to remind myself of the fish and chips that I had from the *Harbourside Café* one year! It was the evening before we left, so I was saving on the washing up by having a quick ready-meal. Joyce said that it looked pretty awful, but I ate it anyway – and paid for it the next day on the drive home, feeling like death warmed up! Even as far away as Ludlow, where we stopped for lunch – mine consisted of a glass of lemonade. 'Nuff said'!

It was at the end of one of those Barmouth holidays that I managed to cause myself an injury that has since re-appeared on too many occasions! I think it had turned to rain on the Wednesday, continued on the Thursday – and was forecast to continue. So we decided to head for home on the Friday, first 'in tandem' with Eileen and Mike, before splitting up around the Gloucester area. We eventually reached home, having driven the whole way in incessant rain. Not wishing to get soaked whilst unloading the car, I raised the garage door and backed the car up as far as I could, until the boot lid was under cover. The trouble was that Joyce's car was still in the garage and I was silly enough to try lifting the heavy cases out of my boot and over the back of the second car! That proved to be a big mistake, as I must have pulled something in the lower back, which developed into sciatica. I started going to a chiropractor, Jonathan Field, of *'Back to Health'* down in Petersfield, and happily he was able to alleviate the symptoms, those of a nagging pain all the way down into the leg – particularly nasty when lying in bed at that time! Since then, about 1994, I have had slight flare-ups of the problem but, thankfully, Jonathan has been able to keep things from getting any worse, by regular 'tweaks' of my lower back.

Family get-togethers

Summer holidays were also a time for everyone to get together, while the kids were young enough to still go with us! 1976 must have been the first occasion for this, when we all went down to Bracklesham Bay and stayed in some old railway carriages right on the sea-front. At night, you would be swept to sleep by the sound of the pebbles being gently moved up and down the beach by the tide. And woken by the rush of wind through the gaps in the floorboards below! Good fun though. Looking back, it wasn't really a 'summer' holiday, it was based around the Whitsun Bank Holiday.

Later that year we went down to Aberporth, that's mid-Wales in Cardigan Bay, along with June, Wack and family. Also staying not too far away were my Dad and Cliff and I recall them coming down to Aberporth on their first day. It rained (of course!) and Dad bought himself a new mac – which he didn't have to wear again! We also drove up to Aberystwyth one day to meet up with them. Another place we visited during that holiday was Tenby, with at least part of its old walled town still well preserved. If I remember correctly, the Davis family had all stayed separately for a week, but then Wack and Kevin returned home, leaving June and Karen to share our chalet. How we all packed into my old *Corsair* for the return trip via Reading, heaven only knows!

Anyway, it was one day after Wack's departure that Joyce, June and children went and picked some 'cockles' along the rocks, brought them back to the chalet and put them on to boil. The smell was certainly a bit 'different' and brought the site owner, Mr Smith, to the door. He took one look at the 'cockles' and told us that if we'd eaten them, we'd have all been poisoned! (The shellfish in question may have in fact been periwinkles.) He was kind enough to then bring us some freshly caught mackerel, free of charge, which we had for our evening meal – a close call!

1977 saw another Whitsun get-together, this time sharing a large house on Hayling Island with the Gillards and Rocketts during the Queen's Silver Jubilee year. The same three families also shared a fortnight in the summer, at Duporth Bay, just outside St Austell in Cornwall. Again we had a large house, of split-level design, with an equally large garden, and the weather was excellent that year. It was also the first time that Geoff came over from Australia with his new wife Sheila. We met up with them on Plymouth Hoe and Geoff treated us all to a fish and chip lunch. Then, a few days later, they paid a quick return visit to Duporth, along with Sheila's sister Viv and her husband Kevin.

Looking back on that year, we must have only spent the second of two weeks at St Austell. For our first week, Joyce, the girls and myself had a week staying at a farmhouse in Polruan. Joyce remembers it all too well – and for all the wrong reasons! On our first evening down there, we ventured down to the beach and found a large pool of water, obviously left there by the ebbing tide. I don't like the sea that much anyway, so Joyce and the girls went in for 'a dip'. That water was so cold that Lorraine and Michelle soon came out, but Joyce stayed in for quite some time. And didn't she suffer later that night? She was in agony with this pain in her side and eventually I had to raise the lady downstairs to call in the local doctor. He gave Joyce an injection to deaden the pain and said that she must have caught a chill in her kidney. If I remember correctly, she spent the whole of the next day in bed, recovering.

The next year, 1978, saw the same three families together once more, this time at Mullion Cove, down on the Lizard Peninsular in Cornwall, while 1979 it was 'something similar' at a little village called Trelights. Again this was in Cornwall, but much more to the north, not far from Padstow, which eventually started to play a large part in the holiday curriculum in later years. Then finally, in 1980, the last family get-together (well for a summer holiday at least) came down at a caravan site near Manorbier, in Pembrokeshire. The weather that year was pretty abysmal for the whole fortnight and the following year, I think everyone had by then decided, not surprisingly, to head for the sunshine of Continental package-tours!

Going abroad for the first time

It may not have just been the bad weather at home that summer (1980), because earlier in the year I had a wonderful two weeks in Cyprus, courtesy of my being in the Territorial Army at the time. *(I've covered this episode somewhere in my military memories!)* Anyway, the next year, 1981, we took the plunge and booked a two-centre holiday in Italy. By this time, Lorraine had outgrown our company, so it was only Michelle that came with us – although it was to be the last time she accompanied us too. We had one week up in the mountains, near the Swiss border, at a place called Livigno. For some reason unknown to me, the town was a duty-free area. One day we did a coach tour into Switzerland, calling in at St Moritz. There was one place, I remember, where we had just come down a steep mountainside and into a town, when the coach had to stop for a road accident. Some poor motorcyclist had come off his bike and skidded under another coach, it looked quite nasty. I recall that, in St Moritz, I was able to practice my German, when asking a policeman where we could get a coffee!

The 'interchange' journey from Livigno in the north, down to our next destination of Diano Marina (DM), was something of a nightmare, taking just about all day long and ending in stifling heat! It also ended in 'panic stations' for me! I was desperate for 'the loo' – none on the coach – and in some sort of agony by the time we reached the hotel. Then we were prevented from going to our room until we'd shown our passports, which were at the bottom of one of our cases! How I managed to hang on is still a mystery! DM was – well, it still is, I guess! – on the Mediterranean coast, just along from the French border, and another coach tour during that week took us to Monaco and Nice.

Monaco was a bit of a disappointment, even the palace looked quite ordinary! I remember the coach park overlooked the harbour, which was full of yachts, and there was a large hoarding, advertising a soccer match between Monaco and another team. One surprise was that for the ladies to get through to their toilets, they had to walk through, just behind the backs of the men who were busy at the urinals! In Nice, we wandered along the *'Promenade Anglais'*, or whatever it is called, and the beach seemed full of naked elderly women! It was baking hot that day, but then the sky became as black as pitch and the heavens opened! It was a short-lived storm however and we were soon able to walk up through a large park and gardens. It's amazing what you remember from some of these trips! At our Livigno hotel there was an English

68

couple, he was a dentist called Brian, and his wife did nowt but complain at the food
– *"I can't eat this muck!"* at a dish of pasta! Why do they go abroad? Actually, the
food at the hotel was of excellent standard, though a little sparse by English measures.
In the town, purchase of the Italian *gelato* (ice cream) proved a little disappointing,
as we were expecting something really special. It was nowhere near as good as the
normal *Walls* ice cream at home!

At DM, the town's water system broke down! We were okay in our hotel 'up the
hill', but some people nearer the seafront had to walk up to our hotel to bathe. At every
mealtime, a young Italian waiter called 'Michael' would bring us 'fresh fruit' - but it
was always plums! That was all right at first, but paled a bit around day five! We all
moaned at him and pulled his leg and finally, the day before we were due to leave, he
came around with a beaming smile and a bowl of apples. When we all 'complained'
that we now wanted plums, he found our English sense of humour a bit of a puzzle!
The food here **was** a bit hit or miss, Joyce and Michelle weren't too keen on the fish,
garnished with olives and tinned tomatoes! Breakfasts were of the 'continental' style
– so many guests took to walking down into the town each morning, where there was
a little café that served a 'full English'!

1982 saw us abroad again, following the footsteps of Eileen and Janet, who had
gone on holiday to the Mediterranean island of Ibiza the previous year. On their
recommendation, we flew to Ibiza, accompanied by June and Wack, and enjoyed a
lovely fortnight in the sun. Our hotel was situated in a fairly quiet spot, from where
we used to walk around the coast and into the main holiday town. The harbour looked
quite pleasant, but not the town centre, which seemed to be full of drunken Brits. The
nicest thing was to be able to walk away from all that! Close to our hotel we found a
small bar, where we used to stop in the evening for brandy and cokes, which seemed
to be huge when compared with what you were served back home. Needless to say,
we managed to sink quite a few of these before staggering back to bed! One evening
we took advantage of an organised coach tour, which ended up at some 'rancho' up
in the hills, where there was a buffet and entertainment laid one – the type where
they tip wine down your throat from a goat-skin held above your head! When we
arrived, there were obviously coaches from all over the island, all there for the same
purpose. Imagine my surprise when I bumped into Eddie Alecock – an old pal from
the Liverpool Institute!

The next year (1983) saw us making the long flight to Florida. Sue and Des had
settled out there, in South Miami, and offered to put us up for a couple of weeks.
Unlike most of the local population, Joyce and I actually got out and walked a fair

bit – we must have seemed like freaks to the locals, who used their cars for even the shortest journeys. This was our first experience of those large shopping malls that had an internal 'food area', a seating section, surrounded by all different types of food outlets, such as burger bars, pastas, pizzas, cookies etc. They have since become very popular here in the UK too. Des did a bit of a 'travel agent' job on our behalf, by booking us in for a couple of days at Orlando, where we spent a great day out at Walt Disney's *'Magic Kingdom'*, followed by another at the *EPCOT Centre*. The motel we stayed in was one of the *Howard Johnson* chain and we were amazed to find that the room had two large double beds - luxury indeed! And another surprise in the morning, when we found our American allies eating large helpings of eggs 'easy over', bacon and hash browns – all covered with sticky and sickly maple syrup!

Following that, we flew to Nassau in the formerly British colony of the Bahamas for a couple of days, which became a bit of a story in itself! As soon as we landed, we got on the airport bus with a bunch of Americans. Well, the driver was a typically laid-back islander type; he just put his foot down and quickly built up a fair bit of speed. To us, this was fairly normal, but of course the bus was on the left, as per British custom, and traffic was whizzing along in the opposite direction at much the same speed as us, with a gap of a mere couple of feet down the centre of the road. To the Americans, this was virtual suicide, used as they were to four- and six-lane highways! No wonder it was a white knuckle trip for them, with expressions like *"Shit, man!"* every few hundred yards.

When we reached the hotel, we were hit by some local taxation rates, which certainly hadn't been advertised in the brochures! Then, reclining on the beach at one stage, checking out the luxury cruise liners arriving at the port and discarding their passengers, we were approached by a young native lad. He insisted on 'giving' us some rather small green bananas, as a token of the love between the locals and their previous Colonial rulers. It was only after we'd accepted this 'gift' that we were asked to pay up, I expect anyone who was white and 'in town' must have appeared like a rich tourist! In the evening we went off for a walk and ended up in this sort of 'shanty-town', away from the tourist areas. Old folks were sitting in rocking chairs on their verandahs, and of course our white faces stuck out a mile. Some small children came up, saying *"Sing you a song for a quarter, Mister"*. I guess we were glad to get back to the hotel area and, on reflection, shouldn't have ventured into the unknown like that!

I do recall that we went into a *McDonalds* for a milk shake – and they were enormous! We took them outside to drink and of equal size were the cockroaches that scuttled around our feet, they seemed the size of saucers! We only stayed in Nassau for a couple of days, and even this ended up in a rather hairy return trip to Miami! *Bahamas Air*, the local airline with which we'd flown, 'went bust' that same day and when we got to the airport for the evening return flight, we were told there wasn't going to be one! Now this is when the American passengers came into their own. Unused to such treatment, they virtually put the airline staff 'up against the wall' and threatened all sorts of retribution. It ended up with the liquor bar being opened and we were all handed duty-free miniature bottles of every type of spirit! Then the nearby *KFC* bar was visited and a take-away meal bought for everyone of us! Thankfully, a flight was eventually arranged and we flew off back to Florida. The big problem was that we ended up landing at Miami airport around four o'clock in the morning. I'd previously warned Sue that there were problems with the flight, but certainly didn't want to phone again at that time of day, cadging a pick-up! Instead, we jumped into a cab and I told the driver the Herlihy address. *"Where's that?"* came the unwelcome response! I then had to try and remember just where Sue and Des lived – somewhere off Dixie Highway, if I now remember correctly. It ended up with the cab dropping us off at a postbox that I thought I recognised, and we set off up this side street. Major mistake! All of a sudden two enormous Rottweilers came padding out of a front garden – and we did a smart about turn and legged it back up the highway!

Amazingly, we did eventually manage to 'get home'. Must tell you though that the Herlihy residence was on a virtually blacks-only estate and that their house had bars on all doors and windows! Des did mention that the two dogs were probably protecting a drug-runners home – thanks mate! On another day, Sue and Des kindly lent us their little *Honda Civic*, in which we drove all the way down the Florida Keys, to Key West and back – quite a trip. At one stage, we were driving across Seven Mile Bridge, which is self-descriptive, when a storm blew up on both sides of us and we wondered if we'd make it through! It was only a couple of weeks after our return from the States that Joyce and Michelle took advantage of an offer by Eileen & Janet, to join them and their families for a fortnight in Minorca – you lucky people! It must have been that year, when they all came off the plane and I was there to pick up 'my two', that I was able to tell Michelle of her success in her school exams and that she'd be going on to sixth-form College.

A land down under!

We somehow missed out on a holiday in '84, although I did get away myself on a TA trip to Flensburg in Denmark – this around the time that Sheila & Geoff came over from Oz for another visit. But in the following summer of 1985 we had the pleasure of an extended trip to Australia, accompanying Mum for a period of about four weeks. We stopped off for a couple of nights in Singapore before landing in Perth, WA, where we had a ball, staying at 11 Darling Street with S & G. They had recently extended their house, adding a guestroom, complete with its own shower room, and we settled in there quite comfortably for the month! Mum had a bedroom to herself in the main house and we all had a really good holiday together.

S & G celebrated their 10th anniversary that year, along with Viv and Kev, in the form of a great party, thrown at Linda and Clive's place. The four of them turned up in one of those stretch-limousines, complete with glasses of champagne! Linda is an excellent cook and presented a fabulous spread, while Clive's turn of phrase is legendary! One of the most enjoyable pastimes whilst in South Perth was being able to take a bicycle ride all around the waterfront of the Swan Basin and see the pelicans and cormorants most of the way around. During our visit, we got across to Rottnest Island and down to Mandurah, where we stayed in a splendid up-market hotel called *The Atrium*, and also as far as Albany in the far southwest. The trip to the island was a complete surprise, kindly set up by S & G, with help I'm sure from the rest of the family. We were first taken to Perth International Airport and booked in – at a caravan! The flight was in a small 8-seater plane, but the best moment was watching Joyce's face when she realised we had to climb aboard and she was to sit next to the pilot! Pure magic! Also joining us on 'Rotto', as well as S & G, were Viv & Kev and Linda & Clive. With no cars allowed on the island, any trips out were strictly by bicycle and, for home entertainment, it was either *'Upwords'* or *'Boggle'*! The quokkas were fun too, being a very rare marsupial found only on Rottnest.

The Albany trip involved a long drive, which gave us the chance to see a lot – and I mean **a lot**! – of the countryside down that way. Albany itself used to be a whaling station, it's about as far south as you can get in WA, in fact it was pretty cold in the cottages where we stayed. I recall that Joyce and I went out for an early-morning walk and saw our first kangaroos out in the wild – hopping off into the morning mist! Mum certainly enjoyed herself on that trip, starting up a lasting relationship with Sheila's Dad, Bill Walker! It was only a few weeks after we got back to England ourselves that Bill flew over, and the pair got married at Crosby Town Hall, Liverpool, before moving back together to live in Perth.

It's amazing to think that over the years that followed our first visit to Australia, a 'parting of the ways' took place between, firstly (I think) Viv and Kev, then probably Susan and Ross, then Sheila and Geoff and, finally, Joy and Bob! All the girls mentioned were the daughters of Bill and his first wife. I recall Bob (Appleyard) took

Joyce, myself and Geoff out for a drive in his *'Valiant'* car, a huge American-style gas-guzzler! We ended up at a place called New Norcia, which was noticeable for its monastery and a hotel which, when we asked for sandwiches, got the response *"That's off"* to almost the whole list! You can imagine how astonished I was, just a few weeks after our return to England, to walk into the baker's shop in Petersfield Square and bump into a young guy with a T-shirt with *'New Norcia'* emblazoned across its chest! I had to chat to him of course and he was equally astonished that anyone knew the place – a virtual dot on the map!

In 1986 we again holidayed with June & Wack, this time on the island of Tenerife, one of the Canaries group. Here, at Puerto de la Cruz, we had the strange situation of being under a layer of cloud, yet still able to be burned by the sun if you weren't careful. We hired a car for a couple of days, only a *Fiat Punto*, but it enabled us to get around and see the rest of the island, including the strange landscape near the summit of Mount Teide and most of the other coastal resorts in the far sunnier south. Most of the beaches were of a black volcanic ash, but one spot we visited actually had a golden beach, thanks to the import of sand from the Sahara Desert! I can remember that, just as we got there, the wind was blowing this sand directly into our faces, so we didn't hang around for too long. But most days we were content to just walk down the hill, from the hotel to the seafront, buy an ice cream, then wander along the vast promenade, full of shops and hotels. And I'm sure Wack will never forget his flaming banana!

1987 saw us staying in England, enjoying a visit up at Whitby on the north Yorkshire coast – not quite your continental weather, but as good as any other place to stay at. We went up entirely 'on spec' and were fortunate enough to find a bed and breakfast place up on the main road just outside the town. Two television series over the years, *'Heartbeat'* and *'The Royal'*, both feature the town quite extensively, causing a certain amount of memory recalling! One such fond memory was the fish'n'chips meal we had at *'The Magpie'* café – absolutely delicious.

Colyton, East Devon

The following year saw us 'at home' again, although we managed to fit in a trip to the Lake District, as well as starting associations with two other lovely spots – Colyton in Devon and Padstow in Cornwall. Joyce had worked for a few months during 1988 at *Burley & Geach*, a solicitor's office in Petersfield. She was recommended this place – *'The Grove'* guesthouse - at Colyton, just across the Devon border past Lyme Regis in Dorset. *(It was run by an elderly couple, Val and John Hudson, and it turned out that John had served as a National Serviceman with REME back in the*

73

Fifties. When REME celebrated its fiftieth anniversary in 1992, I took John one of the commemorative ties for him to wear.) Anyway, we gave it a try for a weekend. For the next few years we thoroughly enjoyed many trips down there, accompanied by such as Mum & Bill, Sue & Geoff – yes, Sue! - Helen & Tim, Jo & Dave Howlett and Anne & Derek Newman.

It was such a shame when Val & John eventually retired and their guesthouse closed down, we had some great times down there. It gave us the opportunity to visit many other places in that area, such as Lyme Regis, Seaton, Sidmouth, Beer, Budleigh Salterton, Exeter, Dawlish and Teignmouth etc. All those places seemed to exist in a time-warp, transporting us back to other remembered seaside holidays from years previously. Not that we complained, we found that part of the country very relaxing and managed to get in some lovely walks wherever we went. One particular walk was along 'The Undercliff', between Axmouth and Lyme Regis, where a long-ago land-slip has left this amazing area of outstanding natural beauty that stretches for somewhere around five miles. We actually timed that walk to perfection! It was the weekend that H & T were joining us and we'd arranged to meet them at Lyme, after the walk, to get a lift into Colyton. We literally walked around the corner at the bottom of the High Street to find Tim driving around the same corner at the very same time!

A little tale here that does the rounds every now and again! When you went down to breakfast at *The Grove*, John did the waiting, while Val was cooking in the kitchen. You'd sit down at your table and John, all neat and tidy, would ask what you wanted – *"fruit juice or cereal?"* He was a bit old-fashioned that way! Needless to say, Tim said that he'd have both – which must have bemused John for a moment, I don't think he'd ever been asked that before!

Padstow, North Cornwall

Eileen's next-door neighbours in Reading, Sue & Maurice, have a holiday bungalow in Padstow, and 1988 saw us (just Joyce and myself as far as I can recall) using it for the first time. Since then, Padstow has become a regular holiday home, providing an ideal spot from which to visit other places, such as Newquay, Bodmin, Wadebridge, Truro and Redruth. Again, we have been accompanied there at times, most recently it has been by Michelle & James, and our two grandsons, Thomas & Calum. At the time of writing, we have not long come back from there once more. During the few days, we drove across to Charlestown, just outside St Austell, and revived a few memories of our 1977 visit.

1989 saw us off to Europe again, this time to the shores of the Adriatic at Cavtat, in what was still – just – the Republic of Yugoslavia. We were located just a few miles south of the mediaeval walled city of Dubrovnik, which really was spectacular. One blemish on the holiday was that, from our hotel window, we could watch – and hear – the planes coming in on their approach to the airport! Barely days after we ended our holiday, we were horrified to see TV news coverage of the city being shelled at the start of a vicious civil war.

With 'the Fitzes' at Newquay Zoo

Thankfully, nothing like that happened while we were there, but I've often since wondered – was it something we said?

Over about four days we hired a car and took some good trips into the surrounding areas, finding a town up in the mountains called Trebinje, *"far from the madding crowd"*. The coastline was very rugged, with lots of fiords, so what appeared a short distance on the map actually involved many miles of driving. I recall taking a ferry across one large estuary and got chatting to this German chap – yes, still able to get by – just – in that language! We visited one town that had been recently hit by an earthquake, so there was quite a lot of scaffolding still in situ. We chose 'a quiet café' for lunch, rather than another close by that was very busy. We ordered some fish – which took ages to appear, was scorched on the outside, but raw on the inside! We still paid up of course – having learned the hard way just why that particular café was quiet! We also got very daring that year, participating in some nude sunbathing! We found one nice little café on the harbour in Cavtat, where we retired most evenings for a cold beer – the pizzas were excellent too! We made friends with a couple from Mansfield that year, Jane and Lew, I think there was a connection with Joyce and Jane both being in the school meals service. Amazingly, we still exchange Christmas cards!

The following year was spent back in England, where we first had a week down at Padstow and then drove all the way up to Whitby for another week. Again, we managed to find bed and breakfast 'digs', this time halfway down the hill into town, staying with a nice couple called Sue and John Cole. Sue was attending local pottery classes and we ended up buying a few from her – I'm sure they're still around somewhere! We had some nice long walks on the Yorkshire coast, particularly the seven-mile one down, past Whitby Abbey and down to Robin Hood Bay and back – very spectacular. I'm pretty sure it was that year that we went to see Scarborough too, picking up a couple of paintings by local artists – which now adorn a wall in Michelle's house!

In 1991, Mum and Bill were over from Perth again, this time staying at some accommodation in Sedgeberrow, just south of Evesham in the Cotswolds – I think they were there for four weeks in all, staying in different accommodation every week! The first weekend, our Sue and Tom came down, and I recall Tom (aged eight?) going all around the outside of the accommodation, hiding in a sort of cupboard that ran all round under the eaves. Anyway, we went to see them (M & B) at the weekends, getting out and about to lots of different places within easy driving distance – Evesham, of course, as well as Winchcombe, Tewkesbury, Ross-on-Wye & Cheltenham. We all had a good laugh at a tearoom in Ross, where an elderly mother and her son were in panic mode when the number of customers must have exceed expectations!

While walking around Sedgeberrow, we noticed some buildings being renovated and lots of sculpted stones lying around the place. When we inquired as to their relevance, we were informed that they had been resurrected from the very thick walls of some local houses, which were now being either 'converted' or modernised. Apparently, those houses had been built around the time of the Reformation, when Henry VIII was having all the monasteries knocked down. Those 'sculpted stones' had been part of those monasteries, then used as in-fill for the thick walls! Mum and Bill also came down to Padstow that year and shared the bungalow with us for a few days.

Back to Australia

Later that same year we headed off on the long trip to Australia once again. Having been to just WA in 1985, we thought it would be good to see a bit more of the 'great continent' this time. Our first port of call was Sydney, with its famous Harbour Bridge and Opera House, but it rained for the first day or so, we even had to buy a couple of cheap plastic brollies! But Joyce and I like walking, and we did lots of that, visiting Darling Harbour, The Rocks area, the Queen Victoria Building etc. We also took a boat-trip around the vast harbour, getting across to the narrowest part of its entrance. Over the previous months, our Geoff had been across to South Australia on business and somehow made contact with old pal Harry Hayes. So it was that, after our four days in Sydney, we were met at Adelaide airport by Harry & Angela, who then kindly hosted us for a whole week. Harry took the time off work and was able to show us around the area; we stayed at their place in Coromandel Valley, in the hills overlooking the city of Adelaide. Rachel Hayes, their younger daughter, was still living at home then, and she was good company too.

Mum & Bill took the opportunity to come across and see us all from Perth; they stayed on the coast at a place called Glenelg (note the palindrome!), at the end of a tram – yes tram! – ride from the city centre. Together, we all had a coach-trip one day into the Barossa Valley, wine capital of the area, visiting a town called *(I think)* Hensdorf, which was very much based on the old German style towns. I think I had a lunch consisting of a *bratwurst* and *sauerkraut*, just to bring back memories of earlier days in Germany itself! We also visited the *Yalumba* winery, as well as actually driving over *Jacob's Creek*! It's amazing to see just how popular all Aussie wines have become back home in recent years.

Mum & Bill made it back to Perth, despite the impending closure of *Compass Airlines*, who were trying, unsuccessfully, to compete with the big boys of *BA* and *QUANTAS*. Harry continued to chauffeur us around and we made a good attempt at emptying his small barrel of port! The trouble is, the bugger kept on filling it up again! A few days later we caught our own flight across the wide-open spaces to WA. By this time, Mum & Bill were living in an area called Victoria Park, and that's where we were based for the next couple of weeks. It wasn't too difficult a walk down to the river from there, though I remember Mum insisting on Joyce wearing a floppy hot to stop her getting too sun-burned! By that time, my sister Pam, husband Steve and daughter Sian had also moved to Perth, while Geoff, now sadly parted from Sheila, was 'courting' a nice lady called Sue! Just after Christmas, for a week that covered the New Year period, a whole gang of us stayed at a very large house built on stilts, that overlooked the beach at Yallingup, a good drive south from Perth. As well as all named above, Sue's daughter Sophie also came with us.

Yallingup is famous for its caves, containing large quantities of stalagmites and stalactites, which we made a point of seeing. From the town, Caves Road runs south, parallel with the coast, and at regular intervals along this main road, side-roads lead off to individual wineries. These offer free wine-tasting and sumptuous lunches, so we tended to see quite a few of them! Those WA wines haven't caught on in the UK, as they tend to be quite exclusive, due to the vineyards being small and independent. They seemed expensive even to the locals! I recall one afternoon when we went to visit a lighthouse out on the beach, which involved walking some distance through 'bush' and it was very hot. Not only that, but those Aussie bush-flies were particularly invasive in my case, they just kept on bombarding me, trying to gain access to ears, eyes, nose and mouth - just glad they were the only available orifices! I valiantly tried to keep my head covered and provided many laughs for those horrible rellies of mine! Those cork-rimmed hats make a lot of sense. Also on the visit list that year were Margaret River and Augusta, before we all drove back up to the city. It was a great holiday, though it took us a whole week to get over the jet lag, once back home in Greatham.

Staying in England

There was no way we could 'follow that' as they say, so 1992 saw us having a quiet year. The usual Easter trip to Barmouth was in the company of both Lorraine & Steve and Michelle & James, and we followed that with another week in Padstow during the summer. Our weekend in Colyton was with Jo and Dave; Joyce had her week in Mumbles with her sisters, then almost all of the immediate family went back there in November to celebrate Eileen's 50th birthday. We ended that year by visiting L & S up at their home in Hoddlesden, perched on the Lancashire side of the Pennines.

1993 was another 'England year'. Helen & Tim took us with them for a weekend in Suffolk. If I remember correctly, we called in at some friends of theirs near Colchester (Jan and Pete) before reaching our destination, staying in the wonderful village of Lavenham, where many of the 15th-century buildings have been lovingly restored. On the evening after our arrival, we had the advantage of a personal tour guide around the town – but we were all pretty cold, as it wasn't very summer-like! During the summer we stayed a week down at 'our' Jan's place in Mumbles, then drove down into Cornwall for a second week, this time in dear old Padstow.

In April of the following year, we had the pleasure of some visitors from Oz – firstly Mum & Bill, followed almost immediately afterwards by Sue & Geoff, now married of course. S & G spent a weekend at Colyton with us – remember it Geoff? The last game of the season, two goals down at home to Wimbledon, then Everton scraping a 3 – 2 win to save themselves from relegation. Phew! That was a close call. By then, Mum & Bill had moved into an 'exchange house', in a small town called Nailsea, close to the Bristol Channel in Somerset. We were able to get across there on some weekend visits and got as far as Bath, Wells, Clevedon and Weston-super-Mare. M & B later came across to see us at our place and we took them up to see Lavenham too. We stayed on a farm nearby, we all remember those breakfasts, huge platters of bacon, sausages, tomatoes – the works! We also managed to fit in visits to Cambridge, Bury

St Edmunds and Sudbury. The summer break that year was a complete carbon copy of 1993, firstly at Mumbles and followed immediately by Padstow!

We had an early 'May break' in 1995, going up to stay with Lorraine & Steve again, during which time we visited some nice spots on both sides of the Pennines, including Lancaster and Skipton. Later, during the summer, we headed up to Whitby once again, fortunate to find the same 'B & B' with Sue & John that we'd used on our last visit. That's another couple with whom we exchange Christmas cards! I think we used the Humber Bridge on the way up there, paying a visit to Bridlington. Again, we had some good walks, this time north of the town to Runswick Bay and Staithes. We dropped in at Harrogate for a night and took the opportunity to visit Knaresborough

We drove down to stay with L & S for a day or two, then drove up via Penrith into Northumberland. We were luck enough to find a farmhouse 'in the middle of nowhere' – in fact it was at Catton, not far from Hexham – where we stayed for a few days. The farm overlooked a deep valley and the view from the toilet was spectacular! Located in an area known as 'The Allendales', it provided an ideal spot for walking and the weather was beautiful for most of the time. We visited Hadrian's Wall, hardly able to see farther than ten yards thanks to a descending mist, before heading across towards the coast and stayed at a little place called Craster overnight, as well as visiting Alnwick. Our return journey took us to Durham, then Ripon, before we ended up back at Hoddlesden for a night, before heading home.

We had a long-standing plan to go to Australia again in '96, so hadn't really bothered about planning a summer break. But Eileen & Mike were going off to Ireland for a week and, virtually at the last minute, asked if we'd like to join them, as there was a spare room at their accommodation. They picked us up for the very long drive overnight down to Fishguard and the early-morning fast ferry across the Irish Sea to Rosslare. After a lovely breakfast at a nearby farmhouse, we dropped in at Waterford on the route across the southern counties. We stayed just outside Killarney and had some great days driving, around 'The Ring of Kerry' and the Dingle peninsular. On the way back, we dropped down to the pretty harbour town of Kinsale for a couple of hours.

A third trip 'down under'

And so, in December 1996, we flew off to Australia for the third time. Lorraine had already gone out there for a long sabbatical, following her first ten years with McDonalds, while sister Sue had been with her for the first couple of weeks. Like the previous visit, we wanted to see another part of Oz, so we started off at *The Colonial Club*' in Cairns, up in 'FNQ' (that's Oz for far northern Queensland!). L flew across from Perth to join us, 'enjoying' an unexpected stop overnight at Alice Springs. *(Lorraine has always been 'one up' on us since then, as Northern Territories is the only mainland Australian State that we never visited!)* The complex was very well situated and accommodating – the layout of food at breakfast time was something that had to be seen to be believed. A courtesy bus was laid on for those of us wanting to go down into Cairns itself, which was quite a laid-back sort of town.

Part of the package was to spend a couple of nights at *'Coconut Beach'*, where the accommodation was in stilted apartments, high in the tree canopy. Magical noises came from nuts dropping on the roof above – and feral pigs rustling in the undergrowth below! We had a nice few days, exploring the rain forest and had a trip out from Port Douglas to the Great Barrier Reef, before heading down to Melbourne. Lorraine certainly came in handy as our tour guide, one glance at the map and she was marching off ahead and showing us the sights! Lots to see there, of course, including Victoria Market, the Southgate area and the Italian quarter. We also had a day visit to Philip Island to see the fairy penguins emerge from the sea to their overnight nests. Then it was back to Perth, again stopping with Mum & Bill, they were now living at Ardross. We had a good chance to explore the locality, with several walks around Canning River, between Canning Bridge and Mount Henry. Fremantle was another favourite spot on that visit, and we also managed another visit to Rotto – though the sea crossing was a bit rough!

Geoff had done us all proud with a house rental for the New Year, this time down at Margaret River. Again, the wineries were an attraction, while a day at Augusta allowed us a boat trip on the Blackwood River, where we had to literally 'bump' the boat over the bar! One 'extra' at the family get-together was Kate, Pam & Steve's 'new' daughter! *(When we got home on January 8th, the house had been flooded out during a spell of freezing weather! But that's another story.)* Towards the end of that trip, we went out for a meal with Tony and Heather Domoney. Tony is an ex-apprentice from Arborfield, who served there at the same time as me, 1956 – 1959. We've kept in touch ever since.

It was only two months later that Mum & Bill came over to Blighty for a long stay, again swapping houses with the couple in Nailsea. Again, we went down a few times, fitting in visits to Bridgewater and Minehead this time. Sadly, that was to be the last time that we saw Bill. He'd been complaining of a 'bad leg' during their holiday and, upon returning to Perth, it was found that he had the dreaded cancer. I remember he'd been limping quite badly walking around the local town of Midhurst, so Joyce popped into a shop and bought him a walking stick. We later found that it had been confiscated at Perth airport by the customs authorities!

Summer that year saw us back down at dear old Padstow for a fortnight, with the Fitzes joining us there for the second week. During September, we enjoyed a lovely weekend away with Helen & Tim, over in Amsterdam. The hotel wasn't up to much, very basic – not quite the five-star rating that H & T were used to! But we must have walked along every canal and over every bridge in the city – we were really lucky with the weather, warm, mellow and sunny. We also managed to fit in a couple of canal-boat trips, one during the day and another by night. One morning, Joyce and Helen took the opportunity to visit the Anne Frank museum, while Tim and I sat outside in the sunshine on the opposite side of the canal, enjoying a quiet beer!

In June of '98 we went off with the Goulds again, this time flying from Southampton to Jersey for a few days. The flight through our 'local' airport was very laid back and relaxing, almost like hopping on a bus. We had a hire-car and visited most spots on that lovely island – some of them twice, eh Tim? One memorable visit was to Jersey Zoo, which featured 'endangered species' such as mountain gorillas and orangutans. Of course Joyce made us laugh in later years, by saying that we'd seen these 'extinct species'! The hotel we stayed at, on the northern coast of the island, overlooked a quiet little bay, and we enjoyed a couple of walks along the coastal footpaths in the locality.

Italy beckons again

Our main holiday that year was back to Italy, along with Ei & Mike, Jan & Roy. The first week was a mad dash of coach-tours, during which we became 'culture vultures' – up very early each morning to beat the tourists to Venice, Assisi, Rome, Florence etc. We actually 'entered' Venice by boat, which allowed a fascinating outlook of the waterfront. We were also fortunate enough to take a gondola trip around the famous canals of Venice, accompanied of course by the singing gondoliers. The first hotel we stayed in was outside of Rome's centre, I think it was at Ostria, and we then took a coach-ride into the city. We got caught up in a traffic jam and had to walk pretty quickly on our walking tour that evening! We visited the Spanish Steps and the Trevi Fountains, before dining in a local restaurant. I recall the three girls giving life to that old song *"Three coins in a fountain"*.

The next day, outside the Vatican, I managed to get caught up in a 'fire in the postbox' incident – and so missed the bus-tour around Rome's famous sights! Luckily, I found where the bus was to pick us up, so sat outside this bar nursing a beer and a dish of peanuts, until the others returned from their tour. That evening, our coach took us up to a restaurant, high in the hills above Rome, where we were entertained by the restaurant's own singing group – very good they were too! Florence was well worth the visit, full of amazing sculptures and paintings, the highlight being the statue of David, by Michaelangelo. The later boat-trip from Sorrento to Capri was also memorable - but for all the wrong reasons! The boat rolled all over the place and, apart from me, everybody else was very green about the gills by the time we reached the island. The second week we stayed at Malchesine on Lake Garda, Italy's largest lake, which was slightly more relaxing! Apart from our room that is, which had the lift shaft located in one corner! One highlight of the week was for Eileen & Joyce, who enjoyed an evening out at the opera, set in the magnificent Arena at Verona. All of us had been to the same town on a day-trip previously. Another day we all caught the early cable car up onto a local mountain and had a good walk all along the ridge from end to the other.

In November that same year, we enjoyed another 'continental weekend', along with H & T, plus 'Essex' friends Jan & Pete. We all met up at Ashford railway station, then took the *Eurostar* train through the 'Chunnel' (Channel Tunnel) to the mediaeval town of Bruges. It was a bit cold, with some rain, being so late in the year, but still most enjoyable. Those tempting Belgian chocolate shops were very hard to ignore, that's for sure – while Tim was able to extend his collection of beer glasses!

The next year, 1999, we again joined the Fitzes down at Padstow for a week, during the boys' school holidays. In August we had another weekend away with H & T – being 'chauffeur driven in their new *Mercedes*! We headed up through Essex and Suffolk into Norfolk, then back through Cambridgeshire. Dropped in at Thetford, went into a travel agent – and booked a week in Crete! We stayed at Wymondham overnight, where Joyce and I had a room with a four-poster bed! We also visited some people who had once been neighbours of the Goulds and lived just opposite the Abbey. Then we continued up to Cromer and Sheringham, before heading down to Ely for our second night, then came home via Saffron Walden.

To Crete with the Goulds

September saw us off on that holiday to Crete, again with the Goulds. We stayed at a hotel complex just outside Gouves, on the north of the island. The accommodation was a bit basic – and the hotel food too – but okay for Joyce and I! *(What did you say about 'Stalag XV' Helen?)* Again, we had a hire-car, so we were able to get 'out and about', with trips to Aghios Nikolaas and Rethymnon in opposite directions. We also went into Knossos, with its historical ruins of the Minoan civilisation of 4,000 years ago, and the museum in Iraklion, the island's capital. Having visited the ruins at Knossos, Tim asked our guide if she could direct us to someplace 'native' where we could eat, rather than in the usual tourist spots. She pointed us inland and wrote the name of this small village on a scrap of paper. Initially, we drove right through this place, which must have taken all of ten seconds, without seeing anything likely. So Tim turned around and drove very slowly back and parked at the side of the road. We found this little roadside café - not very hospitable looking, I must say, but we sat ourselves down at a table outside and watched in amazement as ancient lorries drove past, completely overloaded with their burdens of fruit and vegetables. We then proceeded to eat a marvellous meal of fresh salad, olives and chips, all followed by a huge bunch of fresh green juicy grapes, and they tasted beautiful.

We also had a long drive onto the Lasithi Plain, in the island's centre, which seemed like another world, with lots of twisty turns and climbing higher and higher. After quite a while, having looked out for somewhere to have lunch, we had just about given up. But then, on the skyline appeared a café, with lots of international flags flying outside. Again, the meal we had was plain but healthy, and deliciously tasty. The local town of Gouves was nothing to write home about, very much a 'tourist' spot, with bars advertising the fact that they could offer soccer on wide-screen TV! But we strolled down there every evening to one particular bar and enjoyed the delights of *Cointreau* on ice! I think we must have drunk them dry – the young girl in the bar even had to send out for another bottle one evening! On her personal recommendation, Joyce and I took a walk around the town on our last morning, where we found the local 'deli', so managed to take home with us a huge chunk of the local 'hard cheese', very much like the Italian *Parmesan*.

Our turn for visitors again!

Millennium year 2000 saw us in rather quiet mode as far as holidays were concerned. Our usual Easter week was spent at Barmouth and we also enjoyed a few days down at Padstow with the Fitzes. After that we were inundated with visitors for a while – Mum came over from Australia, accompanied by Sheila, and they stayed a while. Sue and Geoff, who also spent some time with us, followed them a little later. During that time, we managed a few days out locally, and also had a visit down to Dorset, visiting Wimborne, Lulworth Cove, Corfe Castle and a 'bed and breakfast' place in Swanage. Joyce and Sue visited a 'monkey sanctuary', while Geoff and I went to see the famous Tank Museum nearby, at Bovington.

In March 2001, Lorraine kindly treated us to a weekend away in the lovely city of Bath, staying at the *Hilton*. It was a bit cold and wet, and I was suffering from a nasty cold too, but we thoroughly enjoyed our time there, walking all over the place

– but warming up in a cinema one afternoon! On the way down, we had called in at Marlborough, Corsham and Bradford-on-Avon. A couple of weeks later we spent another nice weekend up at the Howlett's, taking a trip on the London Eye and visiting Hampton Court, with a lovely walk along the river. August saw us down at Padstow with the Fitzes again, then in September we took a week's break in Tuscany with H & T.

We just love Italy

We landed at Pisa and picked up the inevitable hire-car, then just drove somewhere different almost every day, with the walled city of Lucca our first port of call. We came across some really narrow country roads along the way – in fact some of them were reduced at times to farm tracks, though that may have been down to my reading of the map! By the time we found a hotel that first night, it was already dark – and it was Joyce who saw the neon sign in the distance, was the town called Pescia? Amazingly, most of the villages and towns that we passed through had a *Co-op* supermarket and we would just stop there and pick up our simple lunch. Fresh crusty bread rolls, gorgeous thick-sliced ham, *peccorino* cheese, bright red tomatoes and black olives – while a bottle of *Chianti* to wash it all down seemed almost obligatory! At one such lunch break, Tim almost backed the car into a river – and we sat eating in a bed of reeds!

Highlight of the trip was a three-day stop-off in an old farmhouse near San Gimignano – except for the beds, in Helen's case! We also visited Montecattini (with its cable-car ride), Vinci (birthplace of Len!), Siena and Volterra along the way, then stayed the last couple of days 'on the beach' at the little holiday resort of San Vincenzo. It was there that we heard the terrible news about the terrorist attacks on the twin towers in New York. We walked into the reception area to find the local TV station showing what appeared to be one of those 'disaster movies', but what was actually live coverage of the burning buildings.

Early in 2002, we had a couple of consecutive weekends away. The first was with Lorraine up in London, when we had a good walk along the river, took in an art display at the Hayward Gallery, crossed the newly-opened Millennium Bridge towards St Paul's and then finally paid a visit to the Tower of London. The following week we were up at Sue and Des's at Culcheth. Sue took us into Manchester and we spent some time in the new Lowry Centre, as well as the 'designer outlet' shopping centre nearby. In May we were off again – to see Jo and Dave at their place in Surbiton. We had a lovely day out, visiting Greenwich and Woolwich – Southwark's Borough Market, with all of its foreign produce, was especially interesting.

At the end of the same month, we joined the Gould's – and Eileen! – for a week in a villa on Portugal's Algarve coast. Again we had a car on hire, but didn't use it too extensively, mainly for shopping and eating out! However, we did visit Portimao, Monchique and Silves, but usually stayed locally on some of the many beaches – and by the pool at the villa. Highlight of that week were three visits to a local restaurant at Guia, where we feasted on 'chicken piri-piri'. One platter would be heaped up with chicken pieces in a delicious sauce, another platter was full of chips and the final one with a healthy salad. I certainly cannot recall anything being left over! Portugal's own wine – *Vinho Verde* – was also very appetising.

In October that same year, Lorraine & Phil 'did us proud', when they treated us to a weekend break in Edinburgh. We drove to their place in East Finchley to pick them up, then we all went up to Luton Airport mate! An hour's flight meant that we were up in Edinburgh for about 10 o'clock in the morning, where Phil picked up a hire-car and drove us into the city – we even stopped at *McDonalds* for a late breakfast! We had a great few days there, visiting all the high spots such as the Royal Mile and Edinburgh Castle. That was a bit nostalgic for me, as it contained a military museum for the Royal Scots Greys. On the Sunday morning, we drove down into the area near Holyrood Castle to meet some of L & P's friends, then walked up to the top of Arthur's Seat, which is a hill that towers over the surrounding countryside. We also had a visit to the town of Stirling, with its Castle and William Wallace memorial tower. Another highlight was seeing the old Forth Bridge, very busy with trains crossing all the time, quite stunning.

Early in 2003, after a theatre trip to London with Jan & Roy, we stayed overnight at Eileen and Mike's. Then we drove down to Padstow with them, stopping off at Marlborough for morning coffee, then later having lunch on the seafront at Clevedon (Bristol Channel). Their daughter Susie, and husband Nick, had recently bought a bungalow in Padstow, just down the road to the one we'd always used in the past, so we made full use of it. Later, in the summer, we used it again, this time for our usual fortnight's get-together with Michelle, James and the boys. Just for the record, both bungalows that we've used in Padstow are located in Egerton Road – and Egerton is the name of our doctor, as well as a village we used to pass through between Bolton and Blackburn.

Easter of 2004 saw us off on our annual trip to Barmouth, which coincided with out thirtieth consecutive trip up to North Wales. Just prior to our visit, tragedy had struck that seaside town, with the death of two lifeboat men, caused by high seas in a raging storm. Lorraine and Phil joined us over the Easter weekend, they stayed in a farmhouse just outside the town limits, while we had the benefit of dog-sitting for Jake! We had occasionally taken the electric train down the coast to Tywyn, generally on the Easter Monday for the outdoor market – and usually in the rain! But for a change this year, we drove up to Porthmadog and took the steam train up into the hills as far as Tan-y-Bylch, it was quite spectacular, with splendid views across the estuary. It was only a couple of weeks later that we again had a few days with Ei & Mike, this time down at Padstow once more. Despite dire weather forecasts, we actually had plenty of sunshine, though it was a bit on the chilly side at times. We managed visits to Mevagissey, St Mawes, Falmouth, Looe and Polperro, thanks to the relatively quiet traffic! Oh, and *Rick Stein's* fish and chips are superb! *(Perhaps I should qualify that last remark! Later that summer we had our usual fortnight at the bungalow with the Fitzes. I told them how good Stein's chippy was, and went down to the harbour to pick up an evening meal. Trouble is, I got there just on opening time and, like too many 'chippies' I have used over the years, the evening's first serving was leftovers from lunchtime! Won't make that mistake again!)*

The following week, just after we'd gone home, Susie and Sarah shared a holiday in Padstow. Just up the coast at Boscastle, a horrendous storm dumped literally thousands of gallons of rain on the harbour town in a very short time. Boscastle is fed by two separate rivers, located in deep valleys, and these just couldn't cope with the amount of water. It led to fantastic flood damage, as witnessed by the rest of the UK on television, but thankfully no lives were lost. *(In late 2004 and into 2005, BBC2 ran a documentary series called 'A Seaside Parish' – and it was based on Boscastle. The crew had been filming in the village and, by sheer coincidence, was there when the floods hit. The series was able then to show the effects of the flooding on the local community, followed by the efforts made to re-build their shattered lives. Compelling stuff.)*

A dream Carribean wedding – and holiday

Towards the end of February 2005, Lorraine and Phil had arranged to get married – on the Carribean island of St Lucia! They very kindly arranged our flights and accommodation, so that we could join them for this happy event. Phil's mother and brother, as well as a lot of the happy couple's friends and colleagues, also came along – arrivals and departures were the order of the day! All in all, Joyce and I stayed for two whole weeks and had a thoroughly enjoyable time. The 'hotel' was a resort-style place called St James, at Morgan Bay. Everything was very casual, with a choice of dining areas, and the food really was very good indeed – I'm pretty sure we had fish at some time on every day! Just outside the resort front entrance, we could pick up a local minibus – they came along just about every five minutes and it was 'a dollar a ride'.

So we used this facility quite a lot, either heading up the coast to the Port Rodney Marina or down the coast into the island's capital town of Castries. One day we joined a two-hour catamaran trip to Soufriere, with its drive-in volcano! Another day was spent on a tour of some rain forest, which included a spot of biking. The wedding itself was absolutely memorable, taking place 'on the beach' near Pigeon Island, with accompanying steel band! The fortnight was very relaxing, although Joyce and I did manage to get some walks in too – and Joyce enjoyed a daily dip in the briny most days. We found the people very friendly, a natural thing when tourism is probably the main income, but none the less welcome.

Easter of the same year found us heading once more up to Barmouth, for what was in fact the 'thirtieth anniversary' of our first trip there. Joyce had not long gotten over a knee operation, so it was good that she was able to get out on all the walks – mind you we've all slowed down now – after all, Mike is seventy later this year! During the week we had one very exciting adventure, when we found ourselves almost stranded on the very narrow road leading up from Llanbedr to Cym Bychan! We'd been up as far as the car park (on a farm), where the farmer now wanted to charge £6 for a car and its four occupants! We turned around and then found the road blocked by a car that had been trying to pass a camper van and had 'bogged down' in the soft grass at the side of the track. We tried to get the car back onto the road, but the real problem was that cars were now driving both up and down the track, arriving at the impasse and being unable to turn around! Eventually, with the aid of a tow-rope and lots of judicial reversing by many vehicles, it did get sorted out, but not before we'd had visions of spending the night in Mike's car! The same week, we drove up to visit Jackie and Steve at the *Ozanam Centre*, where we'd enjoyed a New Year's party. On the way back, we took up Steve's recommendation to visit *'Eric's Café'*, just outside Tremadog, which turned out well worth the effort.

In June of 2005, Lorraine and Phil moved out of North London and set up home in Chicago! *(Not quite Chicago itself, but a town called Wheaton, Illinois – birthplace of the famous preacher, Billy Graham.)* Phil's job had increasingly taken him there 'on business' and eventually he asked (or was asked?) if he'd be better off based there. Lorraine also managed to find a project based in Chicago, so off they both went. Joyce and I were absolutely delighted to be invited to visit them towards the end of August the same year, and spent a lovely fortnight with them. The weather stayed very kind to us and we were able to get out and about just about every day.

We did go into Chicago quite a bit – either with L&P or by ourselves, courtesy of the *Metra* train into the city. That was very exciting, with the shoreline of Lake Michigan a very nice place to visit – and a good spot from which to see the skyscrapers! One highlight was a boat tour of the Chicago River, with an excellent running commentary about the 'Windy City'. The walk into Wheaton from L&P's house was very nice, up through a park and past some splendid houses, the type one normally associates with Hollywood films. We also managed to visit a couple of nearby towns, in the form of Naperville and Geneva.

Such devoted sisters!

That title comes from an old *Beverley Sisters* song – sorry if you're too young to remember it! However, it does give a good lead-in to the following little collection of memories. Back in 1985, all of 'the Jones' girls' decided to have a holiday together, coinciding with the autumn half-term school break. I'm pretty sure that all four girls were still employed in the education system in one form or another. Anyway, they booked a week on the Isle of Wight, either at Sandown or Shanklin. I remember them telling me afterwards of the thrill of sailing out of Portsmouth Harbour and across the Solent on the ferry, *"almost like going abroad"* they said. Having enjoyed their week together, they then repeated the experience the following year - again on the Isle of Wight.

In 1987 they again got together, this time heading down to Swanage in Dorset. This was obviously now going to be a regular occurrence and so it has proved over the following years. By 1988, and for the life of me I cannot remember how the choice was made, Jan and Roy were 'in the market' for a 'second home' - or 'holiday home' – and the location chosen was on the beautiful Gower Peninsula, just outside Swansea in South Wales. So that year, the girls headed down to that area and stayed in a large flat at Langland Bay, which is just a bit further around the coast from Mumbles, which is where the Rocketts eventually bought their cottage at No.3 Village Lane. By the following year (1989), Jan and Roy had settled into their cottage, located almost on the seafront overlooking Swansea Bay. The road leading up from the seafront is quite steep, as we have all found out in the years that followed! It is only a small place, starting its life as one of a row of fishermen's homes. But with two double bedrooms, it (almost) comfortably sleeps four – and is often over populated with a party of six, if you throw in a couple of inflatable beds and sleeping bags! In fact, the first occasion must have been that very same year, in November, when Jan and Roy celebrated their 25th Anniversary.

Jan and Roy use Mumbles extensively, they are usually down there every alternate weekend, with the journey being a straightforward one for them, using the M4 motorway. And who can blame them? The Gower is a lovely spot, with plenty of walking along its coastal fringes at bays such as Langland, Caswell, Three Cliffs, Oxwich, Port Eynon and Rhossili, to name just a few. There is the small shopping centre of Oystermouth right on the doorstep, while the city of Swansea itself is only a short drive – or a long walk - away. The sisters have been going regularly now for some fifteen years – the October half-term is still used as the reason for going, despite the school connection being very tenuous nowadays! Joyce and I have been there during the summer a couple of times and, even at 'high season', the beaches and cliff-top paths are usually very quiet and peaceful. And on quite a few occasions, we have joined Jan, Roy, Eileen and Mike in celebrating New Year's Eve at an assortment of local hostelries.

For the 'girls only' trips, it has become the custom for Joyce to do all the driving. Firstly, June and Jan don't drive at all and, secondly, our car has always seemed to have the largest boot! Anyway, it seems convenient for Joyce to drive from here to Reading and then pick up the others, then make the return trip 'in reverse order'. This year (2005) was no exception and another pleasant break was enjoyed by all four girls – I say that because June didn't make it the previous year, having suffered some sort of internal eye injury.

Boscastle revisited

The first day of February 2006 had us heading off down to Padstow once again after a hurried arrangement with Eileen & Mike. With their 'tribe' of grandchildren and Mike's continued sporting interests of table-tennis and bowling (despite his being now 70!), weekend breaks have become a little difficult to set up. However, we had a phone call asking if we could make it and 'bombed' down there after Joyce finished work on a Wednesday afternoon. Light traffic gave us a fast run, se we were able to have dinner together at Susie's bungalow. The weather was dull and grey for the next three days, but at least it stayed dry, enabling us to get out and about as we usually do.

We actually went down and 'ate in' at *Rick Stein's* one evening – glad to say the meal was well up to the expected standard! Boscastle was our first port of call and it is good to see that the village is gradually getting back to normal, following the floods of August 16th 2004. I bought a small book about those events, proceeds going towards reconstruction work. We also popped into Port Isaac, but it was closed! Wadebridge was pretty much as normal and we also paid a visit to Truro, which made a nice change after a few years' absence. We had a nice river walk in that area, between St Clement and Malpas, which may attract us there again during a summer.

At the time of writing this particular addition, we have recently returned from 'Barmouth 2006'! It had been 'touch and go' whether or not we actually went this year, as Marcus was even more difficult than ever to track down. It eventually transpired that he had sold up and left us out on a limb. It was just lucky that Eileen and Joyce had picked up a leaflet in 2005, regarding the flat next door – right above the *Isis Pizerria*! Even luckier that, with only a couple of weeks to go, we were able to book up as normal for our Easter break. Ei and Mike had only recently returned from two weeks in Cuba, so Joyce and I went up as usual on the Good Friday. Only a few days previously, I had received a copy of Nana's birth certificate, referring to *'Upper Gashford, Stanton Lacy, Ludlow'*, so we dropped in at the tiny village of Stanton Lacy on our journey north. I was able to chat to someone near the village church, who has said that he will attempt to find out some more details for me – watch this space! *(Unfortunately there was no response from that encounter – lots of people say a lot about what they'll do, but never actually do it!)*

The only 'new' place that we visited was about as far away as we'd ever been – up to Aberdaron, right at the 'Land's End' of the Llyn peninsular. On the way back from there, we stopped off at Abersoch and then Criccieth, making a full day of it. At Criccieth, Mike persuaded us to enter an old church that was being used as a sort of 'curiosity shop', full of old books and such. I had a look through some old postcards, obviously concentrating on those in the pile marked 'Hampshire'. Joyce suddenly handed me a postcard of St Giles Church, Reading, where we (and Ei and Mike) had been married - so that was a bargain for only a pound!

Having been unable to visit Padstow the previous year, Michelle had made sure that she was quickly out of the starting blocks in contacting Susie this year! However, with my 50th anniversary reunion booked at Arborfield right in the middle of the Fitzes holiday, we didn't travel down to meet them as normal. Instead, Joyce took the train from Reading to Bodmin on the Wednesday after their arrival. This happened on the hottest July day on record – and there was no air conditioning on the train! The Fitzes picked her up – but only just, as they first got snarled up in a traffic jam on the way out of Padstow! Apart from that little episode, the rest of the holiday was very good, particularly as the weather was so brilliant. Plenty of sunshine, but not the stifling temperatures that we'd been having further east, thanks to a nice sea breeze. I was able to get away from home at noon on the Sunday, following my reunion, and the week that followed went all too quickly. One memorable addition this year was a lovely return trip by boat between Truro and Falmouth. It was an hour's journey each way and we were able to fit in a three-hour stopover in Falmouth. Just a couple of months later, we again returned to Padstow, with Eileen & Mike, for a pleasant few days.

'Half term' is usually time for 'the girls' to go down to Swansea for a week. But 2006 saw June and Janet heading off to South Africa on holiday, leaving Jan's cottage free. So it was convenient for yet another combined 'Gillard and Gripton' break! Mike decided that he'd like to make full use of his football 'season ticket', Reading having been promoted to the Premiership for the very first time, so we arranged to pick up Eileen from Caversham and headed off down the M4 on a Friday. Mike then joined us late on the Monday afternoon. Apart from some of the favourite walks already taken in previous visits, an added pleasure this trip was to visit the waterfalls in the river valley leading down to the little village of Pontneddfechan – try saying that after a couple of drinks! Another bonus was the pub lunch at *'The Angel Inn'* on completion of the walk. We also had a nice meal at *Verdi's*, an Italian-style restaurant right on the seafront at Mumbles – nothing pretentious, just good food at reasonable cost.

After our usual few days spent at Cosby with the Fitzes over Christmas, it would have been customary for us to 'see in' the New Year down at Mumbles. But with Lisa now being 'looked after' more or less full time by Jan & Roy, that became impossible. Instead, we spent a couple of days at Caversham with Eileen & Mike. My back was rather sore at the time and was particularly painful when we drove over to Marlow. Along with the rain that then came along in gale-force winds, it rather spoiled our visit! The next day, New Year's Eve, we did get a walk in – this time around our old haunts in Reading, taking in Queen's Cottages and the Forbury Gardens – all very nostalgic. Pleased to say that the enforced mobility eased my back considerably - but I still took out the insurance of a visit to the chiropractor when we eventually got back home!

It was back to our usual Barmouth haunts at Easter 2007, though this time we stayed in a large flat on Porkington Terrace – we even had two separate bedrooms as well as the living room! The name of the house is *Tal-y-Garreg* and run by a very nice lady, Norma Stockford – Barmouth born and bred. Suzie and family had been staying at Borth-y-Gest the previous week, and they all came into Barmouth on the Saturday to visit us for a few hours. We did manage to find a couple of different walks this year, both based upon the newly constructed Welsh Highland Railway, which will eventually link up Porthmadog to Caernarfon. We visited the 'station' at Rhydd Ddu, walked about a third of the way towards Snowdon and back – then found a delightful little café in the village. The weather was very warm for most of the week, with only a cooler spell and a drop of overnight rain between the Monday and Tuesday. Ei and Mike left on the Friday, while Joyce and I were away from Barmouth early (5.30) Saturday morning to pick up Mum from Culcheth and bring her back down to Greatham for the week. On that same day, 'our Sue' had a clean-up operation on her troubled knee.

So good, they named it twice!

On the last day of May 2007, we departed on a *BA Club World* flight to New York, at the start of a brilliant tour of the eastern seaboard of the United States, courtesy of Lorraine and Phil. We stayed three nights in the *Hotel Casablanca* – and had a whale of a time, walking all over the place, including Central Park, the Hudson River promenade and the city streets such as 42nd Street and Broadway. We saw 'Ground Zero', scene of the devastating attack on the Twin Towers, went inside Central Station – and took the elevator to the top of the Empire State Building. L&P arrived by car, all the way from Chicago, and we all enjoyed an excellent Indian curry together, before setting out next morning on *'le grande tour'*! This took us up to Rhode Island, where we stayed a couple of nights in Newport – I'd remembered it from the 1958 Jazz Festival that took place there, giving birth to the film *'Jazz on a Summer's day'*. Little did I know that Lorraine would later send me the DVD of same!

There is insufficient space here to mention all the details of our trip, but it took in Portsmouth (New Hampshire); Portland (Maine); Boston (Massachusetts) and Burlington (Vermont), before we crossed the border into Canada. There, we took in Montreal, Toronto and Niagara, before the final drive back down on the long journey to Wheaton. Looking back, every place we visited was associated with water – either a river or lake – and each place we ate at was something special – apart from the *Quality* bagel!

July 18 saw us once again heading down to Padstow, to share a few days with the Fitzes, who had been down there since the previous Friday evening. Having had wet weather for what seemed like months, it was no surprise to find Cornwall in pretty damp condition! As it turned out, we got off rather lightly. On the Friday of that same week, Worcestershire, Herefordshire and the surrounding areas were hit by some devastating floods - while we were basking in sunshine! Overall, we had some intermittent rain, but enough sunshine to enjoy. Another visit to Boscastle showed the remarkable progress made in the village, since their own remarkable flood of 2004.

Late September saw us, along with the Gillards, fulfilling one of Joyce and Eileen's cherished dreams! Off we went to the Isle of Wight for a week – in a caravan at Sandown and Shanklin! Ei & Mike left their car in our garage and we then drove down to Southampton, to pick up the ferry down the Solent and across to Cowes. The first half of the week saw bright sunny days, after which it became a little grey and damp at times. But it didn't stop us from getting out every day, and it was bliss to drive around on reasonably quiet roads – not deserted by any means, but no mad rush of dual carriageway and motorway. I think we got around to all the main spots on the island – and recalled just how lovely it is over there.

One spot that we definitely visited – or re-visited – was Brighstone, where we had holidayed with all the children, way back in the early Seventies. Sadly, the old holiday camp is long gone now – the buildings having been transformed into a retail outlet for pearls and jewellery! In the village centre, we happened to drop into what must have been the 'Church Hall', where a little craft fair was being held. I think that both Joyce and Eileen bought a hand-made cushion from one of the ladies, and have since had another one sent over by post.

In late October, Joyce and I joined the 'Gillard clan' down at Lynton, North Devon, for Sarah's wedding to Andy Joule. This was the first time we had been down to that part of the country in many a long year, and we thoroughly enjoyed the whole weekend. We stopped at Cirencester for lunch on the way down there, and then later were able to explore the charming National Trust village of Selworthy, with its excellent teashop! Soon after our return, we found out that the flat we stayed in at Barmouth earlier in the year was likely to be unavailable. Fortunately, Eileen and Susie used the Internet to find another place, which is located just a few doors down from Tal-y-Garreg, on Porkington Terrace. Watch this space!

Back to the States

At the end of our holiday in the States in June, Lorraine & Phil were just about ready to move from their house in Wheaton to another one in nearby Naperville. And so it was that, on December 20th 2007, Joyce and I set off across the Atlantic once again, to spend Christmas and New Year with the Le Bruns! Basically, it was a very relaxing couple of weeks – especially with Phil showing off his culinary skills! There was quite a lot of snow during our visit, but it didn't prevent us from getting out for a walk most days, taking Jasmine for her exercise! L&P took us into Chicago one night, where we stopped at a very nice hotel and attended a live 'Blues' performance at the *Kingston Mines* club.

Looking back at the holidays detailed above, I realise just how fortunate we have been to visit so many exciting places, both at home and abroad. 'Family and friend' influences have obviously dictated a lot – with Geoff having gone off to Australia in the first place, followed by Mum and Jack's decision to settle 'down under' too. Then there has been Lorraine's adventure of living in the United States and the influence of Helen and Tim Gould on certain European trips; not forgetting several other holidays with the 'Jones girls' side of the family – Ibiza, Tenerife and Italy spring to mind. I have to finish the chapter now, but we look forward to a few more holidays in the future – wherever they may take us!

Aunty Betty with Mum and boys, Grange-over-Sands, 1953

Dad's family – the Griptons

Dad's parents, Jane (or Ginny) and Joe, had once lived in No.10 Cromwell Road, Walton, just three streets down Stuart Road from Milton Road. But all my own memories of them are from when they lived in a nice semi-detached place in South Parade, Crosby, at the northern end of Liverpool. We never ever had our own transport, so all of our journeys were taken either by tram, train or bus. And it was 'the bus' that used to take us to visit Granny and Granddad at Crosby. We would pass through Bootle, Seaforth and Litherland, before dropping off directly outside No.47, the last house before the name changed to Northern Road. It was – and still is as far as I know - an attractive little pebble-dashed house, with a gated front drive and a back garden – only small, but a garden nevertheless, which was certainly a step in the right direction compared to our back yard! It's a pity that the view over the garden fence was only of the back of what appeared to be a large office block, I think it was part of the *Littlewoods* empire. I recall that all the interior doors were of a highly polished wood and that there always seemed to be a nice flowery smell about the house. Granddad had a garden shed and loved growing sweetpeas and carnations; both he and Granny were small in stature, just over five feet tall, but big in heart. I recall Granddad once handing over to me an old mildewed linen bag, full of foreign coins, which he had stowed away in the garden shed, but I can't recall what became of it.

Their only daughter, my Aunty Betty, lived with them and it was quite an occasion when we were invited up to Crosby for a Sunday lunch, but my memories are mainly of those Sunday afternoons when we were all sat around the table for 'high tea'. This was almost always a salad as far as I can remember, I know it was very much a treat, because, as far as I remember, we didn't have many salads at home. The salad was always accompanied by a bottle of *Crosse & Blackwell's* salad cream, and then followed by jelly and custard, or blancmange, and a slice of cake. A special treat was when Betty made a 'milk jelly', using a tin of *Carnation* evaporated milk! Another treat at Crosby was a refreshing glass of *Ribena*, again I can't recall having it at home. (N.b. Mum later told me that we did have the occasional salad at No.5, but that little boys were never the greatest salad eaters – she must have meant Cliff and Geoff!)

The meal would inevitably be followed by a game of *'Fish, flower and fruit'*, which seemed to be a family favourite, or *'Lotto'*, played with little cardboard counters, to the cries of *'housey, housey'*. Betty was herself a schoolteacher, who had not been allowed to marry, but instead stayed at home to look after her parents – another fact I didn't know during my innocent childhood years! Betty taught at a girl's school in Anfield, which no doubt accounted for the fact that there were always copious supplies of paper and pencils, a luxury beyond most households at the time. As far as I recall, Betty always had white hair, despite the fact that she couldn't have been all that old and I think that she eventually died of cancer, that sad event taking place sometime in the summer of 1972, when she was around sixty-four years of age.

Rhymes and things!

Betty used to recite certain rhymes to us, some of which remain in the old memory bank right till this day! I'll see if I can quote them correctly!

"One, two, three, Mother caught a flea,
She put it in the teapot to make a cup of tea,
The flea jumped out, Mother gave a shout
And along came a bobby with his shirt hanging out!"

"Oh Aunty Mary, look at my Uncle Jim,
He's jumping in the teapot to learn how to swim.
First he does the sidestroke, then he does the breast,
Upsets the teapot and he can't do the rest!"

"ABCD goldfish, MNO goldfish, SDR goldfish, RDL goldfish"
Which translates into:

"Abie, see de goldfish?
'Em are no goldfish.
Yes de are goldfish.
Are de 'ell goldfish!"

There was another little saying that Betty used to recite, which was I suppose rather rude for its day, but of course we boys used to take great delight in repeating! It went something like this:

"I chased a bug around a tree,
I'll get his blood, he knows I will".

96

Just say it fast and you'll know why we remembered it!

There were a few other 'rhymes' that did the rounds in those days and I can still remember them well enough to quote them to my two grandsons, Thomas and Calum, some sixty years afterwards. I'm pretty sure it was Dad who passed them on to we three boys – and it's possible that they will continue to be handed down through the family tree in future years. Tom in particular finds the following words very entertaining!

"One fine day, in the middle of the night,
Two dead men got up to fight.
Back to back they faced each other,
Then drew their swords and shot each other."

Another very similar version, but more extended, went (and still does!) something like this:

"One fine day, in the middle of the night,
A fire broke out in the ocean.
The deaf man heard it, the blind man saw it
And the man with no legs ran to get the fire bobby.
The fire bobby came along, riding on two paralysed donkeys,
Ran over a dead cat – and half killed it!"

Granddad was just about completely bald, with a large 'walrus-type' moustache that always smelled of the thick black tobacco that he used to smoke in his old pipe – kissing him took a lot of courage! His local pub was the *'Endbutt'*, not far away in Endbutt Lane, where they kept his seat available for him for many years, he was part of the furniture. I still regret not having known Granny and Granddad better, they certainly must have had a few tales to tell! I can't remember their exact ages when we first started to pay visits to Crosby, but they must have already been in their sixties when I was born in 1940. Poor Granny eventually succumbed to loss of memory, so conversations with her became nigh on impossible; she died around 1964, so must have been almost ninety years old. I think 'old Joe', who was around five years younger, remained fairly sharp right up to the end – he had certainly been a very fit man in his prime. He must have died around 1967, just about the time that I left the Army to settle into civilian life.

Granddad was originally from Shifnal in Shropshire and quite a bit of background information on him is recalled in my Uncle John Gripton's memoirs, which can be found on Page 106. However, from my own childhood memories, later reinforced by

Granddad in WWI uniform

Mum, I can now add the following. Joseph had a brother, John (though commonly known as Jack), who was around three years younger (b. 1883). It was Jack who was married to 'Aunty Annie' and they lived on a farm called Wheatley Grange, near a town called Wellington, nowadays pretty well overtaken by the large 'new town' of Telford, also located in Shropshire. I have no real recollection of Jack, while Annie appears in my memory as a figure dressed 'all in black', probably an indication of wartime deprivation.

Mum (Ruth) informed me that Annie was a really mean person, while Jack had 'a heart of gold' – a strange combination eh? Apparently, while we were once stopping down there, Ruth's own mother (another Annie!) arrived on a visit. Later, when Mum was due to leave for Liverpool, she asked Aunty Annie for a turkey egg to take back with her – and Annie promptly charged her three shillings for it, a princely sum in those days! I can vaguely remember an 'Aunty Nellie' living close by in Shropshire, and this turned out to be Annie's sister. I'm pretty sure that we 'went visiting' on at least one occasion, but all I can see in my mind's eye regarding Nellie is a large goiter, which the unfortunate lady carried around her neck. *(From the Oxford English Dictionary, I found that a goiter is an 'enlarged thyroid gland'.)*

Annie and Jack had three children of their own – the eldest was estranged from the family, but the next son, William, lived at home with his mother for as long as anyone can remember, tending to the cattle and their milking and all the other odd jobs around the farm. It was William that I later 'found', living in Oakengates, whilst visiting old Army pal Dave Howlett, then based at Donnington, in August 1984. There was also a daughter, Ellen, inevitably named Nellie, whose own daughter Patricia, was sadly killed by a car when alighting from a bus and running around the back of that same vehicle.

Uncles – both known and unknown!

Dad's four brothers were, to quote the modern parlance, a 'tale of two halves'. The eldest, Jim, and his wife Hilda, I can hardly remember at all, though I do know that he was quite well off and became a respected member of the fruit and groceries trade. I can vaguely remember Jim having a daughter called Jacqueline, but never really got to know her. I have the feeling that she used to visit friends in Northern Road, just a few houses along from Granny and Granddad's place, but it's a long time ago! The family eventually lived in a large house on Burbo Bank Road, on the river at Blundellsands, what you would call a 'posh area' (that information came from Geoff), though Mum also remembers them living at 'The Byway', at the end of the Northern Road, Crosby.

Bill, despite living not too far away from us in Walton Village, was another virtual stranger to us, though I have vague recollections of occasionally seeing him 'along the road' and that he was a gaunt looking chap, with hardly an ounce of flesh on him. I'm afraid his wife, Clara, doesn't even strike a chord with me. My memories of his sons include Billy, who had a bit of a 'tearaway' reputation, Kenny and Ronny, who later married a girl called – I think - Maureen Minshull, who hailed from the other side of Breeze Hill, possibly Buchanan Road. I'm pretty sure that Billy Gripton was involved in an unsavoury incident at a public house at the bottom of Spellow Lane, where one chap was kicked so savagely that he lost an eye. I think Billy ended up in jail as a result of the ensuing investigation.

Bob was married to Joyce, and they lived in a flat in South Albert Road, Aigburth, down towards the southern end of Liverpool. I seem to recall another couple (was it Rene and Geoff?) being around at the time, I think they must have been Joyce's relations. We were fairly regular visitors there, again arriving by bus after what seemed like a long journey around Queen's Drive, then through the Old Swan area. Their flat wasn't far from both Princes' Park and Sefton Park and we sometimes went out for a walk there if the weather allowed, visiting the glass-houses and aviary. *(When Lorraine was at Liverpool University, she shared a flat with other students down in that area of town.)*

Apart from my Mum, Aunty Joyce is now the last surviving member of that generation and lives at the family home at No.47 South Parade. She and Uncle Bob had been living there until Bob's death in 1990. At one time, if I'm right, Joyce had served in the 'WAAF', I'm sure I've seen a photograph of her in uniform. I remember on one occasion that 'my' Joyce and I called in on her, when she was still working in the *Gas Board* showroom in Bold Street, just down at the bottom as you approach

The Gripton family around 1918, Jim (16), Bill (13), John (nearly 3), Joe (8), Betty (11) and Bob (5)

Central Station. I also did manage to catch up with the couple at No.47 not long before Bob died, that was when Sue and Des were living in Crosby too. *(I think that Joyce finally went into a nursing home, so what has become of No.47 nowadays I don't know.)*

The youngest of the five brothers, named John, was married to Dorothy, and they had two boys, David and Paul, who were of similar age to Cliff and Geoff. John had served in the Army, reaching Warrant Officer rank, but was later involved in the licensing trade for most of his life and ran several public houses on behalf of *Bent's Brewery*, mainly on the Wirral, that isthmus of land that lies between the Rivers Mersey and Dee. Visiting them was always an adventure that involved crossing the Mersey and, of course, the illicit thrill of a small glass of shandy would make our day! Quite a few years later (1960), Dorothy and John had another son, Charles – the best mistake they ever made, as they would say. It was a tragedy that Charles died from leukaemia at the early age of thirty-one, he'd not long been married and was pursuing a university education. He'd actually spent his 'gap year' at a computer firm, probably *IBM*, down at Havant in Hampshire, which is where I believe his wife came from. I don't think Dorothy ever came to terms with the loss of Charles, it just knocked all 'the stuffing' out of her. She certainly never looked well afterwards, she lost weight and seemingly the will to live, so that her own death early in 1995 was no doubt a blessing.

Uncle John survived a while longer and I am grateful that, before his own death, in June 1998, he was able to provide me with a potted history of his own family and siblings, containing many details that I'd never known myself. This all came about at my request because, by that time, my Dad's memory was fading fast and I suddenly realised that John was probably the best (and only?) one still capable of putting together a 'family history'. I think he found it therapeutic after the death of Dorothy, I'd certainly like to think so, as I always held John in a lot of affection. My thanks must also go to my cousin Paul, who actually typed in his father's words on computer, enabling me to get the story that subsequently appeared. *(Readers will find John's contribution on Page 106.)*

Hard times

Times were obviously pretty hard during the war, as proved by the fact (as recalled by Mum) that Dorothy often used to come around to scrounge some butter or margarine from us! One thing that she loved was Mum's 'meat pies', made from tinned sausages, with the fat from the tin used to produce the pastry. I can still remember those tinned sausages, I'm pretty sure that they were imported from our American allies. I have a vision that they came in a tin shaped rather like a corned beef tin, so that the sausages were of a square cross-section, meaning they could be 'browned' equally on all four sides! I have always thought that they tasted so wonderful, far better than those of today – and they were skinless too, which went down well with we children. When Dorothy's father returned to the Merchant Navy, her problems were solved, as he was sailing on the convoys to the United States and thus able to supplement their food supply. Mum reckons that the main beneficiary of this was Betty, who ended up with whole hams, which she then shared out amongst her teacher friends!

Just thinking back to those 'hard times', I'm pretty sure I remember a crate of apples – big, red and shiny ones - being opened in my classroom at Arnot Street. I believe this was a present to us children from the Canadian government, as I suppose apples had become something of a rare item in wartime Britain. Adding to this, very recently on the television was a programme recalling the day – in 1952 – when bananas finally came 'off the ration'. Most children of my era wouldn't have even seen a banana until then - and must have had to be taught what to do with them! On the same subject, I recall that the 'black market' was rife in those days, whereby goods supposedly 'on the ration' were available from certain quarters, provided you had the money to pay for them. These 'black marketeers' were commonly known as 'spivs', epitomised by the late comedian, Arthur English, who played the part of such a character in a radio programme. Another term used to describe them was 'wide boys'.

When we were growing up in later years, visits to John's pub were quite frequent; in fact visiting 'the relatives' must have been our main source of entertainment over several years. The one pub that sticks mainly in my memory was the *'Halfway House'*, situated between Prenton and Oxton over on the Wirral, near to Tranmere's football

Betty, Joyce, Granddad, Bob and Granny Gripton

ground - it was definitely the one we visited the most. Later came the *'Station Hotel'* at Ellesmere Port, which had a huge bar, one of the longest I've ever seen, and the *'Blue Anchor'* over at Hoylake, which had been recently re-furbished and made to look like the inside of a cruise liner! *(Come to think of it, how did we manage to get to those places? - it can only have been by bus and possibly a 'ferry across the Mersey'.)* I know that, at one time, John left the publican business for a while, working at some Atomic Energy place over near Chester. I can recall visiting there with Dad one New Year's Eve and actually going out 'first footing' with John. We even had pieces of coal for friends and neighbours, so it was almost like a real Scottish *Hogmanay*! John later returned to finish his working days at his final pub, the *'Farmer's Arms'*, at Frankby, again on the opposite side of the river to Liverpool.

Early memories of home life

Meals at home were governed by what was allowed on the ration and also by the fact that Dad was just about the fussiest eater ever – to use Mum's own words – no doubt due to his continual battle against ill health. Certainly, while we were growing up, Dad never seemed to be well and suffered with stomach (duodenal?) ulcers – for which he was later to have major surgery. He certainly 'brought his job home with him', always regaling us with stories of office politics, the one name that was often included was a chap called Danny O'Driscoll, while another, Mr Wiseman, seemed to be the major 'fly in the ointment'.

Occasionally, on a Sunday morning, Dad would decide to return to the office for one reason or another, and I can remember accompanying him. We would walk down into Bootle, over Miller's Bridge, and into *Blackledge's* bakery. I used to think it was all so modern, with baked (and half-baked?) loaves moving up, down and along on conveyor belts throughout the building. A special treat would be to bring home some strawberry tarts, when that fruit was in season, they always tasted so marvellous. As Geoff's birthday was in the middle of June, he has always associated that time of year with strawberries.

Sometimes we boys would go out with Dad for walks, these would generally be across Breeze Hill and up the continuation of Stuart Road. On the left were the grounds of a girls' school and some playing fields, that went on for quite a distance – it must have felt as though we were out in the country! Dad would constantly tell us to *'breathe in through our noses and out through our mouths'* - the air must have been a bit fresher in those days! My memory is a little hazy, but there was some sort of sports centre up Stuart Road, I think it was known as Bootle Stadium. I know that they used to have a cycle track and that, on one occasion, I attended a football match there, played between ex-players from both Everton and Liverpool. I think the legendary 'Dixie' Dean actually played a part in it, so at least I can say that I saw him play! Just remembering that name 'Dixie' there reminds me that William Ralph Dean never did like his nickname and much preferred the simpler 'Bill'. In later years he ran a public house in Chester – was it *'The Steam Packet'*? Anyway, I remember going to Chester occasionally on the odd day out and being told that kids used to go into the pub and shout *"Hello Dixie"* – before being chased out again! I can definitely recall him there, standing behind his bar, his hair still in that black tightly curled style of his.

The top end of Stuart Road ran into a junction with Hornby Road and, just a little way along to the right, on the opposite side of the road, was the looming presence of Walton Jail, a place we tended to steer clear of. If we had walked as far as that, we would inevitably turn left and walk as far as Southport Road before heading back home again. In those days, of course, traffic was much lighter than today, so walking along these city roads didn't subject us to the pollution that would be the case today. One particular event that involved Dad stands out in my mind. He had gone up onto 'the rezzy' one afternoon and must have fallen asleep in the summer sunshine. He may have been bitten by either a bee or a wasp, but we never did find out. But whatever happened, he slept through it, only to find when he woke up that his whole upper lip had swollen up to horrific proportions! I guess the effect of the hot sunshine on the sting or bite had caused the swelling, it certainly looked pretty awful for a while.

Some years after we had left Milton Road with Mum, Dad had taken up a job with *Schofield's*, the lemonade manufacturers down on Scotland Road. No doubt he was

Aunty Betty – probably with Jacqueline

doing the job of wages clerk, as he had previously done at *Blackledge's*. Anyway, he was unlucky enough to find himself in a narrow gap as a lorry reversed into the yard, and got crushed between the lorry and wall. His hip was severely damaged and he probably never worked again afterwards. I think he must have got a disability pension for his troubles, but I think the damaged hip caused him problems for the rest of his life. Dad's last few years were spent mainly in, firstly 'sheltered accommodation' followed by a nursing home, and is fairly well documented in other chapters. One thing that caused him no end of pleasure was that Sue, Des and Tommy sort of 'adopted' him and visited him as often as they could, especially 'our Sue', who was a tower of strength for him as the last months rolled towards their inevitable finale.

Footnote

I have mentioned in this chapter that my Uncle John Gripton was able to produce some memoirs relating to his parents and siblings, which formed the main basis of my knowledge about my predecessors at the time. There had been a story that Aunty Betty had carried out a lot of family research and that the earliest recorded Griptons in the family tree had been traced back to a band of Cornish smugglers! Sadly, I have no corroboration of this, and in fact the most traceable family line, as far as I have found, dates back to around 1800 in the county of Shropshire – otherwise known as Salop. This of course is borne out by my evacuation to Wellington when I was a mere baby!

Just after returning from holiday in St Lucia, in early March 2005, I 'registered' with the *Genes Reunited* web-site, and was delighted, within just one day, to receive information regarding the Gripton family from a guy called Neale Sheldon, living in Newcastle-under-Lyme. His mother is (or was?) a Gripton and he had long wanted to make contact with unknown relatives. He certainly had the details correct about Granny and Granddad Gripton, so I made contact with him and am now well into further research back into previous generations. I have been able to produce a family tree dating back to a John Gripton, my great-great-great-grandfather, who must have been born around the turn of the eighteenth century. What has rather confused the issue is that both my father and grandfather were named Joseph – and they both married a Hodgson!

Amongst the research documents, I now have birth certificates for Joseph Gripton (my paternal grandfather, b 1880) and his father, another Joseph (my great-grandfather, b 1850). Also, I have traced and received copies of the marriage certificates of John Gripton (my great-great-grandfather) to Mary Walker in 1847 and of Joseph Gripton (great-grandfather) to Elizabeth Chetter in 1877. Recently I have added the marriage certificate of my grandparents, Joe and Jane, from 1902. How much further back I'm able to go is an interesting question!

Research into the Gripton family

I now have a copy of the birth certificate, which indicates that my patriarchal great-grandfather, Joseph Gripton, was born at Shifnal in Shropshire on January 26th 1850. He was the son of John Gripton and Mary, formerly Walker. On the certificate, it is shown that my great-great-grandfather (John) was a labourer. My great-grandfather (Joseph) was a coal miner and married to Elizabeth (formerly Chetter), as indicated on a separate birth certificate, that of their eldest son, also named Joseph, who was born on December 16th 1880.

The document below shows Joseph Gripton and his wife Elizabeth living in Shropshire, along with three very young sons. I would argue that just above the last shown registration (that of Thomas), should really be that of my grandfather, Joseph, who would then have been at least one year old. From Neale Sheldon's research, sons Thomas and John were both born *after* 1881. *(Strangely, my Uncle John's memoirs indicate that there were only four sons, named William, Thomas, Joseph and John, with no mention of an Albert.)*

1881 Census	Wrockwardine, Shropshire					
38 West Street	Joseph Gripton b 1850	Head	31	Coal Miner, Shifnal,		Salop
	Elizabeth Gripton b 1858?	Wife	23	(nee Chetter)		Dawley
	Albert Gripton	Son	3			Shifnal
	William Gripton	Son	2			
	Thomas Gripton	Son	3m			

John Gripton * – his personal memories

John's two grandfathers were as follows:

Grandfather Hodgson (on mother's side)   **Grandfather Gripton**

1st wife	2nd wife	Only wife
May	Joseph (Joe)	William (Bill)
John	Cissie	Thomas (Tom)
Jane **	William (Bill)	Joseph (Joe) **
Nelly	3 more children	John (Jack)
Harry		
Thomas (Tom)		

John's parents: Joseph Gripton ** married Jane (Ginny) Hodgson, 1902. Six children – James (Jim) b 1902, William (Bill) b 1905, Betty b 1907, Joseph (Joe) b 1910, Robert (Bob) b 1913 and John b 1915 *

Jim (James Hodgson Gripton) married Hilda Clarke; they had just the one daughter, Jacqueline (Jackie). Bill (William Thomas Gripton) married Clara Fitzsimmons;

they had three sons, Kenny, William and Ronnie. Betty (Elizabeth Gripton) never married; she stayed at home to look after her parents. Joe (Joseph Gripton) married Ruth Hodgson (that name again!); they had three sons, Peter Douglas, Clifford Robert and Geoffrey John, followed by a daughter, Elizabeth Susan. Bob (Robert Gripton) married Joyce McDermott; there were no children. John Gripton married Dorothy Harper; they had three sons, David, Paul & Charles

Parents – Jane and Joseph
Jane 'Ginny' Hodgson

My mother, Jane, was born about 1875 in Walton, a suburb of Liverpool, and lived in a place called 'Church Flags' (Smithy Lane?) at the side of Walton Church, in Walton Village. *(It was later confirmed that her birth date was Dec 3 1874. PDG.)* The house had two upstairs and two downstairs rooms, with an outside earth closet. One outside water pump served four houses. In Walton Churchyard was a pair of stocks and a baiting cage, used for punishing people who broke the law. (These were still present until I was about fourteen years old.)

Mother left Walton National School at the age of nine, having become proficient in the 'Three R's'. She then went into service as a housemaid at *'The Beehive'* public house in Church Lane. The owner was a man named Bennett. In the evening, if the pub was busy, she would wash glasses and serve beer, having to stand on a box to reach the pumps. The price of a pint in those days was 2½ pence, or you could buy five pints for a shilling (5 new pence). Mother's wage was 1s and 3d (1/3) per week (about six new pence), she got one Sunday off each month, (8 a.m. to 8 p.m.), in order to go home. (n.b. the money then worked out at twenty shillings to the pound.) The sign hanging outside the pub was of an old basket-weave type beehive, and underneath the sign was a verse that read:

> *'Within this hive, we're all alive*
> *For good malt makes us funny;*
> *So if you're dry, come in and try*
> *The flavour of its honey.'*

Mother left *'The Beehive'* when she was fourteen.

Her father, one James Hodgson, had lost his first wife, Ellen, at the age of thirty-three, and then married again to Elizabeth, a barmaid he met at the *'Black Horse'* Hotel, which still stands at the corner of Church Road and County Road, Walton, almost next door to Walton Church. (Churches and old pubs were often close together, so if you need a drink, look for a church spire!) Mother was about the same age as her newly acquired step-brother, and this seems to be the reason why she never lived at home by herself again. She went off to be in service once more, this time to a family called Mellor, in a house somewhere around Malpas in Cheshire. *(A 1901 census form shows Jane Hodgson living with Ellen Mellor, a widow of 71 years, and her grandson Stanley, aged nine. PDG.)* This was a large house with a lot of land, forming part of a farm, with many greenhouses. Here they grew carnations, sweet peas, black and green grapes, all of an excellent quality. They also had a large area devoted to roses, providing cut flowers to a high-class florist's shop in Liverpool, called *Fishlock's*.

Their shop was in the City centre, next door to the entrance to St. John's Market and opposite Central Station. In those days, most city businessmen would wear a flower each day in their buttonhole. Mother used to take the flowers to *Fishlock's* every Tuesday and Friday, arriving at 8 a.m. The roses, carnations and sweet peas were ready-to-wear, carried in a flat type of handled basket made of willow, known as a 'trug'. She travelled into Liverpool on the train, carrying the trug. Other flowers were carried in the guard's van, and then delivered by railway porters. Mother used to say that quite a number of gentlemen would be waiting for their 'button-holes' to arrive, and as soon as she reached her post, they would choose the one they wanted, handing over just a few coppers to the assistant. She said that the Mellors were lucky to receive more than two pounds for the whole tray-full. By the time she reached the age of twenty, she was now getting some five shillings (25p) per week, with one full Sunday and a half-Sunday off every month.

Father – Joseph Gripton

My father was born around 1880 at Shifnal (or thereabouts!) in the county of Shropshire. His father, John, was a coal-miner, who had sired four sons. Bill and Tom both grew to over six feet tall, but Joe and Jack only ever reached around five foot two inches. Their father was a brute of a man, who would make them sit under the table while he ate and, if they dared move, he would swear at them and kick them. Father tried running away on numerous occasions, living rough until he was caught and taken back home. The last time he absconded, at the age of twelve, he was caught poaching rabbits on a large estate. He was then taken by the gamekeeper to the 'big house'. When the owner heard about his hard life at home, he took pity and offered him a job as under-gamekeeper, with a room in the attic at the head gamekeeper's house. He received his food free, and a wage of two shillings a week, and had never felt so well off in his life. At around the age of fourteen (c. 1894), he heard that his father had been killed, when the roof caved in at the coalmine he'd been working at.

When father reached seventeen years of age, he moved on to become a farm hand at various farms around Cheshire. At one of them, he was driving a milk float when the horse bolted, throwing him out of the float. A broken leg meant that he then had to go into Clatterbridge Cottage Hospital, on the Wirral. *(n.b. This hospital is now one of the largest and up-to-date cancer research centres in the country, the fist to have a 'Cyclotron' scanner. This cost two million pounds, paid for out of donations and fund-raising. My wife Dorothy and I, along with Jill & Les Windsor and others, raised £20,000 for the fund in 3 years. Since then, the public has raised an extra £10 million, for more advanced equipment.)* Returning to my father in hospital! He found himself in the same ward as a Hindu gentleman, who had also been in an accident. This Hindu would not let his two badly crushed fingers be amputated, even though it meant he'd be crippled, as his religion stated that his body had to be whole in order to get to the 'after-life'.

Move to Liverpool

My parents met each other around 1898, I'm not too sure, but it must have been somewhere in the Malpas area. I do know that having met and decided to get married, they then moved to Liverpool. They were married at Barlow's Lane Church, Kirkdale, near the Spellow Lane tram sheds. This is where the trams were sent for repairs and renovation. The shed held about seventy-five trams at any one time, being the largest in the City. Smaller sheds existed at Sheil Road and Garston. By now, mother's father and stepmother had moved to a large house at 29 Lenthall Street, off County Road, and my parents went to live with them. Their fist child, James Hodgson Gripton was born there in 1902. Due to his experience with farm animals, father obtained employment as a cow-keeper for a family called Greenbank, who had a large 'shippon' (cowshed) in Bedford Road, Walton, next door to a cinema called the *'Bedford'*. At that time, the only way to get fresh milk was from a dairyman like Mr. Greenbank, and his shippon was licensed by the City Council to hold twenty-eight milking cows and a bull. I would think that in Walton alone, there would be about ten dairymen and shippons, the average number in each being around ten to twelve cows. This made *Greenbank's* the largest business, and his bull was used to service all the local cows at a fee of a pound a time! The names of other dairymen in Walton, to the best of my memory, included Haygarth, Raw, Fawcett, Thomson, Gadie, Capstick and Rimmer.

My mother's brothers and sisters had a variety of jobs. Aunt May (or was it Mary?) was in service to a Dr. Bradshaw in New Brighton, and later to his son, also a doctor. She was head housekeeper by the time she retired. John and Tom were both shop managers for *Richard Taylor & Sons*, who had a bakery in Buchanan Road, Walton, as well as about fifty shops. Tom used to tell the true story about opening his shop one Monday morning, when a little boy ran in and asked for a large loaf, handing Tom a shilling. Tom told the boy that he must have hot hands, as the coin was so warm. The boy said that it was so warm because his mother had just made it! Tom nearly fell over, but sure enough, on examination he found that the coin was indeed made of lead. When he told the boy that he couldn't accept it, the boy started crying, saying his family hadn't eaten since Sunday dinner-time and that they were all hungry. Tom took pity on him, gave him the loaf and some change, and told him to inform his mother not to make any more, else she would end up in jail.

Tom kept hold of the counterfeit shilling, taking it out from his waistcoat pocket whenever he told the tale. In those days, coins contained real silver to the value of the coin; e.g. a threepenny bit had three pennorth of silver in it. Thus five pounds worth of coins always weighed the same, no matter how it was mixed, threepenny bits, sixpences (tanners), shillings, two-shilling (or two-bob) coins or half-crowns. Today's coins by comparison contain no silver at all. The third brother, Harry, worked on the docks, while Nellie (Ellen) was a daily help at various well-to-do houses. *(Uncle John doesn't mention any of the stepchildren of his grandfather's second marriage, to Elizabeth, but it is believed that there were three sons and three daughters, as indicated on the 1901 census return.)* My uncles on my father's side were Bill, Tom and Jack. Bill, who I believe was a regular soldier in a famous Regiment, never came home from the First World War. Tom was a tradesman, while Jack worked the land, both reserved occupations, so they didn't have to go into the forces. Despite the fact that father was also in a reserved occupation, he joined the Army early in 1917, already aged some thirty-six years. He was fed up with people asking him why he wasn't serving, or passing him three white feathers, a sign of cowardice. He hardly spoke of his Army service, spending it all in France, where I think he must have had a hard time. All of mother's brothers and stepbrothers joined the Army at different times, all coming back alive and well.

The children arrive

My parents had their first child, my eldest brother Jim, while living in Lenthall Street in 1902. Soon afterwards, they were able to move into a small house of their own, at No.10 Cromwell Road, off Stuart Road in Walton. This had quite a good kitchen and back-kitchen, two fair-sized bedrooms, with a back yard, containing an outside flush toilet. The rest of the family were born here, Bill in 1904, Betty in 1908, Joe in 1910, Bob in 1913, followed finally by myself in 1915. At this time (1915), father's wages amounted to a whole guinea (twenty-one shillings) a week, with at least a quart of free milk every day. *(It would appear from later research that there was another daughter, Jane, born between Jim and Bill, but she must have died either in childbirth or very soon afterwards.)*

Jim Gripton

Jim, the eldest lad, left school at the age of fourteen, going to work for a firm called *Glover Hill & Company*, who were fruit and vegetable importers, brokers and wholesalers. Their premises were down towards 'town' in Cazneau Street, where the downstairs consisted of a large warehouse, salesroom, banana ripening room and a small office. Up above, the first floor contained offices dealing with import & export documents, plus the cashier's office. The second floor was used as a storage area for empty containers and other items. Jim got his job there because Mr. Glover, his boss, had visited Arnot Street School in Walton to see the Principal. He was looking for an office boy who must be smart and clean, with a good brain. Jim was sent for, and after an interview, got the job.

When he had fist started at Arnot Street, it was a Liverpool Corporation Council Board School, and my parents had to pay 1d a week for his education. Eventually, this system was scrapped, all schools becoming 'free' and Council-run. Arnot Street was a huge premises, occupying the whole street on one side, from County Road up to City Road. It was built in 1898, with two Infants' departments, each with a head mistress and four class teachers. The classes were mixed (boys & girls), with about thirty-six pupils in each. At the age of seven, the children would then move into one of three Junior departments (boys, girls and mixed). Again each department had its own head teacher and four class teachers. They stayed in these classes up to the age of eleven. Clever children, if recommended, could then sit for a High-school scholarship. The rest went to a boys or girls department, each with its own head and five teachers, except for some brighter pupils, who went into a higher grade directly under the Principal.

The subjects taught were French, Latin, Music, Woodwork, Metalwork, Science, English and Maths. Girls could also learn house-wifery at a purpose-built house next to the caretaker's house, where they learned cooking, housework, sewing etc. This was an important area, because so many girls went 'into service' after leaving school. There were many ship-owners and merchants, dealing in cotton, wool, coal and fruit, as Liverpool was then one of the largest British ports. All of the family, including myself, went through Arnot Street School.

Bill Gripton

On leaving school, my brother Bill joined the GPO. He started as a 'can-lad', making tea for a gang of 14 men who had a huge two-wheeled cart, erecting & maintaining the telegraph poles that carried the overhead lines. The cart carried all their tools and an iron fire-grate, with wood, coal and coke. It was Bill's job to get the fire going and keep a huge iron kettle 'on the boil' for making the tea. The gang worked from 7.30 a.m. to 5.30 p.m., with an hour for lunch, and two 15-minute breaks, morning & afternoon. Bill also ran messages and did odd jobs. He attended night school for seven years and became a 'linesman'. He worked for the GPO all his working life, ending up one of the head men, routing the eventual underground cables around all of Merseyside. He helped install the first automatic telephone exchange in St Helens, around 1924, which was also one of the first of its type in the whole of England.

Betty Gripton

Betty sat the scholarship at eleven years of age, but missed by just a few marks. The school Principal granted her a free place at St Edmond's Girl's School, which I think was in Colquitt Street and Rumford Place, Liverpool. Betty was very artistically minded, and could design clothes of all description, as well as knitting patterns. She used to knit *Fair Isle* ladies jumpers, making up the pattern as she went along. At the age of eighteen, she went off to Hereford Teachers Training College, becoming fully qualified four years later. Her first position was at Rice Lane Council School, Warbreck Moor. After teaching at a couple of other schools, she retired from St Margaret's Church School at Anfield.

Joe Gripton

When Joe went into the Boy's Department at Arnot Street, the Head at that time was Mr. Standing. At thirteen, Joe caught acute appendicitis, and was rushed into the old Liverpool Royal Infirmary. He was operated on in the middle of the night by the surgeon, Mr. Jeans. Mother and Father stayed all night, and the operation was a complete success. However, Joe remained quite ill for about twelve days, before recovering and starting on a light diet. This was around Christmas time, and on Christmas Day itself, at teatime, a nurse new to the ward gave Joe some Christmas cake and other rich food. As Joe was hungry, he naturally scoffed the lot – and ended up back in the operating theatre! Apparently, abscesses had formed in his stomach, and the treatment as far as I can remember was the application of 'hot fermentations' for a couple of days. All in all he stayed in hospital for five weeks, and off school for a long time. In fact he was hardly ever at school again, as he left at fourteen.

Jim had put in a good word for him, and he started work as an office boy at *Glover Hill's*. He did all the odd jobs, sorting incoming mail in the morning, then collecting outgoing mail in the afternoon, and taking it to the Post Office. He had to keep a mail-book, entering all the details, together with the price of the stamps. The stamp money came out of petty cash, and everything had to tally by the weekend. He held various positions, becoming 'customs clerk', and responsible for the import & export duty, bills of freight, etc.

Joe stayed at *Glover Hill's* until 1939, before going to work for *Blackledge's* the bakers, who had a large bakery in Bootle, and lots of shops all over the Liverpool area. They specialised in bread, but were also high-class confectioners. This family firm was run by old man Blackledge himself, and his two sons. They gave shares to their workers each financial year, according to length of service and profit for that year. These shares could be sold back to the firm for a pound, or kept for their dividend – it was a private firm, not quoted on the Stock Exchange. Eventually the firm sold out to *Spillers*, who were flour millers. The shares were then valued at a fiver each, so there was a nice profit for those who had held onto them.

Like all takeovers, the new firm made lots of changes and, after a few years, Joe left with a small pension. He went to work for a mineral water firm, *Schofield's*, based in Dalrymple Street, just off Scotland Road – the rough side of town. His job was in the office, but included checking the lorries before they left the yard. He was at this task one day, when another passing lorry rolled him against the wall, crushing his pelvis. After a number of weeks in hospital, he was judged unfit to return to work, and in fact took early retirement. As a point of interest, when Joe had taken a medical for the services, the doctor at the time took one look at Joe's stomach and said *'I see Mr. Jeans has left his mark on you'*. He had recognised the work of the surgeon from years previously. Needless to say, Joe was not passed fit for Military service.

Bob Gripton

Bob also went to Arnot Street, his classes in the Infants, Junior and Senior Schools being all male, with all male teachers. Leaving at fourteen years of age, he took employment with *C & H Crichton*, ship repairers and builders, of Derby Road, Bootle. They had various shops there – coppersmiths, blacksmiths, tinsmiths, electricians, pattern-makers and engineers. There was also a foundry and offices, covering in all a large area. The shipbuilding took place at Saltney, on the River Dee. They built small ships, such as tugboats and barges, used for river and canal work. *Crichton's* was a family firm, looking after their workers. Bob was an office boy in the general office.

His job was a reserved occupation throughout World War II, so Bob never joined the services, but he did do a spell with the Home Guard. He was in the Gunners at a rocket battery, stationed at New Brighton, across the River Mersey. Fortunately, it never saw any action. He progressed with the firm to head costing clerk, his department being responsible for pricing all shipbuilding & repairs. This was quite an important job, vital to profitability. As the years passed by and shipping declined, small companies were taken over. Bob ended up with the *Merseyside Ship Repairers*, a branch of the famous *Cammell Lairds*. He retired from there after a lifetime in the same business.

John Gripton

In 1920, it was finally my time to join Arnot Street School. The Principal then was a real gentleman, Mr. Menny. He lived in an old house on Breeze Hill, walking to school each day at about 8.15 a.m. His route would bring him down Stuart Road and across County Road. He went right up Arnot Street to the top gate, where his office was in the higher grade department, but separated from the classrooms by an iron bridge leading to a complex of rooms. There was a beautiful office with a huge mahogany desk, a big high-backed chair and cupboards, with smaller chairs around the walls for staff meetings. There was also a dining room, with sideboard and dining table, seating eight, on six chairs and two carver-chairs. There was also a fully furnished lounge for relaxation, a washroom and toilet. Mr. Menny had a very high position in the Liverpool Education Department. He really loved children, and on his walk to school would be surrounded by them. He was very old-fashioned in his dress. He wore a morning suit, frock coat, square top hat, highly polished boots, and carried a walking cane. He retired from the school at the end of my first year.

I left school at fourteen, having been promoted to the highest class. I received a good leaving certificate, but in fact never used it. My father had by then given up working as a cowkeeper to start his own green-grocery business, which I helped him run. In those days, time meant little. A typical Friday in summer meant rising at 4.30 a.m., walking to the stable to get the pony ready (twenty minutes), then travelling to Cazneau Street market for 5.30. We would buy vegetables, salads, flowers and eggs from there, then go to *Glover Hill's* to pick up potatoes, soft fruits, apples, pears, oranges etc. There was none of the exotic stuff that you seem to be able to buy everywhere today. We would try to leave *GH's* by 7.30 and get home for breakfast.

We would then sort out the goods and make a display on the wagon, starting to sell at around 9 o'clock. Our main meal, lunch, was at 1 p.m., then we would start again at 2.15, carrying on until we sold out, sometimes as late as 8 p.m. Then it was time to unload the wagon, get to the stable to feed and bed the pony, finishing at 10 at night. Saturday was similar, although we didn't go to market with the pony. If we needed anything, I would go to market on a bike, with front and rear carriers. I might, for example, pick up a dozen 'chips' of strawberries in the front, with a dozen of raspberries in the back. A 'chip' was a small basket, woven from very thin strips of white wood, and holding about ¾ pound of fruit. I worked for father until I reached twenty. We were the best of pals and I knew that the business could be mine eventually, but I was fed up working seven days a week, with no days off or holidays. We had a good talk, and I told him that I'd like a job as a barman, with the intention of becoming the manager of a public house. At that time, brother Jim had a friend who was a supervisor for *Bent's Brewery* at Johnson Street, Liverpool. I had an interview with a Mr MacMillan, and started at the *Farmer's Arms*, Clubmoor, on May 16th, 1936. The wages were a princely thirty bob a week, with a half-day off each week and a week's annual holiday.

This pub was reckoned to be the largest and most profitable in *Bent's* business. The premises consisted of the public bar, buffet, garden hall, smoke-room, bar parlour, saloon, loggia, off-licence, function room, tea gardens and two full-size bowling greens. The staff included fourteen barmen, six barmaids, a gardener, two delivery boys for the off-licence, and a waitress for the function room (used as a dining room). All these were full-time, plus there were three cleaners and four part-time bar staff. The Manager and Licensee was Mr Scrimshaw, assisted by his wife, who looked after all the catering. In the winter there was a function almost every Saturday evening. These were mainly Bowling Club annual dinners, often called the 'prize presentation and hot-pot supper'. The boss would get an extension from the Magistrate's Court, allowing him to serve until 11 p.m. in the function room. Normal opening hours were from 11.30 a.m. – 3 p.m. and then from 5.30 – 10 p.m., Monday to Saturday. Sunday hours were 12 noon – 2 p.m. and 7 – 10 p.m. Pre-war, Sunday was always the busiest day, with the pub being the main source of any local entertainment. Saturdays and Fridays were next busiest, these being usually 'pay-day'.

Eventually my parents bought a new semi-detached house in Crosby, at the northern end of Liverpool, No.47 South Parade. My father had sold his business soon after I'd left, as it was too much work for him. I had a cycle to ride to work; it cost me eight pounds, which I paid off at two-bob a week. I used to stay on at the pub in the afternoons, as there wasn't enough time to bike home. When there was a Saturday function, three barmen would wait on the tables, first serving food, then stripping off the table-cloths to serve drinks until 10.50 p.m. The room had be cleared completely by 11.30, the tables moved aside and the floor mopped and polished, ready for the waitresses to get everything ready for the next lunch-time. I would then bike home, arriving at Crosby about 2.30 a.m. I did various jobs in the pub, becoming manager of the Saloon and Loggia, until I was called up for Army service in May 1940.

When I left the Army, it was as acting Company Sergeant Major, but I reverted to my wartime substantive rank of full Sergeant, that was in February 1946. I had met my wife, Dorothy May Harper, in 1939, when she came to work at the *Farmer's Arms*. We courted until I joined up and decided to marry on 12th November 1940. Our first son, David, was born on 27th August 1942, and then Paul came along on 4th November 1944 (*you must have had some good leaves John!*). Dot stayed with her mother throughout the war, continuing to work at the pub. Upon my 'demob', I returned to work at the same pub, until we were able to get the first pub of our own – the *Cambridge Hotel*, Alt Street, Toxteth. This was followed over the years as follows: *Canon Hotel*, Townsend Lane, Anfield; *Halfway House*, Woodchurch Road, Prenton, Birkenhead; *Station Hotel*, Station Road, Ellesmere Port; *Blue Anchor*, Market Street, Hoylake; *Boot Inn*, Liscard Road, Wallasey – and finally, by a lovely coincidence, another *Farmer's Arms*, this time in Hillbark Road, Frankby, The Wirral.

Without my wife Dorothy, I would never have run all those pubs. We were a partnership, and a good one at that. Eventually, we had a third son, Charles, born whilst at the Station Hotel, on 25th March 1960. *(Charles died tragically at a fairly young age)*. Thus my 'pub' career started at the *Farmer's Arms*, Clubmoor, in 1936, and ended upon my retirement from the *Farmer's Arms*, Frankby, in April 1978 – a full forty-two years after pulling my first pint.

In conclusion, here are just a few added thoughts. Both my mother and father lived until the ripe old age of eighty-nine years. Jim was called up to the RAF at age forty-two, but was forty-three by the time he found himself on a troop-ship on the River Mersey, ready to sail for India. It was announced that nobody over the age of forty-two had to serve overseas, but too late - he had to go! Father worked at *Crichton's* during the War and up until around 1947, mainly as an odd-job man. He was very highly thought of, and when he left, was presented with a cheque for £100 in appreciation of his hard work and excellent time-keeping – not late once in all the years he was there.

John Gripton – 8th January 1996

Footnote by Pete Gripton, son of Ruth and Joe, March 2000

These historic notes about the Gripton family were written by my Uncle John at my request, not long after the death of Aunty Dorothy, March 6th 1995. He later told me that it had proved very therapeutic for him. I am indebted to his efforts – and to his son (and my cousin of course!) Paul, who converted the notes into a Word document on his computer. Having lost the original file, I have enjoyed re-entering it into my own PC! John himself died on June 21st 1998, leaving my own father, Joe, as the last surviving member of the family, apart from Bob's widow, Joyce, who was still then living at the old family home, Number 47 South Parade, Northern Road, Crosby, Liverpool 23. Joe's last few years were spent in gradual decline, so John was the only person who could have produced this short history. I hadn't realised that all the Griptons before me attended Arnot Street School, but I'm proud to say that myself and two brothers, Cliff and Geoff, followed this family tradition.

Joe finally ended his days, quite peacefully, on January 20th 2000. He never did get much further than Bootle – *"where the bugs wear clogs"*, as he used to tell us. My cousin Paul, John's second son, was present at the funeral service. I pass these notes about the Griptons on to the next generation.

The Griptons

Granny Gripton b. 3/12/1874	died June 15th 1964
Granddad Gripton b. 16/12/1880	died c.1967
Elizabeth 'Betty' Gripton b.1908	died July 2nd 1972
Jim Gripton b. 1902	
Bill Gripton b. 1904	
Joe Gripton b. 1910	died January 20th 2000
Bob Gripton b. 1913	died March 29th 1990
John Gripton b. 1915	died June 21st 1998

Postscript

I decided to get in touch with cousin Paul early in 2006 and he was kind enough to fill in some details for me regarding his own history, in the form of the notes shown below:

Paul Edward Gripton, b. 4/11/1944, West Derby, Liverpool (Entry 309)

Anita Gripton, nee Smith, b. 25/11/1947, West Derby, Liverpool (Entry 426)

I was born at 21 Newsham Drive Liverpool - I think that was a maternity home. I married Anita, 21/4/1973, at Frankby Parish Church, Frankby, Wirral, Cheshire

Charles Joseph Gripton b. 25/3/1960, died of acute myeloid leukemia in Southampton Hospital, 21/3/1991. He had married Judy Gripton (nee Allan) on 3/8/1990 at SE Hants Register Office, Fareham. Judy Allan became Judy Hamill, she divorced to marry Charles. After his death, she subsequently remarried.

Paul also sent me a family group photograph that I had never seen before, taken to celebrate his 21st birthday in November 1965. It was taken at the Coach and Horses, Moreton, and shows (from l – r):

Geoff (in the smart suit!); Pat (daughter of Dolly); great aunt Dolly (sister of Dorothy's mother); Uncle Bob and Aunty Joyce (holding hands); Aunty Dorothy; Paul (with young Charles in front); Aunty Hilda; Uncle John; Granddad Joe Gripton; my Dad Joe; Dorothy's father (Ted); Hilary (who was to marry David); Dorothy's mother; David and Uncle Jim.

A family gathering, 1965

Family line / descendants of John Gripton

*(These notes atre based on those originally sent to me (**PETER DOUGLAS GRIPTON**, 6th generation) by Neale Sheldon, whose mother was/is also a 'Gripton'. I have subsequently amended and/or updated the notes for the benefit of myself, and for any later research.)*

Generation No. 1

1. JOHN[1] **GRIPTON** was born Abt. 1780. He married **MARY UNKNOWN.** She was born Abt. 1780.

Notes for JOHN GRIPTON:

As at present, I have little information regarding this John Gripton, apart from a census return from 1841, for the parish of Sheriffhales, in the County of Salop. Shown as living at an address given as 'Littlehales' are:

John Gripton, aged 60 (so born c.1780), Cowman - shown as not being born in that parish

Mary Gripton, also aged 60 (likewise), wife of John - also not born in that parish

Thomas and John Gripton, both born c.1821 - both given the profession of 'agricultural labourer' and both shown as being born in that parish. (Rounding up – or down - of ages, by up to five years, was then common, so these sons' ages could be as far as 10 years apart)

Civil records were not legally necessary before 1837, so trying to trace information from births, marriages and deaths is difficult - and only available where parish churches held on to any of their own parish records. But, provided that John Gripton senior is (1) above, then John Gripton junior would be (2) as shown below. It also follows that if John Gripton senior was aged 60 in 1841, then he would have been born in approximately 1781, as would his wife Mary. Just to confuse things, John (2) also married a Mary!

If all these are facts, then John (2) would have been born in about 1821, thus would have been aged 26 years at the time of his marriage (shown below)

Children of JOHN GRIPTON and MARY UNKNOWN are:

    2.   i. **JOHN**[2] **GRIPTON**, b. Abt. 1821.

        ii. **THOMAS GRIPTON**, b. Abt. 1821.

Generation No. 2

2. JOHN² GRIPTON (JOHN¹) was born Abt. 1821. He married **MARY WALKER** November 7, 1847. She was born Abt. 1826.

Notes for JOHN GRIPTON:
My great-great grandparents.

Christening: Possibly at Wellington, Shropshire, 24 April 1825 (IGI record)

Marriage Notes for JOHN GRIPTON and MARY WALKER:
John Gripton, Shifnal, Shropshire, 4th qtr 1847, XVIII 278

(I have a copy of this marriage certificate)

Mary Walker, as is John Gripton, is noted as 'of full age' (meaning that they were both over 21 years of age and thus born around 1826 at the latest) and a 'spinster', while her father is shown as 'John Walker, labourer'. John's father is also named - as 'John Gripton, labourer' - but as yet there are no further details about him, apart from the supposition shown above.

Children of JOHN GRIPTON and MARY WALKER are:

    3.   i. **JOSEPH³ GRIPTON**, b. January 26, 1850.
          ii. **THOMAS GRIPTON**, b. Abt. 1852.

Notes for THOMAS GRIPTON:

Christening: Feb 29, 1852 Shifnal, Shropshire. Birth: Mar 1852 Thomas Gripton, Shifnal, 6a 556

          iii. **BETSY GRIPTON**, b. Abt. 1860.

Notes for BETSY GRIPTON:

Christening: Apr 19, 1860, Shifnal. Birth: 2nd quarter 1860 Betsy Gripton, Shifnal, 6a 551

          iv. **AGNES GRIPTON**, b. Abt. 1863; d. November 2, 1864.

Notes for AGNES GRIPTON:

Christening: Mar 29, 1863, Shifnal. Death: Nov 2, 1864 / Death: 4th qtr 1864, Agnes Gripton, Shifnal, 6a 417

Generation No. 3

3. JOSEPH³ GRIPTON *(JOHN², JOHN¹)* was born January 26, 1850. He married **ELIZABETH CHETTER** March 5, 1877 in Shropshire (aka Salop), England. She was born September 30, 1857.

Notes for JOSEPH GRIPTON:
My great-grandfather.

Birth: Jan 26, 1850, Joseph Gripton, Shifnal, 1b 157. Christening: Feb 17, 1850 Shifnal, Salop.

(I have a copy of this birth certificate)

Census: 1881, (aged 31) West Street, Wrockwardine, Salop; Occupation: Coal Miner

Notes for ELIZABETH CHETTER:
Father: EDWARD CHETTER / Mother: ELIZABETH HORTON. Birth: Sept 30, 1857 at Dawley, Salop. (great grandmother on father's side)

(I have a copy of this birth certificate)

Possible Christening: Nov 1, 1857, Stirchley, Salop

Marriage Notes for JOSEPH GRIPTON and ELIZABETH CHETTER:
Joseph Gripton, Shifnal, 6a 843, 1st qtr 1877

(I have a copy of this marriage certificate)

Children of JOSEPH GRIPTON and ELIZABETH CHETTER are:

     i. **ALBERT[4] GRIPTON,** b. Abt. 1877, Shifnal, Salop.

Notes for ALBERT GRIPTON:
Albert Gripton, Shifnal, 6a 644 Birth: 2nd qtr 1877

     ii. **WILLIAM THOMAS GRIPTON**, b. Abt. 1879, Shifnal, Salop.

Notes for WILLIAM THOMAS GRIPTON:
William Thomas Gripton, Shifnal, 6a 671 Birth: 1st qtr 1879

4. iii. **JOSEPH GRIPTON**, b. Abt. 1880, West Street, St. George's, Wrockwardine, Salop; d. Abt. 1967, Great Crosby, Liverpool.

     iv. **JOHN GRIPTON**, b. Abt. 1883.

     v. **THOMAS GRIPTON**, b. Abt. 1885.

Generation No. 4

4. JOSEPH[4] GRIPTON *(JOSEPH[3], JOHN[2], JOHN[1])* was born Abt. 1880 in West Street, St. George's, Wrockwardine, Salop, and died Abt. 1967 in Great Crosby, Liverpool. He married JANE HODGSON Abt. 1902 in Kirkdale, Liverpool. She was born December 3, 1874 in Walton, Liverpool, and died June 15, 1964 in Great Crosby, Liverpool.

Notes for JOSEPH GRIPTON:
He was my grandfather.

Birth: Joseph Gripton, Wellington, Salop, 6a 739 Birth: 4th qtr 1880

(I have a copy of this birth certificate)

Census: 1881, West Street, Wrockwardine, Salop

Notes for JANE HODGSON:
Birth: Jane Hodgson, Walton Village, Dec 3 1874, father JAMES Hodgson, mother Ellen Hodgson (nee Matthews)

(I have a copy of this birth certificate)

Jane's parents, JAMES and ELLEN, were married at the Parish Church of Walton-on-the-Hill, Liverpool, on Christmas Day 1872.

On their marriage certificate, JAMES is quoted as 'of full age' (above 21), while ELLEN is 20 years old, so born c.1852.

JAMES's father is stated as being one John Hodgson, deceased.

(I have a copy of this marriage certificate)

Marriage Notes for JOSEPH GRIPTON and JANE HODGSON:
Joseph Gripton married Jane (best known as Ginny) Hodgson, Walton-on-the-Hill, Liverpool, 8b 642, 2nd qtr 1902, at Barlow's Lane Church (St Mary's), Kirkdale, Liverpool. Joseph was aged 21 years and Jane aged 27 years. Joseph's residence shown as Brockton, Shifnal Road, Shrewsbury, Jane's as 29 Lenthall Street (Walton). Their witnesses were Harry and Ellen Hodgson; Jane's father was named as James Hodgson.

(I have a copy of this marriage certificate)

Children of JOSEPH GRIPTON and JANE HODGSON are:

> 5.   i.   **JAMES HODGSON[5] GRIPTON**, b. Abt. 1902.
> 6.   ii.   **WILLIAM THOMAS GRIPTON**, b. Abt. 1905, West Derby, Liverpool.
>   iii.   **ELIZABETH GRIPTON**, b. Abt. 1907; d. July 2, 1972.

Notes for ELIZABETH GRIPTON:
Birth: Elizabeth Gripton, West Derby, 8b 308, 2nd qtr 1907

Elizabeth was unmarried at the time of her death.

> 7.   iv.   **JOSEPH GRIPTON**, b. November 9, 1910, West Derby, Liverpool; d. January 20, 2000, Sefton South.
>   v.   **ROBERT GRIPTON**, b. April 15, 1913; d. March 29, 1990; m. **JOYCE MCDERMOTT**.

Notes for ROBERT GRIPTON:
Birth: Robert Gripton, mother's maiden name Hodgson, ref West Derby, 8b 565 2nd qtr 1913

> 8.   vi.   **JOHN GRIPTON**, b. September 18, 1915, Frankby, Wirral; d. June 21, 1998, Birkenhead.

Generation No. 5

5. JAMES H.[5] GRIPTON *(JOSEPH[4], JOSEPH[3], JOHN[2], JOHN[1])* was born Abt. 1902. He married **HILDA CLARKE**. She was born April 23, 1906, and died February 1996 in Liverpool.

Notes for JAMES H. GRIPTON

Birth: James Hodgson Gripton, West Derby, Liverpool, 8b 328 2nd qtr 1902

Child of JAMES GRIPTON and HILDA CLARKE is:

> i. **JAQUELINE⁶ GRIPTON.**

6. WILLIAM THOMAS⁵ GRIPTON (*JOSEPH⁴, JOSEPH³, JOHN², JOHN¹*) was born Abt. 1905 in West Derby, Liverpool. He married **CLARA FITZSIMMONS.**

Notes for WILLIAM THOMAS GRIPTON:
Birth: William Thomas Gripton, West Derby, Liverpool, 8b 313 2nd qtr 1905

Children of WILLIAM GRIPTON and CLARA FITZSIMMONS are:

> i. **KENNETH⁶ GRIPTON,** b. December 14, 1929; d. March 1999.
> ii. **RONALD D. GRIPTON,** b. Abt. 1934; m. **MAUREEN MINSHULL.**

Notes for RONALD D. GRIPTON:
Birth: Ronald D Gripton, 1st qtr 1934, ref West Derby 8b 639, mother's maiden name Fitzsimmons

> 9. iii. **WILLIAM THOMAS GRIPTON,** b. Abt. 1938, Liverpool.

7. JOSEPH⁵ GRIPTON (*JOSEPH⁴, JOSEPH³, JOHN², JOHN¹*) was born November 9, 1910 in West Derby, Liverpool, and died January 20, 2000 in Sefton South. He married **RUTH HODGSON** Abt. 1939. She was born August 17, 1920.

Notes for JOSEPH GRIPTON:
My father.
Birth: Joseph Gripton, West Derby, Liverpool, 8b 301 4th qtr 1910. Death: Joseph Gripton, Jan 2000, Sefton South.

Notes for RUTH HODGSON:
mother Annie Hodgson, father not named (my mother and father).

(I have a copies of both birth certificates)

Marriage Notes for JOSEPH GRIPTON and RUTH HODGSON:
Joseph Gripton married Ruth Hodgson, 4th qtr 1939, ref Liverpool N 8b 1258.

(I have a copy of this marriage certificate)

Children of JOSEPH GRIPTON and RUTH HODGSON are:

> 10. i. **PETER DOUGLAS⁶ GRIPTON,** b. August 24, 1940, Walton, Liverpool.
> ii. **CLIFFORD ROBERT GRIPTON,** b. July 31, 1943.
> iii. **GEOFFREY JOHN GRIPTON,** b. June 16, 1945.
> iv. **ELIZABETH SUSAN GRIPTON,** b. April 6, 1954.

8. JOHN⁵ GRIPTON (*JOSEPH⁴, JOSEPH³, JOHN², JOHN¹*) was born September 18, 1915 in Frankby, Wirral, and died June 21, 1998 in Birkenhead. He married **DOROTHY MAY HARPER** November 12, 1940. She was born October 28, 1920, and died March 6, 1995 in Birkenhead.

Children of JOHN GRIPTON and DOROTHY HARPER are:

    i. **DAVID⁶ GRIPTON,** b. August 27, 1942.

    ii. **PAUL EDWARD GRIPTON**, b. November 4, 1944, West Derby, Liverpool; m. ANITA SMITH, April 21, 1973.

Marriage Notes for PAUL GRIPTON and ANITA SMITH:
Paul Gripton married Anita Smith, April 21 1973, at Frankby Parish Church, The Wirral, Cheshire - no children

    iii. **CHARLES JOSEPH GRIPTON**, b. March 25, 1960, Ellesmere Port; d. March 21, 1991, Southampton, Hants; m. **JUDY ALLAN HAMILL**, August 8, 1990.

Notes for CHARLES JOSEPH GRIPTON:
Charles died of acute myeloid leukemia at age 31.

Marriage Notes for CHARLES GRIPTON and JUDY HAMILL:
Charles Gripton married Judy Hamill (nee Allan), Aug 8 1990, at SE Hants Register Office, Fareham, Hants - no children. Judy subsequently remarried

Generation No. 6

9. WILLIAM THOMAS⁶ GRIPTON (*WILLIAM THOMAS⁵, JOSEPH⁴, JOSEPH³, JOHN², JOHN¹*) was born Abt. 1938 in Liverpool. He married **DORENE RIMMER** Abt. 1959 in Liverpool. She was born Abt. 1938.

Notes for WILLIAM THOMAS GRIPTON:
Birth: William T Gripton, 1st qtr 1938, ref Liverpool N 8b 585, mother's maiden name was Fitzsimmons

Marriage Notes for WILLIAM GRIPTON and DORENE RIMMER:
Gripton, William T married Rimmer D - Liverpool N 10d 258 marriage 2 1959

Children of WILLIAM GRIPTON and DORENE RIMMER are:

11. i. **KEITH WILLIAM⁷ GRIPTON**, b. Abt. 1960, Liverpool.

    ii. **MARGARET ROSE GRIPTON**, b. Abt. 1964, Liverpool; m. **UNKNOWN ABERNETHY**, June 1986, Liverpool.

Notes for MARGARET ROSE GRIPTON:
Gripton, Margaret R (Rimmer) - Liverpool N 10d 189 birth 3 1964

    iii. **RUTH DORENE GRIPTON**, b. Abt. 1967, Liverpool; m. (1)

UNKNOWN MANNING, August 1989, Liverpool; m. (2) **DAVID WILLS,** January 2002, Liverpool.

Notes for RUTH DORENE GRIPTON:
Gripton, Ruth Dorene (Rimmer) - Liverpool N 10d 285 birth 2 1967

    iv. **JASON RONALD GRIPTON**, b. Abt. 1973.

Notes for JASON RONALD GRIPTON:
Gripton, Jason Ronald (Rimmer) - Liverpool 10d 1769 birth 2 1973

10. PETER DOUGLAS⁶ GRIPTON *(JOSEPH⁵, JOSEPH⁴, JOSEPH³, JOHN², JOHN¹)* was born August 24, 1940 in Walton, Liverpool. He married **JOYCE ANN JONES** August 25, 1962 in Reading. She was born January 16, 1945.

Notes for PETER DOUGLAS GRIPTON:
Birth: Peter Douglas Gripton, 3rd qtr 1940, ref Liverpool North 8b 867, mother's maiden name Hodgson, born Walton Hospital

(I have a copy of this birth certificate)ate)

Notes for JOYCE ANN JONES:
(I have a copy of Joyce's birth certificate)

Children of PETER GRIPTON and JOYCE JONES are:

    i. **LORRAINE⁷ GRIPTON**, b. July 31, 1963, Wokingham, Berks; m. (1) **STEVEN BURGOYNE**, March 7, 1987, Greatham, St. John the Baptist Church; m. (2) **PHILIP LE BRUN**, February 22, 3005.

Notes for LORRAINE GRIPTON:

Birth: Wokingham, Berks, July 31, 1963. Married Steven Burgoyne at Greatham, St John the Baptist Church, Mar 7, 1987 - subsequently divorced (no children). Married Philip Le Brun in St Lucia, Feb 22, 2005.

Marriage Notes for LORRAINE GRIPTON and STEVEN BURGOYNE:
Steven and Lorraine later divorced and she remarried to Philip Le Brun.

12.   ii. **MICHELLE GRIPTON**, b. February 26, 1966, The Grange, Liss, Hants.

Generation No. 7

11. KEITH WILLIAM⁷ GRIPTON *(WILLIAM THOMAS⁶, WILLIAM THOMAS⁵, JOSEPH⁴, JOSEPH³, JOHN², JOHN¹)* was born Abt. 1960 in Liverpool. He married **UNKNOWN INGRAM** Abt. 1983 in Liverpool.

Notes for KEITH WILLIAM GRIPTON:
Gripton, Keith William (Rimmer) - Liverpool N 10d 157 birth 2 1960

Marriage Notes for KEITH GRIPTON and UNKNOWN INGRAM:

Gripton, Keith W, m Ingram - Liverpool 36 0295 marriage 2 1983

Children of KEITH GRIPTON and UNKNOWN INGRAM are:
    i. **WAYNE[8] GRIPTON**, b. Abt. 1984, Brikenhead.
    ii. **NICOLA GRIPTON**, b. Abt. 1986, Birkenhead.

12. MICHELLE[7] GRIPTON *(PETER DOUGLAS[6], JOSEPH[5], JOSEPH[4], JOSEPH[3], JOHN[2], JOHN[1])* was born February 26, 1966 in The Grange, Liss, Hants. She married **JAMES FITZPATRICK** March 20, 1993.

Notes for MICHELLE GRIPTON:

  Birth: The Grange, Liss, Hants, Feb 26, 1966

  Married James Fitzpatrick at Leicester, Mar 20, 1993

Children of MICHELLE GRIPTON and JAMES FITZPATRICK are:
    i. **THOMAS JAMES[8] FITZPATRICK**, b. October 22, 1992.
    ii. **CALUM JOSEPH FITZPATRICK**, b. March 24, 1995.

Unfortunately my own personal line of the Gripton family ends here - that is unless Thomas and Calum take up the Gripton name and pass it on to future generations! Happily, the Gripton name may continues through **WAYNE[8] GRIPTON**.

Research into the Hodgson/Gripton families

The first document (1871) below shows one of my great-grandfathers, James Hodgson, at the age of twenty-seven, living in Walton with his three young sisters. The second document (1881) shows that ten years later, James had married Ellen Matthews. Their daughter Jane, then aged six years old, was my father's mother. By 1891, according to the third document, it would appear that my great-grandmother, Ellen, had perhaps died and James had now married Elizabeth, a much younger lady. *(My Uncle John's memoirs indicate that Elizabeth was a barmaid at the Black Horse!)*

The fourth document (1901) shows Jane working for the Mellor family in Cheshire, then aged twenty-six, as borne out by my Uncle John's family memoirs. The final document, also dated 1901, shows the much extended Hodgson family now living in Lenthall Street. Jane Hodgson married Joseph Gripton in 1902 and I have a copy of that certificate. *(It is interesting to note that, again in my Uncle John's memoirs, he mentions that his parents (Joseph and Jane) later went to live with Jane's father and stepmother, still in Lenthall Street.)*

1871 Census   **Walton-on-the-Hill**

214 Walton Village	James Hodgson b 1844?	Head	27	Gardener/Domestic Servant	Lancs, Formby
	Alice Hodgson	Sis	17		Lancs, Walton
	Kate Hodgson	Sis	15		Lancs, Walton
	Sarah Hodgson	Sis	12		Lancs, Walton

1881 Census   **Walton, Liverpool**

16 Smithy Lane	James Hodgson b 1844?	Head	37	Gardener	Lancs, Formby
	Ellen Hodgson b 1853?	Wife	28		Lancs, Walton
	Mary Hodgson	Dau	8	Scholar	Lancs, Walton
	Jane Hodgson	Dau	6	Scholar	Lancs, Walton
	Ellen Hodgson	Dau	4	Scholar	Lancs, Walton
	John Hodgson	Son	2		Lancs, Walton
	Harry Hodgson	Son	2m		Lancs, Walton

1891 Census   **Walton-on-the-Hill**

33 York Street	James Hodgson b 1844?	Head	47	Gardener	Lancs, Formby
	Elizabeth Hodgson b 1871?	Wife	20		Bradford
	John Hodgson	Son	12	Errand boy	Lancs, Walton
	Harry Hodgson	Son	10	Scholar	Lancs, Walton
	Thomas Hodgson	Son	7	Scholar	Lancs, Walton

1901 Census	Willaston, Cheshire				
17 Streethey	Ellen Mellor	Head	71	Widow, own means	Lancs, W Derby
	StanleyMellor	Gson	9		Liverpool
	Jane Hodgson		26	Domestic	Lancs, Walton
	b 1875?				
	Joseph Merry		20	Gardener	Wellington, Salop

1901 Census	Walton-on-the-Hill				
29 Lenthall St	James Hodgson	Head	57	Gardener	Bedford Lane, Liverpool
	b 1844?				
	Elizabeth Hodgson	Wife	30		Bedford Lane, Liverpool
	b 1871?				
	John Hodgson	Son	22		Bedford Lane, Liverpool
	Ellen Hodgson	Dau	24		Bedford Lane, Liverpool
	Harry Hodgson	Son	20	Clerk	Bedford Lane, Liverpool
	Thomas Hodgson	Son	17	School	Bedford Lane, Liverpool
	Richard Hodgson	Son	9	School	Bedford Lane, Liverpool
	Rebecca Hodgson	Dau	7	School	Bedford Lane, Liverpool
	James Hodgson	Son	5		Bedford Lane, Liverpool
	Joseph Hodgson	Son	3		Bedford Lane, Liverpool
	Elsie Hodgson	Dau	2		Bedford Lane, Liverpool
	Sophia Hodgson	Day	1		Bedford Lane, Liverpool

Mum's family – the Hodgsons

Mum's mother, Annie, my maternal grandmother, lived not too far away from us, down at the bottom of Stuart Road, then across County Road, at number 17 Romley Street, just opposite. It was another two-up, two-down house, with a dangerously steep and curving set of stairs, plus the inevitable backyard with its outside toilet, tin bath and mangle! I can remember that on several occasions over the years, myself, Cliff and Geoff would actually go to her house for our bath – and it would be she who bathed us! If memory serves me right, a bath those days was only a weekly luxury, what we did for the rest of the week, I don't recall – no doubt it would have been just a soapy flannel job! One thing that leaps to mind was that, in those innocent childhood days, we three boys all had 'waggers'! This was Nin's name for penis of course, and it was to be a few years before the more common names for our appendages were learned from the school of life. Thus it was a great source of amusement – and no doubt amazement – many years later when, on the radio during what I think was *'Hancock's Half Hour'*, that droll Australian comedian Bill Kerr was proudly announcing his birthplace as the strangely named 'Wagga Wagga! *(I think this was on the Tony Hancock programme, along with Sid James, though I'll stand corrected if necessary.)*

Although we boys never realised it at the time, Annie had never married, despite the fact that she had two children, Ruth and John. My Mum never did know her father, although she did overhear conversations that perhaps she wasn't supposed to, alluding to the

Mum (Ruth) in the early days

129

My Mum – and hers!

fact that her father was a 'Robert'. She also thinks that she has his surname tucked away somewhere in the back of her mind, although she cannot bring it into daylight at present! Mum also recalls that, during her childhood, two very smartly dressed ladies would occasionally appear on the scene and thinks that they may well have been the sisters of her father i.e. two aunts.

Nana and Nin

Although our grandmother was named Annie, to us children she always went by the name of 'Nin', while her own mother, mainly bed-ridden in her later years when I knew her, lived upstairs and answered to the name of 'Nana'. Looking back and recalling that lethal flight of stairs, it is no wonder that Nana was confined to her bedroom! She was a large old lady who always smelled of a mixture of camphor oil and wintergreen ointment. I guess they were the old-fashioned remedies to everything! She would send me round to *Timothy White and Taylor's*, the local chemist's shop in County Road, 'on a message' as they used to say. This would be for small boxes of saccharine tablets, which everyone used as a sweetener due to the absence of sugar during the wartime rationing. She would more often than enough hand me over a 'tanner' (sixpence) for my troubles, which seemed an awful lot of money at the time.

Before Nana became confined to her bed, I can recall her once having to 'look after' us boys and of course, being boys, we played her up no end, even hiding from her under the bunk bed. She was 'stone deaf' and, trying to chase after us during 'a walk', she was almost knocked down by a lorry going up Stuart Road, just outside *'The Stuart'* pub. She'd obviously not heard the lorry, but still gave its driver a right piece of her mind! Nana died sometime in 1956 at the age of around eighty-six, but I cannot even remember being told of her death. I must have either still been at the 'Inny' during my last year, or perhaps I'd even joined the Army by then, but I guess that younger family members were 'protected' from that sort of news in those days.

In later years, having tracked down a copy of Nana's birth certificate, it came to light that Nana had been born Eliza Griffiths in 1870, at Stanton Lacy, just a stone's throw outside Ludlow, in Shropshire. Her parents are named as Henry Griffiths and Mary Ann, formerly Watkins. According to Mum, her grandmother had appeared on the stage under the nom-de-plume of *'Lila Leonard'* and Mum says that she also thinks that Eliza once performed at *'The Rotunda'* theatre on Scotland Road. Eliza had a sister called Mary - or Polly - and the two girls actually married two brothers, William Henry Hodgson in the case of Eliza and Charles Hodgson in the case of Mary.

(It's quite an amazing coincidence, but when I got the news that Nana had been born in Shropshire – or Salop – it fitted quite neatly alongside the fact that my grandfather on my Dad's side was also from that county, born not too far distant at Shifnal. I guess you could definitely say that I have Shropshire blood coursing through my veins! It's also possible that there was a Welsh connection somewhere, as Nana had been born a 'Griffiths' and her mother was a 'Watkins'. Perhaps that explains why we go to Barmouth every year!)

My 'Nin' (born in Kirkdale, 1895) was quite a character, almost always dressed in an apron, or 'pinny', as it was called, no doubt a shortened form of pinafore. She was well known up and down Romley Street, as she used to run 'the tontine'. This was a sort of savings club, where everyone contributed a couple of shillings (two bob, or a florin!) a week, and every week the whole collection was dished out to each contributor in turn, it must have seemed like Christmas coming early when it was your turn! Mind you, there was no doubt a small commission to be paid to the organiser, as Nin was quite astute! Another sideline, which I obviously didn't know about at the time, was that she used to lend money too! If, for instance, a neighbour borrowed a pound – quite a sum in those far-off days – this would possibly be paid off at a shilling a week over a period of twenty-one weeks, adding up to a total of twenty-one shillings. Thus Nin's pound (twenty shillings) would eventually be transformed into what was known as a 'guinea'. She was always involved in a 'sweep' too, whenever a big horse race, such

'Ninny' (Annie Hodgson)

as the Grand National or Derby, came up. On a personal note, I can remember the thrill of winning the sweep when **my** horse, called *Never Say Die,* won the Derby, I think it was ridden by a very young Lester Piggott.

As I was the eldest i.e. firstborn grandson, Nin used to dote on me somewhat, using the name 'Pedro' as a term of affection. We seemed to often go to her house on Sundays for dinner, which was always a delicious roast beef, Yorkshire pud and all the trimmings. For many years, this was cooked in a huge shiny-black range in the front parlour, the oven heated by a coal fire, which was always blazing on a cold day. That same fire was used to boil a kettle and to heat up the smoothing iron, which normally stood nearby. Again, as eldest, I would often be allowed to stay over on a Sunday night, waking on Monday morning to the smell of hot toast smeared with the most wonderful beef dripping – full of dark, richly flavoured jelly – you don't get it like that today.

One might get the idea that our visits to Nin's house for meals was based purely upon her benevolence, but in fact the costs were shared equally between her and my Mum. I have the feeling that Nin's neighbours used to think highly of her 'generosity', while Nin obviously made no move to change their minds on the matter! At Christmas, it would be Mum that made the plum puddings, the cakes and mince-pies, and then split the costs equally on everything else.

Down at the bottom of Romley Street was a grocer's shop, I'd quite forgotten the

Uncle John Hodgson

name, but Mum reminded me that it was *Lunt's*! I can remember being sent there to buy 'a packet of tea' and can recall that there were no tea-bags in those days, the tea came loose in an oblong packet. One popular type was *'Brooke Bond'*, which actually had a savings stamp on the side, you tore it off its perforated setting and stuck it onto a saver card, goodness knows what they were worth. The other tea I remember well, but which has disappeared now, was *'Golden Stream'* – which came in different colours of packet, depending on the grading of the tea – no doubt we went for the cheapest one!

Uncle John

Also living at No.17 was Mum's half-brother John, some three years her junior, and who had served as a radio operator in the tanks of the 4th/7th Dragoon Guards during the war. I don't think John ever spoke too much about his wartime experiences, but he was probably involved in the Normandy campaign that followed D-Day, through 1944 and 1945. The tanks he operated in were known as 'flail' tanks, because they were fitted with revolving chains at the front, which were used to detonate the minefields, ahead of the advancing troops. My brother Geoff thinks that he also served in Palestine, during 'the troubles' that led up to the setting up of the State of Israel in 1948.

John Hodgson, WW2

One thing I recall was the display of flags and *'Welcome Home'* signs that would be hung outside in the street when it was known that one or other of the soldier heroes was returning safely from the war – no doubt smartly dressed in one of those shiny 'de-mob suits'!

The family name on Mum's side, seeing that Annie never married, was always stated as 'Hodgson'. I guess, financially, our family could never be classed as well off, because Mum had to go out to work, even though Dad had a full-time job. I can remember that she worked just around the corner to Romley Street, as the waitress in a café run by a couple, Mr and Mrs Whittenbury. When school was over for the day, I would go around to Nin's house until Mum finished work and came to pick me up. One day I committed the ultimate sin of not going straight 'home' to Nin's after school, being attracted by the side-shows, swings and roundabouts of the fair which had been set up on the large bombsite opposite Arnot Street school. I must have panicked when it started getting dark and, in my haste to get away, running round the corner of the local fire station, I ran straight into a man on his bicycle. Unfortunately, the bike's axle took a large chunk out of my knee and I ended up at the doctor's having stitches. The doctor in question for that episode was Dr Jones, on the corner of County and Bedford Roads, and I'm told that I screamed blue murder at this – while Mum actually fainted in relief when the last stitch went in! I still carry the scar today.

Mum with her brother John

Our Geoff was another who had an accident of similar nature, this one occurring in Romley Street itself. I have the feeling that there was snow on the ground at the time. Anyway, he was carrying a jar of either strawberry or raspberry jam up the street, no doubt running from the corner shop, as young boys do, when he fell over. The jar smashed and he fell upon the broken glass and gashed his leg quite badly. Trouble was, it was hard to tell the blood from the jam! Geoff was proud of the white bandage he had to wear as a battle decoration for a while afterwards.

I recall that there was another doctor's surgery, also along County Road, on the corner of Church Road West and almost immediately alongside the *'Black Horse'* public house. Outside the pub was a huge public weighing scale, on which horse-drawn carts and their loads would be weighed, they were quite common at the time. The reasons for these weigh-ins are unclear to me now, was it to catch out over-laden vehicles or to protect the animals? The names of the two resident doctors, which I may not be correct about, were Allison and MacNamara.

(I am pretty sure that it was old Dr Allison that I bumped into down at Steadham, West Sussex, many, many years later, whilst out walking through that most picturesque village with Joyce and her sister Eileen. We'd actually passed him in one direction, and I told the girls that I thought I recognised him. When we crossed paths again in the reverse direction, I couldn't resist introducing myself - to his great astonishment of course! But he did recall the name 'Gripton' and told me that his son was quite a high-ranking naval officer, living in the village.)

'Uncle Jack' and 'Uncle Tom'

Across the street from Nin's house lived 'Uncle Jack'. It was only many years later that I found out he was actually John's father, while, as previously stated, my Mum never did know hers! Jack Terry was a caring and loving man, himself a widower, who wanted to marry Annie, but she constantly refused. My only real memories of Jack are twofold. One - that he used to let me look out from his bedroom window onto the railway line, which carried real trains belching out real steam. And two - that

134

when I had rice pudding with sultanas in it, I would be allowed to leave all the plump, warm sultanas round the edge of the dish until last! For some reason, which I always associate with Jack, I called them 'eggs'!

Jack eventually lost his life to tuberculosis (or 'TB'), which was rife in the Forties, dying just three weeks before my brother Cliff was born in 1943. In later years Jack's place was filled, mainly on a Saturday evening I guess, by 'Uncle Tom'. He was a grizzled old gent in glasses who smoked incessantly, and must have been Nin's 'boy friend', though it didn't register with us boys at the time, we were all so innocent in those days! Quite amazingly, some years later to say the least, I actually saw Tom in a dream one night, only to find out the very next day that he had died.

Jack Terry, John's father

I remember that Nin and Tom used to go off on holiday together in the summer, and that their destination was always 'Mrs Jones' guest-house' at Tal-y-sarn in North Wales. Although I can't pinpoint its location, it may have been the one to the west of Snowdon and south of Caernarfon. I can remember her mentioning visits to the Swallow Falls and always wondered about the identity of *'Betsy Code'*! It was only many years later, when I started to visit the area myself, that I found out the true spelling of that beautiful spot was Betws-y-coed. *(Having been visiting North Wales each year for a very long time now, it always brings back memories of the visits made by Nin.)*

Neighbours

Also living on the opposite side of Romley Street was a lady we called 'Aunty Ginnie', I think the family name was Pearcey. She had an adopted daughter called Jean Dobson, who always seemed such a glamorous person, a bit like the film star Veronica Lake, with blonde hair. I remember that she was married to a man named Roy, but that he lived out in Kenya, where he worked on the railway that ran between Nairobi and Mombassa. I recall seeing some photographs that were obviously taken in that far-off land. Mum and Jean knocked around together and Jean often visited our house, along with her two children, Valerie and Jack. Even in my extreme youth, I can recall just how good looking the two of them were. *(Amazingly, in a later conversation with Mum, just after Easter 2005, she told me that she had always had a sneaking suspicion that she and Jean were somehow related! Apparently, Jean eventually went off to live in Australia, so there is little hope now of finding further details!)*

Quite a few of the neighbours in Romley Street became almost as familiar to me as those in Milton Road; I spent lots of time at Nin's house. Next door was a family called Williamson, though for years I was under a misapprehension, because the lady of the house was always called 'Missus Willie', by one and all! Florrie Lamb lived a few doors away and there was another woman by the name of Laycock. The one thing that ties them all together is that all the women then used to wear curlers in their hair, wrapped in a headscarf. This, along with the inevitable pinny, would be their mode of dress all day long, probably until they went down to *'The County'* for an evening's glass of ale or whatever.

Also a few doors away lived the Potter family, I can vividly remember their son

Nin with 'Uncle Tom'

having a bow and arrow, because one day he fired one of his arrows at me and it hit me right in the eye. Reminds me of the old one about King Harold's knight shouting *'Keep blinking 'Arold, it'll come out in a minute'*! I can remember it was pretty painful at the time. At the bottom of Romley Street, on the left, was a shoe-shop, I thought it was a *Timpsons*, but once again it was Mum who, upon reading a draft of this, corrected that to *Playfair*. It probably became *Timpsons* at a later date. Anyway, there was a boy living over the shop that I was quite friendly with, I think he was called Tony Denario.

Crossing County Road and heading up Hale Road, there were some 'pre-fabs'. These were the pre-fabricated buildings that replaced those houses bombed during the war. In one of those lived Nurse Gibson - remember she 'delivered' our Geoff? (Just a quick question comes to mind here – why did our Geoff inherit the name *'Geoffrey Grunter'*?) Nin must have had a weekly job of cleaning this pre-fab, it was single-storeyed and, quite honestly, to me it always seemed such a palace when compared to our own homes. No doubt this is just a childhood recollection, I'm sure the pre-fabs must have leaked badly in places, though they seemed to hang around in some districts for many years.

Back at No.17, there seemed always to be a bottle of port in the side cupboard to liven up the lemonade, and a game of cards going on, the names *'Newmarket'* and another called *'Tuppence ha'penny'* come to mind. Old Tom lived a bus-ride away, somewhere along the stretch of Queen's Drive, which served as an inner-city ring road. Christmas Day would always see the whole family sitting down to dinner, after which the older members would listen to the Queen's speech on the Bakelite wireless. Afterwards, Uncle John would take us boys off down to Walton Hall Park – or 'Wally Hall', as we knew it – for a nice long walk. Then it would be back for cold meat and pickles, with the possibility of a small glass of 'port and lemon' if you were good!

Nin and John kept a cat when I was young, a blue Persian (I believe) called 'Smokey'. Amongst their possessions was an old book, I don't recall the title, but it was full of pictures of a natural history sort – the one I recall so well, even after all these years, was one of a vampire bat! There was another book in the house of a military nature, I think it was a history of the wartime exploits of John's regiment. John also owned an air-pistol – I always assumed it was a *'Webley'*, but our Geoff reckons it was a *'Diana'*. It was always a thrill when we were allowed to load it with small pellets, with their red wooly 'flights', and aim at a target on the back of the kitchen door.

Other family members

Nin had one sister called Lizzie, whose married name was Heaton, and who had two daughters called Norma and Joan. I can't remember too much about them, they managed to get around to Romley Street on visits occasionally. The one thing that sticks in my mind is that Norma and Jean, who must both have been teenagers at the time – though the term probably wasn't even used in those days – used to sit down with me and draw pictures, from which I copied my first attempts at art! The pictures would inevitably be of a large double-decker bus, with the driver somehow perched perilously on the bus's engine cowling.

Another member of her family was her brother Harold, known to one and all as 'Lal', a huge chap who seemed to tower over everyone when he made an entrance at No.17. Those occasions weren't that often as I recall, but I guess he may well have also visited while I wasn't there! One time you could guarantee a visit by Lal was after a match at Goodison, as he went back along County Road – exactly to where, I couldn't even tell you, but it must have been towards Rice Lane I suppose. *(Again here I am indebted to Geoff, who says that Lal lived in a street off the bottom of Breeze Hill, near the Metal Box factory, so I wasn't too far out!)* Lal's wife was called Ada but I do not remember her at all.

After I'd left school and joined the Army at age sixteen, I kept in contact with Nin by letter over many years, occasionally receiving a postal order for half-a-crown – or two shillings and sixpence – which seemed a fortune to me, as my weekly Army pay only came to ten bob! Eventually, the letters from Nin dried up and, when I finally went along to visit her and find out the reason, it was to find that her mind had gone senile. The funny thing is that John, who still lived at home, never thought to write and explain this to me, perhaps he felt rather ashamed, as *senile dementia* wasn't recognised for what it was then, people just thought you'd gone potty – very sad. Nin eventually went into a nursing home, the *'Belmont'* (?), at Anfield and I remember visiting her there with Mum, but Nin didn't even recognise us. Mum later told me that when she first started visiting her mother there, Annie thought she was one of the welfare workers. I seem to remember that, during my brief visit to see her, the mention of 'Pedro' did at least bring a glimmer of recognition. She eventually died at the beginning of 1979.

'Our John'

John Hodgson continued to live at No.17 for the rest of his life, which ended much too soon in 1990. Although he never married, he had had a very long love affair when I was a boy, with a nice lady named Mabel, who I think must have lived in Runcorn. I can recall her coming over to Walton sometimes while I was at No.17, I guess it was 'for tea', as that seemed to be the appropriate time for such family meetings and occasions! Although it didn't really register with me at that youthful time, Mabel was a lot older than John and Nin would 'put the dampers' on any marriage plans by saying that it was a waste of time, as there would be no children!

John worked in Runcorn, along the River Mersey in Cheshire, at a factory that was concerned with leather tanning; he must have travelled there every day by train, because he never ever had his own transport. Apparently there was once a time when he passed his driving test and obtained a licence, after becoming eligible for a company car. However, John never did maintain the confidence to drive it, leaving it garaged near Church Road West. During his career, John went to night school and eventually qualified as an industrial chemist. The firm he worked for was a family affair and I believe Mabel was the secretary in the office. The name of the concern was *Malcolm's* and John eventually became a company director, he was much appreciated. Over the years, *Malcolm's*, like many other small firms, would have been taken over by some large conglomerate.

John was a great follower of classical music, attending concerts at the 'Phil' and always listening to his old valve radio – which I later kept upstairs in my loft for a few years! I recall one time when he took me to the cinema 'in town' – probably the *Odeon* in London Road, to see Harry Belafonte and Dorothy Dandridge in *'Carmen Jones'*, a musical based upon Bizet's famous opera. Evenings would see him off on the bus, along Queen's Drive, to his

Mum (photo by Bill Green), 1953

favourite hostelry, the *'Jolly Miller'* at Broadgreen. He used it for many a long year, even though *'The County'* was only across the road at the bottom of his street. I'm told that John could sink eight pints during the evening, without ever appearing 'under the influence'.

For just a couple of short years in the mid-Eighties, when Mum was living in a flat at Cambridge Road in Crosby, she and John were able to spend a bit of time together at last. It must have been very nice for both of them, especially that John was able to feel, once again, part of a family. My last fond memory of John would probably be during 1984, when the 'tall ships' sailed out of Liverpool, and he accompanied us down to the foreshore to watch that historic sight in front of huge crowds on both sides of the river. He later bought both a painting and a photograph to commemorate the occasion and I'm pleased to say that they now adorn the wall in my hallway, just as you go upstairs.

John's untimely death, early in 1990, came pretty soon after he developed a serious illness, prostate cancer I think. Thankfully he didn't linger in pain for month after month; once he'd been taken into hospital, the end came pretty quickly. Mum was living in Australia at the time, having married Bill Walker in 1985. She came over when it was realised how serious was John's condition and managed to visit him briefly before the end. John's funeral was held at Walton Church, where he had spent a number of years as a 'campanologist' – that's bell-ringer in everyday terms! Apparently he had loved this pastime and become a popular member of the group who rang the bells.

At John's funeral, a 'lady friend' turned up, someone who had been very close to John during his latter days, even though she was still married at the time. They shared a love of classical music and it is likely that their relationship was no more than that – something we shall never know! Having attended that funeral, my brother Cliff and I were asked by Mum to go back to No.17 to see if there were any keepsakes that we'd like to take. I picked up a couple of 'Liverpool' scenes, one a photo and the other a painting, while we still use a pair of scissors from the kitchen! Whilst still at work for my last ten years, I often wore John's 'sports jacket' on a daily basis. I still have it, but it doesn't see so much daylight nowadays! I still try to wear it on occasion, such as when I am visiting the REME Museum up at Arborfield on meetings and/or research.

I never did find those old books that I'd found so fascinating when a kid. One was a sort of Regimental History book, no doubt a souvenir of John's Army days during the war. The other was that pretty old-fashioned natural history book – always remembered (by me) for its picture of a vampire bat! However, I did manage to pick up John's old valve wireless and actually had it working in my office at work for a while. It was eventually 'retired' to the loft, but now I have finally donated it to the REME Museum Telecommunications department up at my old stamping ground of Arborfield.

The Whitley years

It probably didn't register too fully with me, back in the early 1950s, that Mum and Dad were having such serious marriage problems, although I do remember that lots of arguments and shouting matches had been going on over a period of time. Whether or not 'teenagers' had been invented then, I don't remember – but that's what I became in 1953 – always to be remembered as 'Coronation Year'. I was certainly not the 'streetwise' young person you'd expect to find at that age nowadays. The other two boys were even younger than I was, so I guess they were also pretty naïve about the situation. I've mentioned elsewhere that Dad used to 'bring the job home with him', seemingly always talking about 'the office' and the various personnel involved. Dad eventually ended up in hospital for a big operation, I think it must have been for a duodenal ulcer, he'd certainly always been a 'worrier', and that was the eventual outcome as far as I'm aware.

Anyway, he obviously got through the operation, which no doubt was performed at Walton Hospital, and came back home sometime during that momentous year of national celebration. A photograph of Mum, taken along Bedford Road and looking down Makin Street, shows the bunting hanging in the streets. Whether or not there was a serious attempt at reconciliation between Mum and Dad afterwards, I don't really know, but in 1954 a little girl, Elisabeth Susan, was born, so we three boys had the surprise and delight of a baby sister. The other thing that happened, almost simultaneously, was that we all – everyone except Dad that is - left our home in Milton Road!

It was obviously a big upheaval in all our lives, a jump into the unknown in fact. For some time previously, we had noticed the presence of a certain Jack Whitley, he had even built a kitchenette onto the back of No.5, but that obviously wasn't his only mission at the time! Mum must have been seeing a lot of him, I believe it had started when he began going into the café (*Whittenburys?*) where Mum worked, on the block between Romley Street and Arnot Street. Anyway, the upshot of the affair was that we all went to live with him at 60 Cherry Lane, above a small shop that was a sort of general store. Jack had previously been an insurance agent for the *London & Manchester* and the shop was run in partnership with a guy called Dick Blundell, who had also been in the insurance game. *(If memory serves me correctly, Dick was a quiet, unassuming chap - of whom I'm often reminded when I see the character Norris Cole in today's Coronation Street TV series.)*

Although we three boys didn't know too much about things at the time, Jack Whitley was still married, with at least a couple of children of his own. The taking on of another three grown-up boys and a baby girl was obviously a tough responsibility, as he was still then paying maintenance to the wife he had left behind. Although 'our Sue' was definitely Joe Gripton's child, she was brought up as a Whitley, even though it was to be many years before my Mum and Jack eventually got around to being married. We three boys were invited to call him 'Pop', a sort of Americanised version of Dad! I remember that we would be detailed to take Sue, in her pushchair, along to 'Wally Hall' Park, to see our own Dad, but I don't think this went on for too long.

60 Cherry Lane

Life at Cherry Lane brought quite a few changes of course; the route to school now meant that I had to walk through Anfield Cemetery twice a day. Not too bad on a warm sunny day, but quite spooky heading home on dark winter afternoons! I still used to make my way down to Spellow Lane to catch the bus, it made sense, because the 'usual gang' was still using that service, so we could all still meet up together. Another change was that we no longer went to Nin's for a bath! Living with 'Pop' had the benefit of a car – a *Ford 'Popular'* to start with, I think – so I was able to be driven to the public baths at Norris Green, for a proper bath in the luxury of my own cubicle, with lots of steaming hot water.

I was roped in to help out in the shop at times and started to get to know how to handle money and serve the customers. One old woman would come in regularly, always asking for candles; we even got to call her by that name –'Candles'. She was obviously suffering from the onset of senility and we shouldn't have laughed – but of course we did. I remember Jack taking delivery of a huge supply of 'cinder toffee', which we then had to break down into small pieces and place into glass jars, ready for sale. I think the stock must have lasted for months, I know we were encouraging everyone to buy a bag for ages! Nowadays they wrap bars of the stuff in a chocolate coating and call it a *'Crunchie'* bar!

Old pals

It's strange but true that, having left Milton Road, I now got back in touch with fellow 'Old Miltonians', Harry Hayes and John Cowan. We had all now left our old homes, but none of us were too far away. In fact, John was now living just across

Queen's Drive from Cherry Lane, in Wilberforce Road, behind the Ebenezer Chapel. Harry would come along from Milman Road and the three of us started going to the pictures together. There was a cinema just along Cherry Lane, I can't remember its name, but the one we used mostly was the *Ritz*, up on Utting Avenue. The reason for this was so that we could have a quiet smoke, beyond our parents' reach! We used to club together to buy five *Woodbines* (or they could have been *Robin*!), having donned our long macs in order to look old enough, then share them out in the darkness of the *Ritz*, which was a bit of a flea-pit!

I suppose it was around this time that I first started becoming interested in music and girls! Music came in the form of *Radio Luxembourg* (208 metres, medium wave!), when it was broadcasting the *'Top Twenty'* late on a Sunday evening and Mum could be persuaded to let me stay up late enough to listen. You'll recall that John Cowan had gotten into music earlier than me – perhaps he even had a radiogram or record player at Milton Road, though I can't recall ever having seen one. Anyway, those had been the days of Doris Day, Frankie Laine, Johnny Ray and Guy Mitchell (on the American scene), with Frankie Vaughan, Dickie Valentine, Lita Rosa and such on this side of the Atlantic - that was just before Rock 'n' Roll changed the face of popular music forever.

As for girls, well I was hardly very successful in that line, being far too naïve about those matters at the tender age of fourteen. How things have changed today, with teenagers ruling the world, or so it seems. I suppose I did have a 'crush' on Jeannie Longworth, who lived just a couple of doors away, she was into high heels and such at an early age! However, I remember that it was probably her mother, Connie, who was trying to 'get us together' - perhaps she thought that I came from a wealthy background, what with going to grammar school, working in the shop and all! Connie's own mother, 'Granny Gow' I think was her name, also lived at the same house – I can't recall a man on the scene, but the two ladies were definitely of Scottish descent. Anyway, despite what our Geoff would have you believe, nothing really transpired between Jeannie and myself and the last I heard of her, after I'd joined the Army in 1956, was that she was going out with a lad called Robert Ashworth.

I've often wondered about what made me make the decisive step to become an apprentice tradesman in the Army, but I remember being encouraged by Pop that it would be good for me to 'learn a trade'. There was also the fact that he had been in the Army himself, serving with the Royal Horse Artillery. Anyway, this all took place just after my sixteenth birthday, by which time we had all 'upped sticks' once again and moved out to a new house on a new housing estate, still under construction on the other side of the Aintree racecourse, to a district known as Old Roan. It was quite a change of environment for us all, being at the outer edge of the city at what was then its northern limit.

Tonbridge Drive

We lived at No.8 Tonbridge Drive, a typical three-bedroomed semi-detached 'modern' house, with a garage on the side, a front and a back garden, both with real grass! There was even enough room on the drive to have a makeshift game of football or cricket. Another thrill was when Peter Farrell, Everton's Irish captain in those days, occasionally paid a visit to the people who lived next door. I can't remember too much detail of many of our neighbours, but there was a policeman living just down the road, whose bike I borrowed one day, when I had to get all the way to the other end of the city, for a school sports event of some sort. Just across the road lived a couple who went by the name of Woolahan, if that's the correct spelling. The husband, Pat, was an Irish guy with a peg-leg, who ran a cobbler's shop somewhere in Bootle, possibly on Hawthorne or Stanley Road. His wife, Cathy, was a largish woman, and she and Mum must have struck up some sort of neighbourly friendship. Cathy was the sort who could get quotations completely wrong, giving us cause to have a laugh. Mum often recalls the statement *'Patience is a virgin'*, when what was really meant was that it was a virtue!

On leave at Tonbridge Drive, Old Roan, c 1958

With the whole estate being brand new, there were still lots of unfinished houses under construction all around. Having joined the Army, then coming home on leave periods, Jack would entice me along during the dark evenings to raid these new building sites, where we would carry off barrow loads of timber, which then disappeared into the roof of the garage! On one evening, during such a nefarious escapade, who should we bump into but the local bobby – who was doing something similar with a barrow of his own! I can remember at one time that we actually took a whole kitchen unit out of one house, if we'd have been caught, goodness knows what would have happened to us.

I'm pretty sure it was that same policeman who lent me his bike one afternoon. I was supposed to attend a school sports event down at Mersey Road, Aigburth, which was on the other side of the city from Ainsdale. So, I borrowed this bike, which was a bit of a bone-shaker, and set off. I probably could have gone a more direct route, but then I wasn't too familiar with the roads in those days. So, having made my way down through Aintree to Walton, I turned left along Queen's Drive – I definitely knew that road led to Aigburth, because I had been on the bus that way often enough, to see Aunty Joyce and Uncle Bob! No doubt I returned by the same route, and I can remember feeling pretty tired at the end of the day.

A short visit 'across the border' to Scotland sticks in my memory for a couple of reasons that will become apparent. I can't remember exactly how many of us went up there, but I remember going through the famous Gorbals area of Glasgow, and then Coatbridge, before ending up in Edinburgh, where we probably only stayed the one night. Early the following morning, Jack took me up to the Castle, where the Royal Artillery Boys' Band was rehearsing for the Edinburgh Tatoo. It was a marvellous sight as the Band marched away, accompanied by the swirl of the pipes, into the early morning mist. I can next remember sitting in a café, somewhere along Prince's Street, I'm sure that my sister Sue – or was it Pam? - was with us. We'd had our morning tea, or perhaps it was coffee, when the next thing I remember is Jack telling us to sneak the cups and saucers under our coats! They were a light green in colour, I can see them to this day, and no doubt took pride of place in the café in County Road at some later date! I don't recall too many other events of the time, but I'm sure we made our way home down the eastern side of the country, via Durham and Yorkshire.

Learning a trade!

As already mentioned, I joined the Army in the summer of 1956, although I didn't exactly get off to a flying start! All packed up and ready to go, I caught the *Ribble* bus into town, where I reported to the recruiting office, which I think was in Ranelagh Street. When I got there, I found that all I had to do that day was pick up my rail ticket – and then report back the following day. I duly caught the bus back to Old Roan and, when I walked in through the back kitchen door of Tonbridge Drive, Mum burst into tears, as she thought I'd been rejected! I eventually did make it into the Army of course, but that will be covered in another chapter. Looking back, it can be figured out that Pop must have leaned on me a bit to 'join up and learn a trade', as we were all then competing for Mum's time and affection, which was all purely natural. Despite the fact that I was now in the Army, and self-financing as it were, there must have still been financial pressures at home, because it wasn't too long before the family moved back to Walton, to live 'above the shop' at 213 County Road.

The shop in question was a café, or snack bar, which then took the title of *'Jack's Snacks'*. At some time during this period, our Cliff was either silly enough, or brave enough, to stand up to Pop, actually throwing a baby's milk bottle at him. This happened while I was away in the Army, so I wasn't privy to all the details, but the upshot was that both Cliff and Geoff then moved back to Milton Road to live with Dad. Meanwhile, planned or not, and with Susan only a little baby of a few months old, Mum was bearing three more children in pretty quick succession, a daughter Pamela in 1955, followed by yet another two sons, Russell (1957) and Stephen (1958). All this took place against a background of Mum being literally tied to that bloody café day in and day out, serving from behind the counter, making pots of tea and such delicacies as beans on toast, as well as having to do all the domestic chores.

I would come home on leave, although I was hardly 'welcomed' by Pop, to find Mum almost totally exhausted, standing behind a mountain of ironing. Her health was none too good, I think she had a bout of pleurisy around that time, and it later also transpired that Jack was gallivanting out to clubs and pubs, as well as 'carrying on' with other women! Just how Mum survived those days, I'll never know, it must have been a total nightmare for her. I used to get home as often as I could and try to 'do my bit', helping out in the café, washing up, etc, and would often head back south on a Sunday, leaving Mum in tears at the prospect of another miserable week or fortnight ahead. As already mentioned, I was hardly the most welcome visitor in Pop's eyes, I recall many a weekend when he couldn't even be civil enough to speak to me. It seemed that all he wanted was Mum running round in circles, at 'her master's beck and call', with no outside interference from anyone else. But life's a funny thing, Mum stuck with him through all that time and, eventually, they began to enjoy some better times – how ever did you do it Mum?

When I did go home, mainly at weekends, Mum would always try to act as normally as possible. She would send me along to Frank Kelly's butcher's shop, just a short distance away towards Walton Church, for *"a pound of fillet steak, minced"*. This would then be mixed with the most wonderful onion gravy and served with a plateful of home-made chips and garden peas, accompanied by a couple of rounds of bread and butter, always a treat after being on Army grub! And they were real chips too, fried in real lard - absolutely scrumptious!

146

During my early Army days, I became friendly with a guy called John 'Dinger' Bell, who lived next to the recreation ground down Rice Lane, near the end of Hornby Road. Dinger had been the very first boy I had bumped into, on my arrival at the camp at Arborfield – he was digging the plot outside

'Dinger' Bell (left)

the Guardroom, as punishment for one of his many misdemeanours! We began to knock around together for a while, I remember us both buying leather jackets which, along with our blue denim jeans, made us look like our screen idols, Marlon Brando and James Dean. I distinctly recall us going to the cinema down at Walton Vale, just past the *'Black Bull'* pub, to see *'The Tommy Steele Story'*. Coincidentally, I was given a photograph many years later, showing Dinger under the bonnet of an old Army *Jeep*!

Another Army mate was Billy Armstrong, who lived in Winslow Street, about fifty yards from Goodison Park. I think Billy must have been an adopted child, his 'parents' certainly seemed quite an old couple. I remember walking with him all the way down to the Pier Head one summer's evening, where we enjoyed a burger from one of those greasy bars that operated there. Pretty sure we walked back too! I know that, during our summer leave periods, we would go across to New Brighton on the ferry, loitering around the funfair, trying to be noticed – quite unsuccessfully! - by the girls. *(Amazingly, after meeting up with Ken Anderson during my research for my 'Arborfield' history book during 2003, we got into contact with Billy, who had been in the same intake (58A) as Ken at the Army Apprentices' School. Bill, now living in Wokingham, joined us for a pint at the 'Bramshill Hunt' one day – and we have kept in touch by e-mail ever since.)*

Friends reunited

Strangely enough, it must have been around the same time that I made contact, once again, with Harry Hayes and John Cowan, by now embarked on their working lives. I would generally hitchhike home in those days, or pay for a lift from a soldier called Mick Swords, from Birkenhead. I would try to ensure that I was home in time for Saturday afternoon, with maybe a match at Goodison to watch, leaving the evening free to go out with my two old buddies. We would meet up in the *'Clock Inn'* in London Road, a *Younger's* pub opposite the *Odeon* cinema, I think we all drank 'brown mixed' in those days, which was a bottle of brown ale poured into a pint glass and topped up with draught mild. There would always be a visit from a guy from Southport, selling fresh shellfish – well, he told us they were fresh - and the potted shrimps did taste good! We would also occasionally be visited by members of the Salvation Army, or 'Sally Ann', as they were popularly known, selling their *'Warcry'* magazines.

From the pub we would mostly head along Lime Street and then up Mount Pleasant, finishing up in the *'Mardi Gras'*, one of the many clubs in the city centre, with its bar and dancing. They always had these ultra-violet lights in there, so the girls would make sure they wore see-through blouses and white bras, to show off their figures! Most of the music played there at that time was traditional jazz and skiffle, with a guy called Clinton Ford being a big favourite at the time. This was just before the explosion of 'Mersey beat' and all the Liverpool groups who followed in the footsteps of the Beatles – Gerry and the Pacemakers, the Searchers, the Swinging Blue Jeans and many others. I'm afraid I just preceded that era and had to follow the local scene from a distance, especially when I got posted to Germany in 1961. *(Quite amazing that, while I was in Germany, the Beatles were beginning to make their name in Hamburg – not too far away from where I was stationed. And of course, Paul McCartney and George Harrison were both ex-members of 'the Inny'.)*

Harry and John had picked up a couple of girl-friends by then, I think Harry was going out with a librarian who worked in the branch on County Road, just along from the bottom of Arnot Street. One weekend they introduced me to a girl called Valerie Lonnie, who lived all the way out at Maghull, just behind the big cinema there. Having the job of taking her home, I accompanied her on the bus all the way to that far-flung outpost and bagged my first real kiss – she was quite passionate about it, but I was probably in deep shock! Particularly when I realised there were no buses back to Walton and I ended up having to walk a pretty long way home. On a couple of occasions at least, I'd accompany 'the gang' by bus up to the two main dance-halls in Liverpool then - the *Grafton* and the *Locarno* – were they on Smithdown Road? I have a vague recollection that we bumped into old pal Alec Hurley and his elder brother Tommy up there once, but my main memory was of the fights you'd have to avoid outside a nearby pub known as *'Ma Kelly's'*.

My weekends would always end outside Lime Street station at around midnight on the Sunday. I always made sure that I had booked a lift back to camp, I don't think hitching a lift at that time of night would have been much good! It was generally Mick Swords who did the honours. Four of us would pile into the back of his little 7-cwt. *Ford* van, with another couple in front, then it was off through the Mersey Tunnel and heading south. This was pre-motorway Britain, so our route took us past Chester, through Whitchurch, Newcastle-under-Lyme, Castle Bromwich, the Coventry by-pass, Warwick and Oxford, on the way back to Arborfield, located a few miles outside Reading, in Berkshire. Sleep was just about impossible in the restricted space of Mick's van, so we'd inevitably sit chatting and smoking ourselves silly all the way back. I can remember coming across Nettlebed Common, between Oxford and Reading, around daybreak, listening to the dawn chorus of birds. We would stumble out of the smoke-filled van and just about have time to lie on our beds for a brief spell before a bugler, playing *Reveille,* sounded and it was time for work. Somehow, I don't think there was a lot of work done on those Mondays following a Liverpool weekend!

The leaving of Liverpool

Eventually I suppose, Jack Whitley must have realised that there wasn't a lot of money to be made in the 'snack bar' business, and so he turned back to the far more lucrative insurance game. The 'shop' at 213 County Road was converted into an office and, I think I am right in saying that the property above was bought outright, having previously been only rented. In 1965, Mum and Pop bought another new house, out on the Pinfold Estate at Ainsdale, just north of the Formby by-pass and small airfield. I can remember my first visit there around August of that year, Joyce and I had two-year old Lorraine by then and Joyce was around three-months pregnant with Michelle. We still have a set of four photographs, each one showing Lorraine with one of her aunts and uncles – Susan, Pam, Russell and Stephen. I can't remember that Pop made us particularly welcome, but as he was at work down in Walton all day, we somehow managed to enjoy our visit!

In fact, we must have visited quite often over the next few years, but Pop seemed to get harder and harder to live with and alienated just about every member of the family. One thing that sticks vividly in my mind about those visits to Bowness Avenue was the morning ritual of coughing! Both Mum and Pop smoked like the proverbial troopers, and each morning would be unable to start the day without inhaling the dreaded nicotine, followed by a bout of coughing – it sounded pretty scary.

Sneaky visits

In 1975, along with Joyce's two sisters, Eileen and Janet, plus their husbands and children, we all paid a visit to Barmouth, North Wales, for an Easter holiday. *(Little did we know that Joyce and I, along with Eileen and Mike, would still be doing that trip thirty and more years later!)* I can't remember if we began the same year but, because North Wales wasn't too far from Ainsdale, we used to head off to see Mum at the end of our week in Barmouth. We would leave Wales very early on the Saturday morning, driving up through Dolgellau and past Bala Lake, before stopping along the roadside for a breakfast of cold toast and a flask of tea. Then it was on via Ruthin, Mold and Queensferry, through the Mersey Tunnel and Liverpool, and on up the coast road. Hard to believe, but we would then make sure that Pop had left for the office, so that the coast was clear for a sneaky couple of hours with Mum before we headed back home!

By the late Seventies, our Pam was working at 'the office', which was what 213 County Road had now become, and learning the insurance business. She and Steve had taken up residence in the upstairs flat, and, for three years running (1979 – '81), we took the girls up there with us over the August Bank Holiday weekend. Brother

Joyce at Ainsdale, 1965

Geoff had gone back to Australia around 1969, settling down well in Perth, the capital city of Western Australia, and later getting married to Sheila Walker in 1975. Around 1980, Mum and Pop went out there for a holiday and Pop must have decided that Perth was the place he would settle in when he reached retirement. I remember that Joyce and I met up with them at Windsor to say farewell, along with a couple of their friends, Joan and Eddie Bullen. This event took place at the end of November in 1982, and it looked as though Mum was finally going to have a peaceful 'place in the sun' – not that she ever liked the sun that much!

Unfortunately, that state of affairs didn't last too long, as Pop's many years of heavy smoking and drinking finally caught up with him. He died in April 1983, only a few short months after moving to Australia, and left Mum with the big decision on 'what to do next'. So what did she do? Find out in another thrilling chapter!

Sisters and brothers, nieces and nephews

Elizabeth Susan – 'our Sue' - was born in April 1954, at around the same time that Mum made the break from Joe Gripton and moved in, along with three growing boys, with Jack Whitley above a grocery-style shop at No.60 Cherry Lane. We still retain one photograph of Sue taken during that era, probably just across the road from the shop. *(And it is amazing that, when Lorraine reached the same age, they could have been identical twins, if it wasn't for the years in between!)* As far as we were all concerned at the time, Sue was 'a Whitley' and she was certainly brought up as one.

Toddler Sue at Cherry Lane

Despite the fact that I can remember taking Sue in her pushchair to Walton Hall Park to see my Dad, it probably didn't even dawn on me at the time that Sue was Joe's daughter. Just shows you that it was definitely the 'age of innocence' in many ways! Those visits didn't last too long however, particularly after the newly increased Whitley family had moved out to Old Roan, Aintree. I'm pretty sure that, in those early childhood days, Sue never realised that she was only a half-sister to the other three children. As far as I know, none of them were treated any differently, they were all brought up together under the same rules and regulations – and pretty strict ones, knowing Jack Whitley!

Family footsteps

Sue certainly 'followed in the footsteps' of myself, Cliff and Geoff, in that she eventually gained entry to Blackburne House, which was the 'sister' school to the Liverpool Institute – our much-loved 'Inny'. In fact, though she may correct me here, I have the feeling that she successfully worked her way to the dizzy heights of a *Margaret Bryce Smith* scholarship, definitely 'one up' on the rest of us. *(Sue was able to confirm that she did indeed pass that scholarship, prior to sitting her '11-plus' exams.)* With me being away in the Army from summer 1956 onwards, I never really had the pleasure of seeing any of the four children growing up – but it all seemed to happen pretty quickly, that's for sure! I used to see them during leave periods of course, and once I'd met Joyce and then later we got married, we both used to visit as regularly as we could. I guess Cliff had become the surrogate 'big brother' in my absence.

I remember that, not long after Joyce and I had moved into our house in Longmoor Road, both Sue and Pam came down for a visit that ended in our digging up some trees from nearby Blackmoor – and then transplanting them into our back garden. Today we are still living with the consequences of that move, with the silver birch trees having since grown to immense proportions and dropping their seeds and leaves every year and driving Joyce mad in her effort to maintain a tidy garden! I'm sure both girls can also recall walking up Butser Hill, on the way down to Hayling Island, as my old *Morris Minor* (split windscreen and side-valve engine!) couldn't make the hill fully loaded! Sue and Pam would have just about been into their teens then, where have all those years gone?

Growing up – and away

It wasn't until Sue began her university education, a few years later, that we began to see her more often – and that was mainly down in London. She first took up residence in Halliday Hall, located on the south side of Clapham Common, and from Hampshire that wasn't too far to drive, even in the old bangers I always owned! We would drive up the old A3 to Guildford, then turn off on the A24 towards Dorking and Leatherhead, eventually going though Raynes Park, Wimbledon, Morden, Tooting Bec and Balham (gateway to the south!), before ending up at Clapham. One thing that was memorable was the splendid 'high tea' provided by Halliday Hall – sandwiches and cake! The place was actually a 'hall of residence, belonging to the university, where students would stay for part of their three-year further education.

(Just digressing here for a moment! The reason I mentioned "Balham, gateway to the south" was that it reminded me of the old Peter Sellers album, "Songs for swinging Sellers", which I used to love many years back. Around 2002, whilst on holiday up at Barmouth, Mike and I paid our annual pilgrimage to 'The Cob' record store in Porthmadog. I casually asked the guy behind the counter if that album had ever been issued on CD. He checked his catalogue and the answer was in the negative. "But I've got a copy on vinyl", he told me. Needless to say, I snapped it up and have it at home – still as funny as ever!)

Pam – or Pamela Helen, to give her full name – was born the year after Sue. By the time she reached the age of one year, I'd left to join the Army. The first 'major incident' I can recall concerning Pam was when the family had returned to live 'over the office' at 213 County

'Swee'pea' leaving home

Road. Joyce and I had met by then – we may even have married. Anyway, we were on one of our visits to Liverpool and Pam was a very sick little girl. I think she had been diagnosed as having gastro-enteritis, but both Joyce and I were convinced that she had something worse. We convinced Mum of the severity of things and called the local doctor at his surgery next to the *Black Horse*. It transpired that Pam actually had peritonitis, which was, to say the least, life-threatening and she was rushed away into *Alder Hey* children's hospital along Queen's Drive and thankfully made a full recovery.

My earliest memories of Russ (Russell Charles) and Steve (Stephen Robert) are mainly linked with No.8 Tonbridge Drive, up at Old Roan, when they were just toddlers. I do have a couple of old photographs of the children playing in the garden up there. But the 'most famous' photo is the one of Stephen, standing in the back yard of County Road, coat around his shoulders – as he prepares to leave home! Steve was a great 'crawler' as a baby, and was given the nickname *'Swee'pea'* after the similar character in the cartoon series, *'Popeye the Sailorman'*.

Another series of photos shows our daughter Lorraine, being held by each of the four children in turn. These would have been taken around 1965, after Jack, Mum and family had moved to their new house in Tonbridge Drive at Ainsdale – there was still lots of building works going on all around the newly-developing estate. An incident that comes to mind concerning Russ is the time that he fell with a knife in his mouth, badly lacerating his lip. By the time the photo with Lorraine was taken, he had just about healed up and was so pleased that the photo showed him looking normal again!

London lodgings

Pam always had an interest in the theatrical side of life and, after Sue had settled into her university studies in London, it was Pam's turn to make a similar move. She came south to study drama at the *Maria Gray* Teacher Training College in Twickenham – it is strange that I now regularly drive along St Margaret's Road, which is where she used to live. I have a feeling that both Sue and Pam also shared 'digs' for a short spell, somewhere near Wandsworth Common, although my memory of that is rather vague! I do remember being up on a visit to London and we were out walking with Pam, when we 'just happened' to bump into this bearded 'hippy' along the street in Twickenham. Pam later married her hippy, Steve Nicholas, in 1978. Despite having been brought up around the Cheltenham area and being a Bristol City fan, he very quickly converted to 'Evertonianism'! This was quite a sensible move when you consider that all other family members – except Russell of course – were 'True Blues'.

My memory on the timing of events is a bit hazy now, but I am sure that, at one time, Pam was involved with Liverpool's famous *'Everyman'* theatre, which has been involved in the careers of many well-known actors, actresses and playwrights. I'd better not try and quote any names here, as I'm bound to be wrong on some counts. One play that I think Pam was involved in was *Major Barbara*, by George Bernard Shaw if memory serves me right. (Thinking of it, surely this was **after** her training in London, but I could well be wrong!) I think Sue left Halliday Hall to move to a flat at Tulse Hill, just a bit further along the South Circular Road. When we went up there to see her, Sue took us to the nearby *Horniman Museum*, which at the time had a very interesting exhibition of South American arts and artefacts. From the nearby park, which I believe was at Dulwich, there was an excellent view across central London.

I'm not too sure of the facts here, but I do believe that Sue had met up with Des Herlihy when they both shared bus trips to and from their schools in Liverpool, and then got together again in later years, after Sue had started her studies down in London. This was after Des had completed his Degree at Portsmouth Polytech, just a few miles south of us here in Greatham! The pair of them supported each other through postgraduate training, before both becoming teachers. I have a feeling that we helped them move into their first place – or was it the second? Anyway, it was in Brixton and I think we carried a bed on the roof rack of whatever car we had at the time!

Anyway, they eventually married at Lambeth Town Hall (I think!) towards the end of 1975. I recall being in Brixton for 'the party' – our Steve was there too, along with Pam and Steve, who were then living together over at Hounslow, Hanworth, or some other such place – it was definitely directly under the Heathrow flight-path! At some point in the afternoon, I somehow got roped in to give Pam and Steve a lift home – *"It's only about twenty minutes"*, said our Sue (she'd had a few by then!) 'Our' Steve volunteered to join me and we duly dropped off our fares on the other side of London. The trip back, without passenger guidance, was a bit of a nightmare – I'm positive we went over Kew Bridge about three times! By the time we got back to Brixton, it was time for Joyce, the girls and I to head home.

While Pam was still in the London area, I recall one visit to see her, when we paid a visit to Kew Gardens – with an entrance fee then of 'tuppence'! As documented elsewhere, Joyce and I also caught up with Pam and Steve on a few occasions, starting in 1979, after they had moved back up north to live over what was now 'the office' in County Road, Walton. On one of those occasions, I recall visiting a sort of 'farm' in Calderstones Park. Sue and Des must have stayed in London for a bit longer, ending up in the Holloway area. The journey up there used to take us over Blackfriars Bridge, up along Fleet Street and past the *Sadler Wells* theatre. I think I'm right in saying that one Sunday morning Des took us all, including Lorraine and Michelle, to our first ever visit to a *McDonalds* restaurant. It was (again, I think!) only the second ever to open in England (the first at Woolwich in 1974?) and was located on Seven Sisters Road.

The first time we visited that flat, we spent ages looking for it and actually sat in the car for a long time, hoping to spot the Herlihys and find out where the place was! It turned out that the entrance door was in a side street – not, as the address suggested, on the main Tollington Road. The house was located between two sets of traffic lights on a very busy London main route. Having gone to bed, we lay there listening to the sound of cars and buses revving up as they raced from one set of red lights to the next – a bit of a nightmare that our two girls have never forgotten I'm sure! One good thing about that place was its proximity to Highbury, home of 'the Arsenal', which did allow me to accompany Des on a couple of visits to see probably both Everton and Liverpool. (Yes, I'm afraid Des is another Redneck!)

Both Russ and Steve had left home in the intervening years and I was little involved with either of them very much. Prior to that, there was one memorable occasion when the two of them actually came down to stay with us for a week down here in Hampshire. I think Mum had been tearing her hair out with them and had asked whether they could come down for a break – the break being her very own I think! Anyway, they did come down here and, as far as I recall, made very good use of *The Queen*, our village pub just around the corner – and especially its pool table!

Two weddings in Germany

Russ went on to join the Merchant Navy and started training at a place in Anglesey as far as I know – a shore-based 'Training Ship' by the name of *Indefatigible* or *Indominatable* – one of those 'old Empire' style names. My knowledge of the affair is scanty, but apparently Russ was 'accused' of having drugs in his possession and ended up leaving that particular line of work! Deservedly or not, he became something of 'the black sheep of the family'. The next thing I knew was that he was out in Greece somewhere, where he languished in jail for a while and was almost cut off from the rest of the family. He was eventually to settle down in Germany and married a girl called Angelika (or Angela for short) towards the end of 1989 – following the birth of a daughter, Lisa, just a couple of weeks earlier.

Meanwhile, 'our' Steve had joined the Army, basically as a driver with the Royal Corps of Transport (RCT), doing his basic training at Naunton Manor barracks in Taunton, down in Somerset. *(Joyce and I drove past these very barracks late in 2007. We were on our way down to Lynton, North Devon, for Sarah and Andy's wedding.)* Early in 1979, Sue and Des got tickets for us all to see *'Elvis'* (a musical) in London. Later that same year, Steve was due to get married to Jacquie Headridge out in Minden, Germany, where he was then serving – I think he was a Lance Corporal by then. I remember that Mum and Sue drove down from up north to catch a flight from Heathrow to Germany, to attend the wedding. They had arranged to stay with us overnight and Joyce and I kept on anxiously looking at the clock as the hours passed by and there was no sign of them.

Eventually there came a phone call – there were no such thing as 'mobiles' then of course, Sue had had to knock on someone's door in order to use their phone! It turned out that they had driven through some torrential rain on the journey south between Warwick and Oxford and, just outside Kingsclere, Sue's *Mini* had decided that it didn't want to go any further. I had to drive up there and, thankfully due to having 'messed around' with cars a bit, had some idea of what the problem might be. The distributor on the *Mini* was located rather senselessly right in front of the engine and prone to filling with water in wet weather! A quick strip-down, followed by a wipe with dry rag and they were back on the road – with me to guide them the last few miles. Mum and Sue then joined Pam and all three did eventually attend Steve's nuptials.

Now Jacquie and Steve went on to have two children, Leanne and Craig, neither of whom we ever met for many a long year! Amazingly, it was in fact to be the year 2000 before we finally met up with Jacquie, when she and Steve came down to London to help celebrate my 60th birthday. Even meetings with Steve himself have proved very few and far between over the years, it's just a sad fact of the different lives we both led. We did manage to catch up with each other at Uncle John's funeral in 1990. Catching up with Russ has proved even more of a rare occurrence and only a couple of times immediately leap to mind. Once was at a party thrown for Sheila and Geoff up in the Crosby area (was it the *Blundell Sands Hotel*?), I guess that could have been in 1984. And then in 1997 he joined Mum, Bill, Sue, Joyce and myself for a dinner at a pub near Nailsea, when Mum and Bill were over on their last visit together in this country and staying in the Lovell's place for the second time.

Born in the USA

I can't remember the exact year, but it must have been around 1980, that Sue and Des made the exciting decision to go and see whether or not they could set up home – and survive – in the United States. Des was born in New York before moving to the Southport area as a young lad, and still had some family members over there. Anyway, they ended up at Miami in Florida, where Des began teaching and Sue went to do admin work in the IT department for some banking and mortgage company. In November 1982 their only son Thomas was born out there – Mum and Jack Whitley were over there at the time. It must have been earlier in the year that Lorraine also visited them, along with school friend Maura. The pair also went to stay with Maura's relations in St Louis. The following year, Joyce and I went to see Sue and Des on a two-week holiday, which is covered in the appropriate chapter on holidays!

I think it was the American education system, with its possible negative effect on Tommy, which helped decide Sue and Des to return to England once again. *(Sue later told me that Des had learned that his mother, then living in Southport, had been diagnosed with terminal cancer, so obviously that was a big factor too.)* This they did and moved into a house in Crosby, at the north end of Liverpool. I can't recall the exact date, but it must have been after Mum's return from Australia in August 1983, following the death of JCW, and before her move back to that country with Bill Walker in 1985. In fact, the Herlihys stayed with Mum for a short while, before settling down in Ascot Park, just along The Northern Road from where Granny and Granddad Gripton had lived, at 47 South Parade, all those years previously – quite a coincidence when you come to think of it. Around the same time, Pam and Steve moved into York Road, also in Crosby, so Mum and her two daughters were able to see each other more easily for a while. It was early in 1985 that Pam and Steve's elder daughter, Sian, was born.

Sue and Des eventually moved to a second place in Crosby, the road was called Morningside, but later moved away from Merseyside altogether to settle in a brand new house at Culcheth. Now I must admit that, until they moved there, I'd never even heard of the place. It's basically about halfway between Liverpool and Manchester, not far from Warrington, in the county of Cheshire. The 'village' is really quite large and certainly has all the required amenities – just ask Mum, who now lives in the same village, having come back from Australia after Bill Walker's sad death towards the end of 2002.

Looking back, it is amazing how quickly the years – seventeen in all – passed, between Mum's marriage and subsequent second move to West Australia and her final return. I'm not too sure of the reason myself, but Pam and Steve decided to also head off 'down under'. I guess that must have been during 1986, because prior to their departure, they had moved to a flat down near the ferry-port at Seaforth. I remember visiting there with Joyce while Sian was still at the 'toddler' stage. Pam had spent quite a long period in learning the 'insurance game', starting before her Dad's death, while Steve has long been involved in the teaching of handicapped children. The Nicholas family has been out in Perth ever since and, during that time, we have spent a couple of Christmas holidays in their company, in 1991 and 1996. Between those dates, another daughter, Kate, came along in 1994. There have also been 'reciprocal' visits to UK by the Nicholas's, around the New Year of 1993 and 2001. With Sian now 'all grown up' and living with her boyfriend James, it will be just Pam, Steve and Kate who were due another UK trip towards the end of 2004.

I think 'our' Steve must have served his full twenty-two years in the Army. Certainly, towards the end of his service he was posted up at Catterick (now there's a name to treasure!) in Yorkshire. Having left 'the mob', he got fixed up with a job at Ardentinny, up in the wilds of Scotland near the famous submarine base of Holy Loch, where he worked at some sort of 'Outward Bound' centre, organising sporting activities. We never did get to visit those parts, though I'm sure that Sue and Des made the effort on a few occasions.

It is only fairly recently that Steve became less than enamoured with the job up there, and he and Jacquie have now settled in North Wales, between Port Madoc (or Porthmadog) and Caernarfon. Steve now oversees *'The Ozanam Centre'* on behalf of the *St Vincent de Paul Society*, a charity that offers visitor accommodation and leisure activities to various groups. It is hoped that 'the family' can use the place as a base for a get-together at the end of 2004, while Pam and Steve are over here – perhaps we'll also finally get to meet up with Russell's family. Pam and Steve duly arrived at Heathrow on Sunday December 5th, along with Kate, and they stayed with us for a few days before heading off via Winchester to Salisbury. By then, we'd heard that it is only Russell that will make it to North Wales!

A family reunion

So, on New Year's Eve 2004/05, Joyce and I found ourselves on familiar territory, driving all the way up the route that we always take to Barmouth at Easter. We had our usual pit-stop at the *Little Chef* at Hope-under-Dinmore and then later took a slight diversion in order to visit the small town of Montgomery, where we enjoyed a splendid bowl of butternut squash soup. Then it was up to Dolgellau, through the Coed-y-Brenin to Porthmadog and on to Llanllyfni.

All in all it turned out to be a splendid get-together. Mum came along with Brenda from next door, who has become an honorary family member. Then there were Sue and Des, along with Pam, Steve, Kate and Russell. Lorraine and Phil brought Jake – of course – while Michelle, James, Thomas and Calum also made it. Steve and Jacquie were obviously there, working extremely hard at making everyone welcome and well-fed, while it was nice to finally catch up with Craig, who had travelled down from Scotland to join the party. It was amazing to find out, from Jacquie, that her Dad had been serving with the Royal Scots Greys way back when Joyce and I were with them at Fallingbostel, back in 1966/67. On New Year's Day, for those who struggled from their beds in time, there was an adventurous walk down the lane on which the *Ozanam Centre* is located. Spotting a footpath sign, marked 'Tal-y-sarn ½ mile', Joyce led us all off across the fields to a neighbouring village. Unfortunately, on the return route, the wet weather set in with a vengeance, as it often does in 'Wet Wales'

– and everyone got soaked! Good job then that Jacquie held the fort with bowls full of steaming hot homemade vegetable soup – really delicious!

Since that reunion, things have not turned out too well for Steve, as he has been suffering from severe arthritis in his knees, which have led to a lot of pain and some horrific-sounding treatment. One good thing, I suppose, is that Craig has been on hand to alleviate the situation, while Jacquie has obviously had to shoulder a lot of the work-load. In the meantime, Sue and Des have bought themselves a caravan on a nice site in the Lake District, where they can now spend some leisurely time together. They were kind enough to let Michelle, James and the two boys stay there for a few days in the summer of 2005.

In mid-November 2005, at the beginning of what was the coldest weather for a good few years, Joyce and I paid a visit to Culcheth to see Mum, staying over with Sue and Des for three nights. Sue had recommended a visit to Wilmslow, so Joyce and I took Mum across there for a couple of hours. That evening, the five of us enjoyed an excellent meal at *'The Packhorse'*, a local inn situated just far enough from the village centre so as not to attract the more yobbish clientele! On the Saturday afternoon, it was nice to have a flying visit from 'our Steve'. He had ridden across from Caernarfon on his motorbike, been 'climbing' with Des in the morning – and then dropped in at Mum's in the afternoon. He was obviously in a lot of pain, but determined not to let his injury get the better of him. He said that it felt really good to get on the bike, unrestricted by the crutches that he normally has to use.

As I sit adding these few words in May 2006, I think that Steve has made some progress with his leg. We had thought that we might drop in on him and Jacquie again whilst at Barmouth, but we didn't make it. Over in Australia, Sian celebrated her 21st birthday in Perth, before moving, along with boyfriend James, across to Melbourne. Sometime soon, I think that there is going to be a 'bit of a do' in Melbourne, as Pam goes over there at the same time as Sue and Geoff take a break from New Zealand – and Lorraine and Phil take a holiday there too! That far-off reunion did take place and we have some photos to prove it! Early in 2007, Sian and James decided to take a chance on coming over to UK, hoping to eventually find work in London. After visiting Culcheth, Liverpool, Richmond (Yorkshire) and Cheltenham, they ended up here at Greatham on April 26th for a couple of days, before heading into London to seek new ventures! I was able to give them a lift into Harrow, where they had booked a hotel for a few nights.

At the end of August that same year, we had the pleasure of another visit from Sian & James, ostensibly to help me celebrate my 'fortieth' birthday – I wish! They arrived by coach at Liphook on a Friday evening and we picked up some fish'n'chips at the local chippy. On Saturday we had a nice day out, split between Winchester and Alresford, then on Sunday we enjoyed the return walk between Chawton and Farringdon. Before they left on Monday afternoon – a Bank Holiday – we managed to fit in a longish walk over Selborne Common and across to Newton Valence. Fortunately, after a couple of weeks of wet weather, the holiday weekend turned mainly fine and sunny. The young couple have both found work in London and are now living in the Highbury area – and both supporting Everton as often as they can!

Return to Milton Road, 1975

Aunty Joyce with 'our Sue, Mum and boys

*Mark, Colette, Lorraine, me and Joyce,
with Roy in front*

Sue and Pam with the girls, 1971

Day out at Windsor, c 1961

162

Pam, Steve, Sue and Russell

June and Stan at home, Reading, late Sixties

Joyce's Dad, Stan Jones, second from left at rear

Mum Jones with Joyce and June

Granddad Jones, with Lorraine and Karen

163

Cliff and Geoff

Back to Milton Road

As I've mentioned previously, once I'd gone off to join the Army in the summer of 1956, it couldn't have been too long afterwards that Cliff and Geoff also 'baled out', going back to live with Dad at Milton Road. My memories of those events are almost negligible, seeing that I was away from it all. But I do recall being told that there had been an almighty blow-up, culminating in Cliff throwing the baby's (Steve's) milk-bottle at Jack Whitley, and that seemed to be the final scene before it was decided that the two boys should return to 'their father'. Unfortunately, this also led to a great loss of contact on my behalf and I can't really recall much detail of the next few years as far as Cliff and Geoff are concerned.

As far as I am aware, Cliff went to work as a shipping clerk down in Liverpool city-centre and he probably worked for the same firm for a number of years. Over those same years, the original firm was taken over, first by one and then possibly by another, of the bigger conglomerates. I seem to recall the name *'Baxter Hoare'* cropping up at one point! The reader will recall that Cliff had been hit on the back of the head by a house-brick when he was very young, going on to suffer a form of epilepsy in later life. No doubt this was kept under control by constant medication, but I do recall once that he was a passenger on a bus into town, standing on the platform, and was unable to remember where he was supposed to get off.

Cliff continued to live with Joe Gripton for a very long time. I remember going up to Milton Road with Joyce and the girls in our old *Ford Cortina* one summer, that must have been in the early seventies and was the first time I'd been back there in years. I still have the photograph to prove it! By then, Geoff had gone off to Australia on his own and I suppose No.5 was just about adequate for only Cliff and Dad. However, a few years later, they moved into an upstairs flat at Cromwell Court, just 'across the border' into Bootle, where Breeze Hill splits off with Balliol Road. They must have stayed there for quite some time. Probably the last time that I visited there was when Uncle John Hodgson died in February 1990. After the burial service at Walton Church, Cliff and I went round to a 'chippy' in Hawthorne Road and picked up some fish 'n' chips – they must have been cooked the old-fashioned way in lard, they tasted absolutely delicious, just how you always remember them as a kid!

Cliff never seemed to have had too many girlfriends, although he did bring one such young lady, Alison, down to our place at Greatham one weekend. We still have a photo of her looking over our garden fence at some horses – one of them was called 'Corky' at the time, if memory serves me correctly. Cliff made such a fuss around that girl, plumping up cushions and almost cutting up her food for her, it was a bit embarrassing really. I suppose at one time he had been used to looking after the other four younger children (Sue, Pam, Russell and Steve) in earlier years,

Geoff and Cliff with Joyce and girls, 1971

and the habit had sort of stayed with him! There was one other girl that comes to mind, but I cannot remember her name. Joyce and I went to meet them for a drink at a pub out at Sefton – was it the *'Nag's Head'*?

Cliff finds a partner

I'm not too sure as to when Cliff hitched up with a widow by the name of Sylvia, but she already had a ready-made family and lived not too far away, again in Bootle. Anyway, he was obviously taken with her and they eventually got married. It was probably around that same time that Dad moved into sheltered accommodation, just off the roundabout at the junction of Linacre Lane and Northfield Road, while Cliff set up house with Sylvia in her own place. When Dad later became more infirm he moved again, into a nursing home further down towards the docks, which is where he was to end his days. Joyce and I did manage to visit him there on occasion, but by then he had become very frail and his mind had started to wander.

It must have come as a shock when Cliff was made redundant soon afterwards and it is then that the 'parting of the ways' came between the two of us. I don't think anyone of our family (apart from Cliff of course!) was particularly taken with Sylvia. To say that she is overpowering is an understatement! But it wasn't just that particular fact that got my back up. Cliff 'borrowed' some money from me, promising to pay it back once he had got a new job – I think there was supposed to be one 'in the pipeline' at the time. Looking back, the old saying *'neither a borrower nor a lender be'* should have warned me off. If Cliff had asked for the money purely as a gift, I don't suppose there'd have been a problem. But he'd said he'd pay me back and I took him at his word. *(I think that Mum had previously fallen for the same line of patter!)* The next thing I heard about him and Sylvia was that they were having a new fitted kitchen and an extension at the back of their house! Now, that costs money, so where was it coming from? The upshot of it all was that I got a bit pissed off to say the least and, although I got a very small proportion of money back, I have never seen the rest of it. In hindsight, I should be thankful that the 'hundreds' weren't 'thousands'!

When Dad finally died, in January 2000, it was inevitably Cliff and Sylvia who handled all the funeral arrangements. Our Sue and son Thomas had made a rapprochement with Joe a few years previously, which certainly brought a lot of joy into his later years. Apart from her own feelings, I know that Sue wanted Tom to feel that he 'belonged' to a family that stretched back a little longer in time and provided him with a grand-dad. So, along with Sue's husband Des, they had kept in close contact with Joe, right up until the time he died. *(We never did get those millions that Dad had stashed away in the States though, did we Sue?)* Joyce and I went up to the funeral and that was the last time we have had any contact with Cliff. It's sad really, as we always got on well together in earlier years, but these things happen in all families I suppose.

My cousin Paul, son of Dorothy and John Gripton, kindly also put in an appearance at his Uncle Joe's funeral. That brought back a few memories. When we three boys were all young, we met up with Paul and elder brother David on many an occasion, usually when visiting pubs run by Aunty Dorothy and Uncle John Gripton.

Geoff's story

I know that Geoff at one stage worked for *'MANWEB'* (Merseyside and North Wales Electricity Board), that was possibly his first job after leaving school, but you'd have to ask him on the veracity of that. I also know that, around 1969, Geoff eventually decided that there were better things in life than hanging around Walton for the rest of his days. I think that at the time he was working for *Littlewoods Pools* (or was it *Vernons*?), when he and another two guys 'upped sticks' and went off in search of adventure. They 'hitch-hiked' across Europe and India, finally making their way down to Singapore and catching a boat to Australia. I remember receiving at least one postcard from Geoff, when I think he went to stay at some rich Indian Nabob's house in the hills. But the details are scanty as far as I am concerned - again you'd have to ask Geoff for a detailed account of his once-in-a-lifetime trip!

I think I recall Geoff telling me that they got off the boat at Fremantle and it was in neighbouring Perth that he settled down to his new life. So it was probably quite a surprise to everyone when Geoff arrived back in England on March 26th 1971. It was rather unfortunate timing actually, as Joyce's Mum died at her home in Reading only two days afterwards. I seem to recall that Cliff also visited around that time, in fact it's likely that he came down to pick Geoff up and take him back to Liverpool. I have a photo of the pair of them sitting on our 'back step' that must have been taken during that visit. Geoff's reasoning at the time was that he just wanted to give the old country a final chance to hang on to him, during a six-month trial period. I guess he must have gone to live back at Milton Road and I think he went to work at *Nelson's* jam factory out at Aintree for the period. That brings to mind a story that Dad used to tell us, when we were much younger. Apparently, there was a guy working at *Hartley's*, another jam maker, whose job it was to 'make' the little wooden pips to put into raspberry jam! Thinking of the wartime conditions when that story got told, it may even have been true! But it also makes you wonder about the actual contents of those jars of 'raspberry' jam!

Anyway, *Nelson's* obviously couldn't hold a candle to the lure of sunny 'down under' beaches and a girl called Kerry – at least that's how I remember it. Despite Everton having just beaten Southampton by a score of eight goals to none, a few days later, on November 24th, Geoff again left for Australia, this time for good. I'm pretty sure that Joyce and I took him up to Heathrow for his flight, but when we turned around, there he was – gone! Geoff was never one for prolonged good-byes! My other memory of that visit to the airport is that we saw two reasonably famous people there that day. One was Marty Feldman, the now-departed pop-eyed comedian, and the other was Doctor Ian Paisley, who is still 'making waves' in Northern Irish politics to this very day, more than forty years later.

It was to be another six years before we saw Geoff again. By then, he had married Sheila Walker in Perth on August 2nd 1975, with Cliff having flown out to be their best man for the occasion. Then, during the summer of 1977, Sheila and Geoff, along with Sheila's sister Viv and her husband Kevin, all came over to England together on holiday. They actually stayed at our house for at least one night, while we were ourselves away on a summer holiday, down at Duporth Bay, near St Austell in Cornwall. Cliff had driven down to open our house to them – the instructions for turning off the gas supply still remain on the gas-tap in the garage to this day!

Sheila and Geoff later met up with us on Plymouth Hoe one day. Apart from seeing us, another reason for them being in Devon was that Sheila's family had once lived down there in Plymouth. Geoff treated us to a meal at what was then a *'Bernei Inn'*, a chain that has long since disappeared, though very popular at that time. I recall having a plate of fish 'n' chips, turning over one battered cod to find another parked beneath it! Perhaps that's how they went out of business! Anyway, a few days later, all four 'Aussies' then came over to the house at Duporth Bay on another visit. We were sharing that house with Eileen and Janet and all their children, so it was quite a get-together! In September, later in their holiday, Sheila and Geoff came to stay with us at home for a few days.

I'm not sure of Geoff's employment career during those early years in Western Australia, but he eventually ended up on the management side with the *Goodyear Tyres* dealership, covering all of Western and South Australia at one point, which continued right up until 2000. I remember that Geoff and Sheila once had a house in a suburb of Perth called Wanneroo – a very strange name to our English ears. Geoff brought Sheila across to England again in March 1979 and then during September 1984 while, in between those visits, Mum and Jack Whitley had not only holidayed out in Perth, but had also emigrated there in November 1982. But that was to be a short-lived affair for JCW, who died the following May. Joyce and I, along with Mum, finally made it out to Australia, via a two-night stopover in Singapore, in August 1985. We were able to stay with Sheila and Geoff at their then home, 11 Darling Street, South Perth, where they had had a self-contained extension built at the rear. We had a wonderful month out there, which is well chronicled elsewhere.

By Easter of 1989, not that we were fully aware of at the time, Geoff's marriage to Sheila had obviously run into some trouble. He came over to England on holiday all by himself – then did the very same thing the following year. That year, 1990, he actually joined us at our beloved Barmouth and had a few good walks out in the hills with Eileen, Mike and ourselves. But his marriage was now, to all intents, over with. Fortunately, he then went on to meet up with Sue, a lovely lady with two children, Sam and Sophie, and it has been an upward curve ever since. Happily, Geoff has since stayed on excellent terms with Sheila, which has enabled Joyce and myself to keep in touch also.

In December 1991, Joyce and I went off to Australia for a second time and were thus able to meet up with Sue and her two children, Sophie and Sam. Just after

Christmas, along with the rest of 'the family', we all stayed together for about a week at Yallingup, a seaside resort about two hours' drive south of Perth. In September of the following year, with Sue being a 'Kiwi' girl, she and Geoff flew across to New Zealand and 'tied the knot'. In April of 1994, the happy couple came over to England together, at the same time that Mum and Bill Walker were already staying at their 'exchange' house down at Nailsea in Somerset. Sue and Geoff joined us for a weekend at Colyton, East Devon, during their stay that year. It will always be remembered as the weekend that Everton saved themselves from being relegated, in the very last match of the season.

At the end of 1996, Joyce and I once again flew around the world to Australia, for our third visit. In retrospect now, it was also probably our final visit, as events seem to have transpired against another trip to 'the largest island on earth'. Geoff had organised another 'family get-together', this time in a large chalet-style house down at Margaret River – 'somewhere off the coast of Australia'. Lorraine and Steve were also there that year but, sadly, it was to be their last holiday as a couple, as they decided to go their separate ways a few months later. Towards the end of 1997, Dad's health was causing increasing concern, so Geoff made a flying visit to Liverpool to see him. I was able to dash up to Culcheth and catch up with him at Sue and Des's place.

Amazingly, however, Dad surprised everyone by regaining some strength and surviving for another two years, but Geoff wasn't to see him again. But later that same year, in September 2000, he and Sue arrived in England once again – to be picked up at the airport by none other than Sheila, who was staying with us at the time, as well as Mum! That arrangement came about by Mum coming over to attend my 60th (and her own 80th) birthday celebrations. Bill was unfortunately not well enough to travel, so Sheila had kindly agreed to be Mum's travelling companion. Then, in October, with Mum and Sheila having returned to Perth, Sheila and Geoff came back to Greatham for a few days. During that particular stay, we enjoyed a nice couple of days away in Dorset with them, visiting such places as Wimborne, Corfe Castle and Wareham - and staying in Swanage. At the time, Geoff was hoping to arrive back home to good news concerning a 'pay-off' package from *Goodyear*, upon which he could take early retirement from work.

'Land of the long white cloud'

Happily, things must have worked out well for him and, in July of 2001, Sue and Geoff were able to fulfill their dream of moving to New Zealand, Sue's old stamping ground. They are now firmly established at Omokoroa, on the North Island's Bay of

Plenty, where they have a lovely house that also functions as a 'bed and breakfast' facility. Whether or not Joyce and I will ever have the pleasure of visiting them out there remains to be seen. It's not that we don't want to, but Joyce blanches at the thought of once again sitting in an airplane for all those long hours. We'll just have to wait out on that one!

Early in 2005, Sue and Geoff set off on a long break, first looking up old friends in Perth for a week, then arriving in England on March 30th. Amazingly, they were going to be staying at the Lovell's house in Nailsea (Somerset) that Mum and Bill used on two previous occasions! They arranged their flight so that they eventually landed at Bristol, saving that long drive from Heathrow. We were away in Barmouth for the Easter holiday at the time, so it was two weeks before they caught up with us here in Greatham, just stopping over for a couple of nights. We enjoyed a visit to Midhurst with them, where we introduced them to that longish walk around the outside of town that Joyce and I had previously trekked on several occasions.

The following week, we reciprocated that visit by heading down to Nailsea. It was quite a surreal experience, staying there again after a break of some seven years. At the time, Lorraine and Phil were away in Chicago, settling the final details for their move there later in the year. It meant that we had Jake with us when we went down to Somerset, but he was no trouble. We had a nice long walk with Sue and Geoff, based upon *'The Battleaxes'* pub at a place called Wraxall – good job we didn't take Jake on that one, as it was quite a long trek – and he's no youngster! After we'd left Nailsea, Sue & Geoff were heading north for a few days, dropping in on Jackie & Steve in North Wales before moving on to Culcheth. They were able to stop at Mum's place, as she was then away in Spain on one of her petanque trips!

The Grippos came back for one flying visit to us in early May and we walked over Catherington Down with them. I'd been 'a few degrees under' at the time, with a suspected kidney stone, and although I managed the walk quite easily, it sure left me feeling tired the following day. We managed to get down to Nailsea again later in the month and enjoyed an afternoon's drive down to Street, despite there being quite a lot of rain about. We were most fortunate with the weather the next morning and had a good long walk based upon Tickenham, before spending the afternoon watching the Cup Final on television. Before heading home on the Sunday, we drove into Bristol and visited the magnificent Clifton Suspension Bridge – very impressive indeed. Sue and Geoff were due to leave for home just a few days later – never known a holiday go so fast! They left Blighty on the hottest day of the year and arrived home in New Zealand to cold, wet and windy conditions!

Towards the end of June 2006, there was quite a 'family reunion' taking place in Sydney! Lorraine & Phil had flown out there on holiday, while Sue & Geoff did the same. Sian & James were now living in Melbourne, so were able to fly in too, meeting up with Pam & Kate, over from Perth! Along with Sue's daughter, Sophie, the whole gang spent a couple of days together. This was commemorated by the arrival here of five postcards, all pictures of Sydney Harbour Bridge and all carrying exactly the same message! No need to ask who instigated that little occurrence!

Mark, Eileen, Joyce and Lorraine at rear; Susie, Sarah and Michelle at front

The Jones family

When I first met Joyce Ann Jones, at the Oxford Ballroom, she was still living at home with her family at 17 Queen's Cottages in central Reading, just a few minutes walk away from the town centre. The house was in a very similar situation to 5 Milton Road, where I'd been brought up myself. It too was set in a cul-de-sac and was basically a 'two-up, two-down', although there was an extra little bedroom at the back, just about big enough for a single bed, and situated above the kitchen. I've since been told that during the coldest of winter nights, the bed's occupant would be given the luxury of having an old Army greatcoat as an extra layer of insulation! *(The spider population was rather less appreciated!)* There was a back yard with a shed, some flowers and roses and an outdoor toilet – otherwise known as 'George'. Thus *"I'm just going to see George"* was a very familiar phrase! The front door led directly into a hallway, in which was usually parked Stan's bike! Stan was 'Dad' of course. He seemed to be a huge bloke, having done manual work all his life – and had apparently frightened the life out of many would-be suitors to his daughters over the years! His job at that time was as a fitter at *Reading Gasworks*, just along the River Kennet, which flowed along past the end of Queen's Cottages and out into the Thames, some distance away.

For some reason, that piece of water was referred to by the locals as 'the dannell', obviously a term used in Reading, much like the term 'jigger' was used in Liverpool to describe a back entry. I obviously picked up quite a few of these terms, which seemed strange to me at the time, but now have become familiar. For instance, if you're hungry in Reading, then you are 'gut-founded', while a wood-louse, known up in Liverpool as a 'leather-jacket', now became a 'cheese-log'! I also had to get used to unfamiliar food, such as parsnips – which I'd never even had before – and lardy cake, from *Meabys*, which Joyce swears to this day has never ever been equalled. *(Though she does agree with me that the one we had in Bridgnorth a few years ago took some beating!)*

Joyce's Mum had been christened Juliet Elizabeth, though she was always better known as June, and she mainly worked as an office cleaner for either a local school or doctor's surgery. She used to be accompanied by next-door-neighbour Mrs – or 'Aunty' - Alex (well, Alexander really, but it was almost always shortened to Alex). Mr (Ted) and Mrs Alex always looked very old, even when I first met them. They both 'smoked like chimneys', yet both lived on to a very ripe

Eileen, June, Janet and Joyce – the famous Jones girls

old age, I believe they were both well into their nineties by the time they shuffled off this mortal coil. They had one son named Reg, a daughter Pat, and an adopted son, Terry. Terry must have been of similar age to Joyce, as they both used to go swimming together as children. I remember that when Lorraine was still a baby, if Terry happened to come into No.17, she would always end up crying! He was killed in a car crash around Easter of 1965 - I seem to recall that the car had been stolen. Terry had 'got himself in with a bad lot', or that's how the story was told.

Although I wasn't around to witness it at first hand, the story goes that Mrs Alex had a washing-up bowl that was used for just about every household task, from washing up of course – to mixing pastry and dough! Apparently, one of 'the Jones girls' (Janet) used to go around to eat there quite often – and managed to survive. I expect that her face was often washed after eating with the dish-cloth! There's no doubt that the place was hardly an advertisement for health and hygiene. Some years later, Joyce and I were gifted one of those folding beds, whose frame was full of crawling things – goodness knows what the mattress must have contained, but we never got to find out as Stan helped me dump it in some woods!

With Queen's Cottages being a closed street (or *cul-de-sac* to use a posh term!), neighbours tended to know each other very well, and there were rather a lot of elderly people living there – I'd be pushed to remember many of their names, but I'm sure Joyce could name every one! *(Mrs Blunstone? Mrs Wyatt? Mr Lovelock? Mrs*

173

Tiger?) I do recall that on the opposite side of the 'back yard wall' was a Mrs Walker, who would often shout across to ask, *"Mrs Jones, could I just borrow a cup of flour?"* – or sugar, or tea, as the case may be. 'Borrow' of course was a euphemistic term for 'can you let me have?' After the old lady's death, the house was subsequently occupied by the O'Lauchlan family. Joy was a huge woman, with great rolls of fat around her, while he (Paddy?) was an Irish navvie of sorts – I recall she used to shout at him a lot and it was easy to hear across the space of the two back yards! Joyce and I actually rented the same place for a short term in later years – who can forget the kitchen cabinets of those days, with their drop-down leaf to form a sort of work area? No home should be without one! When we left, a couple we just knew as Pauline and Stewart moved in. I seem to recall that they had the one child but that Pauline died from a brain tumour just a few years later.

Both June and Stan were very down-to-earth people and would always make everyone feel welcome, even though the house must have been very crowded at times. There was one particular cupboard, next to the kitchen, which seemed to contain every sort of household article. Every time Mum opened the door, in my mind's eye I could see the whole lot sliding out onto the floor, although as far as I remember, it never actually happened. *(In retrospect, the presence of so many visitors, albeit them being 'family', must have created quite a pressure on Mum, she could hardly have had much time to herself really.)* Sunday dinner in those days, as it was across the rest of the nation, was a traditional occasion not to be missed. Mum Jones was undoubtedly a good cook when it came to Sunday dinners, a full roast of meat, along with Yorkshire puddings, roast potatoes, vegetables and rich gravy. *(That's when I was introduced to 'parsnips' – which Stan always swore would put 'lead in your pencil'!)* Stan used to be sent to 'do the messages' (shopping!) on a Saturday morning, when he would venture up into the town centre, where I believe *David Greig's*, on the corner of St Mary's Butts, was the favourite trading outpost! I do know that he liked his large wedge of extra-strong matured Canadian cheddar too – always went down well with *Jacob's* cream crackers

However, my one over-riding memory of No.17 was the television in the corner – one of those rented *(Robinson's Rentals?)* black and white sets that sat on four spindly legs, very much a child of the sixties! Reception was a bit of a gamble in those days, and you would have to fiddle around with the horizontal and vertical hold buttons quite a lot, before getting a reasonable picture! In those days of course there was no distraction from the 'goggle box' - it was either BBC or ITV, take it or leave it! Stan used to love his Westerns on the box, *'Rawhide', 'Bonanza'* and *'Gun Law'*

174

spring to mind. Saturday nights was always light entertainment, with programmes like *'Saturday Night at the London Palladium'*. Although I seem to recall that June didn't like Stan watching when the *Tiller Girls* came on with their high-kicking dance routines!

Other 'TV' occasions that were pretty memorable include the football World Cup Final in the summer of 1966. I'd been up to Wembley earlier that year, to see Everton win the FA Cup and we were still in Army quarters at Oakley Road, Bordon. June and Stan must have been down visiting, as we watched England's great victory over what was then still West Germany. Then came the American astronauts, landing on the Moon back in 1969. We must have been up in Reading that weekend, as I distinctly remember watching Neil Armstrong's 'small step for man' in the corner of the living room by the window. I remember one early morning, it must have been a Sunday and probably around 1970, when we set off from Greatham to drive down to Bournemouth for the day. I think Eileen, Janet and families were down there, staying in a flat somewhere, while June and Stan must have been close by in another flat. My memory of the day is basically confined to, firstly, having trouble in locating them all then, secondly, sitting on the beach, near the pier, in deckchairs! Thinking back now, it all seems like a different world altogether.

The Jones girls

Joyce was the youngest of four lovely girls. In fact, when I met her she'd only just celebrated her sixteenth birthday (January 16th 1961). I often heard the story of the patience required by Stan, as he tried to get his daughters ready to go out. It's probably just as well that there was a ten-year gap between the eldest and youngest, dating from 1935 until Joyce's arrival early in 1945. So, by early 1961, the eldest of the sisters, 'really' named June (unlike her Mum!) was already married and living away from home, over at Woodley. If memory serves me correctly, of the other two girls, Janet and Eileen, the latter was still living at home and Janet just across the road, in 10 Queen's Cottages, in a rented house.

As I said, June was definitely married - to Wack – and still is! Where he got the nickname from, I don't really know, but he's been stuck with it for a long time now and it doesn't seem to bother him! As mentioned, they had a home at Woodley, in Fawcett Crescent, but they later moved to the other side of town at Tilehurst, where they have stayed now, at 28 Church End Lane, for the best part of forty years. Their son Kevin was born in 1961 and daughter Karen came along in 1964. From what I remember, Karen's was a difficult birth and it was touch and go for June for a while. I guess they moved house between those two years, I certainly stayed at their house in Woodley on the night before my wedding in August 1962. My 'stag night' was held in the pubs of Reading, after which we went for a Chinese meal at an upstairs restaurant in the town centre. Which is where we bumped into Joyce and her hen-night companions! *(Remember falling over in the ladies' Joyce – and getting a damp spot on your pale green skirt?)*

I'm not too sure as to when Jan married Brian Robbins, but it was certainly either just before or during my early years of 'keeping up with the Jones's'. I know that they lived for a while at a house just about opposite Stan and June in Queen's Cottages. Brian had one of those three-wheeler 'bubble-cars', a *'Heinkel'* I think, as well as a scooter. I remember him giving me a lift back to Arborfield one night on the scooter and he told me how lucky I was, having snared one of 'the Jones girls'. Rather strange that, as it wasn't too long after he married Jan that he began an affair with another Janet! After they had married, they had bought a house in Woodley, at Coleman's Moor Lane – Joyce and I later lived there for a while, as an Army hiring.

The runaways

Being fairly close by to June and Wack, I guess they used to hang around together. Well, this 'other Janet' lived next door to June and was a bit of a man-eater! Brian obviously didn't mind, as he went off with her and left 'our' Jan to get on with her own life. When Brian 'did a runner', there were some concerns as to the ownership of the house. Anyway, a posse was suddenly arranged to head Brian and this other Jan off at the pass! I was found out that the couple had moved down to Bristol and had arranged to have letters, pay packets etc delivered to a Post Office. Eileen accompanied 'our' Jan down there and they waited in a café across the road to the PO. Amazingly, they spotted the runaway couple and Brian was probably so shocked to have been caught up with, that he immediately signed a document that Eileen had written, ensuring that our Jan was indeed left as owner of the house in Woodley.

Fortunately, there were no children involved and Jan later met Roy Rockett, when they both worked together at a place just along the river from Queen's Cottages – *'Greenslades'*, I think it was called. Roy went off to try his luck in South Africa (SA) and Jan joined him out there – a very brave move in those days I guess. An old photograph shows Jan walking across the runway to board her plane at what is now Heathrow – it's certainly changed since then! I think she and Roy lived in both Cape Town and Johannesburg for a while, they certainly got married out in SA, in November 1964. Their two daughters, Colette and Lisa, arrived on the scene in 1965 and 1968 respectively, in fact Colette was born out there in SA.

Eileen was 'going out with' Michael – or Mike or Mick, take your pick! – when I first met Joyce and he kindly performed the duties of our 'best man' when we got married in August 1962. It was to be the following year that they took their own vows, at St Giles' Church in Reading, the same as us. They'd already bought their own house in Woodcote Way, Caversham, are still living there now, and it's hard to imagine a happier couple. They have three children – and a hell of a lot of grandchildren – eight at the last count! Their son Mark was born in 1965, while daughters Sarah and Suzanne joined the family in 1967, then 1970.

I hardly ever got to meet up with any of the parents of either Wack or Roy. I think that their fathers were already deceased by the time I came onto the scene and I recall only seeing their mothers on very rare occasions. Mike's parents lived in York Road, just off Caversham Road in Reading – I can remember going there for a 'calming drink' just prior to going to my wedding! Bill Gillard had worked on the railways for many years and liked to take a pint in his local – was it *'The Temperance'*? – just along the road. (Mike later confirmed to me that it was actually *'The Moderation'*.) Mike's Mum suffered terribly with arthritis, but was a really friendly soul. Both Mr and Mrs Gillard seemed a fair bit older than my own parents, with Mike about six years older than me anyway. Both Mike and Wack had served their country during the days of National Service, with the Royal Berkshire Regiment. They had both been in Cyprus during the battles with Greek Cypriots fighting their war of independence from the remnants of the British Empire.

I only seem to remember one other relative in any detail and that is Mike's sister Roslyn – or Ros. She was married to a chap called John and they eventually moved up as far as Cumbria, settling in a place called Dalston, just south of Carlisle. I remember visiting their lovely house just the once, it must have been in 1987, as we were on holiday at Ambleside that year, along with the Gillards and Rocketts, and drove up to Dalston one day. I know that Ros had a 'granny flat' on her property, which I think both her parents lived in towards the end of their days. Mike's Dad was the first to die and it was only about six months afterwards that news came through that Mrs Gillard was very ill too and not likely to survive much longer. It must have been arranged that Eileen and Mike would go up to Cumbria and we were up in Caversham, ready to look after the children. Eileen and Mike had only just left home when we had a telephone call to say that Mike's Mum had died, so there was no need for their journey! I remember getting into the old *Capri* and belting up the road after them, catching up with them just outside Wallingford – fast car that *Capri,* when you put your foot down!

Ros and John have children, but I can't say that I know a lot about them, except for the one daughter, Jill, who studied music down at Chichester. We once met up with her down at the Festival Theatre, where she was part of the youth orchestra, playing the accompaniment to the show *'Chicago'* – before it became the famous show/film/DVD that it has since become. It was only earlier this year (2004) that John died, although I think I'm right in saying that he had been suffering in a few different ways in previous years.

Ancestors and relatives

There were a fair number of Jones' (or perhaps I should say Lailey?) relatives living in the Reading area, though all of them were on June's (Mum's) side of the family. Stan had a rather more awkward childhood, not knowing his father and being sort of 'fostered' as far as I can make out. He was born in 1910 and, on his birth certificate, his mother's name is shown as 'Elisabeth Jones, formerly Goodman', but the space reserved for 'father's name' is annoyingly blank. June's maiden name was Lailey and her birth certificate shows her mother's name as 'Rosetta Maud Lailey, formerly Peppiett'. Mum's birth certificate also shows her being born at 46 Francis Street in Reading and when she and Stan were married in 1933, both of them are shown as resident at that same address. It is believed that old 'Grandfather' Lailey came from the Wallingford area, just a few miles north of Reading, while 'Granny' is thought to have originally hailed from London, but moved down to Wallingford into 'domestic service'. (How often that term crops up on old documents!) With a name like 'Peppiett', it is quite possible that there was a Continental connection in the past, possible French or Spanish. Rumour has it that someone in the old lady's family used to buy meat-pies from Todd's pie-shop – and we all know the story of Sweeney Todd, the demon barber, and what is supposed to have gone into his famous pies! Another story was that a long-distant relative had put his signature on the nation's banknotes, being the Governor of the Bank of England. While there has also been a story told that there was a family relationship with Sir Edward Moseley, famous Nazi sympathiser of pre-war days! Who knows?

Mum had three sisters, Violet, Vera and May, who I got to know on an occasional basis. In fact May used to visit Queen's Cottages on virtually a weekly basis, along with her daughter Edna, who was sadly a *Down's Syndrome* child. I say 'child', but in fact she was I'm sure of a similar age to perhaps Janet and June. Vera was married to Frank and they had two children, Anne and Tony, who were of course cousins to 'the Jones girls'. Violet was married to Walter – or Wally, as he was better known to one and all. They had two sons, providing the girls with two more cousins, Roy and

178

Kenny. I'm pretty sure that I must have attended a couple of weddings from that list, probably those of Kenny (to Lavinia?) and Tony – to Jenny. I also vaguely recall that June had a brother called Romeo. *(If you recall that 'June' was really 'Juliet', then there seems to have been a Shakespearean tendency in the family!)*

As with all families, there are always the 'legends'! Wally was the not-so-phantom farter by all accounts! He used to dress up as Santa Claus at Christmas time, but all the kids knew exactly who he was from the rumbles and smells that came their way! And even nowadays, if someone is being a bit secretive in eating say sweets or chocolate, they are quickly compared to 'Aunty Violet'. It is told that whenever she had some sweets, rather than share them with others, she would slink off to the toilet and eat them all to herself! *"You're just like Aunty Violet, you are!"* Handed-down tales revealed that all the cousins were apparently a close-knit lot when they were still children. *(Now of course they hardly ever see each other, but that's common to all families as we get older.)* Joyce talks of going to her Gran's house in Francis Street for Christmas, where the kids were never allowed to sit with the elders. They would be sat in a room apart, using planks of wood suspended across dining chairs to make the extra seating required. No need to announce that the older kids, Roy and June I think, got the best of the grub – and poor Edna probably fobbed off with the worst! Joyce also recalls that when Eileen was really small, she would be put to sleep in one of the drawers from a chest-of-drawers. One favourite tale that Joyce often tells is of going down to Barry Island (Glamorgan, South Wales) in Uncle Frank's car. The car in question would have been one of those old *Ford Prefects* or some such like, Joyce and Eileen have both described it as a 'biscuit tin on wheels'. Despite that, the number of adults and children crammed into the biscuit tin seems to grow larger each time the tale is told – was it eighteen at the last count?

A long courtship!

When I first started 'courting' Joyce and going back to her house, we usually had the use of the front room, which was pretty tiny. At the very beginning, it wasn't unusual for the door to be knocked, with one of the family having to *"put a shilling in the meter"*. Well, that's true of course, as the gas meter was in a corner cupboard, but I couldn't help but think that it was an excuse to be weighed up as a suitable candidate for Joyce's attention! I must have passed muster, thank goodness! As already explained, I was to fly off to Germany after only a few weeks of knowing Joyce, and I didn't get back to England until my first leave, in the August of 1961. Having already 'popped the question' to Joyce – ah, romantic days! – I was grateful to be offered somewhere to sleep during my leave. That was on the sofa in the front room! I was to spend my following leave periods at the same venue, right up until we married at St Giles' Church, Reading, in August the following year. Totalling things up, I must have spent just fourteen weeks with Joyce before getting married!

It was generally accepted with the Jones's that Friday was 'fish day'. So when I was 'at home', I usually got the task of walking up Queen's Road to the fish'n'chip shop. I can remember thinking what a scruffy little chap he was, the guy who ran the chippy, but I can't fault the produce! On Sundays, Mum Jones always cooked the traditional Sunday roast – and she was damn good at it too. When I say that her cooking was as good as I remember my own Mum's and grandmother's, then that's a big compliment!

Joyce and I were eventually to rent Jan's house at Coleman's Moor Lane in Woodley, while I was on an Army course at Arborfield. This meant that Joyce could quite easily hop on a bus for the journey 'into town', so she was able to pop in at No.17 most days. Dad was usually able to get home from the gasworks for his lunch, riding that trusty old bike of his, with the inevitable 'roll-up' hanging out of the corner of his mouth! A packet of *Rizla* fag-papers and a tin of *Old Holborn* tobacco would provide the smoking material. Come to think of it, there was hardly ever an occasion when one or another of the girls wasn't visiting, the house always seemed pretty full to me! We were up at Woodley when Lorraine was born, at Wokingham, in July 1963. I was still without a car in those days, although I did have a 'funky moped'! But what comes to mind is the bus ride between Woodley and the town centre, with Lorraine balanced on our knees in her carry-cot – that must have gone on for quite a time.

When I later got posted down to Bordon, in May 1964, trips to Queen's Cottages didn't cease, they just became slightly more complicated – and longer! We first had to catch 'the green bus' *(Aldershot Traction Services?)* from Bordon to the bus-station in Aldershot. There we would change to 'the red bus' *(Thames Valley* I think) for the longer trip via Fleet, Hartley Wintney, Bramshill and Riseley to Reading. The whole affair would take around two hours and, of course, there was always the return journey to look forward to! Journeys between Bordon and Reading were not just confined to the Griptons of course. I don't think Stan ever passed a full driving test, but he did have a licence for two-wheeled vehicles. He thus bought a scooter – either a *'Lambretta'* or a *'Vespa'* – and he and June would often take a spin down into Hampshire to see us for a few hours. No doubt about it, Stan was no 'Rocker', he was always a 'Mod'!

Later, on the strength of his two-wheel licence, he was able to buy one of those three-wheeled *Reliant Robins*, a bit like the one owned by 'Del-boy' in *'Only fools and horses'*! It was the apple of his eye, though we all worried that one day he would turn it over, they were the most unstable of beasts. I think I'm right in saying that he actually had two such vehicles, one after the other of course. The first one was bright yellow and we all called it 'Buttercup'. After Stan's death some years later, Joyce and I actually had the use of the second one, a dark blue colour, for a few short months.

Other members of the family also came to visit us at Bordon. I recall one weekend we had a gang down, and we all went down to Hayling Island for the day – I was on the back of Mike's motor-cycle if I remember correctly, either a *'James'* or an

Kevin and Lorraine (with Joyce), Hayling Island

'AJS'. Wack drove down in his *Hillman Minx*, how many he crammed into it I hate to hazard a guess! I do know that it turned to rain, because we still have a photo of Kevin and Lorraine, sat on the merry-go-round, complete with plastic macs! When Michelle was born, at 'The Grange' in Liss, in February 1966, Mike rode his motorbike down in the pouring rain one night, and the matron almost refused to let him in, as he looked so bedraggled! The reason he was on his own was that Eileen was already down at our place – 'looking after' Lorraine and myself. We always have a laugh over that, because it was more like me looking after her!

Christmas with the Gillards

For a number of years, it became traditional for us (that's Joyce, the girls and me) to spend Christmas Day up at Eileen's house in Woodcote Way. The morning would be spent at one or other of the neighbours' houses in the street, sort of rotating on an annual basis. There were Sue and Maurice next door, with son David and daughter Teresa; the Cousineau family just a few doors up, that was Colleen, Alan and brood; Judy and John with their adopted family; or Jackie and Mike, with children Michelle, Steven and Duncan. Fairly copious amounts of drinks were consumed on occasions, as I remember, making it difficult to stay awake after dinner! I can't remember just how many of us sat down together at dinner every year, but it probably varied somewhat. If you count the Gillards and Griptons at the very least, that added up to nine – and I know that Jan and Roy would be there too some years. Mike would provide some afternoon or early evening entertainment by getting out his projector and showing some old slides on the front-room wall.

As detailed elsewhere, over the years the whole family – where possible – used to get together on holidays, especially when all the children were young. Nowadays of course, they're all grown up, most of them with kids of their own, so they don't get to meet each other too often. I suppose it's the same with all families. All of the most recent family get-togethers must have taken place at the inevitable raft of weddings that took place over the years, which provided some memorable occasions. It's a shame, but neither June nor Stan Jones lived long enough to see any of their grandchildren married. Just as sad, of course, is that not many of their grandchildren can have any clear memories of them either. When June died in 1971, she had been ill with cancer for quite some time before that, having had an operation about eighteen months previously. But even so, her health deteriorated very rapidly towards the end and it was a great shock to all the girls. Joyce took it particularly badly, it took a lot out of her. Amazingly, she was taking her driving test around that time and had so much on her mind that she didn't have time to worry about the test, sailing through at the first attempt. She was smoking far too much and lost a lot of weight, so it was even harder when Stan died only three years later.

In between time, he had actually got married again, to Doris – who, like me, was born and lived in Walton, Liverpool! *(In fact she had once lived in Hahneman Road, just a few hundred yards down Stuart Road from Milton Road – small world eh?)* They married at Reading Register Office on June 17th 1972. Stan had just been down with Doris to visit us at Greatham one weekend, in July 1974, and went off home feeling a bit 'under the weather'. Joyce must have had a bad feeling about that because I remember her phoning Eileen to ask her to keep a check on him. But a fast heart attack hit Stan and he died only a day or so later. Neither June nor Stan had been a great age by today's standards, so those few years proved very sad indeed.

An expanding family

Over the years that followed, all of the cousins continued to grow up at what seemed a remarkable rate and of course the family was able to get together at one wedding after another! Looking in my 'diary of events', the order of weddings went like this: Kevin, Lorraine, Colette, Karen, Lisa, Mark, Sarah, Michelle and Susie – from 1986 right through until 1994. Unfortunately, as if to fit in with the statistics of the day, regarding unsuccessful marriages, each one of the four separate families was to suffer one separation too. But there was always the happiness of a continual arrival of new grandchildren, and these came along as follows: Natasha, Rebecca, Abigail, Lucy, Owen, Thomas, Imogen, Daisy, Jacob, Calum, Brogan, Erin, Samuel, Joshua, Neve, Amber and Fern! All seventeen births were spread over the period between 1987 and 2000, quite an achievement! And of course the Gold Medal must go to Ei and Mike, whose three children have, between them, contributed an octet of grandchildren to the total! Keeps them busy too I'm reliably informed!

Even now, in 2004, it seems only a fleeting moment ago that we attended the first wedding of the series, that of Sonia and Kevin, at Tilehurst in July 1986. Sadly, that union was probably the first one to suffer too, and it has been many a year since the couple split up. From what we know, Sonia went on to re-marry and provide a stepfather to daughters Natasha and Abigail. It still came as quite a shock when June rang us one evening to inform us of the sad news that Sonia had died just a few days previously. Sonia had long suffered from diabetes, but it is not yet known if that contributed to her demise. We all hope that the two girls can be happy once again after the sadness of two tragic events in their short lives.

It is not all gloom and doom on that side though. After Sonia's death, the two girls decided that they were happy to stay under the care of their stepfather – and Kevin was eager to see them settled in this way. On Saturday 11th December 2004, Kevin married again, to his long-term girlfriend, Emma. That ceremony took place in Guildford and the couple has now settled in Woking. I think I must be correct in saying that Kevin has been working for HM Customs and Excise for all of his career so far, which seems to have been most successful. In the early days, he was away from home a lot and has told us tales of dashing about in fast cars, hot on the trail of drugs-runners and other such miscreants. Karen has been married to Graham Hughes since December 1988 and they have gone on to produce two daughters, Rebecca and Lucy, and a son Jacob. As far as I know, Graham has worked for the Post Office all of that time. The family still live in Tilehurst, having moved from their first home, which was 'just around the corner' to June and Wack. They are still not that far away though and June finds her hands full on many an occasion!

Moving swiftly across to the Gillard clan, Mark seemed to have set his early sights on being a photographer, but later went into the garden landscape business with an old pal, probably from school. He married Corinna Gay in August 1991 and they now have two daughters, Erin and Neve. Corinna has since returned to her career in teaching. They still live in Reading, over in Earley. Sarah married Stephen in July 1992 and they went on to have three children in rapid succession between 1994 and 1997. Daisy and Brogan are the two girls, with Joshua being both the son and youngest child. Unfortunately, even these three happy events didn't prevent their marriage breaking up and Sarah now lives, with the children, not far away from us in Alton. As I re-scan this, early in 2007, she has a new partner in her life, a chap called Andy, and they are presently looking forward to purchasing a house together. Meanwhile, the three children are 'shared' between Sarah and Stephen on a regular basis – an unusual arrangement, but one that seems to suit all concerned as far as I know.

Susie is another triple-header! She married Nick Pocock at Goring-on-Thames in October 1994 and they managed to break the trend by having a boy first! Samuel now has two younger sisters in Amber and Fern. Nick used to work with his father, but now spends his time chasing electrical contracts all over the place. He's obviously been very successful at it too, they have recently converted two side-by-side bungalows into 'Pocock Palace', on the outskirts of Reading. Also, much to the benefit of such as ourselves, they purchased the bungalow down in Padstow, which has already provided us with many happy holiday moments.

For the final lap, I change over to the Rockett girls! Colette got married to Mark Gifford in June 1987 and they have two children, son Owen and daughter Imogen. They used to live just the other side of Basingstoke and we did manage to visit them there on one occasion. They have since moved down near Calne in Wiltshire – we occasionally meet up with them when we go down to Swansea for the New Year at Jan's cottage. Mark was a policeman at one time, but has been employed in a variety of jobs over recent years – the last we heard, he was interested in thermal heating from under the ground! Lisa married Martin Howard on a hot summer's day in 1989, but sadly the union didn't last too long as Martin sought pastures new. In the last few years, Lisa has been suffering with Multiple Sclerosis (MS), but appears to be managing her life very well now after early complications. In the summers of recent years, we have joined in sponsored walks on behalf of the *Reading MS Society*, along with Jan & Roy of course, plus Eileen & Mike in the main. Lisa divorced Martin and eventually had a new 'chap', Gary, in her life.

After Stan died in 1974, Doris stayed on at Queen's Cottages for some time, but eventually sold up and moved back 'up north' – in fact to Wallasey, Merseyside. Joyce and I visited her just the once up there, I think she was sharing a house with her daughter Hazel. The family eventually moved down to Shropshire, and we dropped in there a few years later, to the little village of Lydbury North, not too far from Ludlow. We regularly pass that way on our Easter trip to Barmouth, so it was 'on route'. Doris died sometime in the 1990s and we haven't heard from Hazel for ages now, we assume that she may have died too, as she had suffered from breast cancer. Ten years ago (as

I write!), in January 1995, all eight of us (that's June & Wack, Jan & Roy, Ei & Mike and Joyce and myself) met up for a meal at *'The Crown'* pub out at Playhatch, on the occasion of Wack's 60th birthday. Quite a milestone of course, but one that has since been overtaken by all the rest of us bar one! Now, in January 2005, it is Joyce's turn to reach that same milestone - hard to believe that 'the baby' of the family is sixty years of age! In the event, we shall all be meeting up again, at exactly the same venue, to celebrate the fact that we have all survived so far! Wack has recently passed into his seventy-first year, having survived a cancer scare and operation back in the summer of 1992. We hope, of course, that there are still a few celebrations ahead of us too!

I have to backtrack a little here and make a couple of additions to the family tree! Since Kevin re-married towards the end of 2004, his new wife Emma has given birth to two children, a son Matthew in 2005 and the latest edition, daughter Amye in August 2006. Considering that Kevin was born in 1961, that means that he started his 'second' family at the ripe old age of forty-four years! We take our hats off to him.

Mumbles retreat

When Jan and Roy bought number 3 Village Lane, down at Mumbles on the beautiful Gower Peninsula in South Wales, it became the focal point for many happy times. As detailed elsewhere, the other girls have used it consistently around the end of October each year for a 'girls only' holiday. New Year has also proved a popular visiting time, when Jan and Roy have invited Joyce and myself, with Eileen and Mike, down there for a few days. It gets a bit crowded of course, but Joyce and I generally take blow-up beds down with us, as we've become used to sleeping on them at Michelle's! We have enjoyed seeing in the New Year at Mumbles on quite a few occasions now, mostly at local hotels, which have put on an evening's repast and 'disco'. I think 2006 was the first time that we actually stayed 'at home', only venturing down to the promenade to catch the fireworks going off all around Swansea Bay. That trip was memorable due to the fact that Jan had accidentally scalded her foot, whilst carrying tea and biscuits upstairs. This actually happened before Christmas and Jan had to attend the local hospital, which fortunately had a burns unit – one of the few around the country. That meant that she had to stay at Mumbles but, by the time we all got down there for New Year, the burn had mostly cleared. But Jan was still advised to use a fold-up wheelchair to protect her foot, so we all took turns in pushing her around!

As documented elsewhere, early 2006 saw us down at Padstow with Ei & Mike. We'd only been down there one day, when Eileen woke up, complaining of what appeared to be a touch if sciatica. It failed to stop her from joining us on our normal round of trips and walks. We also had their company at Barmouth over Easter, and

Ei was still in some discomfort, but also managing to get around with us as usual. She continued to have the problem 'on and off', but came down to stop with us for a couple of days in early May. It was after getting home after that visit that her 'sciatica' really started to play up – and she has been laid up with it for the last four weeks or so. I think 'a scan' is now on the cards, let's hope she's suffered no permanent damage.

It is good to be able to report that, by early September that same year, Eileen appeared to have shaken off her earlier 'sciatic' problems. Just after my ex-Arborfield 50th anniversary reunion at Sonning Common, Joyce and I then popped over to Caversham for a few hours. Mike drove us all up to Wallingford, where we spent a couple of hours, including a walk along the river. Then, just a few days later, Eileen came down to see us at home – and was quite happy in walking along Southsea promenade with us, with no obvious problems. The following day we drove down to Emsworth and, after traversing the harbour, we then walked all along the coastal path to Langstone and then back via Warblington, a two-hour round trip. We are planning to head down to Padstow again later in the month, so hopefully there will be no re-occurrence of the problem.

Sad news about Lisa

On a much sadder note, Lisa's condition has deteriorated rapidly these past few months. Jan & Roy took her to see a specialist in mid-June and the prognosis is not very good at all. Despite still having her own house and a 'boyfriend' (Gary), Lisa has become increasingly dependent upon her parents and really cannot now look after herself in any real sense. Only a couple of weeks ago, she was fit enough to start phoning the whole family, leaving a message on our answering service, which was really a cry for help. I'm pretty sure then that Lisa knew what she was facing and was just desperate to let everyone know that she was still 'a person'. Sadly, that no longer seems the case as her MS takes an increasingly downward spiral.

Just a couple of weeks after writing the above, Jan & Roy have had to move Lisa back in with them, as she is really now incapable of looking after herself. It is very sad that, due no doubt to her deteriorating mental condition, she blames Jan & Roy for all her problems, accusing them of locking her up and taking away her freedom. It really is a horrible situation for them and it looks, sadly, that Lisa will have to be put into care at some time soon – it is certainly all too much for Jan & Roy, who must be taking a terrible mental battering.

By mid-July 2006, Lisa had voluntarily moved 'into care' at a psychiatric unit at Prospect Park Hospital in Reading. Joyce and I accompanied Eileen on a visit and, despite the circumstances, I feel that Lisa enjoyed seeing us, even though her trains of thought seemed pretty illogical at times. At the time, Jan & Roy had taken the opportunity to have a well-deserved weekend at the Mumbles, but of course they now all face an uncertain future that doesn't appear to have any satisfactory conclusion to look forward to. That same afternoon, we took Eileen over to visit Susie and her children, aware that Sarah and her three would also be present, so a nice chance to catch up with them all. Unfortunately, our arrival coincided with Susie's little dog having managed to escape down the adjacent footpath and directly under the wheels of a passing car! Needless to say, when the children were all told about it, there was lots of sobbing all round, so we three decided to beat a hasty and tactical retreat!

July 2006 saw us staying at Susie's bungalow in Padstow again, having missed out the previous year. About halfway through our second week there, we were delighted to meet up with Karen and Graham, along with Lucy and Jacob, who had arrived to stay at our 'old' abode – Sue and Maurice's bungalow! It must have been years since Joyce and Michelle had seen them all, although I'd actually bumped into Karen myself fairly recently. The 'reunion' was completed on the Friday, when June and Wack arrived with Karen's other daughter, Rebecca – and haven't the kids all grown up now!

Towards the end of September, we once again ventured down to Padstow, meeting up with Eileen & Mike, who had arrived the previous day. Despite some changeable weather, it stayed pretty warm and we managed to get out on a few walks. This included the 'round trip' up to Little Petherick, as the Gillards finally showed us the proper path on the other side of the creek – avoiding the mud that Joyce once dragged me through! We also enjoyed a visit to the *Eden Project*, over near St Austell, where an old clay quarry has been converted into a visitor centre that includes two huge 'biomes' that contain plant-life from the humid tropical zone and the temperate desert zone. We spent quite a long time exploring what are, in effect, two very large greenhouses!

Around the end of October, with Lisa now living back 'at home' – that's with Jan & Roy – J&R went off on a much-needed holiday to South Africa with June & Wack. Fortunately, they had been able to obtain residence for Lisa at a respite home called *'Brambles'*, which was down near Gatwick Airport in a little place called Horley. Eileen & Mike were very good, visiting Lisa there on a few occasions. Eileen also took the opportunity to visit us for a few days and we were able to visit Lisa with her over the final weekend while J&R were still away. Lisa was in pretty good spirits and one could tell that the stimulus of having lots to do, along with plenty of company from other residents, had cheered her up no end. It is to be hoped that some 'day care' can be arranged nearer to home, where Lisa can get similar company – and give her parents some leisure time of their own.

By July 2007, Lisa's condition was certainly getting worse and Jan & Roy must have been exhausted from looking after her on a full-time basis. The managed to find a holiday at reasonable cost and went off to Costa Rica – again accompanied by June & Wack. Once more, Lisa was able to spend a couple of weeks at *Brambles*, and again we took Eileen over there with us. By this time, Lisa was in her wheelchair just about permanently and there certainly seemed to be a 'loss of spark' when we compared her to our previous visit there. Upon J&R's return from holiday, talk turned into them having their garage converted into a permanent room for Lisa, as she had by then gone into hospital again, suffering from some infection. It wasn't too long afterwards that the decision was made to move Lisa into a permanent care home and, the next time we went to see her, this was at Beacher Hall in Reading. Jan & Roy had found it increasingly difficult to handle both Lisa and her situation – particularly when Roy had to go into hospital himself in October, this for a knee replacement operation.

Meanwhile, on a happier note!

Towards the end of October that year, Joyce and I drove down to Lynton and Lynmouth, on the north Devon coast, to join the Gillard family, on the happy occasion of Sarah's marriage to Andy Joule. The couple had been 'living together' for some time, over in Alton, and the fact that Andy gets on so well with Daisy, Brogan and Josh made marriage inevitable. We were fortunate enough to attend the wedding in Lynton Town Hall, as well as spending a few happy hours with Eileen, Mike and their now newly extended family! After the wedding service, Andy's father – another Mike – read out the following extract from an Irish poem, stripped of its religious overtones – but very fitting for the occasion:

May you live as long as you want, and never want as long as you live.
Always remember to forget the things that made you sad,
But never forget to remember the things that made you glad.
Always remember to forget the friends that proved untrue,
But never forget to remember those that have stuck by you.
Always remember to forget the troubles that passed away,
But never forget to remember the blessings that come each day.
May the saddest day of your future be no worse than the happiest day of your past;
May the roof above you never fall in and may the friends gathered below it never fall out.
May you have warm words on a cold evening, a full moon on a dark night,
And the road be downhill all the way to your door.
May you live to be a hundred years – with one extra year to repent!

May you live as long as you want, and never want as long as you live.

Back to the future?

Towards the end of 2004, we went up to spend a day at Caversham, with Eileen and Mike. It was only a couple of weeks before they were due to go on holiday with Jan and Roy – off to South Africa for three weeks or so. No doubt that revived many old memories for the Rocketts, of when they got married out in that country some forty years previously. Ei & Mike took us up to the little town of Wallingford for a couple of hours, where we had a walk around and visited the ruins of the castle, about which I had no previous knowledge. It was also during that trip that it came to light that, according to Eileen, the Jones girls' granddad, old Mr Lailey, may have been resident at Wallingford in his younger years, possibly working as a farm labourer. It is also likely that his bride-to-be had moved down from London to take up a post in service at a local 'big house'. Quite amazingly, it turned out that none of the Jones girls even knew their granddad's Christian name! However, Ei & Mike had obtained the address of someone who may have been able to help on family research around Wallingford and I later contacted the gentleman, David Beasley, who lived at Crowmarsh Gifford. Unfortunately, the information gleaned didn't shed too much light on the Lailey family history, but I was later able to obtain a copy of the wedding certificate for June and Stan from the General Record Office in Southport.

Their marriage took place at St Giles Church in Reading in 1933 – and names June's father as George Lailey. It was also stated that at the time he (George) was 'a pensioner', so he must have already been of fairly advanced (at least sixty-five?) years in 1933. Having checked the International Genealogy Index since then, I came across reference to a George Lailey, born at Bucklebury, Berks, in 1850. This gentleman, if he had survived that long, would thus have been aged 83 in 1933. Looking at an old photograph, which appears to have been taken just after that 1933 wedding, the 'father of the bride' would certainly appear to have been of similar age – and Joyce always reckoned that her granddad was 'getting on a bit'.

Another reference to a George Lailey shows a wedding at Chievely, Berks, on November 17 1890 - though I cannot trace a Peppiett entry on the same date. On the same 1933 wedding certificate mentioned above, Stan's father was named as George Jones – although this may not be biologically correct! But using that marriage certificate as a starting point, I later obtained the birth certificate for Mum – Juliet Elizabeth Lailey, born October 24th 1911. Her mother is named as Rosetta Maud Lailey, formerly 'Peppiett', although the spelling of that original surname may be slightly suspect. Juliet – or June – was born at 46 Francis Street in Reading and, according to the later wedding certificate, she and Stan were both resident at that same

June and Stan on their Wedding Day, 1933

address some twenty-two years later.

I subsequently also obtained Stan's birth certificate, which named his mother as Elizabeth Jones, formerly Goodman. Stan's father is not named on that certificate, which corresponds with what the girls always had in their memories. Stan's date of birth was stated as February 3rd 1910 and the address is given as 12 Bedford Road, Reading. Early in 2007, after I had tracked down the above information myself, Ei & Mike started to do some research of their own, checking the 1901 census returns at the Museum and Library in Reading. What they found was hardly conclusive, but very interesting nonetheless! In fact I joined Mike at the Records Office in May and we were able to obtain a printout of the census return that had caught his attention. It shows that at No.44 Francis Street, next door to No.46, lived a family by the name of 'Peppiatt'. But none of the names seem to have relevance to what is already known! The head of the household is stated as James Albert Peppiatt, then aged 45 years and originally from Bethnal Green in London, while his wife is named as Elizabeth, aged 42, also from Bethnal Green. At the time they had six children living at home – namely Alice (17), Harriett (15), Joseph (12), Lilly (10), Thomas (5) and Charles (4). It's hard to say if there is any relation, but the Francis Street connection is most intriguing!

Arborfield – the Apprentices' School and afterwards (1956 – 1961)

Having left 'the Inny' in the summer of 1956, for reasons not immediately known to me at the time, I then joined the Army! This wasn't to be for any gung-ho all-action future, but probably because I had been encouraged by Jack Whitley to *'learn a trade'* – and my being in the Army would see me off his hands too! Anyway, whatever the rights and wrongs or circumstances at the time, I certainly have no regrets about joining the Army and actually went on to serve for the next eleven years. That may seem a strange length of time, but the nine years 'man's service', for which I'd signed on, actually started at the age of eighteen (in 1958), at which time I still had the final year of my apprenticeship to complete. That apprenticeship was for a three-year period, after which I was to become a member of the Royal Electrical and Mechanical Engineers – or 'REME', as it is usually referred to. I eventually passed out from the School (which was to later gain the status of 'College') as a Radar Technician – one of the highly respected electronics trades. So the trade training must have been pretty intense, especially when coupled with all the other stuff that was going on – like the standard Army education and military training. But I'm leaping ahead of myself a bit, so back to the beginning!

'Joining up' itself certainly proved a bit of a nerve-wracking experience, having to attend the Recruiting Office in Liverpool city centre at Ranelagh Square, followed by the indignity of 'the medical', which took me to a building somewhere near Exchange Station. In those days of course, compulsory two-year National Service (NS) was still in vogue, so there were literally dozens of rather disgruntled young men attending for medicals, a good few years older than me in most cases. Burly dockers and building workers surrounded this scrawny callow youth, making me feel both immature and insecure!

Off to a false start!

My previous grammar school education had obviously stood me in good stead for training of a technical background, so after passing the statutory psychological and general knowledge tests, I was accepted as a raw recruit to the Army Apprentices' School at Arborfield. This was based near Reading, in rural Berkshire – but it could have been on the moon for all I knew! I remember that we were then living at Old Roan, a district up at the north end of Liverpool, beyond Aintree Racecourse. Having been told to report to the Army Recruiting Office, I left home and caught the bus into town, carrying a suitcase containing 'all my worldly goods' - and a mac over my arm. When I got to the office, I was handed a travel warrant – but not to be used until the next day! So I caught the bus back home, walked up Altway and into Tonbridge Drive. I knocked on the back kitchen door and, when Mum opened it, she burst into tears – she thought I'd been rejected!

The next day I was on my way for real, taking the bus into town once more, then into Lime Street Station to catch the train to London's Euston Station. This was quite an adventure, being on the express train to London all by myself, watching the countryside flash past in a blur and listening to the rhythmic rattle of the train over the tracks. And of course the trains were still steam-powered in those days, so occasionally the view would disappear behind a cloud of smoke and steam. The stations at Crewe and Stafford had reasonably familiar names, but then came places like Bletchley, Leighton Buzzard, Tring and Hemel Hempstead, which all sounded pretty foreign at the time!

Then it was the *Northern Line* tube from Euston to Waterloo and a *Southern Rail* train to the little town of Wokingham – much bigger nowadays! I was picked up on an Army lorry and dropped off at the Camp gates at Arborfield – my home for the next three years, and a bit more as it turned out. The first person I happened to bump into was a scruffy looking lad who seemed to be digging a patch of brown soil just inside the gates. He looked up at me and said, in a menacing tone, *"Where are youse from lad?"* Luckily for me, John 'Dinger' Bell was a fellow 'scouser', so when I mentioned my Liverpool upbringing, his face changed into a smile. Otherwise, he'd have probably landed me one!

A three-year apprenticeship

How can I begin to describe the next period of my life? I would literally have to write a book on the subject (which I eventually did!), so much happened. I started off as a 'Jeep' (that's a nickname for all juniors) in Headquarters Company, along with dozens of other young lads in much the same boat as myself. In other words, totally baffled and wondering why we'd joined! There were accents from all around the country, Jocks, Taffies, Geordies, Scousers, Cockneys and Brummies – the lot. One young lad – I think his name was Bob Hanson - tried to explain where he was from, but none of us could find 'Berkup' on the map. Turned out he was from 'Bacup' in Lancashire, hardly a million miles from Liverpool, but he could have been from another planet!

The next three years passed by in a blur of activity. Initially, the new lads were put into Headquarters Company as 'Jeeps', which was the common name for all new arrivals. We scrubbed floors, polished floors, blancoed webbing (belts and gaiters), bulled our boots and shone our brasses. We learned our trade, at which I was to eventually become a Radar Mechanic (the Technician part was a later change). We studied our education with Warrant Officers from the Education Corps and Physical Training Instructors chased us around the sports fields until we dropped. I almost wrote 'drooped' there, and perhaps I should have! There were parades, inspections and 'fatigues' almost on a daily basis, the week lasted from Monday morning until Saturday dinner-time, and even Sunday mornings were often taken up by church parades!

Eventually of course, even the junior boys gradually climbed the ladder and became senior boys, with all the privileges and advantage that this provided. No longer did everyone 'gyp' you in the queue at mealtimes, as the three years progressed, you actually found yourself gypping the boys junior to you! These steps 'up the ladder' occurred every six months, as there were two intakes per year. Having joined in the second intake of 1956, we forever became known as '56B'. If, dear reader, you wish to get a flavour of what happened during those three Arborfield years, well don't forget I have written the definitive history of the place – so all the lurid details are somewhere in there!

It wasn't quite 'all work and no play' of course. After the initial six-months term, when you made that first step up from being a 'Jeep', one had the privilege of being 'allowed out', when a bus trip into Reading seemed like a step into wonderland! We used to go into the record shops, such as *Barnes & Avis* and *Hickie & Hickies*, where you could ask for a record to be played, while you listened to it from within a soundproof booth. I recall one particular Saturday when I bought a 78 rpm version of 'Diana', by a very young Paul Anka. I managed to haul it around safely for the rest of the afternoon and evening, even on a pub-crawl, before arriving back in my barrack room. There, I threw the record on my bed – then promptly sat down upon it! Sadly, in those days, records were breakable!

Around the early summertime of 1959, not too long before we were due to finish at the School, we were all sent out to 'camp' under canvas at what I now know as Hankley Common, not too far away from Greatham, up the A3 towards Godalming. I remember pitching a two-man bivouac with Bob Lennon the first afternoon, some way down a bit of a slope. That night – inevitably – it rained, and we had water running through our tent, which didn't make for a comfortable experience. Part of the camp period was 'confidence building and initiative tests', in which we were sent out to accomplish various tasks. Bob and I were sent out to gather information regarding Guildford Cathedral, which I remember we were able to get from the verger, who had obviously been primed to expect such visits! We went into the town centre and I recall sitting in a café having some tea and toast, whilst listening to the news that Swedish boxer Ingemar Johansson had just won the world heavyweight boxing title from the American, Floyd Paterson. I think we picked up a lift back to the camp area, and I recall the driver pointing out the spot where Mike Hawthorne, a world champion racing-driver, had been killed, when he drove his car into a tree on the Guildford Bypass.

The next morning, Bob and I set off again – I think we had a 'free' day just to ourselves. Again, we were lucky in getting a lift, and ended up down at the far end of the A3, at Southsea. I remember that it was a very warm day and that we were dressed in denim trousers and 'woolly pulleys', which must have looked a bit incongruous to say the least! Anyway, we walked all along the promenade, eyeing up the girls on the beach - or what passed for a beach, as it was (and still is) all shingle! We hitched a lift back too, being picked up by a Naval gentleman in uniform, who treated us to a pint on the way back, at a pub on the hill in Petersfield, now long vanished.

One of the highlights – well THE highlight - of each term was the leave period! During the weeks leading up to the 'great escape', one would eagerly reckon up just how much one would be taking home in 'credits'. The train journey home was often a blur, as all us 'Scousers' used the buffet-car bar to great advantage on the journey north from Euston to Lime Street. It didn't matter which intake you belonged to at that stage, we'd been through another term together and were now free to enjoy another session in our home city. The feeling of exhilaration as the train crossed the railway-bridge over the Mersey at Runcorn is still something for the memory to savour.

Most of the guys I served with, plus the hundreds of other 'ex-boys' that I have met up with over the years, look back on their Arborfield days (or daze?) with affection,

194

while there are others who hated every minute of it. But there is no doubt that you had to grow up fast and learn how to survive, otherwise life there could be very tough indeed. Me? Well, I don't think it did me any harm. I certainly 'learned a trade', as had been the original intention, and I learned other things too – how to keep my head down when the muck and bullets (figuratively speaking of course) were flying. And so, having joined as a member of intake 56B, I still remember those days quite vividly. The old place has an Old Boys' Association, which was sort of resurrected in 1977, having been in the doldrums for a few years. Since then, I have attended numerous reunions over the years, meeting up with ex-contemporaries, some of them on a regular basis, such as Dave Howlett, Doc Houghton and Jock Dodds.

Back in 1996, Doc and I managed to get in touch with as many of the 56B guys that we could and held a reunion of our own in the Sergeants' Mess at Arborfield, it was a great success, the 40th anniversary of our joining up. Indeed, it was so good that we did it again in 1999, which was forty years after leaving. Since then, quite a few of us have got together again, most notably at Rod 'Smudge' Smith's 'bash' at Sonning, for which he paid the whole bill. *(The reason for Rod's hosting of that event will become obvious if you read the whole chapter!)* Plus hotel weekends at Reading, York and Redditch so far, with another planned at Diss, Norfolk, in 2004. So it can't have been all bad, eh?

Another eighteen months

I earlier mentioned 'three years and a bit more'. That was because, on leaving boys' school, a handful of us continued serving at Arborfield, when we attended Ordinary National Certificate (ONC) training at the adult Training Battalions and Reading Technical College. So it was four and a half years at Arborfield in total, plus later 'Upgrader' training for a few months around 1964 – couldn't get away from the place! Not that I have any serious complaints about that extended sojourn at Arborfield, life tended to be pretty good during those days. Those of us who had left the boys' school together first moved to 3 Training Battalion at nearby Bailleul Barracks. Accommodation there was exactly the same as what we'd left, so it was all pretty familiar. And of course, now that we were all 'trained soldiers' – and Lance Corporals to boot, we thought we were real cool guys! We shared a room with several slightly older guys doing their NS, all they thought about was when they would be demobbed, ticking off the days on their wall calendars – or 'chuff charts', as they were popularly known. We must have driven them mad with our devil-may-care attitude. After all, three years of boys' school had left us quite knowledgeable in 'how to skive' and get away with things.

'Posing' at 3 Battalion REME, Arborfield, 1960

It was during those few extra months at Arborfield that I started to get interested in 'modern jazz'. Dick Morris and Jim Rampling were very much 'into it' - Dick even had his own drum kit and would sit there playing along with his favourites, such as Miles Davis, Sonny Rollins, Thelonius Monk, Gerry Mulligan, Stan Getz and the like – the sound is still 'cool' even fifty years later!

Dick and I also shared an interest in football and even attended a couple of matches up in London. Mind you, that showed what ignorant 'provincials' we were! Once, heading to see a game at Tottenham, we caught the tube to Tottenham Court Road, walked up into the bustling city centre and asked a policeman, *"Where's the football ground?"* We did eventually get to White Hart Lane, but the copper's face was a picture! Another trip to Stamford Bridge to watch Chelsea started off with us poring over a tube map. We found a station called Stamford Brook and logically decided that 'a bridge must go over a brook' – wrong again! Amazing to us at the time, it turned out that the nearest tube station to Chelsea's ground was Fulham Broadway – funny people, those Londoners!

It must have also been while we were at '3 Batt' that we had a coach-trip down to Southend, I think it was on a Sunday. The group of lads who had preceded us out of boys' school were then at '5 Batt', but asked us if we'd like to join them for a day out. Which of course we did! I remember that when we got there, we parked near a funfair, I think it went by the name of *'The Kursaal'*, or something like that. Anyway, we decided to work our way along the seafront, stopping off for the occasional pint along the way. There was a visit to one of those tracks where we drove some 'racing cars' around for a while, then a few of us decided to go to the pictures. I recall that it was an old-style gangster film, starring Edward G Robinson, but can't remember the plot. We'd all downed so much beer that we slept right through most of the film! It was then time for the return trip along the seafront, probably calling in at all those pubs we'd missed on the first pass! Eventually, everyone made it back to the coach and we made our way back to Arborfield. I guess it was sometime during 1960 and there was a popular Lionel Bart musical doing the rounds at the time, by the name of *"Fings ain't what they used to be"*. Anyway, one of the lads, Archie Naylor, kept jumping up and yelling, *"All together now ... ..."*, at which the whole lot of us would break into a chorus of *"They've changed our local Palais into a bowling alley, etc etc"* – goodness knows how many times we sang that song on the way back to barracks!

One of the 'funnies' to come out of that trip was probably only made up, but it's still worth telling. It was possibly Jimmy Walker, one of the 5 Batt guys, who had a go at the shooting gallery and won first prize of a tortoise. Like the rest of us, he'd had a few too many and the story goes that next morning, back at camp, he told the rest of his room-mates how much he'd enjoyed *"that crunchy pie"* the previous evening! As I say, the truth will never be known, but it has always raised a smile for me! I still have a photograph or two of the Southend trip, quite a day out!

Our education continued in two ways. Most of the term was spent under the guidance of a few NS Sergeants, who carried on from where we'd left off at the School – Maths, English and technical training. The classes took place in cold wooden buildings and our first task each morning was to light the stove that warmed the place up! But we'd also go off to Reading Tech College for practical work in laboratories and on equipment unavailable to the Army. Mornings would see us taking the bus into Reading, where we would make a stop at the *Joe Lyons* teashop in Broad Street for some breakfast. At lunchtimes, we would walk towards the town centre and have a 'pie and a pint' in one of the local pubs. Then in the evening, we would arrive back at 3 Batt and make our own suppers in the cookhouse. This was inevitably a big fry-up – chips, eggs, bacon, sausages and chips, all washed down by a pint mug-full of ice-cold milk from the big walk-in fridge. Happy days!

Not that we did very well educationally! I could be wrong, but I think that it was only Rodney Smith who 'made the grade' at the end of the Reading Tech episode. And it certainly paid off for him in later life, when he went on to become the Chief Executive of a large computer firm in California and a multi-millionaire into the bargain! He'd gone off to the USA around 1971, having been 'head-hunted' by the *Fairchild Corporation* as an electronics expert. At some later stage, along with some other guys, they'd set up their own company and it obviously became very successful.

Eventually, Rod became 'Mister Big' of his own *Altera Corporation*, involved in the manufacture of computer chips – good for him! When the 'lab work' coincided with a Friday, this gave us the opportunity to rush through the work in the morning, then set off home for an extended weekend break. In fact, if I recall correctly, one of the NS Sergeants who was 'instructing' us was also heading off to Manchester at the same time! *(I think his name was Jed – and Rod Smith later gave me a photo of the same Jed, standing outside of one of the 3 Batt barrack blocks used for instruction.)* I've lost count of the number of times that I used to hitch-hike all the way to Liverpool – often in uniform in those days, as this usually helped to gain a lift as well as some sympathy. If you told the driver you were NS, this could lead to a stop at a café somewhere, where a cuppa and pasty may come your way!

Hitchhiking was a bit hit-and-miss of course. One week you may get a lift almost all the way home, another time you would hardly get a lift all day. I recall being stranded once at Wednesbury, somewhere in the Midlands, when it started pouring with rain and there was poor visibility, so nobody wanted to pick up a bedraggled squaddy. I had to catch a local train into Birmingham – Snow Hill station, I think it was – then another train as far as Crewe. From there I 'phoned home' –no 'mobiles' in those days, it was pennies in the slot and 'press button A!' I was lucky enough to find Jack Whitley in good enough mood to come all the way down to pick me up. Going back to camp was another matter. I always made sure that I had arranged a lift directly back, usually with a 'regular' soldier who had his own car – or van! If I remember correctly, the guy who provided most of the transport was named Mick Swords, who came from Birkenhead. The pick-up point for this lift back was generally outside Lime Street station in the city centre, at around midnight on the Sunday. The journey would be through the Mersey Tunnel, then down the old A5 route via Chester, Whitchurch, Newcastle-under-Lyme, Castle Bromwich, the Coventry by-pass and so on, down past Oxford and so back to Arborfield. We'd arrive just about in time for morning muster parade, then spend as much of the day as possible dozing in class! *(I think I've covered this bit in another chapter, but what the heck!)*

One fact that springs to mind was the number of fags that we'd smoke whilst on the journey, we'd just keep handing them round, one after the other – and nobody ever seemed to refuse. The back of the van must have been just a blue haze all through the journey and when the rear door was finally opened, we'd all stagger out surrounded by a smokescreen! That reminds me of a saying commonly used up in Liverpool – and no doubt used by Scousers in the Army too! If you were offered a fag and didn't want

198

to smoke it just then, you'd take it anyway, tuck it behind your ear and say, *"I'll keep it for the judy's ould feller!"* – that's the girlfriend's or wife's father by the way!

I recall one particular trip in the back of that van, it must have been a winter's night when we were travelling back south to Arborfield. Somewhere on the road between Coventry and Southam, in Warwickshire, the back wheels must have hit a sheet of black ice and, suddenly, the van was spinning round - literally, because it seemed to go round a few times at least. Thankfully, there was no other vehicle near us and we managed to avoid any collision with walls, trees or other obstacles, as we finally came to rest with the rear of the van pointing in the direction we were supposed to be going! There must have been a communal sigh of relief – and no doubt a few extra fags were smoked on the rest of the journey!

Of course there were no such things as motorways in those days, perhaps a blessing when you consider the problems we have on those so-called fast roads today! If I remember correctly, the first part of the M1 opened in 1961, and during journeys on the train between Liverpool and London, you could see the construction taking place. Once it opened, with no speed limit as far as I'm aware, motorcyclists used to race along it at speeds of up to 100 mph – hence the term used to describe them – 'Ton-up kids'. Certainly, whilst travelling home in the back of Mick's van, we'd be lucky to get up to sixty – and thought we were doing great if that happened!

Recreation – Berkshire style

All that travelling was okay, but a bit wearing, and so more local attractions in Reading started to beckon. There was no shortage of pubs in Reading and, in my time, I guess I must have gone into most of them! If you timed the bus journey from camp just right, you'd arrive at St Mary's Butts just in time for opening hour. *The Allied Arms* was right on the bus stop, so it would be the first stop. A nice pint and a pork pie, with lots of mustard, would see you through the TV programme *'Six-five Special'*, which featured all the top music of the day. It was mostly skiffle then, with a dash of trad jazz, with other acts such as the Dallas Boys and the Vernons' Girls. Then the pop scene started to feature such as Tommy Steele, Marty Wilde and Billy Fury – yes, those were the days all right!

A walk along Broad Street usually included a stop at *The Peacock*, and then we'd end up in *The Star,* in London Street, for a game of darts and more drinks – while 'egg banjos' and pickled eggs were a couple of favourites. The landlord of *The Star* at the time was a chap named Bob, and he always gave us a warm welcome, unlike some of the Reading pubs, where groups of young lads were looked upon as trouble-makers. Eventually we'd end up further up London Street at *The Foresters*, which was basically a dancing club, but also a bit of a dive really! But the music was great, all the big American stars – Elvis, Gene Vincent, Eddy Cochran, Little Richard and the rest. The lights were so low in there that you could jive the night away quite well, however poor a dancer you were! And it's probably just as well that we couldn't see who we were dancing with most of the time! They used to have a break in proceedings, when you could have the back of your hand stamped, go out to the *Barley Mow*, then get back in for the last session. Of course, you could do your dancing with a little more style at one of the larger Ballrooms, such as the *Olympia, Majestic* or *Oxford*, but the music there would be by a live band – pretty tame stuff when compared to *The Foresters*. Still, the big advantage was that they all had bars that stayed open about half-an-hour longer than the pubs, so it was worth the admission fee for that reason alone!

It didn't happen too often, astonishingly enough, but there was the odd occasion when the 'last bus' would be missed and it was a case of 'shanks' pony' all the way back to Camp. Having had a few beers, it never seemed too bad, even though it was a walk of around seven miles. But most times we made that last bus on time and inevitably it would be packed with squaddies. We'd all enjoy a good singsong on the way back, with songs like *'Maybe it's because I'm a Londoner'*, *'Maggie May'*, *'I belong to Glasgow'* and such like. There would then follow a short period of trying to sober up before walking into the Guardroom to book in.

Another incident that suddenly came to mind was a trip across to Burghfield, near Reading. I believe it was Colin 'Fritz' Fry's elder brother who came back to Arborfield for a weekend, driving one of those open-topped sports cars – did it have only two seats or a full four? Anyway, he asked us if we'd like to go out for a drink and a handful of us managed to squeeze into this car, a couple of us actually sitting on the bodywork at the rear – all highly illegal of course, but we were very devil-may-care at that tender age! We must have ended up at one of the two pubs in Burghfield – better known in those days for its WREN camp! - either the *'Six Bells'* or the *'Old Hatchgate'*. The trip back to camp proved most memorable, as it turned out that the car had no lights on it! So you can imagine what it must have been like, riding along those country lanes, having had a few bevvies, in near darkness! It must have been summer-time, otherwise I probably wouldn't be sat here writing this now!

The 'Boys' School' at Arborfield long ago started up its own 'Old Boys' Association, but which withered on the vine somewhat towards the end of the Sixties and on into the Seventies. However, the arrival of a Commandant who was himself an 'old boy', in the shape of Colonel Barrie Keast, rejuvenated things in 1977 and the Association has gone from strength to strength since then. A Reunion is held every year and I have been to most of these since 1977. Apart from meeting lads who were there at the same time as oneself, friendships seem to build up with other faces, familiar by their annual presence.

A twist of fate

Early in 1961, those of us who had attended the ONC training were preparing to be posted to our first units, most of which in those days seemed to be in Germany – BAOR, British Army of the Rhine. However, fate had decided that, just two short months before we were due to embark across the Channel, I was to meet Joyce Jones – *'the girl from the Pru'*! (*Prudential Assurance*, I think was the full name.) I shouldn't even have been 'out and about' on the Saturday evening in question, January 28th, because I had been selected for Fire Picket duty at the Garrison Cinema, the *Globe* (or 'Gaff' as it was popularly known). However, someone asked me to swap duties with him, and a request by Jim Rampling to join him in Reading that evening fell on willing ears. No doubt we did the usual 'pub tour', before ending up at the *Oxford Ballroom* – and in particular its upstairs bar!

Whilst sitting there nursing a whisky and orange, the head of Jimmy 'Jock' Gardner appeared up the staircase and we asked him to join us. He declined at first, saying that he had not one, not two, but three girls with him! Doreen was 'his' girl, Pam was her sister, and Joyce was the third of this trio of girl singers known as the *'Grifftones'* (an amalgamation of 'Griffin' and 'Jones'). Having met Joyce on that Saturday, of course I then had to do the cinema duty at Arborfield the following night. But we'd already agreed to meet on our first 'date' on the Monday, when we went to the *Odeon* cinema in Reading, to see *'Tunes of Glory'*, starring Alec Guinness – would you believe, a story about soldiers! I think we went on to visit the 'flicks' just about every night that week, it was certainly a popular pastime in those days. It wasn't long before I was invited around to Joyce's house 'for tea' and, of course, for the family to run the rule over me!

I tried to see Joyce as often as possible during the next few weeks, knowing that I'd soon be off to Germany on posting. Romance blossomed very quickly and I astonished myself by asking Joyce to marry me, after an evening at the *Majestic Ballroom*. Thankfully she said *"Yes"* and I think we've since managed to prove that there is such a thing as 'love at first sight'! The rest, as they say, is history! An old Liverpool saying describes Joyce – *"She's the best girl in seven streets"*! And what's the old song? *"We've been together now for forty years – and it don't seem a day too much"*!

Coincidentally or not, but Jim Gardner went on to marry Doreen, while Pam married another Arborfield boy, in the shape of John Teasdale! When we first settled in Greatham, we often used to drop in on Pam and John, living on Basingstoke Road in Reading. Tragically, they had a little boy, John, who was born with a hole in his heart and died at an early age. I remember that they came down to visit us on a few occasions too, particularly when I did a spot of apple picking at *Blackmoor Estate* – as John joined me at least once! Jim later did his 'Tiffy' course at Bordon, so I saw quite a lot of him in the camp, while he and Doreen lived down towards the bottom of Chalet Hill. Some years later, Jim got commissioned into the Medical Corps and we visited the family in quarters at Mytchett.

Day out at Southend, 1960

Serving in Germany (BAOR 1961 –1963)

My group of ex-Arborfield Apprentices embarked for Germany on March 28th 1961, firstly making our way by train to Harwich. From there, we boarded the troopship *'Empire Parkstone'* (I think that's what it was called, although it could have been *'Parkeston'*), which took us across the Channel to the Hook of Holland. I honestly cannot remember too much about that sea crossing, except that it seemed smelly, interminable and pretty damn uncomfortable! Once back on dry land, it was back on the railways again, this time by what was called the *'Blue Train'*, run by the British military authorities, across Holland. I can recall seeing what appeared to be hundreds of cyclists, whenever the train crossed a level crossing. Then it was over the border and into Germany, ending up at the town of Minden. We were to be housed there for an overnight stay, before continuing our respective journeys to our eventual units the following day.

I think the Army unit we stayed at that first night was called 27 Special Tels Workshop – the 'Tels' meaning Telecommunications or, to put it simply, radio repairs! Anyway, we were fortunate enough to bump into Norman 'The Dude' Dewdney, an old boys' school acquaintance, who volunteered to take us out 'on the town' that evening. It turned out that the town of Minden itself was 'off limits' at the time, due to some previous problems with *The Cameronians* (or was it the *Black Watch*?), who had upset the local townspeople with rowdy behaviour and fighting with other Army units in the town. It was definitely a Scots regiment and they were referred to in the German press as the *'Gitzwerfe'* – poison dwarfs! So instead we went out to a little place called Buckeberg and enjoyed our first sample of German beer – it all looked so innocent, a nice golden colour and lots of froth, in those seemingly tiny glasses, not a bit like the good old English pint! But looks can be deceptive and there were a few sore heads the next morning as we set off for other places! I think we split into just two separate parties, one lot going off to the Baltic coast up near Hamburg, while the rest of us ended up at 94 Locating Regiment Royal Artillery (RA), in the old German town of Celle.

94 Regt, Celle

The barracks, or *'Kasserne'* as it was known, was a huge building, at least six storeys high and it seemed to stretch for about half a mile from end to end, with two twin towers in the centre, pointing up to the sky like a pair of space rockets! This was to be our home for the immediate future and, to nobody's surprise, the REME Workshop accommodation was based on the bottom floor at one end, while our accommodation was on the top floor at the other end! I suppose it was meant to keep us fit - or at least out of the way! The official name of that huge building was 'Block 14' and included both cellars and attics for its full length. There were other buildings of course, which housed the Messes and Headquarters, with others dedicated to providing cover for the military equipments. The whole lot was named Goodwood Barracks and there was another separate camp, just a short drive away across town, called Taunton Barracks, home to 115 & 152 Locating Batteries, both also part of 94 Regiment. Another site, as far as I can remember, was where the Education Centre and Garrison Library were located. This lay out on 'Route 3' as you headed towards Bergen-Belsen, home of the infamous Nazi wartime concentration camp.

The main function of '94' was to use radar sets to locate enemy artillery positions and then guide our own Artillery onto the same. The Workshop was literally full of ex-boys from the School at Arborfield, so it really was like 'home from home'. By the time I arrived there, I had already been away from boys' school for 18 months, so the single stripe on my arm immediately became two and I settled into a life of work and pleasure! The work was quite easy to handle, but the pleasure was difficult – keeping on top of a bar-tab in the Bombardier's Mess! *(For those of you not of a military bent, a 'Bombardier' is the RA equivalent of a full Corporal).*

It was far too easy to be drawn into a life on the booze, however hard one tried to keep away from it! I can recall one particularly great weekend when the unit soccer team was invited to take part in a friendly match against a youth side from one of the outlying villages near Celle. As usual, a handful of us had met up in the Mess on the Saturday evening, to find it strangely quiet – until we found that a lot of the guys had gone to this soccer match. We also heard that there was an evening's entertainment arranged at the village *Gasthaus* (German pub!). Not wanting to miss out on the fun, we picked up a crate of *'Silvertop'* (the bottled beer with the silver-foil top, properly called *Bavaria Export* if I remember correctly) and caught a taxi out to this village.

The 'party' was inevitably very much based upon lots of beer and we weren't too late to partake of a few rounds! It must have been in the early hours that three of us found ourselves almost alone, the party was now over and we were more or less marooned at the pub. Luckily it was a very rural place and just around the back was a barn with a huge haystack inside. We climbed up on top of it and slept like tops! When we woke the next morning, we couldn't believe our luck when we found that the elderly lady in the pub was calling us over – and inviting us in to a cooked breakfast! This we managed to wash down with a few more beers – hard to believe I know, but we were only young once! We could hardly muster a *pfennig* between us, but no worries, it was 'on the house'. What splendid people ran that particular pub.

I can remember that the rest of the day turned out to be pretty warm and we hardly fancied walking all the way back to Celle. Luckily we found the local *Bahnhof* (railway station) and boarded a train back into town. It was a great relief that nobody thought of asking us for tickets, either getting on the train, during the journey, or at the main station in Celle! Walking back to camp, we bumped into a couple of other lads, who asked us to join them at the *Zillertal* – another watering hole in the town! Quite how long we stayed there I can't now remember – nor who paid, but it certainly wasn't me!

Drinking became one of the great pastimes in those days and it certainly made the evenings and weekends go past in a blur! I recall that during one particular weekend, Celle held one of its regular *'Shutzenfests'*. In fact many towns and villages held these shooting fairs, as they would be in English, an event where the locals would set up shooting stalls and compete to find the best shot. Of course there were many other stalls around too, like the beer tents and *'Schnell Imbiss'* stalls – literally 'fast food' outlets.

Now I can only go on other people's stories here, but apparently I'd been entered into a drinking contest at one of the beer tents and eventually ended up lying on the floor! A sergeant called Jim Ford found me there and helped me back to Camp. But on the way back I'd escaped his clutches and chased some ducks across the lake in the grounds of *'Das Schloss'* (the castle)! I guess it must have been true because my trousers later required dry-cleaning! Just going back to those 'fast food' outlets – or *'schnellies'* as we squaddies called them. Those in the town centre used to do the most wonderful *bratwursts*, smothered in *zenf* (German mustard), paprika and accompanied by either potato salad or french fries - I can still savour the taste now, so many years afterwards. (A *bratwurst* is a fried pork sausage, while a *bockwurst* was very similar, but boiled rather than fried – both quite delicious!)

My one saving grace during those days was that, before heading for the Mess, I used to sit down and write several pages of love letters to Joyce – that must have been just about every night, even when out on 'schemes' (military exercises, away from the camp). That kept me sane and the next leave period was always eagerly awaited. I can recall that my very first leave from Germany during the summer of '61. I was most grateful for the fact that 'air trooping' had just been recently introduced, run by an airline called *British Midland* I think. Hanover airport wasn't too far away from Celle, so it was most convenient to get there and fly directly to Gatwick. Looking back, that must have been the very first time that I'd been up in an airplane, so it was quite an exciting experience, even though the flight time was only around an hour in duration.

From Gatwick, I picked up one train directly into London and then another west to Reading. I'll always remember the train trip from Waterloo to Reading South, looking down into all the back gardens along the route. Later, I took Joyce up to Liverpool with me, which must have been to County Road, because I remember walking with Joyce down to Walton Hall Park on my 21st birthday. And that same day, we had decided to get married the following year, buying our engagement rings in a jeweler's shop in Paradise Street, down near the city centre. Jack Whitley, for some unknown reason, didn't think much of the idea, he thought we were far too young – especially as Joyce was only seventeen. His words went along the lines of *"It'll never last"*, but I guess we proved them wrong!

Out on the town

It wasn't **all** boozing of course! Having arrived in Celle, it was great just to go into the town centre and stroll about, taking in the different sights and seeing how the German people lived. If I'm honest, in those days there was still a bit of a 'them and us' atmosphere, a mere sixteen years since the end of the war. One of the things that particularly told us apart was the mode of dress. The Germans always seemed to dress so smartly, whatever time of day, and the men's suits always came in some rather strange shiny colours (browns, greens and even mustard!) when compared to the traditional blues and blacks of the English-style clothing. Nowadays of course, everyone seems to have adopted the international dress code of T-shirt and jeans!

One thing that impressed me was the proliferation of coffeehouses and restaurants. With our 'overseas allowance' we always seemed to have a few marks (around 11.5 to the pound if I remember correctly) in our pockets and it was a nice feeling to go in and order a quarter or half chicken, depending on appetite! I think the best place for those was called the *'Goldring'*. The place for coffee, tea and lovely cream cakes was the *'Konditorie'*. I got a liking for the German fashion of drinking plain black tea – no milk or sugar – served with a slice of lemon in a press device. Funny that, because when I went home on my first leave and told Joyce about this delicious 'lemon tea', she volunteered to make me a cup. Only trouble was, she must have squeezed a whole lemon into one cup of tea and my eyes haven't stopped watering since! I seem to remember that her Mum and Dad had a damn good laugh at my expense at the time! Despite that, I have kept to drinking 'neat tea' ever since – along with quite a few other members of my family, including Joyce and both of my daughters. In fact I couldn't even bear the taste of milky tea nowadays, it just seems like dishwater to me.

The Workshop was due to go out on an exercise on one occasion and, for some reason or another, I was in the position of having to jump down off the back of a 3-ton *Bedford* Army truck. Unfortunately, the signet ring on the middle finger of my right hand got caught on the top of the tailboard and almost ripped my finger off! (The said ring – with a nick in the ridge from where it got caught up – still holds its position!) My hand immediately swelled up and was pretty damn sore, so I was told to return to barracks and miss that particular exercise. One of the other lads in the workshop was one Benny Allhouse – another ex-Arborfield boy – and he was also not included on the 'scheme'. So, for a couple of days, he was able to take me out in another 3-tonner, the infamous *Commer* Z-wagon, and do a spot of driver training. That was a bit of an experience – no synchronous gears on those old wagons, gear changing was all achieved by double-de-clutching - and the pressure needed on the clutch pedal made it all pretty hard going! But it was nice to get out into the countryside around Celle for a while.

I think it must have been around that time that I thought of buying a car. One of the lads, a Scouser vehicle mechanic called Jim, had an old *Volkswagen 'Beetle'* that he was willing to sell me for a small sum. He tossed me the keys and told me I was welcome to try it out, it was parked outside the barrack block. So off down the stairs I went and found the said vehicle nosed in about a yard from the block wall. However hard I tried, the car just kept inching forward towards the wall, as I tussled to find reverse gear. In the end I gave up, gave Jim his keys back and told him that I'd decided to leave it for now. What I hadn't realised was that the *VW* reverse gear was in a different position to that of the *Commer*! In my innocence, I thought that all gearboxes followed the same pattern.

There were a number of people at the Workshop that made an impression – some good and some not so good! In charge of the Radar Section were some Warrant Officers. Eddie Broomfield was one and, although not aware of his background at the time, I later met up with him at several Arborfield Old Boys' Reunions! Malcolm Body was a quiet gentleman and I used to baby-sit for him on occasion, it was nice to just sit in a civilian environment for a change – although the German TV programmes made little sense! I'd usually enjoy a beer or two from his fridge as I wrote a letter to Joyce.

Then there was 'Granny' Jones! I remember that the radar sets, 3Mk7s, had an entrance door and you had to step up about eighteen inches off the ground to get in. It became the natural thing that, once you'd finished working on some internal task, like fault-finding or setting-up, you automatically stepped down backwards from the same doorway. On this particular occasion, a number of sets had been placed onto low-loaders, ready to be back-loaded, and were now sat awaiting collection on the vehicle-park. 'Granny' was doing a last check on paperwork I suppose and, forgetting that the radar was now an extra four or five feet up off the ground, reverse stepped out of one and fell pole-axed to the ground! Maybe his pride was hurt more than anything physical, but it must have shaken him up quite a bit. Funnily enough, I recall somebody else telling me that, when he was on guard at 3 Batt, back in Arborfield, the very same Granny Jones had come cycling down towards the main gate. He had his nose buried in some book, or maybe an EMER, and crashed straight into the barrier across the camp entrance! It certainly sounded true to me!

When I arrived at the Workshop, the guy in charge was a WO1, who was known to us all as 'Wobbly' Wells. His title then was 'PWF', which stood for Principal Workshop Foreman – I had never heard the term before and don't know if it is still used today. The Chief Clerk was a Sergeant Ron Seabrook, who I later caught up with again when I joined the TA at Bordon many years afterwards. If I remember correctly, I was put into the Workshop Office to act as Chief Clerk for a while, when Ron must have been away sick or something. Quite enjoyed it too – much better than working on radar sets! Our 2i/c in those days was a Lieutenant Reeks – no surprise that he went by the nickname 'Stinky'!

We had another guy called Joe Geary. Rumour had it that he had been a Warrant Officer with the Artillery during the war. Now, for some reason, he was a Corporal Tels Tech in REME. Trouble was, he was also an alcoholic and it would only take one large bottle of German beer to 'top him up', so he used to spend his days in a bemused state – it was all very sad. Just thinking back, that beer that Joe used to drink came in a bottle with a wired ceramic top and rubber sealing ring – reminded me of the old 'pop' bottles we had as kids. Our workshop welder was a Wilf Thornton, who had once served in the Navy, if you believed his tattoo collection! He had a bunk-room to himself and had a live-in 'girlfriend', who went by the name of 'The Animal'. Can you believe it? His best mate was a Scouser, another Corporal, in the Ordnance, called Battersby. What an obnoxious pair they were, always on the piss and sneaking loose women into and out of camp! *(Amazingly, I read in 'The Craftsman' magazine, early in 2006, that Wilf had recently died – I wonder just how he had survived that long!)*

I remember once having to act as one of the guards for someone who had been caught after going absent, he may well have been a Gunner, I can't clearly remember. What I **do** remember is that he literally stank! Two of us were supposed to stay in the room with this guy, perhaps for his own safety, I don't know. But wow, it was my safety I needed to ensure, because the smell just knocked you over! Another guard I was part of was looking after a REME SSgt, I think his name was Pete Rofe, who had unfortunately killed a German woman in a car-crash and was awaiting a Court Martial.I have already mentioned that 94 had more than its fair share of ex-boys from Arborfield. Obviously, we used to hang out together in many instances – better the devil you know! Pete Tidey was one such ex-boy, he was one of those guys whom had been on the famous day-trip to Southend, along with Jimmy Walker. Pete was married to Pat and they lived in what must have been a hiring, not too far away from the camp, out on the road towards Braunschweig I think. A few of us would be invited to their place for the evening and we'd take a few *'Silvertops'* with us, loading them up in the bath, full of cold water to keep the beer cool. I can still see all those green bottles standing there, with the labels having soaked off and all floating on the surface!

Other names that just about stick in the memory were Dave Cahill, 'Tanky' Moir, Jim Cliff and a few others – plus of course some 'regular' soldiers and National Servicemen. At some point in time, I was attached to one of the RA Batteries located at Goodwood Barracks, this was just a short trip away from the main barracks. There was one National Service (NS) guy over there, I seem to recall that he was from the Birmingham area. He was an Anglo-Indian by birth, but that may **not** have been the reason why everyone knew him as 'Smokey' Sinclair! Because the other thing about him was that he always had this huge pipe stuck in his mouth, so that he was permanently surrounded by a haze of dense smoke. Poor Smokey – he was one of the last few NS lads left in service as that type of two-year Army service headed to its closure. All the NS lads kept what we called 'chuff charts' on their walls – calendars on which they dutifully ticked off the days of service as their return to civvie street all-too-slowly approached. Then the 'powers-that-be' suddenly found that they were going to be short of trained technicians in certain trades, and subsequently extended their stay by another six months. It certainly broke Smokey's heart, along with many others I'm sure.

Pipes seem to have gone completely out of fashion nowadays, perhaps it's all part of the whole anti-smoking campaign that has been in the public domain these last few years, but how many old briars do you see being dribbled into at present? Anyway, another pipe-smoker comes into my memory and that was Frank Stanway, he was a 'regular' soldier - he hadn't come from an Army Apprenticeship – who was also at Celle. If I remember correctly, he came from Staffordshire and sadly died but a few years later. He had a wife called Heather and, when they at one time got posted back to Arborfield, we once found Heather working at the *Marks & Spencer* store in Reading.

21 Regt, Fallingbostel

It wasn't too long – January 1962 - before I 'got posted' to another RA Regiment, just a bit further north on the Luneberg Heath at Fallingbostel. The unit had originally been a Medium Regiment, and was recently based at Rhyl in North Wales. They were now being set up as another Locating Regiment and a few of us were sent up from Celle as an advance party to set up the REME Workshop. I guess we must have had six months with very little to do except sort out toolboxes and EMERs! We were under the command of two newly qualified 'Tiffy' Staff Sergeants – Jim McLauchlin and Ivan Holmes. Jim was full of himself and not much liked, while Ivan was a much quieter and approachable sort.

Dave Howlett was one of those sent to 'Fally' with me and that was the start of a lasting friendship that was still in force when he and his wife Josephine – or Jo – celebrated their 40th wedding anniversary at *Denbie's Winery*, Dorking, Surrey, in June 2003. At the time, Dave was converting to Catholicism, as Jo was a Southern Irish girl, and he was always driving back to Celle for 'conversion' lessons, or whatever you'd call them.

The Godawas

To assist in language interpretation, the local German priest arranged for Dave to meet up with a young German lad called Karl-Heinz Godawa, who lived close to the previously mentioned Kasserne. He used to go and stay with the family at weekends – and I was most fortunate to be invited to join him on one occasion. This quickly developed into a regular weekend trip and it was wonderful to be able to share a family lifestyle with 'Mutti and Poppa', K-H, Gisela, Rita and Ulrich – or 'Ully' as we called him. The Godawas were most friendly, and had other visiting soldiers from Holland and America at various times – we used to call them the *'Family International'*. Dave has kept in touch with the family more closely than I have, but both Joyce and I have met up with some of them in the intervening years. Just after we got married and Joyce joined me in Germany, I had to go off on 'exercise' and Joyce stayed with the

Godawas – speaking no German, while Mutti spoke no English! But they got along pretty well, considering! It was years later that I found out that Gisela spoke pretty good English, but she didn't let on at the time!

Poppa was employed as the caretaker at a Catholic school in Kanonenstrasse, which wasn't too far away from the Army camp – in fact just about five minutes' walk through a local park. Dave and I often stopped over at weekends, usually on a bed made up on the floor and sleeping under a duvet – certainly my first experience of such bedding and vastly superior to an Army bed with sheets and blankets. Remembering that this was still not all that many years after the war, many items of food were still very difficult for the German people to get hold of. Thus, in return for their kindness and hospitality, Dave and I used to take them what were then 'luxury' items – such as coffee and jam – purchased from the NAAFI shop, just down on the river in the town centre.

Breakfast was a wonderful meal with 'Familie Godawa'. Mutti would place a huge loaf of bread on the table, along with butter and cold meats, and we would all just help ourselves. I particularly liked the German mustard – called *'senf'*. The family owned (I guess) a sort of summer residence, a wooden chalet, at a place called Marwede. (Must admit, I'd forgotten all about this, until chatting with Dave many years later!) I couldn't place it on a map now, but it wasn't too far out of Celle, located near a lake and nestling in some typically German pinewoods.

Sometimes we had to work!

One Army exercise (or 'scheme') that I went on was a three-week affair, taking us down towards the town of Kassell, towards Frankfurt. As a Radar Tech, I travelled in the front of an *AEC 'Matador'* truck, which towed the radar set behind it. Uphill was a right struggle, but downhill was brilliant – the driver would knock the gear into neutral and coast down hills at increasing speed, the truck being pushed along by the weight of the radar set behind it! Highly illegal of course, but we never got caught. The driver in 'our' truck was another fellow Scouser, Harry Kruse, while the 'odd job man' was a Gunner from Reading, by the name of Johnny Ward – we all got on very well together. The cab of our vehicle usually contained a crate of German beer, just to keep us going you understand! I recall us driving into location late one night and having to manouvre the truck – and trailer-mounted radar – into position in between some trees. When we got up next morning and saw the location, it was an old orchard, full of apple and plum trees. Just how we had managed to locate the equipment where it ended up, in pitch blackness, is still a mystery, because it took us ages to get back out again with all the benefits of daylight!

'Schemes' provided lots of fun and entertainment, on top of the daily routine. Even when out in what seemed like the middle of nowhere and supposedly waiting for 'the enemy' to attack, there could usually be found time to sneak away and sample the local scene. Once we had our whole section, towing vehicles, radar set and generator, parked beneath the largest tree one could imagine. 'Camming up' was a doddle, we simply draped the camouflage nets from the lower branches and everything was well hidden. A few of us found our way to a local Gasthaus and happily started to enjoy a few bevvies. But suddenly, someone burst in and shouted that, *"The Yanks are dropping in by parachute, let's go!"* We had to account for everybody of course, and we were most fortunate to find Geoff 'Taff' Culverhouse lying fast asleep in a cornfield on our way back to the campsite!

On another occasion, we'd all been asleep in our beds one night when the alarm was given for *'Quicktrain'* – which meant that the whole Regiment had to de-camp and head out onto the heathland, ready to repel the advancing Russian Red Army! Trouble was, the officer in charge turned in the wrong direction immediately upon leaving the camp – and we all ended up totally lost! I also recall that one of the RA Sergeants, a guy by the name of Robertson, always made sure he took his complete Army bed out on exercise with him. One night he must have fallen asleep whilst smoking and the next thing we knew was that his tent had caught fire!

The actual work on those schemes didn't add up to much in my case – once the radar had been set up, there was little else to do. So I took it upon myself to help out with the cooking – all done on petrol-based burners, housed in a pit dug out for the purpose. *(These makeshift cookers were known as 'Bengazis', as they had been used in the North African desert by Second World War troops.)* The main grub was 'compo', which was all tinned stuff such as Irish stew, Mutton and veg, and steak and kidney pudding. But, thanks to Danny Booth and 'the Inny', I used to speak a fair bit of German and so I was able to supplement the meals with fresh eggs and lots of fruit, swapped at local farmhouses for bars of chocolate and sweets from the compo rations.

In those days, smoking was neither a habit nor a pastime – more a way of life! Perhaps we should have guessed that it wasn't doing us any good, but there were no 'health warnings' or anti-smoking campaigns to oppose the tobacco influence. As far as service in Germany was concerned, fags were so cheap (a shilling for twenty, if I recall correctly) in the NAAFI that everyone smoked. We'd even buy them in tins of fifty - *'Sobranie'* came that way, I know.

When in the Mess for a session, guys would just throw a packet on the table and everyone would help themselves throughout the evening. Both Joyce and I smoked when she joined me in Germany, but I think we just became so sick of them that we both gave them up overnight. Joyce did later start again, around the time that, first her Mum and then her Dad died, but later gave up altogether.

Just going back to Karl-Heinz Godawa, I do remember once going up to Hamburg with him, I'm pretty sure it must have been in Dave Howlett's car, the one he'd bought from Ron Scott, also of 94 Regt. If I recall correctly, we also dropped in at a village before hitting the city, where K-H wanted to catch up with a girlfriend if his. I can't recall the date, but it followed fairly soon after Hamburg had been very badly hit by floods. In fact, down towards the seafront area, you could still see the 'tidemark', high on the side of many buildings. I also remember going into a 'gents' (*Herren* in German!). I was just having a 'wee' when this woman walked past me! Turned out she was a cleaner and she just walked around both the ladies (*Damen*) and the gents, irrespective of whether they were in use or not. That custom was certainly different to anything I'd met in England and I was so astonished that, in theatrical terms, I 'dried'! Walked around for the rest of the day with half a wee swilling around inside!

Another place that I visited, either from Celle or Fallingbostel, as it was roughly halfway between those two towns, was Bergen-Belsen, previously mentioned as one of the Germans' infamous concentration camps during the war. I always remember just how quiet it was there, there appeared to be no birds singing at all. It certainly wasn't the sort of place that one enjoyed visiting, but it served as a reminder of the horrors of war.

A spot of leave – and a wedding!

In August 1962 I took three weeks of leave and went to Reading to get married! This happy event took place on August 25th at St Giles' Church in Southampton Street, with our reception held in *'The White Hart'* hotel in St Mary's Butts, slap bang in the middle of Reading town centre. That place has long since gone, as well as *Wellsteed's* department store that stood alongside it – all part of the massive redevelopment work that most towns have gone through these past forty-odd years. If I remember correctly, it was Jack Whitley who gave us a lift to Reading Station, from where we caught the train to London's Paddington Station. There, we jumped into a taxi and asked the driver to find us somewhere to stay! We ended up stopping overnight in a lady's flat, somewhere in Belgravia, before making our way next morning to what was then called London West Air Terminal – now, of course, better known as Heathrow! In those days, you still walked across the tarmac to get onto the plane – and that's

The happy event on August 25th at St Giles' Church

certainly what we did, as we took a flight across the Irish Sea to the Isle of Man. Our honeymoon was only for a week and then it was back to Reading and eventually another tearful departure (for me) back to Germany.

Having now become 'married', there were no married quarters available in those days, so I had to look around for a 'hiring' – in other words, paying rent to the German owner. Our first 'home' was actually a converted garage, owned by a Frau Biermann, who looked for all the world like one of the sadistic guards you'd imagine in a concentration camp! There was just enough room for a bed – which itself was two singles pushed together – the rest of the place seemed to be taken up by an old-fashioned cooking range, which had to be kept stoked up with coal or coke. I do remember that Joyce made what she has always reckoned was her best ever Yorkshire pudding on it! But the place was a shambles really, the condensation used to pour down the windows on the inside and we couldn't stand it for too long. I think we stayed there for about a week, before finding a much better place up at the top of the hill going out towards Soltau. It was a two-roomed little place, right up in the attic of a large house, owned by Frau and Herr Schwarz – he was something to do with newspapers. His wife – the Frau – was Swiss and the rent we paid went straight into her purse, no doubt as pocket money! But at least the place was reasonably comfortable, we had an electric fire that seemed to throw out an enormous amount of heat.

Most evenings – after the hour or so it used to take Joyce to 'put her hair up! - we would catch a black *Mercedes* taxi up to the cinema at the camp, that was about the extent of entertainment available. (Although we did go out for a splendid meal one evening, along with the rest of the workshop, at another small local town called Walsrode.) At lunchtimes, Joyce would walk all the way down into Fallingbostel from our hiring, then uphill towards the camp, where we'd meet up at the *Church of Scotland* canteen for a bite to eat. We'll always remember the kids in there, whose lunch consisted of a big plate of chips and a bottle of *Coca-Cola*! The other memorable thing about our stay in 'Fally' was that Joyce had become pregnant. So the then very fashionable ski-pants soon became a bit uncomfortable for her. But she did start to learn a little German, with the phrase *"Ein kleines weissbrot, bitte"* – *"a small white loaf please"*. It has stuck with her these past forty-odd years!

A very severe winter

Also memorable was the fact that the winter that year, 1962-63, was one of the most severe on record, so that Joyce's walks to and from the hiring were set against a constant backdrop of snow and ice. One couple that we became friendly with, Nancy and Joe Redfern, lived in a mobile home just outside of 7 Armoured Workshop

– the Army had just made these available as its short-term answer to the quartering problem. But it was so cold that winter that the water supply pipes just seized up completely, so that drinking water had to be carried from inside the Army enclosure. One of the guys attached to the Workshop, I can't remember his name but he was in the Ordnance (RAOC), had very blonde hair and also lived in a flat down in the town – and was the proud owner of a car. He offered me a lift into Camp occasionally and it was a bit of a nightmare really, negotiating the slippery and virtually constant icy conditions. That winter seemed interminable and I remember the snow was still thick on the ground when we finally left Germany around April.

February of 1963 had brought quite a shock, with the unwelcome and unwarranted news that I was now considered a 'security risk'! Just how this was supposed to have come about, I never did find out, however hard I tried to query it with REME Records. The end result was that I was suddenly posted back to Celle – what difference was that supposed to have made? – while Joyce had to just as quickly return to the bosom of her family in England. Fortunately, with the help of the Godawas, I was able to find another hiring in Celle and Joyce joined me again after a break of only a few weeks. However, this 'flat' was hardly the stuff of dreams! Its location was in one of the scruffiest parts of town called *'Im Kreise'*, close to a couple of seedy taverns – one known as *'Smokey Joe's'* and the other called *'Krone und Schanke' (Crown & Anchor)*. We shared our toilet with the gaststube downstairs, the shower had what appeared to be mushrooms growing out of the walls – and the bed was just about wide enough to sleep on, provided you didn't make a false move. With Joyce around five months pregnant, life was far from ideal! No sex please, we're British – and afraid of falling off the bed!

Help was on hand from the Godawas again, who found another place for us, out in the countryside a few kilometers from town, at a place called Garssen. It was located quite a long way down a cart track called *Spiegelei Weg* – literally *'Fried Egg Way'*! All our worldly goods were transported for us from town to country courtesy of old mate George Vince – in his *Austin Mini-Cooper*! The way it used to bounce up and down that track was something to be seen. Joyce used to come into town to meet me at lunchtimes again, but this time using the local bus. Ever seen a queue for a German public bus? Very orderly, everyone lining up strictly in the order of arrival – that is, until the bus arrives! Then all sense of orderliness disappears and it's just a fight to see who can get on first and grab a seat. Quite amazing to both Joyce and myself! Mind you, another German term was now learned – *"Allerbrucke zuruck, bitte"* – this asking for a return ticket to the bridge over the River Aller, in Celle town centre, where the Forces NAAFI shop was located. It also gave Joyce the opportunity to go and visit Mutti & Poppa Godawa and family.

But not for long! My security vetting was still 'up in the air' and, in its wisdom, the Army had decided that I should change trade from Radar to Control Equipment. This meant that I was to return to Arborfield for a conversion course – but it also meant that Joyce would be able to have our first child at home in Blighty. So you lose a few and you win a few, it all worked out okay in the end. The end of the Germany saga brought us back into George Vince's *Mini*, as he kindly took us down to RAF Gutersloh in mid-April of 1963, for the return flight to England. Imagine, if you will, sitting in the back of a *Mini Cooper*, with all the suitcases and paraphernalia crammed in with us. If you can picture that, all the time, George is zooming down the Autobahn, overtaking huge lorries – their wheels towering above us – at probably about 70 mph, then you'll also know about the headaches that were suffered at the airport while waiting for departure!

It wasn't until after I'd started my trade conversion training at Arborfield that I realised that the new tank just coming into service, the *Chieftain*, was still on the secret list. Indeed, when it was transported around the country, it was always under tarpaulin wraps to keep it safe from prying eyes. Now if I was such a 'security risk', why was I now training to work on secret equipment? It's a question that I've asked myself – and others – many times in the years that followed! I never did get a decent answer though.

Old Pals

(The story below was written as a separate article for the Arborfield Old Boys' Association Newsletter. I have included it in this 'family' history, as the Howletts, Jo and Dave, have become almost 'part of the family' over the years. I apologise if some material is repeated elsewhere.)

Although Dave (Howlett) and I joined up as Army Apprentices at the same time, back in late Summer 1956, we weren't destined to meet until the following year, as he had the unfortunate experience of being sent first to Chepstow! Things took a turn for the better for him in 1957, when he was sent to join the start of '3 Div' at Arborfield, joining my class of trainee Radar Technicians. We spent the next two years becoming fairly good mates, but then that applied to all of us at that time. 'Boys' School' tended to make you become a tightly bunched group of mates - you always had to stand together against those 'Senior Div' lads who had already been through it all and were now 'cocks o' the walk'. And boy, you couldn't wait to be up there in that exalted position yourself!

When we eventually came to that sadly sweet day of the 'PoP', both of us had our Mums there for the Parade, and I recall us all meeting together one evening – remember *'The Peacock'* Dave? Fortune had decreed that, at that stage of our careers, due to the advent of ONC training, we – that is, all our group of 'Technicians' – should all be posted together to the great outside world – in Arborfield! Yes, we were destined to spend yet another eighteen months 'in training', split between those great pillars of education, Nos. 3 and 5 Training Battalions REME and Reading Technical College. Ate well in those days didn't we Dave? *Lyons' Teashop* in Reading's Broad Street for breakfast; a 'liquid lunch' at *'The Mitre'*; then a slap-up self-cooked evening fry-up in the cookhouse! Eggs, bacon, sausages, mushrooms, fried bread – all washed down with pints of cold milk straight from the walk-in fridge. I can also remember Jim Rampling, sitting in the back of class at Reading Tech, eating fruit salad directly from the tin – with his fingers!

Finally, the training was over and, at the end of March 1961, we were off to our first posting. Via Harwich to 'the Hook' on the old troopship *Empire Parkstone* and across Holland on the 'Blue' train into Germany, where we spent the night at 87 Special Tels Wksp at Minden. One of our old 56B mates, Norman Dewdney, took us out for the evening. I think it was to a town called Buckeburg, Minden being still 'off limits' thanks to the escapades of the infamous 'poison dwarfs' of the Black Watch – or 'Gitzwerfen' as the locals called them! Anyway, that very first taste of Deutsche bier sure went down a treat – I think *Watney's 'Red Barrel'* had just been introduced in Blighty, so readers will know what I mean! The following day we were split up into two parties, sadly saying farewell to those lads heading up to the far north, to Delmenhorst with 12 LAA Regiment, while our party made the rather shorter trip to 94 Locating Regiment at Celle.

Both Dave and I had left sweethearts back home and wedding plans were in the air. Dave had decided to change to RC in order to 'marry in church' and, to this end, was advised to see the local German Roman Catholic priest. Due to language difficulties, Dave became friendly with a young local lad, Karl-Heinz and soon became a regular guest at Karl's home, not far away from the Army Kasserne (Camp). One weekend he me along too and that was the start of a relationship that has lasted, although rather tenuously, until the present day. Mutti and Poppa have both visited England, as well as Gisela, who now lives in the States, and also Rita and her husband. I myself visited Ulli and his wife, on a TA trip back to Germany in 1979. Good friends, the *'Familie Godawa'*.

218

After a few months in Celle, both Dave and I were designated to move to a new location at Fallingbostel – the dreaded 'Effing-B'! 21 Regiment RA was moving out from Rhyl in North Wales, re-mustering from a Medium Regt to another Locating Regt, like 94 at Celle. We were to act as the advance party for the new REME Workshop. Without equipment for the first six months or so, we had a pretty cushy time, with plenty of opportunities for going down to Celle on weekend visits. It must have been around that time, Dave, that you bought your first car – that yellow *Ford Anglia* – from Ron Scott. After some time in Fally, it was inevitable that Dave and I would eventually have to go our separate ways. Sure enough, and for reasons that I won't go into here, I was forced to go back to Celle and told I must change my trade to Control Equipment – or 'ECE' as it was termed in those days.

I eventually returned to Arborfield for a basic ECE course, followed immediately by Upgrading – our course was known as 'Fed Up 9'! Dave and I never served in the same unit again, but happily our meetings continued over the years, during our subsequent marriages and the bringing up of our eventual families. At one time, Jo and Dave lived above the Army Recruiting Office in St Mary's Butts, in Reading town centre. That was a weird place Dave, I can remember you showing us around its many crooks and nannies! Then there was the time you visited Joyce and I at Queen's Cottages in that old *Hillman* shooting-brake – the one where you had to put an umbrella up when it rained! Didn't Jo once borrow numerous coats and scarves for a drive back to Gillingham, one bitterly cold night – and can we now have them back?

I left the Army, being rather disillusioned by that change of trade and the mysterious way in which it all happened, at the 9-year point, having decided on a civilian instructional job at SEME Bordon in Hampshire. Joyce and I bought a house down that way and have been there ever since 1967. Dave, however, continued his Army career in REME, going on to gain a commission and ending up as a Major, finally retiring from that life in 1997. During those in-between thirty years, we've managed to keep in touch and had quite a number of memorable occasions together in a variety of places. A lot of them have been memorable due to the laughs we have shared, so just a few to recall here. The fancy-dress party at Winchester, probably in 1974, where I failed to recognise the 'well-dressed bird' in all her feathers and finery, plus make-up, who turned out to be Derek 'Lofty' Newman from 56B! Then there was a trip to Malvern, where I managed to back my car into the biggest tree, on the widest of avenues – and that before we'd even reached your Army quarter!

There was a weekend in Woolwich, which included a trip to the theatre to see your young son Adrian appearing as one of Fagin's kids in a version of the Lionel Bart musical *'Oliver'*. And a visit to Donnington up in Shropshire, where we managed to track down the farm to where I'd been evacuated during the war. We even managed to find and say hello to my long-lost cousin Bill! It's amazing how the memories keep flooding back. After many years of living on Kingston Hill in a block of apartments, Jo and Dave have recently made the short move to Surbiton and are currently busy at the task of re-furbishing their 'dream cottage'. Thanks for all the memories and good times Dave and I just hope that this article, when it appears in the *OBAN*, encourages you to put together that long-promised article of your own. (Get the house finished first mate!)

Postscript

I originally wrote the above as a small article for publication in *OBAN* (*Old Boys' Association Newsletter*) in the first issue of 1999. Checking back, I find that Jo and Dave actually moved to their new place at Surbiton during 1997, because we first visited them there early in 1998. Well, now it is early 2006 and we have just been up to see them again, a visit that included a trip to Canary Wharf and the Docklands Museum, which proved very interesting, followed by a tour of the Guildhall art gallery.

Looking back over the years, we have enjoyed visiting some very entertaining spots in London, during all the years that the Howletts have lived there. Just trying to name them all would prove extremely difficult, but I shall try to recall some of them! I remember that when their eldest daughter Maria got married to Dominic in 1990, this took place at Woolwich Garrison and we stayed the night at the Garrison Officers' Mess. The next day we took a trip around the Greenwich area, including the *'Cutty Sark'*. When we got home later, I found that there was no film in my camera, so no photographic memories either! It must have been about twelve years later that we visited the area again – and this time have the pictures to prove it!

Alex is their younger daughter and began training as an actress at an early age. Despite her not getting into the business for a career, she did appear in many plays over the years, and this enabled us to visit a variety of small theatres and playhouses to see her. But I cannot recall where most of them were located. I do recall going back to Winchester to see her perform in *'Educating Rita'* in December 1998, while one of her performances took place above a Chelsea pub! Other places of interest have included the London Eye, Richmond Park, Hampton Court, and Borough Market at Southwark. At one time, through his Army connections, Dave was able to get cheap theatre tickets, and we joined the Howletts on various occasions on trips to 'theatreland'. I mentioned Adrian earlier, when he appeared on stage. Well, he went on to find work in the hotel business and that brings back another couple of memories. One was the opening of a restaurant called *'Rainforest Café'*, to which we were invited just before it opened to the public. Then there was Dave's retirement party at an Irish theme-pub in Soho in 1996 – I think it was called *'Waxy O'Connor's'*. Adrian was involved in the running of both places.

As I sit reading this over, it is the weekend of the Arborfield Old Boys' Reunion and this year is the fiftieth anniversary of the year we first joined. Dave has promised to put in an appearance and, hopefully, there will be a good turnout of several other old pals. Later this year, we hope to meet up again at another get-together arranged on behalf of Rodney Smith, who accompanied us to Reading Tech all those years ago – then put it all to good use by going on to become a millionaire in the United States!

Joyce at Windsor Castle, 1961

Further Army Service (1963 - 1967)

At the time that we returned from Celle to Reading, Joyce would have been around six months pregnant, so it must have been a great relief to her, returning to the 'bosom of her family', so to speak. Another relief was to get away from that terrible winter that we'd endured in Germany. *(That's not to say that England hadn't suffered too. In fact, Mike was later able to show us a photographic slide that he'd taken, showing the Thames frozen over at Caversham Bridge.)* With me about to start a training course at Arborfield, we were fortunate in being able to stay with her parents, June and Stan, for a short while, at their little home in 17 Queens Cottages. I'm sure that it wasn't the ideal arrangement for any of us really, as the house was only really a two-up two-down place, but Mum and Dad (as I called them too!) were kind enough to allow us to stay with them until we got things sorted out. Stan used to be an avid fan of *Alf Garnett* on the telly (remember *'Till death us do part'*?) and used to refer to me as *"you long haired Scouse git"* – but all in fun of course!

At that same period, Joyce's older sister Janet was having problems of her own. She had married Brian Robbins some three years previously, but Brian was always a bit of a 'ladies' man' and had eventually gone off with another Janet, who had left her own husband, Reg. They had all lived in Woodley at the time, as well as Joyce's eldest sister, June, with her husband, whose given name was Maurice, but has always been known to one and all as 'Wack'. *(It had been at June and Wack's house in Fawcett Crescent – I think! – that I stayed on the night before my wedding the previous year.)* In fact, Reg and this other Janet were June's next-door neighbours.

I guess we must have looked around in Reading for a 'hiring', there being no Army quarters available, much the same as it had been in Germany. I can recall looking over one large flat up near the old football stadium at Elm Park, but it was hardly anything to write home about. As it was, things fell into place quite nicely, as Jan kindly offered us the use of her house in Coleman's Moor Lane, while I think she went off to stay with Eileen and Mike at their place in Caversham for a while. Eileen was the next to youngest of the four 'Jones girls', with Joyce the 'baby' of the family. Eileen and

Mike must already have had the house in Woodcote Way, Caversham, as they didn't marry until the following month – at the same church, St Giles', as us.

So we moved into the house in Woodley on May 11th 1963. As we were 'renting' the house, it qualified as a hiring in Army terms, so they paid a special addition to my wage to cover that hire charge – which of course went straight to Jan, so we were all more than happy with that arrangement. Number 1 was right on the corner of a junction, with a fair bit of garden and certainly very comfortable for just the two of us, and so we settled down to virtually a 'civilian' style of life. Arborfield wasn't too far away, so I bought a 'moped' (*Paloma*?) and began riding it to and from work, a distance of some five miles each way. Brian Robbins had left behind an old leather 'flying jacket', which I wore on the moped. It was warm enough, but hardly waterproof, so I got a few soakings for my pains. It was hardly the most reliable form of transport either, the plug used to foul up quite often on the two-stroke mixture, so I was always having to stop, remove the plug and clean it up! But apart from that, it was quite an experience, riding through the lovely countryside between Arborfield and Woodley. Most of the time I'd head out through Barkham and onto the main Reading road at what used to be *'Crimpy Crisps'* – that was the factory that used to stand there, now replaced by a *Sainsbury's* supermarket.

There was a Staff Sergeant (was his name Key – or perhaps Keys?) on the permanent staff who also lived in the Woodley area, and he was kind enough to give me a lift in his car on the odd occasion. I think his car was one of the old *Ford Populars*, which were probably amongst the first mass-produced family cars in the country. The course at Arborfield actually proved a bit of a 'doddle' for me, after all I'd already trained as a Radar Mechanic, so going through the basics of Control Equipment electronics and electrics was bread and butter stuff. The rest of the lads on my course were 'first timers' and I can only recall a few of them. There were two Fijians, one's name was Simpson and the other was a great guy, very good sportsman, by the name of Jim Vakatali. There was a chap from Jamaica too – he was actually white, but definitely spoke the patois. Then there was a tall West Indian called Eric Ricketts, he actually came from Stroud in Gloucestershire and it was only years later that I found out that he was also an ex-apprentice.

One memory was of sitting in the NAAFI canteen at morning break time, stuffing cash into the jukebox and playing, over and over again, the *Beatles' 'I want to hold your hand'*. Needless to say, we accompanied the song – not very tunefully but definitely loudly! Those were the days of 'Merseybeat' music, with pop groups from Liverpool and the surrounding area sweeping the world with their versions of rock'n'roll. The

Liverpool Echo - you remember me talking about cinema adverts on the front page? Well, these had now been replaced by notices of which group was playing at which venue – and there were far too many for me to put down here. But, as well as the *Beatles*, we had such others as *Gerry and the Pacemakers*; the *Swinging Blue Jeans*; the *Searchers*; the *Merseybeats* – I could go on and on, it really was Merseyside that ruled the musical world in those early Sixties.

Meanwhile, things were 'developing' on the home front as Joyce's pregnancy reached into the final stages. Living at Woodley, she had been able to regularly take the local *Thames Valley* bus into Reading, visiting Mum & Dad during the day while I was at work. With it being the summer months, she had also been keeping the garden in a good state for Jan and in fact was still digging and weeding right up to the very day of our first daughter's arrival! Thus it was that, on July 31st, 1963, we welcomed Lorraine into the world, this happy event taking place at the Maternity Unit at nearby Wokingham Hospital.

Afterwards, we continued the routine of visiting Mum & Dad at Queen's Cottages of course, with Lorraine now accompanying us on the bus in her carry-cot, which also doubled up as a pram when mounted on its wheels. On Sunday mornings it became quite regular for me to be proudly pushing the pram along the river, over the bridge, then up through Forbury Gardens and into Reading town centre. Back at Woodley, we weren't too far away from *The George*, a pub situated alongside the river, to where we would occasionally take an evening stroll and treat ourselves to a drink. Life was pretty good!

Having completed my trade conversion course, I was able to persuade REME Records that, because I had been forced to change trade, I was now at a disadvantage in the seniority stakes, when compared to my peers. This was resolved by my staying on at Arborfield for an extended tour, in order that I could attend an 'upgrading' course at my new trade, now known as 'CET' (Control Equipment Technician). That started in January 1964. Once again, I cannot recall all the members of that course, but I do know that Bob Ord and Dick Emmett were part of it – two guys I had known at 'boys' school' a few short years earlier.

Serving at Bordon (1964 - 1966)

As the end of my upgrading course at Arborfield approached, I started thinking about how much I was enjoying being back in England and how nice it would be to maybe stretch that out for a bit longer! So I again went back to REME Records, with a bit of a sob story, bemoaning the fact that I was missing out on completion of my training for the Ordinary National Certificate (ONC), for which I had started back in

224

1959. *(Of course I didn't tell them that I'd managed to fail the exam, along with most of the other lads, having been far more interested in messing about!)* I asked for a posting in England and thankfully that's just what I ended up with! And so, around the middle of May 1964, I was posted as a Corporal CET to SEME Bordon, down in Hampshire.

My arrival at the SEME (School of Mechanical and Electrical Engineering) was a bit of a shock to the system, to say the least. I had travelled down there with a travel warrant that involved me using three separate buses – firstly Reading to Camberley, then on to Aldershot, and a final one south to Bordon. It must have taken me most of a whole morning. Anyway, I booked in at the RDO (Reception and Dispersal Office) and was sent to occupy 'the bunk', in the corner of a barrack room, situated at the far end of the regimental parade square. From there, and to my great surprise, I'd been told that I could get changed into civvies and go back home, as I had rather inconveniently arrived at a holiday long weekend!

However, just as I was happily changing, who should arrive but a jumped-up Provost Sergeant of the permanent staff - an almost exact replica of Sgt Fred Silver from my old boys' school days! The room I was in was apparently one occupied by cooks, who are probably the world's worst offenders when it comes to personal hygiene and overall tidiness. I hadn't really looked into the barrack room, too eager to get changed and back home, but now this strutting little Sergeant was pointing it out to me. It was certainly a shambles, stuff piled high everywhere, no semblance of the orderliness that I'd always been accustomed to. And to cap it all, this Sergeant was yelling at me that, as 'the room Corporal', I wouldn't be allowed home until the place was tidied up!

After he'd charged out in a cloud of steam, spewing expletives, I realised that these cooks had probably gone off themselves on leave and that any 'tidying up' that needed doing was obviously down to me – having been 'in charge' of the room for all of five minutes, maximum! I marched myself down to the RDO and managed to grab hold of a Major, immaculately dressed in his civvies, as he was just about on his way home for the same holiday weekend. I told him my story and he was immediately on my side - he told me not to worry, he would sort things out with the Sergeant the following week - and offered me a lift as far as Fleet, where he lived! I jumped at the chance of course, took the lift and he dropped me off at a convenient bus stop, from where I travelled directly back to Reading.

Following that weekend, I was moved down to Martinique Barracks (long since demolished!) and found myself in charge of a room full of Nigerians! Despite the weird music they played on their gramophones (record players – even that sounds old-fashioned too!), they were far easier to live with than cooks, I can assure you! In one of the other barrack rooms was a course of Upgrader students – vehicle mechanics no doubt. I remember being taken out with some of them on a couple of occasions – once to the *Seven Thorns* public house, up on the old A3. This later became *The Spaniard* – which eventually caught fire. I recall that once, when Sheila and Geoff were still together, and over here on holiday, we went there and Sheila had a very hot curry! I don't know if that was the cause of the fire, but the burned-out shell is still there to this day! Another visit was to *The Agincourt* dancehall in Camberley, a sure-fire place for trouble!

As a CET, there wasn't much electronics work at Bordon, so I was asked instead to report to the Electrics Department, for an interview with the civilian supervising instructor, an ex-Navy guy by the name of Bob Hunt. He was a gruff sort of fellow, who seemed ancient to me, with a hearing aid. Bob must have thought he was still in the Forces, as he called everyone by their surname. In the mornings, as the hour for starting work approached, he'd stand at the top of the stairs outside the Electrics Branch, checking up on who was late for work. It was just as though he was standing at the top of a gangway in his Navy days! Anyway, on interview, he asked if I'd be interested in doing some instruction on basic electrics and I agreed to give it a try. The rest, as they say, is history! *(Bob died shortly afterwards and I remember going to his funeral service at Blackmoor Church.)*

And so I started another phase of life, as an 'instructor', by sitting in with various other instructors, a lot of them were elderly gentlemen, full of experience, and I seemed to fit in very well, even though I was probably the youngest-ever member of staff at the time! Around the same time, I was promoted to Sergeant and eventually was able to face up to my first classroom full of students. The trade of electrician had just been abandoned and vehicle mechanics were now given responsibility for vehicle electrical systems – and it was at this level that I started my instructional career. It wasn't long before I decided that 'this was the life for me' and that I would leave the Army at the first available date (in 1967) and try to get a job as a civvie instructor.

Back in those days, the Electrical Section was located right at the top end of the camp, it had a two-tier flight of steps going up to it. There was one old chap, Jeff Shove, who suffered from emphysema. He could just about manage to make it up the first flight of steps in one go, then needed to rest a while before he made it all the way. And then he'd lean against the rail and light up a cigarette! I think that it was eventually arranged to deliver him by car at the back entrance, by the battery shop, to prevent his morning climb! That Battery Shop was the 'Kingdom of Joe Coleman', who was the resident instructor there.

Most of those old civvy instructors I remember with affection. Reg Morrison was probably the first one that I 'sat in' with, as I set off to learn the ropes. He was resident in a practical classroom and knew all there was to know about ignition systems. Frank Gillians had his leg in 'an iron', so clumped about the place a bit. Joe Coleman ran the battery shop for more years than anyone was able to remember. Then there was dithery Wally Long – known to all as 'Lolly Wong'! Bill Pepperall ran the 'B' vehicle layouts - he was to later die whilst on holiday in Spain with Pat McGuirk. Pat later left to run a guesthouse down at Ilfracombe in North Devon and quite a few of the Electrical Section had a coach-trip down there one weekend in May 1979.

Norman Dibb was a gentle soul, he wouldn't say boo to a goose, who later became one of the supervisors. His one overriding regret in life was that he couldn't work out just how a single-phase motor was able to work! One of the worst instructors you could meet was Les 'Dodger' Green, although one could like him a lot as a character. He used to smoke this old pipe and was interested only in railways and engines – how he ever held down a job as an instructor, I'll never know. I had occasion once to deliver a message to one of his students and, when I walked into the classroom, there was Les, drawing on the blackboard, while all his 'students' were apparently fast asleep – or pretty near it! I'll give Les one thing though, his blackboard drawings of the RB310 control box were a thing of beauty and a joy forever!

As mentioned, a lot of the instructors were already elderly when I started work and I can recall them sitting around in the rest-room, discussing whether or not they would retire 'that year'. There seemed to be a train of thought that went, *"If I just stay on for another year, that'll increase my pension when I finally retire"*. The trouble was that so many of them then failed to survive long enough to get their pension! I think I started thinking then that I would endeavour to eventually retire at as an early age as possible   - which of course I did! One thing about working there – starter motors and dynamos could always be brought in for repair - new brushes, skimmed armatures, one only had to leave the devices with old Reg and you could be sure that by knocking-off time, it would be as good as new. Spark plugs could be sand-blasted to order, ignition distributors timed to perfection, with new contact breaker 'points' – not like nowadays when you can't even get at any electrical components on your car, never mind take them off for servicing.

It seemed to be a tradition that we always gathered together at Christmas, usually at the *Angel Hotel* down at Midhurst. Those of us who lived in the Bordon area used to organise an Army coach to pick us up and then deliver us home again afterwards. That always seemed to be a hell of a long trip to me, via Liphook and Fernhurst, but nowadays by car, of course, it's a lot shorter. I remember one occasion, we even ran a 'quiz night' at one of the functions, I think it was in the days under the command of Major Sparkes – now there's a good name for I/C Electrics!

At one point in time, the trade of Electrician was dropped by REME, and vehicle mechanics had to be taught how to cope with vehicle electrics. In order to boost the staffing requirements for the enlarged training staff, a number of Army sergeants were posted in to the Section. Just thinking back, they included John Eaton, Geoff Hudson, George Stone, Frank Smith, John Howarth and Maurice Hilliker. It was Maurice who had the job of teaching electrics for the newly issued FV432 Mk1, while John Howarth later returned as a civvy instructor and became one of the supervisors. Another few names recalled are Frank Rybka – Polish Joe! – Ron Woodfield and Pete Watkins.

Back to College

On the personal side, I was also able to finally gain my ONC by going to Guildford Technical College on day-release from my job. That in itself was a bit of a struggle, as getting to Guildford each day involved a very early start, firstly to catch a bus into Farnham. Then I would catch a train into Guildford – a journey that had to be repeated in reverse in the evening. However, one of the guys on the course was about my age, named Ralph and ex-Navy, who had this big motor-bike. I got friendly with him, most of the others were a lot younger, and on a number of occasions he would give me a lift back along the A31 'Hog's Back' road between Guildford and Farnham at he end of the day. I can remember sitting on the back of his bike, doing 'a ton', with my briefcase sort of hanging in the slipstream behind us! Later, I found that there was a guy from Bordon on another course at Guildford, who owned one of those new-fangled *Citroen* cars with the hydraulic suspension – and began to travel with him in a lot more style and comfort!

When I had arrived at Bordon, Joyce and I were pretty pleased to be soon offered an Army 'pad' – the term used for married quarter. By that time, having two stripes on my arm and a young baby too, I was owner of enough 'points' to qualify for the quarter. And so we moved into No.9 Exmoor – known locally as Coronation Street! These houses were in a terrace and must have been put up around the time of the Boer War! They were pretty dark inside and very old-fashioned. We lit a fire to heat the water – and were still waiting for it to get hot about three weeks later – not joking either! Thankfully it wasn't too long, well six months actually, before we moved to No.4 Oakley Road early in 1965 – an absolute palace by comparison. It even had a garden at the back and was reasonably well appointed. And of course by now I had the benefit of three Sergeant's stripes on my arm, which made life a little more comfortable with reasonably good money coming in.

A Wednesday afternoon with the Army has always traditionally been 'sports afternoon' and at Bordon I used to make use of that break to do the shopping! From Oakley Road, I could reach the NAAFI Shop in no time at all and I remember staggering home from there, carrying a couple of large shopping bags – not the plastic ones used today – both filled with the week's supplies and costing less than a fiver for the lot! If we had a free weekend, we'd 'take the bus' up to Reading and stop with Mum and Dad. In fact it was two buses, 'the green one' as far as Aldershot, where we'd change over at the bus station and get 'the red one'. The whole journey used to take a couple of hours in all, but it all seemed so normal, as we didn't have a car then.

One episode that occurred during those years as a military instructor is well worth a mention – though it still brings tears to my eyes! One of the 'new' vehicles being brought into service then was the FV432 – FV standing for Fighting Vehicle. It was – and still is – a troop carrier, but was also adapted for many other roles. These included a self-propelled gun (the FV433 *'Abbot'*), the FV434 Recovery vehicle and others fitted with radar sets and missile launchers. The chief military instructor at the time was Artificer Sergeant Major (ASM) H A V Williams, who later became Mr Harry Williams, the Head of Department of the Engineering Science Department.

One afternoon, the ASM and I went up the Armoured Vehicle section to check out some electrical circuits on one of those FV432s. While in the process, I was suddenly hit by this almighty pain in my side, it felt as though I'd been run through with a sword – and then someone was twisting it! I was obviously as white as a sheet and must have appeared to be dying. Harry had a couple of other guys to help me into his car and immediately dashed me down to the nearest medical assistance, which happened to be at Longmoor Camp, just up the road to where we now live. Anyway, the Medical Officer diagnosed a 'kidney stone' and gave me a pain-killing injection and sent me home to bed. Harry drove me home to Oakley Road and, by the time we got there, I was so 'knocked out' by the injection that Joyce thought I'd been brought home drunk! Whatever it was, it worked and I was right as rain the next morning.

Being on the permanent staff at SEME Bordon brought me into contact with lots of guys who I'd already known previously and in fact I even ended up teaching some of them over the next few years! One of the earliest was Klaus Pennington, who must have been one of those vehicle mechanics now having to learn electrics. During my time there, one day I was introduced to a new civvie instructor, just arrived, and he turned out to be Colin Drasutis. What an amazing coincidence – not only had he and I gone to the Liverpool Institute, but we had also served at boys' school together, where he made RSM. And now here we were, instructing on the same subjects at Bordon. Colin had been invalided out of the Army, having caught some sort of horrific stomach-bug over in the Far East. Prior to coming to Bordon, he had been working as a civvie electrician at the Command Workshop up in Liverpool – at Daysbrook Barracks, if I remember correctly. *(We are both retired now of course, but Colin still lives at Liphook, just a few miles away from Greatham.)*

Time passed by quickly and Joyce was able to present me with another daughter, Michelle, in February of 1966 – the year that Everton won the FA Cup and England the World Cup. (If I remember correctly, Stan and June must have been visiting that weekend, I'm sure I can recall us watching that World Cup Final together.) Things were obviously going too well and fate intervened with the news that I was going to be posted to Berlin! Now this didn't go down too well at all. After all, I was due out of 'the mob' the following summer, I intended to pass directly into civvie street doing the same job as I was now doing, so what was the point of going back to Germany for just a few months? And so I began to fight the move, using all the ammunition that I could lay my hands on – and eventually the posting was cancelled. But about six weeks later I was told that I was going back to Fallingbostel – the dreaded 'effing bee'! The logic of this has always escaped me, but it was to no avail. REME Records stated that there was a dire lack of CETs at my rank and experience in BAOR, so at the end of October I found myself back at 'Fally', with the Royal Scots Greys, a tank regiment of long and illustrious history. As it turned out, despite my reticence at being there, those few months spent with The Greys weren't too bad at all!

Back at 'Fally' for a brief tour (1966 – 1967)

Returning to 'Fally' with The Greys, the 'myth' of my being deemed essential to the trade was immediately proven, as I actually spent most of my time running the battery charging shop – as well as learning how to handle the crossword in the morning paper! There was an Artificer Staff Sergeant, Archie Schofield, running the electrical side of the workshop and he told me that he had far too many Corporals crawling over his tanks already and could hardly ask a Sergeant to do the same thing! Therefore, he asked me how I'd like to take charge of the battery shop, not too difficult a task! *(I hasten to add that I was very well informed about batteries after a couple of years at SEME teaching the theory about them!)* For the first month or so, I stayed in the Sergeants' Mess, one of only about three living-in members. Each morning I would wake to the smell of a cup of tea on my bedside table and some young squaddie whispering, *"What would you like for breakfast, Sarge? It'll be ready when you come downstairs."* So, after a wash and shave, it was downstairs to a leisurely choice from freshly cooked bacon, eggs, sausage, a 'fried slice', beans etc - I think they call it 'the life of Reilly'!

I'd only been there a couple of weeks I guess, standing in the Mess one lunchtime, when came the letter from old mate John Howarth, with some really great news. While still at SEME, I had been in a 'pools swindle' and, upon leaving, I'd left enough money in the kitty for one final week's gamble. What a surprise to find that 'the syndicate' had won around £17,000 between them and that my share was a cheque for £651! Even though it was 'drinks all round' at the Mess bar later that night, the bulk of that money was definitely a lifesaver. We were later able to use it towards a deposit on our house – yes, the one we still live in today at Greatham.

About a month after I'd arrived at Fally, Joyce and the girls joined me in an Army quarter up on the main road down towards the little town of Fallingbostel itself – the one up which Joyce used to trudge, backwards and forwards, a few years previously. We had just a few months there – thinking back, I reckon that by sending me out to The Greys, REME Records had hoped I would be persuaded to 'sign on'. But by then the die was cast – we'd see out our time at Fally and then it would be back to Bordon for demob and a crack at me being a civvie instructor.

That Army quarter was huge! I think the barracks had originally housed some German cavalry soldiers – and seemed to have plenty of spare room for their horses too! Each block was split up into four separate quarters – you opened the main door to be confronted with a wide corridor, covered in some highly polished green material and long enough to hold a dance in! I can't remember exactly how many rooms ran off each side of that corridor, but sufficient to say it was large enough for Joyce, two small girls and myself! Above us was an attic and, on one occasion, a young German girl hid herself away up there, apparently 'on the run' from the authorities. I think Lorraine's memory still stretches back to that story, even though she must have been only three-years old at the time.

The block also had a basement, which contained the central heating system. If I remember correctly, each 'flat' occupant would take it in turns for a week at a time, keeping the boiler stoked up with coke during the cold weather. Having the two girls with us meant that going out to functions as a couple wasn't easy, not unless we could get a baby-sitter. There was one guy, a young Geordie recovery mechanic, who 'baby-sat' for us one night – but when we got home, he'd helped himself to all the beer in the

At Linda and Bob Owen's wedding, Bracknell, 1967

fridge and the below-stair neighbours had had to step in when they'd heard Michelle crying! I don't suppose we bothered going out after that! Although mostly we were able to depend upon Corporal Bob Owen, a really nice bloke, with whom we have always exchanged Christmas cards over the years. We even attended his wedding to Linda at Bracknell in 1967 and, many years later, on our way to a holiday up in Yorkshire, we astonished Bob by dropping in on him at his home near Scunthorpe! Just going back to the 'trade' question of why I'd been sent to Fally – there were CET Corporals attached to every Troop and Squadron. So many that you couldn't place a piece of paper between them, so the need for a Sergeant was superfluous – no wonder I was asked to work in the battery shop!

One function that we definitely did attend was the 'Burns Night Supper' in January 1966. With the regiment being historically of Scots descent – they were at Waterloo in 1815 – this particular occasion was celebrated every year with all the 'pomp and circumstance' you'd expect. 'Tatties and neeps', plenty of Scotch whisky and the piping in of the haggis – yes, we had it all. Trouble was – it just went on –and on - for so long! Traditionally, nobody was allowed to get up for a 'natural break', not as long as the RSM was still sitting down at his honoured position at 'the top table'. No doubt his bladder was highly trained for such an occasion, because he just sat and sat and sat. We lesser mortals just had to sit in stoic silence, bladders straining at the leash, until finally, the event came to a conclusion. You've never seen such an explosion of bodies, as the biggest proportion of Mess members made a dash for the gents! Which of course was far too small for such a crowd, so I was definitely one who relieved himself on the parade square, amongst many others seeking relief! I'm pretty sure the RSM knew all about what went on, but thankfully he was still inside the building and we all got away with our military indiscipline!

The Royal Scots Greys were an Armoured Regiment and, back in 1966, were equipped with the old *Centurion* tanks, no doubt (to use the parlance) around Mark 13s. These were supplemented with *Ferret* Scout Cars for reconnaissance tasks and backed up with a variety of other cargo-style vehicles. I hardly ever got near a tank, except for one session of a few days when I went out with a Squadron to do some radio suppression testing on Hohne ranges. It was quite boring really – you'd drive around to different locations, test the radios and write reports on the reception in each area. I suppose this was to make sure of good communications, should the Russians ever come rumbling across the border – believe me, that was a real threat in those days.

The Colonel of the regiment was a 'gentleman' in every sense of the word. I remember being interviewed by him both at the start and end of my short tour and was very impressed by his demeanour. Colonel John Stanyer later became 'CIGS' (Chief of the Imperial General Staff). Amongst the other regimental officers, the Adjutant was none less than Edward, Duke of Kent – 'Steady Eddie' I think the lads called him! One of the young subalterns was a member of the Player family – remember *Players'* cigarettes? It is rumoured that once, having written off a *Ferret* in an accident, he just wrote a cheque for its replacement!

There were two 'QMs' (Quartermasters) with the regiment, one who dealt with the technical stores and the other non-technical. Both had 'come up through the ranks' and were, by custom, allowed to use the Sergeants' Mess as well as their own Officers' Mess. They would sit up at the bar and invite you to join them in a game of 'pokey dice' – at least I think that's what it was called. I know it involved a lot of deception and bluffing – followed by copious drinking! I got stuck in a game one evening and when I woke Joyce up on my return home, she mumbled *"Oh, you're early"*. I certainly was early – it was about six in the morning! I must have slept a few hours, it being a Sunday – and I remember playing football for the LAD (Light Aid Detachment) that afternoon – life was a bit different then!

I find it hard to recall many other members of the REME personnel then serving with The Greys. Two of the vehicle artificers were John Ambler and Tony Hughes – the latter also became an instructor at SEME in later years, when I found out that he was also an ex-apprentice from Arborfield. I still catch up with him at reunions. I believe that there were two junior ranks, 'Spud' Battle and 'Farmer' Pike, who later actually left REME and joined The Greys, such was their affection for the regiment. I'm really having to rack my brain here, but I have the feeling that, not long before we were due to leave Germany, we were paid a farewell visit by Familie Godawa – well at least Mutti and Poppa. They must have come up from Celle, possibly with Karl-Heinz and maybe even with Dave Howlett, it's a long time ago! *(It was to be another thirteen years until I saw them again, but that tale is in another chapter!)*

Not long after I'd left the Regiment, restructuring of the Army enforced their combining with the 3rd Carabiniers to form the Royal Scots Dragoon Guards. This move didn't suit The Greys at all, they considered themselves as much the superior of the amalgamated pair – and I'm told that, over a period of time, they gradually subsumed the other lot into what can still be proudly called 'The Greys'. Many years later, on a visit to Edinburgh with Joyce, Lorraine and Phil, I took the opportunity to visit the Regimental Museum, located in Edinburgh Castle.

Me, meeting the Duke of Edinburgh at Bordon, 1969

Life as a Civilian Instructor (1967 – 1979)

I was actually due to be 'demobbed' from the Army on my twenty-seventh birthday in August, having completed my nine years 'with the colours', but a month's 'embarkation leave' actually brought that forward to July 1967. Thus, on my return from BAOR in April, I was nominally posted to the REME Depot at Arborfield, from where I would be officially 'demobilised'. I didn't really fancy hanging around the Depot for three months and, having spoken with the appropriate authorities, I was given special dispensation to return to SEME Bordon and carry on with some teaching, in readiness for applying for a civilian post. During that short period we were lucky enough to hire out No.18 Queens Cottages to live in, right next door to Joyce's Mum and Dad!

One incident that took place there still brings back the shivers. Michelle was still a toddler, about eighteen months old, and one day just fell backwards and hit the back of her head on the tiled surface of the backyard. Instinctively, I must have read about it or seen it demonstrated, I began to administer the 'kiss of life', as she'd totally blacked out, and managed to get her sorted out. That incident also brings back memories of when Lorraine, while we were still at Oakley Road, had managed to fall with a toy broom-handle in her mouth, jamming it down her throat! There was blood and panic at the time, but again fortunately, no lasting damage or after-effects.

While living at No.18, I was still in the position of being without my own means of transport, and used to depend upon lifts between Reading and Bordon. A guy called Dave Meadows had a hiring up near the *'Granby'* cinema at Cemetery Junction. He was actually on the permanent staff, stationed at Arborfield, but was attending a course down at Bordon, so his daily travel plan fitted in quite well with me. One thing I remember is him having to 'drop in' at a house in Newton Valence, I think one of his wife's family lived over there. It really seemed 'out in the sticks' at the time – but in later years became the focal point of many a walk over Selborne Common. There was one trip from Bordon that sticks in the mind. A couple of other lads were in the car with us, either they also lived in Reading or were heading to the railway station to catch a train connection. Anyway, it was a warm late Friday afternoon, so we decided to stop for a drink at a pub along the road. The one we eventually chose was the '*Leather Bottle*', still there nowadays at a place called Mattingley. One of the lads, happy to be on a weekend break, walked into the pub whistling – and the landlady had the temerity to say that she didn't allow music in her bar! Needless to say, we all smartly 'about turned' and marched back to the car.

I had actually started to learn to drive in Germany back at Celle, when an old mate from boys' school, by the name of Benny Allhouse, used to teach me, behind the wheel of a *Commer* Z-wagon. That was a horrible old beast of a vehicle with a crash-type gearbox and very unstable to say the least! But at least it gave me the rudiments of driving. The only other tips I'd ever picked up were from Jack Whitley. I can remember him telling me about automatic gearboxes, racing changes and double de-clutching, probably driving along the Formby bypass between Walton and Ainsdale – seems like a lifetime ago now!

I'd also, at one stage, taken some civilian driving lessons in Reading, with a guy whose name I can't remember, but who had previously given lessons to at least one of the Jones family – probably Janet. The trouble was, as soon as I got into the car, I tried to drive it like the old *Commer* – double de-clutching and ramming on the brake pedal! However, my instructor persevered with me and I soon got the hang of synchromesh gears and hydraulic brakes. I recall driving along Caversham Road on one occasion (a little less busy than it is today!) and hitting a pigeon that flew right under the car. I was then commended on not panicking and braking, although the pigeon probably wouldn't have agreed! Even so, I later failed my test miserably, attempting an obligatory 'hill-start' at the top of Prospect Street, over towards Tilehurst.

So I was very fortunate when, one day, Major Dougie Hopwood (who was then the Officer Commanding 'A' Company) called me in for an interview, prior to my job application. He asked about my plans – where I would live etc – and found out that I had no driving licence. Quick as a flash, he picked up the phone and contacted the MT Driver Training section. With me still being (just!) a soldier, he was able to fit me up with an intense course of driving. So I spent a couple of weeks – or was it more? – driving all around Hampshire, in a *Land Rover* alongside my instructor 'Sandy' Powell, who had at one time been RSM of the Scots Greys! And to my eternal gratitude, I was able to pass my test down in Portsmouth and get a driving licence. On the day of the test, I was completely unaware that I'd be taking it that particular day. We'd driven down to the coast as usual and dropped in at the NAAFI Club for 'tea and wad' as our lunch. When we got back to the *Land Rover*, Sandy tossed me the keys and walked away! It was only then that I noticed the driving examiner sitting in the passenger seat. With no time to think or worry, I drove a 'perfect' route around Portsmouth and Southsea and was handed my licence at the end of it.

(A notification in the REME magazine 'Craftsman', at the beginning of 2008 and just as I was submitting this book for publication, told of the death of Dougie Hopwood, well into his nineties. God bless you Sir.)

The time eventually arrived for the interviews and I was joined on 'the board' by other military staff in the Electrical Department, who were also due to soon leave the Army. Amazingly, all four of us were accepted – no doubt our experience of already having worked there in uniform helped just a little bit! The others were Ross Crapnell, Vernon Maw and Derek Rogers. It was Ross who offered me an old *Opel 'Kapitan'* (we christened it *'Herman the German'*), for the princely sum of £50, as my first car. I still remember the thrill – and not a little fear – when I picked the car up, all on my own, from the back of the married quarters, up near the main A325 road in Bordon. And so, for a little while at least, I began 'commuting' from Reading and back each morning and evening. If I remember correctly, I'd put a pint of oil in at the start of every journey! This would usually be purchased at the roadside garage in Alton, situated just after having turned left past the railway station into the town centre. The garage is still there, but has long since ceased selling oil and petrol – it's now a tyres, brakes and exhausts outlet.

The amount of traffic on the roads was then considerably less than it is today, and it was sheer pleasure, driving down from Reading to Bordon each morning, in charge of my own vehicle at last. The *Opel* was one of those old cars with a bench-seat right across the front and a column-mounted three-speed gearbox, but to me it seemed like a 'chariot of fire' as I whizzed down the thirty-odd miles of mainly country roads. Mind you, I did slow down a bit going up Worldham Hill in the evenings, I guess the engine was 'a bit' worn (to say the least) and the traffic was always a little heavier at that time of day, having knocked off work around five p.m. Coming back down that hill of course was no problem, I'd even manage to get up quite a bit of speed. However, on one occasion, it was a good job that I wasn't going too fast! About halfway from Worldham to the Oakhanger turn is a house on the left and, approaching it one day, a little girl had wandered out into the middle of the road. Thankfully I was able to slow down and stop, before taking her in to her mother.

We were still living at No.18 then and I remember one afternoon I decided to knock down an old wooden shed in the back yard and then saw up the old wood for fire lighting. Whatever it was – sawdust, insects or something – I came out in the most horrible rash – red blotch spots all over! I went to the Jones's local doctor in Southampton Street and, as I sat in the waiting room, the other patients sat as far away from me as possible. Luckily, I'd just had an allergic reaction – as I say, probably to the dust – and it soon cleared up.

The move back to Bordon

Once I'd settled into the job as a civvie, in the Electrics Section at SEME, the next move was to look around for a house in the locality. An ASM in the Section, HAV 'Harry' Williams, who later went on to become Head of Department 'upstairs' in the Headquarters building and was also a very nice chap, showed me around some housing down at Cowplain. While Bert May, another civvie instructor, put me onto a house at Four Marks. Now that place was brilliant – a detached place with a nice garden backing on to a disused railway line, which was up on an embankment at the back. But financially it was just beyond our reach and we finally decided on the first place we'd seen – and we're still living here at Chapel House, Longmoor Road, Greatham, nearly forty years later.

Just thinking back to the financial situation, I was fortunate in that Dougie Hopwood had signed some papers to say that I would (as a civvie) be earning so many pounds a year. Now he had quoted the 'top rate', which I was not to reach for about seven years or more! But it did the trick, allowing me to take on a larger mortgage than would normally have been allowed – and for a period of thirty years! I'd been saving with the *Leeds Permanent Building Society* for some years, but they weren't prepared to offer me the mortgage terms I wanted. So it was eventually the *Leicester Permanent* that came up with the goods.

The supervising instructor at that time was George Armitage, newly arrived from Chepstow, and he was living in the house next door. With the prospects of sharing cars on a weekly basis to reduce costs, plus the fact that it was only about four miles from Bordon, it wasn't too hard a decision to buy Chapel House. And having George next door was a great bonus when I consider all the old cars I was to have over the next twenty years! He was an ex-Royal Engineer and could turn his hand to just about anything. I only had to put my head under a bonnet and George would be there, ready to help a hand. Sadly he had been a long-time diabetic and the insulin he took eventually destroyed his kidneys. He fought bravely, even had a couple of transplants, but died in May 1988.

238

Our own house

Once we'd bought the house, and taken possession on October 31st 1967, we had to move all our stuff down from Reading, in a number of separate journeys of course. I used to pop down to the house from Bordon during the lunch break with a few bits and pieces. On one of the other trips, on November 5th, I had the back seat full of chairs, with Joyce and the girls on the bench-seat alongside me at the front. Coming down the Basingstoke Road in wet conditions, a van pulled out in front of us and then, without any signal, just stopped to turn right near to the *Gillette* factory. We smashed into the back and poor *'Herman'* was a write-off – I'd only had it for three months! Fortunately, none of us were hurt. Someone gave me a lift back to Queens Cottages, we managed to raise Wack on the phone – no mobiles then – and somehow we all managed to get into Wack's old *Hillman 'Minx'* and he brought us down to Hampshire. I think he and Mike eventually got the *Opel* down to the scrap-yard the next day. (I'll cover the rest of my cars in a separate chapter!)

Looking back now, Joyce and I just cannot believe how quickly time has passed by since we moved into Chapel House. The years have flown by so fast that it is difficult to chronicle all that has happened. Sufficient to say in this particular chapter that, in 2004, we are celebrating thirty-seven years here! The two semi-detached houses, Chapel House and New House next door, were built around 1965. I guess the

Wesleyan Chapel (now Chapel House)

Armitages bought their place when it was new – and we weren't too long afterwards. The family that lived here before us was named Blamey, I think that's the correct spelling.

Prior to the building of these houses, the site was occupied by a Wesleyan – or Methodist – chapel, constructed from corrugated iron on a wooden frame, probably dating back to the early 20th-century. Hence the name *'Chapel House'* of course. We did think of changing the name when we moved in, no doubt I wanted to call it something suitable, like *'Goodison'* or *'Dunsoldiering'*, but we never did change it, leaving its historical link firmly in place. Many years later, at *'The Maltings'* fair in Farnham, which takes place on the first Saturday each month, I actually found a good photograph of the old chapel. It felt quite eerie at the time, but I was really pleased to find it.

Buying the place was a bit of a struggle, I had to supplement my wages by working part-time at *'The Silver Birch'*, then a thriving pub in the village, well sponsored by the many soldiers serving at Longmoor Camp, just up the road. I also used to earn extra cash by instructing evening classes at SEME, for soldiers trying to pass what where known as 'pot Art' exams – potential Artificer to give them their full name. We managed to extend our mortgage loan a couple of years after moving in – using the money (£500 if I recall correctly) to buy a small parcel of land to extend the garden to around three times its original size. There's still a photograph somewhere, showing Joyce in shorts and wellies, as she dug over the virgin ground!

In hindsight that was a good move, as later years saw two houses being built alongside ours, but their gardens have had to 'stop short', as our extra garden space runs behind them. Without that, we would be overlooked, which would rather spoil things. Behind the garden is a large field that, thankfully, has seen off a couple of planning applications over the years. It remains just grazing land and mainly supports horses, which provide a nice sight most of the time. Sadly, the opening of the dual-carriageway A3 trunk road in 1996, bypassing Petersfield and Liphook, now provides a constant background of noise from morning to night, a permanent reminder of 'progress'! Luckily, soon after the road's opening, we were able to join a local 'pressure group', which successfully gained a compensation award for many villagers. It just about paid for the house to be completely double-glazed, so at least the noise is abated indoors. We'd already had some double-glazing fitted some years previously, but the new PVC-clad windows are far more convenient – no painting and far more easy to keep clean.

Life as a civilian instructor couldn't have been better, it was a job I loved doing, passing on knowledge is certainly most rewarding. The thing with teaching Army students was that, in the main, they **wanted** to learn – not always the case in civilian schools I know. I graduated from teaching 'basic principles' and was always keen to teach armoured vehicle electrical systems and new equipments as they were introduced. This meant lots of research into new types of electrical systems, as vehicles became more and more sophisticated as solid-state (or transistorised) control systems came into their own. I also progressed to teaching Artificer students – now they **were** keen to learn – and would invite their instructor to end-of course 'parties', which was hardly ever turned down!

At one point in time, the Shah of Iran was still in power and decided to buy *Chieftain* MBTs (Main Battle Tanks) from the United Kingdom (UK). He sent over squads of technical officers to learn all about them and, as I was well into tank electrics by then, I found myself standing in front of a class of pretty high-ranking Iranian officers, all hanging on to my very word! At that time too, a civilian firm called *MTS (Millbank Technical Services)*, had a contract to maintain the vehicles out in Iran. Trouble was, they managed to copy a lot of training precis and notes from our staff, so much so that we said that the 'MTS' stood for 'mind-tapping specialists'!

As an instructor, I started off teaching the basic subjects and, as I became more experienced, so moved on to the more technical side – as with that officers' course just mentioned. Possibly the most rewarding course to take was the 'Tiffy' course. The students would be well motivated and mature, being Sergeants wishing to move up a vital step in their careers. Being of similar age to many of them, I was able to build up rapport and really enjoyed spending some six weeks or so with the same bunch. However, it did have its pitfalls! I walked into the classroom one morning, to find a cheap plastic 'Christmas fairy' on my lectern. Around her neck was hung a sign, with the one word 'NUFF' written on it. I could sense the giggling from the lads and recognised that they obviously knew something that I didn't! When I asked for an explanation, it went along these lines. *"Sir, whenever you explain something and then ask us whether or not we understand, you finish it off with 'Fair enough?' So that's what you have on your desk – Fairy Nuff!"* Well, I had to see the funny side of that of course, it showed that everyone picks up these little habits, without realising that they have them. It's certainly something that has stuck in my memory all these years and I have enjoyed telling the tale to many audiences.

One of the oldest instructors at Bordon was a guy by the name of Tommy Groves. I'd first met up with Tommy when I was changing trade and on course at Arborfield.

We had to go down to Bordon to see the electrical 'mock-up' of the *Centurion* ARV (Armoured Recovery Vehicle), on which Tommy was the expert. Now that I was an instructor myself, he was now a colleague – even when he later became one of the supervising instructors, alongside George Armitage. At one stage, Colin Drasutis and myself had to go off and visit the FVRDE (Fighting Vehicle Research and Development Establishment) over at Chertsey, in order to learn all about the *Chieftain* electrical systems. Here, we were guided by an ASM in the MAG (Maintenance Advisory Group), a chap called Joe Price.

Joe later came to Bordon as an instructor himself and, as he lived in Aldershot, he used to travel in a car-sharing scheme with Tommy G and another chap, Pat Maher. Having been in Chapel House for a few years, I'd decided to block in the porch outside the front door. I was looking for material from which to construct it, when Joe told me that he was extending his kitchen and had a spare window – which seemed to fit the bill. I remember Joyce and I going to Joe's place in our *Morris Minor*, fully equipped with roof rack. How we got the window, still in its metal frame, with its wooden sill, back to Greatham, I don't know! It was a huge thing and overhung the car both front and back. But manage we did and, having had to saw the middle portion out, that window is still there some thirty-odd years later.

Pat Maher was a nice guy, he had served in the RAF and, despite his Irish brogue, always said that he was from Norwich. Once he gave me a 'brass rubbing' that he'd taken in Norwich Cathedral and was always saying 'you must go there'. *(It was only in 2004 that we eventually did!)* At one point, I can't remember exactly why, but Pat and I started going to the pictures! I guess we were both tied up with young families and not able to get out that much. So I would drive through Weybourne (Farnham) and pick him up outside a pub called *'The Running Stream'*, then we'd continue onto the cinema in Aldershot. One film we saw was *'Tora, Tora, Tora'*, all about the Japanese raid on Pearl Harbor and the Battle of Midway that followed. We also went to see a film starring George C. Scott, when he played the part of General Patton.

At some point, probably in the early Seventies, I was enticed into resuming my cricketing career, which had been severely curtailed back in my 'Inny' days by a certain 'Squinty' Morgan! This came about by my friendship with Colin Drasutis, who had settled down to live in Liphook, after first living at Liss. Colin had always had an interest in cricket and was currently playing for their 'Second XI'. One of the main attractions was that the lads met up rather frequently at Liphook's *'Green Dragon'* pub and I don't mind admitting that I enjoyed a pint or two there, in pursuit of cricketing fame and fortune!

I suppose one of the main reasons behind being actually chosen to play was the ownership of one's own transport – with the obvious ability to give some other lads a lift to the away matches! The captain of the team at that time was an older chap called Harry (can't recall his surname), who picked his sides on two abilities really – drinking and driving! Anyway, despite the above qualms, I did spend a couple of seasons with Liphook Seconds and, in the main, it proved quite enjoyable. Home games were at the Recreation Ground, while away matches included some really nice locations. One such idyllic spot was down at '*ICI Verdley*', actually in the village of Fernhurst, and I think that when I played there, Joyce and the girls, along with at least Eileen and family, came along as spectators for the afternoon. Another nice spot was down on the common, just north of the Chichester Festival Theatre. Apart from Colin and Harry, I really cannot remember the names of any others, except for Malcolm 'Bomber' Webb. He gained his nickname by bowling one ball that went straight up in the air, before falling directly onto the stumps at the batsman's end!

As mentioned, the social side of events seemed to figure large, and I recall joining a coach load of players, friends and family, on a trip to the AWRE at Aldermaston, to participate in a 'pub quiz' evening. But most of the socializing (i.e. drinking!) took place at the *Green Dragon*. It's lucky for me that, in those days, the Longmoor Road was pretty well dead straight between the edge of Liphook and the gates of Longmoor Camp! The drinking and driving laws hadn't then come into effect, so it was probably a damn good thing that my 'career' lasted no longer than a couple of seasons!

Back at the 'work-face', for a few years in the late Seventies, I moved out of the classroom environment and became one of the 'practical' instructors. That involved demonstrations, maintenance, supervision of practical work etc, both on real vehicles and realistic skeleton models, which included all the electrical apparatus. I recall one day, having been 'putting faults' onto a circuit, inside a vehicle framework, I stood up right under a metal corner and made a large dent in my head! Blood was running down everywhere and I had to be taken down to my own doctor at Liss for stitches! Eventually, after I'd been teaching in the classroom – and on practical work – for a number of years, the scent of promotion started to drift across my nostrils and I decided it was probably time to move on! But before I move on in the story – the following 'interlude' is included!

A spell in the Territorial Army (1979 –1986)

Just why I decided to re-join the Army – well, the Territorial Army (TA) anyway - having been so happy as a civilian for about twelve years - I don't really know! I was away on a training course at Beaconsfield, up in Buckinghamshire at the time, and went for a few pints in the Sergeants' Mess one evening. Somehow, Terry Burns persuaded me that I was still young enough (at thirty-nine!) to get into the TA and earn myself some extra cash for what seemed very little actual service – a two-week summer camp each year, plus two training weekends.

Well, whether it was the beer or not, when I got back to Bordon, in January 1979 I went over to the TA Headquarters at Broxhead House and signed on! I was taken in at the rank of Sergeant, but the trade I settled on was Electrician – after all, I'd been teaching the subject at SEME for a number of years! My unit was 9 Field Workshop REME, what was termed a 'sponsored unit'. This differentiated it from those 'independent' units that were usually associated with the local area of whichever towns they were based in. The unit was actually a Regular Army unit, based at Bordon, but one that could be quickly reinforced by part-time soldiers, as the need required. Many of the part-timers were just that, having had no previous military experience, but were good at their particular trades. Then there were a few ex-soldiers, like myself, whose experience and previous military training could be put to good use.

Helping the recruits

As it turned out, being almost 'on the doorstep' of Bordon, I was able to fix up quite a number of extra weekends of work, all paid for at the standard Army pay for my trade and rank. The 'work' consisted of assisting with the initial enrolment of men who had come to join the TA for the first time. I would usually pick up a minibus at Bordon on the Saturday morning, then drive to either Farnham or Liss railway station, to pick up the new recruits as they arrived on their trains. Then it would be back to HQTA to book them in. This would be followed by medical examinations – or 'PULHEEMS' as they were known – at which I would assist with such things as measuring height and weight, eye-tests and urine tests – no, I'm not taking the piss! By the time this had been done for maybe two or three busloads of guys, the morning would have passed by and it would be time for lunch. This involved taking the new lads to the cookhouse, where we 'recruiters' would tuck in to a good meal as well! My usual mate on most of these weekends was none other than Jim Scurr, with whom I'd served as a boy-soldier back at Arborfield – we made a pretty good team together! After dinner, it would then be time for kit issues, so it was off to the Quartermaster's (QM's) stores, where I'd again assist, this time in making sure everyone got all their kit – hopefully of the correct size!

Then came the bit that the new recruits dreaded – the assault course! They didn't actually have to 'pass' a test as such; it was just to give them a taste of what would be expected of them when they got attached to a TA unit. Most of them were dead keen on joining, so they made a good effort at completing the course, however hard they found it. Then would come the tea meal, again in the cookhouse, by which time everyone would be chatting away as though they'd known each other for years, rather than a whole day! Finally it was time for them to return home, now carrying all their kit-bags with them of course, so a 3-tonner lorry would take them back to their respective railway stations.

This whole affair would be repeated on the Sunday, with another bunch of hopeful recruits. I recall one Sunday morning, sitting in the minibus outside Farnham station, awaiting the first train of the day. I was reading the paper when there was a tap on the window and a voice asked *"Is this the transport for Bordon?"* Replying in the affirmative, I told 'the voice' to climb in the back – then wondered where he'd come from, as there was no train yet in the station. It turned out that the guy had stayed overnight with a mate in the area and then I suddenly recognised his face! It turned out to be a guy called Valentine Bullen, who I'd known as a mate of Harry Hayes in the days when we'd knocked around together about twenty years previously! And, do you know, I don't think I've ever seen him since!

Back on Luneburg Heath!

Anyway, apart from those 'recruiting weekends', I also had some 'real-time' serving to do, with my first two-week camp taking place in BAOR in September 1979. The exercise was termed 'Steel Trap' and took place out on the heathland of Soltau, an area well known to me from my regular service at both Celle and 'Fally'. The Regular Army ASM (Artificer Sergeant Major) of 9 Field was a lad called Mick Elton – who had been a mere 'grunt' with 94 Locating Regiment at Celle when I'd been there as a technician. Over the middle weekend of the camp, as tradition demanded, there was a two-day period of 'R and R' – rest and recuperation. Most of the TA lads headed to the fleshpots of Hamburg, but I didn't really fancy that at all! Instead, I asked Mick if he fancied going back into Celle.

He jumped at the chance and we travelled down there in his own Land Rover, obtaining permission to stay overnight in the Sergeants' Mess. As he checked in at the Guardroom, I innocently got my camera out to take a few pictures – and was almost arrested as a spy! Security had certainly been stepped up since my last appearance at 94 and, despite Mick and I both being in (rather scruffy!) uniform, the alert guards must still have wondered what was taking place. It was all settled amicably of course, once I'd explained who I was and the reason for my being there. But I don't think I ever did take any photographs!

After we'd booked in at the Mess, then showered and changed, Mick was happy just to stay in the bar for a few beers and talk over old times, but I set out to track down the Godawa family! I walked around to Kanonen Strasse, to the school where they had lived, only to find they had moved on, to another town not too far away, but of course impossible for me to get to with my limited time. Fortunately, the new occupants of the flat over the school had a phone number and I was able to call through and tell Mutti that she was speaking to 'Peter-Scouse'! She was absolutely amazed of course, it had been more than 12 years since I'd left Germany and been in touch.

Mutti declared how sorry she was that we couldn't get together, but gave me the address of Ulli and his wife. Ulli (short for Ulrich) was 'the baby' of the family and still just a young boy when last I'd seen him. I returned to the Mess, had some tea, got myself washed and changed and called for a taxi. It turned out in the end that I had to guide the taxi-driver down to Ulli's place – I knew Celle better than he did! Imagine my surprise when I got there to find that Mutti and Poppa had driven down from Hildesheim to meet up with me! They had brought a photo album with them, so I was able to catch up with all their news for a couple of hours. Eventually, Ulli offered me a lift back to the Kasserne, but not before we stopped off at a bar in town for a couple of excellent beers!

A memorable trip to Cyprus

My next TA 'camp' was in May the following year and turned into the 'trip of a lifetime'! I was over at HQTA one day, on some sort of business, when I bumped into Staff Sergeant (SSgt) Pete Breedon – who had been on a tiffy (Artificer) course under my instruction just recently. It turned out that he was now in charge of individual training with the TA, so 'where did I want to go?' Like a flash, I told him that I'd never been overseas with the Regulars – you can't call Germany 'overseas' can you? – so what were the chances of a visit to Cyprus? Enough said - that's where I went for a fortnight!

I think there were twelve of us in the party, three of us were senior ranks, and we were all from different units. I remember sitting on the plane from Brize Norton, just in front of Bob Monkhouse, who was going out there on 'forces' entertainment'. We flew out on a Friday and we senior ranks were shown to our individual bunks in the Sgts' Mess at RAF Akrotiri, which was also used as the base for 48 Command Workshop. The accommodation was pretty basic, just a single room on the ground floor of a three-storey block. There was one of those huge rotating cooling fans on the ceiling and we were warned to switch them off before going to bed. Apparently, if you slept without covers, which was required in the heat, there was the danger that the fan would have you so cool by next morning that hypothermia could set in!

That first night, one of the other sergeants, Joe Smith of the Pay Corps, asked the other two of us to join him at one of the ritzy hotels on the sea front in Limassol. Joe knew the island well from previous experience and introduced us to 'brandy sours' – served in salt-rimmed glasses and very palatable! We were sat at the bar, when in came a couple of faces well known to me, Ginger McCleod and Derek Simpson, both still in the Regulars and serving with the Workshop. It just so happened that Derek's daughter had just been married that very day – would we like to attend the reception? That was one of those offers you can't refuse and a great time was had by one and all! We had a great meal, plenty to drink, and were entertained by a group of Greek dancers in the traditional style! We also got to meet an American chap, who invited us to join him on his yacht the following afternoon! This we did of course, enjoying a splendid cruise around Buttons Bay in the warm Mediterranean sunshine!

It all had to end and, on the Sunday, we had to don our uniforms (all twelve of us now) and join one half of the Workshop on what was termed its 'summer camp'. This took place on a sandy strip just along the coast, called Pissouri Bay. There was absolutely nothing there at that time, but I believe it has now been developed into a tourist spot, full of hotels. Anyway, our accommodation was a little more basic – tents! The power was supplied by the usual diesel-engined generating sets, noisy old things, but they did the job! I remember having the job of connecting up all the lights around the camp area.

For the next few days, we TA lads joined in with the Regular members at such activities as football, volleyball, sailing etc! I even took part in an air-sea rescue demo! Picked up by a helicopter, I had to drop into the bay from a height of some 30 – 40 feet, then float in my life-jacket until the chopper crew came back to pick me up, winch me aboard and return me to the cliff-top. We also did some map reading exercises, one at night, which was interesting, marching on a compass heading only. Came the Thursday, and we were asked if 'the TA' would like to enter a team to join in a 30-kilometre 'route march'. I jumped at the chance and, our team of three included a TA chap, a fellow-Scouser called Harry Henderson, and a Regular SSgt known to one and all as Ziggy – he looked a bit like Charles Bronson, you know, the *'Death Wish'* actor.

Anyway, we set off very early in the morning, suitably dressed in trousers, long-sleeved shirts and floppy hats – all to ward off the blazing sunshine. I remember going up a terraced hillside, built to house the grapevines that seemed to grow everywhere, when Harry froze with his foot in mid-air. He'd almost trodden on this huge black snake and was petrified! Whether or not it was poisonous, we never found out, we were just happy to avoid it. There was map reading involved, as well as the walking, and it proved a pretty demanding day, I can tell you! But we were very proud to finish in the second-fastest time! I recall that, when we got to the finish, it was in a small village up in the mountains, and the booking-in table was located in an orchard. Now, I'd spent the last four days at least 'bunged up', if you get my drift, probably due to the change of water and routine! Sufficient to say that there is one particular tree in that orchard that got a lovely load of organic manure that afternoon!

When we returned to Pissouri, the OC (Officer Commanding) of the Workshop paid a visit and, when he heard that the 'TA team' had done so well, he sent us all back to Akrotiri that same evening, rather than waiting until the end of the 'camp' on the Sunday. Not only that, but he ordered a Scots lad to act as our driver, using the Workshop minibus, and to be at our disposal over the next couple of days! Needless to say, we made full use of that and acted just like tourists, visiting a Roman amphitheatre at Curium, the birthplace of Venus and the lovely resort of Paphos, at the western end of the island. We also had a good evening out at the 'Kolossi Castle' – a pub run by an English guy, just outside Akrotiri. I think we watched Notts Forest win the European Cup on TV that same night – I seem to remember it was a 1 - 0 win over Swedish club Malmo.

When Monday eventually arrived, we all thought that we'd actually have to do some work in the Workshop. But no such luck – we were left to our own devices for the rest of the week! On one of those days a few of us 'borrowed' a *Land Rover* and I drove us to the Army base at Episkopi to pick up some pay! On the way back, one of the tyres 'blew', just after we'd navigated a treacherous hairpin bend that first dropped alarmingly to sea level, then rose steeply upwards again, I think they called it 'Happy Valley'. The job of changing the wheel was none too easy, the jack on the vehicle must have last been used on one of Boudicea's chariots! Fortunately, we were parked on a sandy stretch alongside the road, away from the traffic, so no danger to anyone. Then a real piece of luck – coming along the road was an *Eager Beaver*, a motorised forklift truck. The driver pulled over and simply lifted our vehicle off the road and, within the turn of a few nuts, the new wheel and tyre were re-fitted and away we went.

Another day saw us piling into the workshop minibus once more, with one of the Greek drivers taking us into the island's capital, Nicosia, still split then by the United Nations' (UN) 'green line' between the Turks in the north and Greeks in the south. We didn't stop there too long, only long enough to have a drink or two in one of the bars along 'the strip' – can't remember the proper name for it, but it was a notorious place full of sleazy bars and pick-up joints, I was none too impressed with it. *(During 'the troubles' in Cyprus in the Fifties, it had been known as 'Murder Mile'!)* After that, we were driven up into the hills of Troodos and stopped at a roadside café for a meal. It must have been the worst meal ever! It was actually 'cooked' by a UN soldier, I can't remember his nationality, who was the boyfriend of the girl who was supposed to be running the place. Anyway, he didn't have a clue and ruined whatever it was we'd ordered, so we all refused to pay and just walked out.

That was a pity really, as all the food we had on Cyprus during our two-week stint was delicious, except for that once. On the return trip, the Greek driver decided to show off his talents as he drove down the steep mountain roads at breakneck speed, hardly using his brakes at all – we all sat in the back wondering if we'd get home safely. It really was a 'white knuckle' ride - I've never been so terrified! During the rest of that week we managed to get as far as Larnaca for a few hours and, on the same trip, dropped in at Dhekelia, where 48 Command Workshop had a sort of off-shoot. At the end of it all, the Workshop threw a 'going home' party for us and we were able to look back on a fabulous fortnight, one I'll never forget, that's for sure.

A couple of other things I remember from that trip, one of them being the small yellow scorpions that scuttled about near the accommodation block, so that one always checked ones boots before putting them on each morning. And, on the subject of boots, buying a couple of pairs of desert boots – or chukka boots, as they were also known. They were light in weight and of suede covering, one pair in sand colour and the other in grey. Lots of the soldiers serving in Cyprus actually wore them as part of their uniform, along with shorts, which were *de rigeur*!

Other trips

Nothing quite lived up to that 'camp' and the rest of my TA service paled by comparison. One other 'camp' actually took place at Bordon and Tidworth, but I did go back to Germany again, to a place called Heide, and managed a day-trip to Hamburg. This took the part of a sightseeing trip, mainly around the harbour and its overhead railway – memories of Liverpool – as well as being able to admire some pretty up-market shopping centres. Another trip took me to Flensburg in Denmark, where I remember driving one of the workshop lorries for a very long distance, the trip took us over some remarkable bridges, from one island to another – though I'd have to look at a map now to try and recall their names! We got quite close to Copenhagen towards the end of the first week and hoped to make a visit there for 'R and R' – but the Officer Commanding (OC) put the mockers on that, saying that we had to stay within the workshop accommodation.

Strangely enough, that OC, Major Brian Garden, had actually taught me on a computer course at Blandford just a couple of years previously, in his civilian capacity. He was a bit of a miserable sod, and that refusal to sanction a trip to Copenhagen probably decided me that I'd had enough of part-time soldiering, I was now 46 years of age so I packed it in. But it had been an interesting time in the main! I had even taken advantage of my position to arrange some HGV (Heavy Goods Vehicle) training and actually held an HGV licence for a few years. Even used it on one occasion to deliver an old computer system to Salford University! And, of course, as detailed above, I used it to do quite a bit of driving during the rest of my TA service.

Something amusing that occurred was during one of my visits to Germany. Washing facilities while on exercise were limited and it was customary for trips to be arranged to visit local Army garrisons for showers. On this occasion, we had driven into Hohne and there I was, under the lovely hot water and probably with soap in my eyes, when a voice alongside me piped up, *"Fancy seeing you here, Sir"*. Turned out he was a soldier who had only recently been on a course under my instruction back at SEME Bordon! And it's not often that a Sergeant is addressed as *'Sir'*!

It was probably at the end of my final TA trip that I joined ASM Jesse James in driving back to Blighty in the Workshop Machinery Wagon. Now Jesse was a 'bit of a lad' on the quiet and had managed to hoard away tons of booze and cigars in every nook and cranny of that old wagon – I think there was even some stashed away under the engine bonnet! The journey out of Germany and onto the roll-on-roll-off ferry across the North Sea passed without incident. Jesse then asked me to do the driving off the ferry, which I did with my heart in my mouth as we drove into the Customs shed! But Jesse had a cunning plan! As the Customs officer approached our vehicle, Jesse climbed down from the cab clutching a large map. He then lay it across the front of the vehicle and engaged the officer in finding out the best route away from Harwich and across towards Hampshire.

Anyway, his cheek paid off because we were then waved through Customs without having the vehicle inspected. I recall that we had landed in the early hours of the day in question and, rather than trying to negotiate a route around the outskirts of London, we (well I) drove right through the city centre and eventually onto the A3. It was still dark when we got as far as Farnham and I think it was the very first time that I'd driven along the Farnham by-pass and found the traffic lights at green! I never did find out whether Jesse had kept his swag or sold it on, but I was just grateful to have not been nicked for smuggling! *(As an aside here, Jesse's real name was Mervyn and his wife Shirley worked in the kitchen at Bordon alongside Joyce!)*

Promotion – and computers (1980 – 2000)

Just after the Christmas recess of 1979/1980, old pal Colin Drasutis came to see me. *(You may remember that Colin had been at the Liverpool Institute at the same time as me, and then also at the Apprentices' School at Arborfield. His rather strange surname, he told me, was that of a 'lapsed Lithuanian Catholic!)* Colin had already left the electrical section on promotion and was now working as a 'course designer' in the SEME HQ building – commonly known to one and all as 'The Kremlin'. During the leave period, an elderly former instructor called Ron Girling had sadly died and someone was now urgently required to fill his post as the School's statistician. This meant looking after student records and other things – I won't bore anyone with the details! It was a bit of a one-off task that Ron had been doing for a number of years, working away much to his own methods, in a room upstairs next to the Technical Library. The trouble was that nobody had a clue as to how he had actually done the

Opening of the SEME Computer Centre, Bordon, 1982

job, he'd left no written instructions anywhere – and there was certainly nobody else around to refer to!

Colin informed me that interviews would be taking place in order to fill the vacant position and asked *"Was I interested?"* The obvious answer, otherwise I wouldn't be telling the story, is that I was! And so, a few days later, the Canadian Major who had conducted the interviews (Gary Bingham) called me into his office and said that the job was mine if I wanted it. I must admit to a certain amount of trepidation, but once I got stuck into the job, it became very interesting. The main thing too is that I actually wrote down a complete set of instructions on how the job was being done – by me anyway – so that it could later be picked up by any successor with not too many problems. In the event, this actually happened the following year, when I was succeeded as statistician by Eric Wealls – who had actually been my room NCO (Non-Commissioned Officer) at boys' school back in 1957! It can't have done him any harm either, as he eventually gained promotion on the instructional side and moved away to Deepcut (not far from Camberley).

During my tour of duty in the Statistics Room, it became evident that the chance of promotion would eventually come up, to replace a guy called Jack Wickham, who was then the Supervisor, Internal Validation. But the job was going to change with his successor, as the School was soon going to purchase a computer system to assist with the training system. *(Colin Drasutis and Gary Bingham were actually involved in the project to purchase the computer.)* So what 'they' needed was a young upstart (my term!) who was willing to not only take the promotion, but also to get trained up on computers! Just a couple of months later, I therefore attended my first computer course at Blandford. It was all about the basics of computing, but far removed from where computer technology is today, and took place at the 'DADPTC' (Defence Automatic Data Processing Training Centre) – known locally as 'Dad's Army'! It was good to be housed in one's own private room at the Officers' Mess, where at least we received good treatment and plenty of good food.

That course was only three weeks long, but it was really hard work and seemed a hell of a lot longer! Most of the other members of the course were already part of the computing world, mainly from a programming background, so the terminology was at least familiar to them. Some were civilians, while others were military guys from the Army, RAF and Royal Navy – it was pretty high-powered! I was accompanied on the course by an older chap named John Thayer, who worked next door to me, in the SEME Examination Centre. He'd already served a full 22 years in the Army before becoming a civilian instructor, and must have been around the age of sixty I guess, maybe nearer sixty-five. At the time of the course, we didn't even have a computer at Bordon, so we'd never handled a keyboard before either, which didn't make life any easier!

With flow-charts, top-down systems design and basic programming techniques, I'm afraid it all went right over John's head, he was completely flummoxed. He lived down in Barnfield Road, Liss and, during the two weekends of the course, when we were allowed to come home, I went around to his place to try and help him with the coursework that we'd been set. He was almost in tears, saying that he should never have been persuaded to attend the course, it was well beyond his capacity. Luckily, once we both got back to SEME, he never really had to put any of it into practice and gratefully retired when his time came up!

In February 1981, a promotion board was finally set up for the previously mentioned Internal Validation vacancy. There were quite a few volunteers from within SEME and other external candidates too. I was one of the protagonists and managed to pass the board with flying colours. Over the years that followed, many of those other guys who attended that promotion board told me how grateful they were that they hadn't passed! When they saw the amount of work that was involved, they were pleased that they remained in the mainstream instructional side of life. One of those guys was Bob McLeod, who retired early in 2006. I went to his 'retirement party' at *The Cricketers* in Kingsley – and he was still thanking me, even then, twenty-five years later, for getting that job!

The Computer-less Manager!

And so I was now a fully-fledged Supervising Instructor – but with no instructors to supervise – as well as being the Computer Manager, with no sign of a computer to manage! However, this didn't prevent the School from sending me on another course at Blandford, this time for a whole six weeks! This one was termed 'Basic Systems Design and Analysis' and proved a real brain-wrecker! The day's work would usually end about 4 p.m. and I would gladly put on some sports gear and go for a run all around the camp perimeter, it was just so good to get away from the 'head banging' for a while. Then it would be back to the Mess for tea and cake, but then there would be a session of course-work to do before the evening's late dinner.

I must have gone home every weekend during the course, I remember the trip there and back with great clarity. I was driving my *Ford 'Capri'* at the time and it was quite a pleasure taking the route across via Alton, through Winchester city centre and the Salisbury ring-road, then down through pleasant countryside to Blandford. That trip would be on the Sunday evening, with fairly light traffic, so I was able to get my foot down and make it in good time. At the end of it all, I was delighted to receive a certificate of competency from the National Computer Centre. So I must have learned something, despite all the headaches!

In October of 1981 I was again back at Blandford for another three-week course, this time on Project Management. It was far in excess of what I actually needed at that stage, but at least offered a good grounding for the future. Most of the other 'students' were high- ranking officers from all three services and the food was excellent! We even had *lobster thermidor* one evening in the Mess – the one and only time I have partaken of that particular dish! Most of the course consisted of presentations by visiting experts in their field and it was all very interesting, to say the least. We also had a couple of 'visits' out, one was to the *Westland* helicopter head-quarters, I think at Yeovil, where we looked at 'computer aided design'; I think the other place was at Street, but I can't recall what we did there! *(It must have been on this course that I came across Brian Garden, who I mentioned earlier in his TA guise – of which I had no knowledge at the time!)*

Back at Bordon, during the early period of my job 'in computing', I shared an office with some soldiers who were part of the External Validation team. They were all Warrant Officers, mature guys, and it was a good time, very friendly all round. One of the ASMs was a guy called Barrie King – who I didn't find out was an ex-apprentice until an old boys' reunion many years later! Nick Scantlebury is another I remember, because he bought the *Vauxhall 'Viva'* from me.

Early in the following year (1982), surprise, surprise, the computer hardware actually began to arrive at SEME! It was manufactured by an American company, *Data General (DG)*, and their software people were responsible for taking an existing package used at Princess Marina College, Arborfield and, with my 'assistance', change it to suit Bordon's particular requirements. The hardware itself presented initial problems and it was ages before the CCTA (Central Computer and Telecommunications Agency), a Treasury-sponsored organisation, agreed that it was 'up to the job'. I then had to go off on *DG* courses in order to learn how to handle the specific computer system installed at Bordon. Then it was time to sit down with the *DG* programmer, a young lady by the name of Diane Lightfoot, while we thrashed out the necessary software changes. All very time consuming, but it eventually paid off and we got most of what we wanted.

As things developed over the next few years, the 'SPEC' system at SEME (Student Performance Evaluation by Computer) became the benchmark for similar systems throughout the Army educational system. I feel that I played quite a big part in setting up a system that eventually stood the test of time. Across the training system, we set up the SPEC User Group, which included personnel from Bordon, Arborfield, Chepstow, Harrogate, Chatham, Minley Manor and the Military College at Sandhurst. We used to meet up at regular intervals, at one location or another, and it all proved very interesting. By the time that I retired in 2000, SPEC and its successor 'SPEX' had been running for almost twenty years and doing a very good job of maintaining the School's internal validation system. It was to be replaced by a new networked system just around the time I was 'out of the door' and, on subsequent visits to SEME as a 'retiree', the moan was that the staff would all like to see SPEX back up and running!

'The Jays' netball team – Joyce holds the cup

A new career!

Around the beginning of March 1998, I spotted a notice pinned to the telegraph pole in the front garden outside of the house. It announced a meeting to discuss what was called a *'Village Appraisal'*, to be held in Greatham Village Hall. I was none too sure as to what this entailed, but decided to attend the meeting and find out for myself. A lady called Jo Dixon, on behalf of a group called *'Rural Action'*, gave a presentation of what this Village Appraisal was all about. Essentially, it asked local people to get together and discuss what they wanted for their future community needs – such things as local transport, education, leisure activities, health and services – just about anything really. Apparently this had all started up after John Major, Prime Minister at the time, had attended a conference in Rio some years previously. A Village Appraisal invited people to look at their community – maybe even to peek into its past – and come up with viable ideas on how things could possibly be improved in the future.

To cut a long story short, there were sufficient people interested – me included – who thought that this was a good idea and we arranged to meet up the following week to discuss how the Appraisal could be set up and supervised. For my sins, I ended up as Chairman of the ten-strong Steering Group, reporting to the Parish Council. Over the next few months, we diligently prepared a questionnaire, based upon those questions that were mainly asked during our research. The questionnaire was produced, then delivered (in February 1999) to every household in the parish. Later, of course, it had to be collected after completion. Another member of the Group, David Dumaresq-Lucas, used his computer to analyse the results and eventually we produced a report, with conclusions and recommendations, on what appeared to be the main concerns to residents of the village. The eventual outcome of this was the setting up of another group – *'GLAMA'* (Greatham Leisure Area Millennium Appeal) – in order to raise funds for what had been shown to be Greatham's most immediate need – a children's play area with adult leisure facilities. This would be based alongside the Village Hall.

256

There was finally a satisfactory outcome to all this and, along the way, I was pointed onto the path of another career – that of an author! Because, before presenting the findings of the Appraisal to Rural Action, whilst reading the 'small print', I found that, as Chairman, I was expected to produce a brief history of Greatham, as background information to go with the report. Having lived in the village for just over thirty years, you'd have thought I must have known something about the place – wrong! But I was sufficiently interested to start my own investigation regarding Greatham's history. With many acts of assistance from innumerable sources, many based on personal experiences, I found myself becoming more and more amazed at the fascinating amount of material I was collecting.

Fortunately, Lorraine and Phil had by this time presented me with a PC (Personal Computer), which enabled me to start putting all the information into one place – and hopefully into a sensible format. Around the start of the new millennium year of 2000, I had probably enough material to produce a book on the subject and that was now what I was hopefully going to do. As part of the project, I asked an ex-Arborfield colleague of mine, Brian Hornsey, to put my book together with the aid of his desktop publishing system, on his computer over in Basingstoke. However, it proved no cheap or easy task to have a book published. I visited one publisher in Windsor and the cost was in the order of £6,000. Despite my efforts at getting sponsorship or some form of funding through the Parish Council, or local Historical Societies and other sources, I ended up with 'the book' just 'put onto the back burner' for the foreseeable future.

Retired – well, for now!

When my 'early' retirement eventually came up in the summer of 2000, I had to step down as the 'SEME Rep' on the Arborfield Old Boys' Association (AOBA), of which Brian Hornsey and myself had been members for a number of years. The Apprentices' School (or College, as it had later become) had wanted a definitive history produced for about the last eight or nine years at that time. Thus, at many Committee meetings, I had gone on and on *ad nauseam* at successive Chairmen on the subject – *"What's happening with the College history?"* Well, now that I was stepping down, and with his knowledge of my 'expertise' with the Greatham history, Brian suggested to the Committee that I was the guy to produce their history for them! (Or, in other words, 'put your money where your mouth is'!) Needless to say, they almost bit my hand off at the thought that here was someone who could possibly bring an almost dead project back to life! The previous 'volunteer', Victor Brooke, had suffered from ill-health for some time and, despite a promising start around about 1993, had never really got much achieved.

I was fortunate enough to start with a booklet called *'A Brief History'*, which had first been produced by a guy by the name of Bryn Richards a few years previously. This eventually became the framework of the complete and definitive history that I hoped I would be able to produce. First of all, I brought the 'brief history' up to date (2000) and then started to 'flesh out' the history from the 'bare bones' provided by Bryn, using many different sources. One great source was the *Old Boys' Association Newsletter (OBAN)* that had been resurrected in 1992 and issued about two or three times a year ever since – full of personal anecdotes of experiences, both at the School/College, as well as in later service. Then there was the regular edition of the School/College magazine, each one presenting facts and figures about what had been going on at Arborfield at the time. From these sources, I was able to keep adding to the overall story – a task that kept me busy (ask Joyce!) for a full three years. *"Retirement? What retirement?"* But it did prove to be a 'labour of love' and I enjoyed the challenge immensely.

Early on in the project, I had made an announcement in the *OBAN* about the task I had undertaken and just how much work and time I thought it would take. I was delighted to receive an e-mail from Rodney Smith, of my own intake 56B, who undertook to cover a lot of the expenses that would be involved. Thus, over the next three years, I kept Rodney updated as to the progress and cost of the project. I am happy to say that he 'came up with the goods' to the eventual tune of £5,000, which certainly oiled the wheels, so to speak!

Towards the end of that project, I was lucky enough to have the assistance of Ken Anderson. Ken had been a young soldier just behind me at Arborfield and had obviously done well for himself in later years, becoming a 'multi-media consultant'. He had already taken up the post of 'webmaster' for the AOBA, running an extensive web-site on its behalf. Now, he offered his help with the publishing of my work, for which the Committee must be eternally thankful – I know I was! Over a period of quite a few weeks, we would meet up at the REME Museum and sort out the photographs from the archives, picking those we thought most suitable to complement the story of Arborfield. That was quite a labour intensive effort. The archive photographs were all kept in envelopes, themselves stored in cardboard boxes, stacked up on racks in the Museum. I did the sorting, while Ken, nodding in approval (most of the time!), then 'scanned' each one into the Museum's computer. He then had to copy them to compact disk and take them back home to 'edit' into the text. I think we did a good job in the end.

Back on track with Greatham book

On one such occasion, we were having lunch in the *Bramshill Hunt*, when I must have mentioned my 'latent' book about Greatham, still lingering on Brian Hornsey's computer at Basingstoke – as well as 'the original' text on my own PC at home. Ken's interest was aroused and it ended up with my e-mailing some chapters across to Ken's home at Worcester and, all of a sudden, he was hooked! He soon offered to publish it for me and then, with the enhanced 'state-of-the-art' software that Ken had on his system, he was able to copy many of my local photographs and postcards into the Greatham story. It just so happened that, on the day that the first 'Arborfield' books were delivered to Ken at Worcester, I was up at nearby Redditch on a reunion get-together with a few of my old Arborfield mates from 1956. Ken kindly brought a few books over to Redditch and the 'official launch' of *'The Arborfield Apprentice'* started there and then! Since then, the book has been for sale through various sources – many through the REME Association shop at Arborfield and over the web-site. I have also been able to sell around fifty copies myself and feel that I've certainly done my bit for the AOBA! And, of course, it wasn't long afterwards that my *'A History of Greatham'* book was also published and it has been a great success around the village.

Since then I have been presented with another task! Another ex-Arborfield boy, John Dutton, who joined up in 1943, later found himself serving in 'the forgotten war' in Korea, 1951-53. He later gathered plenty of stories from other REME soldiers and, together with his own memories, put them together with the hope of publishing his own book. Unfortunately for John, the manner in which the 'book' was presented left a lot to be desired, it didn't really hang together as an articulate tale. Ken Anderson got to know of this and asked me if I'd be prepared to take John's original manuscript and, hopefully, make it readable, with all the correct grammar, paragraphs, punctuation, etc. This is something I am working on now, as 2003 fades into 2004 – and it could be a couple of months yet before I'm happy with it. Whether or not Ken will ever get it published on John's behalf, I don't know – but it won't be for the lack of trying on my part! *(As a footnote to that, the proof copy arrived back here during March 2004 and, having posted some relevant amendments, the book was printed and published very shortly afterwards. It is called 'The Forgotten Punch in the Army's Fist'.)*

Yes, my 'career' as an author came about quite unexpectedly, but has given me an enormous amount of pleasure and pride. And it hasn't stopped really. The evidence is that you, dear reader, are looking at another endeavour of mine, to write down some sort of life history of my own. In my own mind, I never did get to know my own family well enough, but I am determined to hand down to my own descendants some account of the family history. Perhaps, one day, someone will be able to say, *"This is the book what my ------ Granddad wrote"*!

My 'talents' in the writing area brought me another unexpected task, one that is now giving me great pleasure. I've already mentioned the *'OBAN'* somewhere above and I now have the honour of being the editor of that magazine, while Ken Anderson covers the publication. Between us, we bring out three editions each year and it has begun to look very good in its presentation, with a full-colour illustrated cover and glossy format. I hope to carry this on for a few years to come – either until the old brain and/or eyesight become too suspect, or until the other old boys get fed up with what I'm doing! What the job entails is receiving articles, letters and e-mails from many other ex-Arborfield boys, then making sure that it is all edited and suitable for Ken to publish. I'm amazed at the amount of material that arrives regularly – mainly in response to something published in the most recent magazine. I also contribute quite a lot of stuff myself, but try to 'spread it around' and not hog a whole issue! What has been good is my ability to persuade my own 56B lads to make a few contributions, even from guys living as far away as Australia, Tonga and South Africa. The whole job certainly keeps my brain active and enables me to keep in touch with many ex-colleagues from all over the world – and of course their stories make fascinating reading.

Postscript

Little did I know it, but I have recently become self-employed! This all started when Tim Gould asked me, a few years ago, whether I'd like to input some data onto his computer at the factory in Alton. This involved entering data from job-cards onto a database and was done, generally, at the end of each working month - just a couple of hours or so. At some later date I 'filled in' on some cleaning at the factory too, as the regular cleaning lady had left. Then, around the spring of 2003, Bill Marie retired from the workforce and, at the same time, Ken Williams broke his leg in a motorcycle accident. That left *Gould and Williams* short of manpower on the shop floor. Up until then, Tim had carried out the deliveries and pickups associated with their light engineering business. Now, he had to get back onto the shop floor to turn out the products – so asked me whether I'd fancy doing some driving. Needless to say, I agreed to the request and have been doing that, quite regularly now, for eighteen months or so. To 'keep things legal', I had to register as being self-employed – so I'm once again a taxpayer for my sins!

Most of the driving is naturally in the south, with one regular run up to *Sheen Instruments*, in the Ham Common area in London, taking me through Twickenham and Richmond. I often sit and have my lunch whilst sat near the pond on the Common – a quiet haven of peace in the busy city. But prior to that, I often make a stop in Twickenham at *Sandy's* fish-shop! Tim and Helen obviously like their fish and it's no real problem to stop for a few minutes and do a spot of shopping! The other advantage is that Joyce and I have become quite regular fish consumers too. Not that I always buy from *Sandy's*, as it's hardly what you can call cheap, but the fish is always excellent and well worth the occasional purchase. Apart form that, we are mainly happy to buy fish from *Tesco*, their salmon is fine and a new fish, 'Jamaican red talipia', is particularly tasty.

The most regular run is fairly short – just down to an industrial area at Langstone Harbour, just at the bottom of the A3(M). Another run that crops up occasionally takes me into Oxford Road, Reading – which is where I first met up with Joyce! It's also just 'around the corner' from June and Wack, so I have been able to drop in and see them from time to time - something that we just don't seem to get around to nowadays. I've been able to build up a good knowledge of the local roads, so that I am able to vary the journey at will and sometimes this becomes essential when the local radio station warns me of 'trouble on such and such a road'! Other places that come to mind are Alresford, Andover, Eastleigh, Farnham and Gosport – with one trip once as far as Hayward's Heath, over in Sussex – that turned into something of a wild goose chase!

In early November 2005, I was off on one of my regular trips to *Sheen*, heading up the Blackwater Valley Relief road (A331), when the van's engine blew up – a conn-rod came out of the side of the crank-case. I suppose I was lucky, in that I was able to coast over to the side of the road near the Frimley exit and use my mobile phone to call back to Alton. In the event, Tim came out in his 4WD and towed me back as far as Farnborough Business Park. There, we unloaded the equipment into his wagon, and he then had to drive up to Ham Common to complete the delivery. On the return trip, of course, we had to stop and pick up the van, which Tim then towed – with me steering it – all the way back to the factory! I think the van is a write-off and, unfortunately, Dougie at work managed to prang the second van just a few days later – and that could be a write-off too! *(Just to add here that both vans were eventually put right – and I am still driving them now, in May 2006!)*

The story continues ....

Following the success of my book *'A History of Greatham'*, I was pleasantly surprised to find that it circulated well beyond the reaches of Greatham itself. I think that quite a number of people sent copies of the book to friends and relatives who had moved out of the village in previous years. Some of those recipients of the book were so pleased with the memories that it evoked, that they wrote back to me with their comments – mostly favourable, I hasten to add! By gentle persuasion, I was able to get several people to send me their own reminiscences about their lives in Greatham. To cut a longish story short, the result of much correspondence finally persuaded me to put together another book, simply called *'Greatham Memories'*, which is now available for publication in these early months of 2008.

Cars what I have owned!

When you get to my age (approaching sixty-eight!), I suppose one could quite easily base a whole life history around the cars one has owned. I haven't quite done that, but certainly each car that has passed through my hands has always had some sort of story to tell. So here they are – and in chronological order of ownership too!

1957 Opel 'Rekord' (444 ALX)

I suppose the first car you buy always has a special place in one's memory, and so it is with *'Hermann the German'* as we called it! German built, as suggested by the name, but part of the American *General Motors (GM)* lineage. I bought it from Ross Crapnell on August 4th 1967, having just started my career as a civilian instructor at Bordon on leaving the Army. I was still living in Reading, so used it on a daily basis, morning and evening. Ross was still a sergeant in those days and I remember picking it up from outside his quarter after work one day, 'she' cost me a whole fifty quid! *(Why do we guys always refer to our cars as 'she'?)*

What an exhilarating feeling of freedom it was, to finally be driving my own car, especially as the roads weren't so clogged with traffic then. On my way home at night, she used to struggle a bit up Worldham Hill, but then she had only a three-speed gearbox, operated by a shift on the side of the steering wheel, what used to be called a 'column change', long out of fashion nowadays. She was a bit of an oil guzzler though! I used to turn into Alton High Street each evening, where there was a roadside garage just around the corner from the station. *(The business is there today, but only for tyres, exhausts and batteries.)* There I would buy petrol – and a pint of daily oil! At first, I thought the yellow oil-warning lamp was just for company! I had the *Rekord* for just three months before 'pranging' it on the Basingstoke Road coming out of Reading on Bonfire Night – as detailed elsewhere.

1952 Morris 'Minor' (PPP 815)

This was a quick replacement for *'Hermann'*, bought only five days after the accident and write-off, as I seriously needed my own transport – once the bug has

263

Michelle on 'Betsy'

bitten, you can't shake it off! We were now living in our own home at Greatham, but wanted to get out and about to explore the new world around us. She was pretty old even then, with a split windscreen and a small side-valve engine that had definitely put its best days behind it! It used to chug around, I don't suppose it was ever that powerful. When Sue and Pam came to visit us – now in our new home at Greatham – we decided to go down to the seaside one day. The car was affectionately known as *'Betsy'*, but she certainly didn't want to go up Butser Hill with all of us inside.

It ended up with the girls getting out while I drove *Betsy* to the top of the hill and they all walked up behind me – or did they make it first? I recall George from next door giving me a hand, I think we tried to 'de-coke' the engine. Being a side-valve, it needed special tools to compress the valves, so we struggled a bit – and I doubt if it ever made that much difference. But we tried! At least it got George and I to work when it was my week to drive. I can't remember where I bought her - nor where she ended up – but I do have a photo or two to prove that she existed!

Vauxhall 'Victor' (66 HKM) – no known date

With the little *Minor* not being very powerful, we came to the conclusion that something a little larger was required, although we managed to get one summer's motoring out of Betsy before replacing her. I can't recall how we heard about the *Victor*, but in September 1968 we bought her from a guy at Whitley in Reading – he sort of 'bought and sold' cars (wrecks?) from his front garden on a council estate! Perhaps we should have known better, but at first she really seemed like 'luxury' to its discerning new owners!

Similar in style to the *Rekord*, it came from the same *GM* family. She looked quite stylish with her two-tone colour and rakish body style, as well as having those plastic windshields on either side, so that you could wind down the window and still be streamlined. We actually kept her for exactly two years, but fought an endless battle against rust! We later found out that the particular range of *Vauxhall* cars during those years were renowned for being rust-buckets, there was just no answer to it. I eventually drove her down to a scrap-yard at Buriton, from where I came home with the number-plate – which still hangs in my garden shed!

Morris 'Minor' (VGT 455) – no known date

And so, in September 1970, I was looking for another car. Just around the corner on the main Petersfield Road was a garage run by Ray Flack. I reasoned that I would get a reasonable deal from my 'friendly local garage', and I think she only cost me another £50. *'Betsy Mk2'* was slightly more modern than the first one, a light green in colour. But it wasn't long before bits started to go wrong! Our Geoff came back from Australia in March of 1971 and later that year, he and Cliff came down to visit. They stayed with us and, one day, accompanied us for a day-trip to Reading – they in their car, we in ours. We were going down Southampton Street when there was a loud clattering noise from under my bonnet and no way that I could find a gear!

It ended up with us borrowing a van from Eileen & Mike's neighbour Maurice and then me towing Geoff back to Greatham, while Joyce and the girls must have come home with Cliff. What a perilous journey that must have been, but somehow we made it back the thirty-five miles to Greatham. I found another gearbox in a scrap-yard (they figure a lot, don't they?) and George helped me fit it. After that, whenever I took off in first gear, it sounded like a tractor – but at least it went! I can't remember when MoT tests came in, but the *Minor* was eligible for it that year, but was rejected for 'holes in the chassis'. A Warrant Officer at SEME, a Scots chap named Bill, with a huge walrus-style moustache, said he'd try to weld up the floor for me. But when it came down to the work, he told me that *"there's more holes than bodywork"*! So I'm afraid *Betsy Mk2* met a similar fate to my previous cars!

1965 Ford 'Cortina' Mk1 (NNO 816 C)

In November of 1971 we took ownership of a dark blue *Cortina*, it was purchased from a house down Bat and Ball Lane, on the turning just before Wrecclesham Hill down into Farnham. It was a fairly well to do area and the car was only six years old, so at last we'd joined the true motoring society – Ha! Ha! From a reliability point of view I suppose we could say that we got more than three years out of her, but at the same time I was doomed to learning all about the working parts of cars from George next door! Mind you, George – and son Clive – were always working on their cars too, and our front drives must have seemed like garage workshops at the weekends, we were always pottering about with something or other between us. The *Cortina* developed a nasty habit of leaving a smokescreen behind it, the reason was (as I found out) that it was burning oil. I think what finally polished it off was a trip to Plymouth in January 1975, to watch Everton play an FA Cup-tie. I took a carload with me, including Argyle fan Derek Barenski, and just about made it home with the cars dying gasp! Again it was George to the rescue, as we stripped down the whole engine. The old piston rings just literally fell out in little bits. Despite a re-bore and new rings, it was definitely on its last legs and so I decided she'd have to go!

1969 Ford 'Corsair' (URE 360 G)

One of the Colonels at Bordon was advertising his *Corsair* for sale. It was silver in colour, with a black vinyl roof and - for those days – definitely in the luxury class! It had a V4 2-litre engine, which was certainly 'man enough' to cope with a growing family. I bought her in March of 1975 and the first trip we made in her was up to Barmouth in North Wales that Easter – a tradition that has lasted until this very day (but sadly not the *Corsair*!) I do recall how good the engine was, you could literally drop the speed down to walking pace whilst still in top gear, then pull away effortlessly as required

1963 Austin 'Cambridge' (311 MPO)

With Joyce about to start a new job as 'kitchen assistant' at Bordon, we decided to go for a 'second car' and in August 1976, during the height of a drought, we went down to Fernhurst and bought the old *Cambridge*. The chap who'd owned her had been an estate manager for *ICI Verdley*, a place where they tested herbicides, weed-killers, insect killers and such like. He was retiring and going for a new car, but the Cambridge had hardly really been used, except for driving around the *ICI* estate. So, for its age, it had remarkably few miles on the clock. Built like a bus, it was very stable as you drove it along – and the engine was as quiet as the proverbial church mouse. Just after we'd picked her up, we had to stop at a junction outside Liphook and it was so quiet I honestly thought the engine had stalled!

1972 Vauxhall 'Viva' (APY 442 K)

Things get a bit vague after we became a two-car family! I can't remember now just which one of the two went first, but in March 1977 I bought a small family saloon from Dougie Gilbert at SEME, he was a Staff Sergeant at the time, serving down in 'B' Branch, so I knew the car had been pretty well maintained. There was nothing remarkable about it and I don't know how long we kept it, before I sold it on to Nick Scantlebury, who was another soldier serving with me at Bordon, he was being posted to the West Country and needed a cheap little runabout.

Thinking back, that must have happened after the end of 1979 and possibly not until 1981, because Nick was in my office after I'd taken over the Internal Validation post at Bordon. The other event that dates it was my first ever TA Camp, towards the end of 1979. I was in Louisberg Barracks at Bordon, awaiting the move down to South Cerney, when I phoned Joyce to say 'Cheerio'. She'd been out to Petersfield and had a 'prang' in the *Viva*. Another car had run into the front offside wing at the junction that joined the old A3 and A325. The other driver was an Army officer and he and his son moved Joyce's car to the side of the road – she thought that was very kind of them, especially as it was the other driver's fault. Obviously though, there was an ulterior motive because, later this officer, a real gentleman I guess, swore blind that it had all been Joyce's fault. Needless to say, we never did get any satisfaction and ended up having to pay for the front wing to be replaced.

I think it must have been the *Viva* that gave us a bit of a laugh! We'd been up to see Mum at Ainsdale and had a roof-rack on top, because we were picking up one of those stainless steel kitchen sinks. We dutifully tied the sink onto the roof-rack and set off down the Formby by-pass, before turning left across towards Maghull to pick up the motorway link. We were mystified by a slight 'knocking' noise and so pulled over at the side of the road. What had happened was that the plastic sink plug was hanging down on its chain and gently tapping away on the roof as we drove along!

1973 Ford 'Capri' Mk2 (ORD 624 M)

In the summer of 1978, we enjoyed a family holiday down at Mullion Cove, Cornwall, along with Eileen & Mike and Jan & Roy, as well as all the children. Roy was looking to sell his car and it was such low mileage that I decided to buy it from him – although I did this over a period of time, he was kind enough to allow me to do that. I kept that 'lean, mean, green machine' for fourteen years and well had my money's worth out of her! I recall having a test drive in her before we left Cornwall and the bonnet seemed to stretch away in front of me for miles! And she could certainly go a bit, with good acceleration and a fair lick of speed. For quite some time though, we could always smell petrol and in fact the two girls always felt a bit sick in the back. We put this down to the shape of the body, which only supported small side windows for the rear passengers. Jan had also remarked that her two girls, Colette and Lisa, had the same problem. We eventually found that the fuel pipe from the filler-cap was not correctly fitted and that, whilst 'filling her up', petrol was leaking into the boot! After sorting that, the problem eased off, but there was always a bit of a niff!

The only major job I had done on her was a new overhead camshaft, which had got very noisy at one time – apparently it was a common fault on that type of engine, because the oil feed up to the camshaft used to get blocked. I drove up to a place in South London, one of those 'under the arches' garages that specialised in the job. I left it there for a few hours and walked around the area, having some sandwiches in a local park. They must have done a good job, I certainly don't recall having any problems afterwards. When the time eventually came for the *Capri* to go, it was Colette's husband Mark who bought it for a nominal sum, but I don't think he kept it for long afterwards.

1975 Ford 'Escort' (MPL 650 P)

I'm at a bit of a loss here with my memory, I know we then still had the *Capri*, but in the summer of 1983 we had to replace 'the other car'. Looking back, it must have been the *Cambridge*, I'm sure the *Corsair* had long since disappeared – correct me if I'm wrong! (See postscript!) Mum had returned to England after the death of Jack Whitley, and was staying down here at Greatham for a short while. She kindly put up some money for me to buy the *Escort*, which was white in colour, with a black vinyl roof. I bought it from a girl called Sally, who worked at Bordon and lived down at Liss Forest. Not a bad little car, quite cheap to run and, as I recall, pretty reliable.

1982 Vauxhall 'Cavalier' (FRV 916 X)

I'd just returned from Christmas leave in 1987, when I heard Fred Mills, another instructor at Bordon, saying that there was this *Cavalier* for sale. It belonged to another guy, Vic Goffen, who had not long retired, and lived just along the road to Fred, in Petersfield. *(As an aside here, Fred went on to die whilst playing the 18th hole at Blackmoor golf course – what a way to go!)* Anyway, this chap who'd retired, I knew that by reputation he would have had the car regimentally maintained, so I gave him a call and we agreed on a price. That definitely became 'Joyce's car' and she really loved it. The bodywork was lovely, a deep maroon, and Joyce kept her religiously washed and polished for many years – probably about fourteen, so it lasted as long as the *Capri*.

By 1989, Jan and Roy had bought a small house in Mumbles (Swansea) as a 'holiday home', and Joyce and her sisters have been going down there around October each year ever since. Inevitably it has been Joyce who has picked the other girls up and provided the transport. Luckily, the *Cavalier* had a cavernous boot, which was an absolute bonus when you needed room for the cases of four 'girls'! Towards the end though, apart from the engine, which I think would have gone on for ever, everything else had started to fail and water was leaking into her all over the place. Joyce couldn't bear to watch me drive it away, but I had to! I took it up to Brian Chiverton in the village, who had an outlet means of scrapping cars – for which you were now charged twenty quid!

1988 Vauxhall 'Cavalier' (E 841 KOR)

In September 1992 we'd finally lost the *Capri* after fourteen long years, she'd been an excellent servant. By now, Dougie Gilbert was a civvie – but still working at Bordon, and still selling cars! I knew he had this *Cavalier*, and Joyce had been so pleased with hers that I bought this one from Dougie. I remember the first trip in that was down to Colyton, Devon – one of the many visits we made to *'The Grove'* guesthouse, run by Val and John. She proved equally as reliable as any car we'd had, and of course had the same huge boot as Joyce's car. Not surprisingly, she eventually developed similar leakage problems and went on the same route to the 'car graveyard' via Brian Chiverton!

1997 Vauxhall 'Vectra' (R 804 WVU)

When I retired in July 2000, I had the advantage of a few quid in my pocket, thanks to the civil service 'gratuity'. I had always said that, when that time came, I would treat myself to a decent car. Helen's Mum had been married a second time and earlier that year had become a widow for the second time too. Her husband Eric had the *Vectra*, which had pretty low mileage and was still in excellent condition, so Tim put me 'on the waiting list' until the probate on Eric's will had been sorted. So in September I was able to take possession of the *Vectra*, which was the first automatic gearbox car I'd ever had, and a pleasure to drive. So of course, Joyce has just about taken it over, having told everyone that she'd never drive an automatic!

The one big problem with the more expensive cars of course is that they are more expensive to fix! No more lying about on the drive outside, struggling to fit clutches, gearboxes and brakes etc – it's all far too complicated nowadays and the only way to get faults sorted out is to pay someone to do it. All the engines are now controlled by electronic systems and, if they go wrong, there's nowt you can do but cough up the cash! Then there are emission control systems – the catalytic converter on the *Vectra* fell apart and it cost £500 to have put right! That would have bought me ten cars a few years back!

There was one particular episode that comes to mind about 'unfixable faults' on cars! At Easter 2002, we were heading for Barmouth in the usual fashion on the Good Friday. Around the Newbury area, the *Vectra* ignition just cut out on three separate occasions. Each time, I was able to re-start the engine and off we'd go again. After that, we got all the way to our usual stopping place, the *Little Chef* near Leominster, for breakfast. Then it was the usual route past Ludlow and a run across to Welshpool, where we picked up the hot-cross buns as normal. By now, I'd assumed that the ignition fault had just been a one-off (well, three-off actually!) and we carried on over the mountain pass at Dinas Mawddwy and down the steep road that drops into Dolgellau. Almost reached the bottom of the hill when the warning light came on once more and we were 'coasting'. I managed to steer into the car park at the *Cross Foxes* pub and was able to restart once again. The fault then occurred once more on the road to Barmouth and by then I'd decided enough was enough!

Being a Bank Holiday weekend, the only 'assistance' I was able to rustle up was from the local garage, *Bradbury's*. The young chap, Chris, said he thought the problem must be with the engine management unit (EMU) and that he didn't have the equipment to check it out. The nearest places for *Vauxhall* main dealers were either Llandudno or Aberystwyth! I decided to call *National Breakdown* and explain the problem and it ended up with the *Vectra* being loaded onto a trailer the following Saturday, while we were offered a lift home by Eileen & Mike. As it turned out, they had borrowed a huge Japanese Land Cruiser vehicle from Sue & Nick, just for the holiday, so there was plenty of room. I'd asked for my car to be dropped off at Woodcote Way, from where I'd take the chance on driving it the last 35 miles home.

Everything was fine until we got to the outskirts of Leominster and decided to stop for a cuppa. We pulled into a car park and got out of the car. For some reason, Mike went back to open the car and – would you believe it? – it was as dead as a doornail! He then had to contact the AA, whose engineer arrived to tell Mike that the battery in his remote control had packed in. Anyway, we eventually got going again, thank goodness, and eventually ended up back at Woodcote Way, where the *Vectra* was awaiting! I drove it home with no problem, but the fault did re-appear and I was able to get the EMU replaced at no small cost. Not surprisingly, that particular EMU started to cause the same fault a few months later, but was then replaced free of charge, being still under warranty. Oh for the days when you could fix your own car at the roadside, with the aid of a screwdriver and a test-lamp!

Early in 2006 we began to see evidence of a major oil-leak from the *Vectra*. I was told that it was going to be an expensive repair, as the seal between the engine and gearbox required replacing. The seal itself was only a few quid, but the labour costs bumped the price up towards £350. Trouble is, we'd only had it back a couple of days, when the leak appeared worse than before! Obviously it had to go back to the garage, where it was 'found' that the young lad who'd been detailed for the job had, in fact, botched it up - well, that's what we were told – and had now been sacked! It took the best part of another week for the garage to go over the complete repair once again. They now also replaced some other seals, but of course couldn't charge me for labour again!

1989 Peugeot 205, (F 373 RAD)

With the second *Cavalier* having gone to its fate, I suppose we could have made do with just the one car, seeing that I was now retired. But with Joyce still working, we decided to get another one just for me to potter about in, and so bought the *205*. It's a bit of an 'old banger' really and has had quite a few problems already since I got it in 2002. At one point I had another engine fitted but, just after that job was done, the camshaft tensioner broke and I ended up with a couple of bent valve stems! Since then it has been pretty difficult to get her started and running, especially on cold mornings. But Richard, the guy who first sold it to us, has been very good in looking after things and we'll probably try to keep it going for another couple of years, or until Joyce decides to finish working at the hair salon. Looking back with the benefit of hindsight, it has proved to be very useful, in that I have been working as a driver/courier for Tim these past couple of years at least. The *205* has enabled me to get in and out of Alton and earn a few bob at the same time - a great boost to my civil service pension!

1998 Rover 400 (S 982 AOK)

Early in 2006, whilst visiting Cosby, we decided to buy the *Rover* from James. The *Peugeot* had deteriorated quite a bit and was beginning to use too much petrol. In fact I was using the fuel gauge as a rev counter! It had always had problems with water leaking into the floor pan, meaning that the windows were misting up all too often. The *400* is a much nicer motor, one of those that has been 'customised', with special wheel-trims and a rear spoiler – a bit of a boy racer's car really! I'll try not to be one though, as I'm getting a bit long in the tooth for that! But since learning how to operate the CD player, I've been catching up with a lot of my old – and new - favourite music!

Postscript

After I'd written this, Joyce had a read and reminded me that we'd actually had another two cars too! Then I remembered - it was during the time that Lorraine was having a summer break from University and I was able to get her some temporary employment at a research place at Farnborough. I'd bought this red *Hillman 'Sceptre'* from Jim Melhuish at work and Lorraine was using it to get to and from Farnborough. She phoned us one evening to say that it had broken down at Wrecclesham – and I never did get it going again, I think the head gasket had gone, or something drastic anyway. I'd only had the car a matter of weeks at the most and always suspected that

Jim had 'sold me a pup'. It was Mervyn 'Jesse' James who took it off my hands and eventually re-built the engine - and ran it for a few years I think! Thinking back again, perhaps it was 'that' car that had to be replaced by the *Escort* that Mum helped us with. It was certainly around that time, with Mum then living at Crosby and Lorraine at Liverpool University.

The 'other car' wasn't really ours, it was just 'on loan' to us for a while. This happened just after Joyce's Dad died in 1974, leaving his widow, Doris, in possession of a *Reliant Robin*, one of those three-wheelers with the fibreglass body. Anyway, we took over its running, until Doris decided that she needed to sell it in order to raise some cash. The main event that goes with the *Reliant* was a trip to Winchester, when Jo and Dave Howlett were living at 10 Fiona Close. They threw a fancy-dress party – Joyce posed as a St Trinian's girl, while I looked silly as a Bay City Roller! After the party, driving home along the A32 towards Alresford, the heavens had opened and the road was literally awash with large puddles. Three-wheelers don't cope too well in those conditions and I'm pretty sure that the car 'bottomed' in some of the deeper puddles! Thankfully, we got back safely.

Greatham Brownies

Mum's returns – to Crosby and Culcheth

After Jack Whitley had died in April 1983, it didn't take Mum too long to decide that she'd rather come back to England to live, she never much enjoyed the heat anyway. When she did come back, in August that same year, the decision to move back to her Liverpool environs couldn't have been too difficult either. At the time, 'our Sue' was still living out in Miami with her husband Des and young son Thomas, who had been born only the previous November (1982). In fact, recalling that event, Mum and Pop had been present in Miami at the time, it must have only just preceded their move to Australia.

Sue and Des had been in the USA for around six years in all. Des had family connections out there and had then wished to find out whether or not they could 'make a go of it'. I recall that it was the American educational system that finally persuaded them to come home. Lorraine and her school friend, Moira, had visited Sue and Des in 1982, as well as going to St Louis to visit some of Moira's relations. Joyce and I also had a visit to Miami in July 1983, we stopped with Sue and Des in their fortified (!) home in South Miami. Perhaps 'our Pam' and husband Steve had already moved to Crosby by that August of '83, I do recall that Joyce and I had visited them for three consecutive August Bank Holidays, when they still lived 'over the shop' at 213 County Road. That was during the late Seventies and early Eighties. Pam had learned quite a lot about the insurance business and was obviously putting it to good use by 'helping out' with Jack's business.

Whatever – Mum decided to settle in Crosby, moving to a very nice little self-contained flat in Mere Park, Cambridge Road, just off College Road. (We all remember the duck pond, just outside!) It was strange really, as Granny and Granddad Gripton had lived in Crosby all those years before. When Sue and Des returned from the States, the family also moved to Crosby. Then Pam and Steve moved to York Road, so now Mum had both of her daughters virtually 'on the doorstep', it was a neat arrangement. I don't think Joyce and I visited the flat all that often, after all Mum only stayed there for a couple of years. One time when we definitely *did* go was when the

Even Mum was a 'scally' once!

International Garden Festival was held down at Otterspool, on the banks of the River Mersey, in 1984. I remember having lunch in a pub that had been built on the site, I think it was called *The Britannia*, and being beaten by the size of the Cumberland sausage I'd ordered! I also remember going up there with Michelle one weekend, probably in May 1985, when Everton were playing some great football and about to clinch the League Championship!

Lorraine had started university in October 1982, first living 'on campus' down in Aigburth. When Mum later got her flat at Crosby, I think Lorraine went to stay with her for a while – and actually got paid some money for cleaning the stairs! There was also another weekend, I believe it was a half-term (October 1983), when Joyce went up there, accompanied by her sister Eileen. It would have been then that the first thoughts of a 'family history' began as a gleam in Mum's eye, as she told stories of her youth to the two girls. (Pity you didn't write it all down Mum!) I also recall, during another trip, moving some gear for Lorraine, it was either from Aigburth to Crosby or vice versa! We were driving along the dock road – must have been going north now that I think about it – when we were pulled over by the 'scuffers' for speeding! I must have told a particularly good sob story, because I was let off with a warning – after all, if I'd been going 32 miles per hour, that would have been an exaggeration!

Lorraine graduated from Liverpool University in July 1985, so we obviously stayed with Mum at that time, because she went along with us to the graduation ceremony at the Philharmonic Hall – brought back a few memories for me, I can tell you! The Liverpool Institute had always used 'the Phil' as a venue for its annual speech-day. It was probably that same year that we visited Crosby and watched the 'Tall Ships' sail past the foreshore out of Liverpool. Thousands of people lined the banks on both sides of the Mersey, it was a splendid sight. Mum's brother, my Uncle John, was with

274

us on that occasion, it might in fact have been the last time that we saw him before he sadly died. That didn't occur until February 1990, so that time gap seems very long, but the reason was that we weren't up in Liverpool so often then, as Mum had gone back to Australia – heat and all!

Just a few days after Lorraine's graduation ceremony, Joyce and I set off to Australia as Mum's 'guests', where we stayed in 'the annex' at Sheila and Geoff's place at 11 Darling Street, Perth, in Western Australia. That four-week holiday features in a story of its own, but the upshot of it was that Mum 'fell' for Bill Walker, Sheila's Dad – and it was a good job that he 'fell' for her too! It was only a couple of months later that Bill came over to Crosby and the pair got married at the local Town Hall on September 28th. That brief Crosby era was over, as the happy couple went off back to Perth and spent seventeen happy years together, until Bill's sad demise in December 2002.

And another return

During Bill's long terminal illness, it must have been pretty tough on Mum, having to deal with everything – especially when she had to go into hospital herself for a bowel operation, after cancer had been diagnosed. Mum had always insisted that she would return to England after Bill had passed on. But it was still a major surprise to us all when she arrived at Heathrow so soon after the funeral, just a couple of days before Christmas. Joyce and I picked her up at the airport, where she arrived in a wheelchair, looking very frail and miserable. She then spent around three weeks with us, feeling pretty low I'm afraid, before Sue came down from Culcheth to whisk her away 'up north'. Mum stayed with Sue and Des for the next couple of months, while the housing situation was assessed. Eventually, mainly due I'm sure to her physical condition, she was fortunate enough to be offered a small bungalow in Culcheth, only a few minutes away from Sue's place. Lots of decorating and fitting then took place over a few weeks, while at the same time Mum was waiting for her 'goods and chattels' to arrive on the long sea voyage from Australia. On April 9th, she officially moved in to her new home and, at the time of writing, was settling in very well.

Despite still missing Bill – and dog Alfie – tremendously, hopefully she will be happy and comfortable in Culcheth. It is very convenient for the village centre, which is well provided for shopping, and, of course, Sue and Des are very close at hand to offer support, should the need arise. The bungalow in Kaye Avenue is Council-owned and semi-detached, forming part of a row alongside several others. The location means that all the bungalows share a common 'back garden', which is fairly well sheltered and secure from the general public. Mum's next-door neighbour is a lady called Brenda, who somehow got the name 'Maude' from Mum! The good news is that they have become firm friends and share many activities together, such as going to a 'gymnasium' in Warrington – not bad at the age of eighty-four! Another favourite visit is to *Bent's*, a garden centre just a short bus-ride away towards Leigh, which provides an excellent luncheon menu and pleasant browsing.

Whilst still in Australia, Mum and Bill got involved in the game of *'petanque'* – or *'le boules'* – I don't know whether or not the spelling is correct. Looking for a pastime in Culcheth, Mum has managed, with some assistance from Sue and Maude, to set up her own *petanque* club, within the boundaries of the local sports and social club. With the regular visits to the gym and games of *petanque*, this has not only provided Mum with lots to do, but has also improved her mobility no end. During 2005, Mum was able to have operations to remove cataracts from both of her eyes, at two separate times. This appears to have been most successful - in fact she can probably see better than me at the time of writing! Another great benefit was the purchase of new hearing aids – pretty expensive, of course, but they have made the world of difference. Combined with the eye operations, this has enabled her to hear and watch television to a far better extent than was the previous state of affairs.

In the meantime, Maude – or should I say Brenda – has re-married, to a gentleman by the name of Peter Parker, but the couple are living next door to Mum, so she has been able to maintain the friendship. They are all involved with the petanque club, which has been quite a successful venture over the last few years, and now continuing into 2006. As far as I am aware, April should bring a Lottery Award that will allow the club to extend its pitch, as well as providing wheelchair access. As I write this, Mum is looking forward to a visit from Muriel Boyd, an old friend from Perth, who is going to stay at Mum's for a while and also accompany her on a petanque club trip to Spain.

When Michelle turned forty in February 2006, we went up to look after the boys while James treated her to a couple of nights at a health spa, located somewhere between Daventry and Banbury. On the Sunday morning, we picked Mum up at the coach station in Leicester, then we all dropped in at the health spa on our way home. I took Mum back home by car the following Friday – hoping to join the Liobians Reunion at Anfield that evening. Unfortunately we got snowed in at Culcheth and I missed the Reunion for a second consecutive year!

Mum's health has certainly let her down on many occasions since she arrived back in the UK, I think the term for her condition is 'diverticulitis', which means that she will always be prone to bouts of stomach upset that lay her low for a few days. In early July 2006, she had just suffered another flare-up and we headed up to see her for a couple of days. Thanks to Sue and Des, we had somewhere to lay our heads, as Mum's place is basically for a single tenant only. She was sufficiently recovered to join us on trips out to Warrington and Bolton over the weekend.

In August, the 'cunning plan' worked again! It was James who turned forty that month and held a good party at his local gym and health club, which he had recently joined. Once again, on the Sunday morning, Mum arrived at Leicester by coach and we were able to pick her up and bring her down to Greatham for a few days. I think we covered most of the roads in Hampshire that week, visiting the likes of Emsworth, Fareham, Farnham, Midhurst, Petersfield and Port Solent. I was able to book a train ticket and put Mum on a train home from Reading to Manchester. That was the second year running that Mum had been able to celebrate her birthday down here with us.

Early December saw Joyce and I heading up to Culcheth once more and, thankfully, the traffic conditions were very good for both journeys. We stayed at Sue's again for the three nights and were able to take Mum out for the day – mainly a shopping trip to the *John Lewis* shop at Cheadle Royal and then lunch at *Lakeland*, just outside Wilmslow. On the Saturday afternoon, Marjorie Barlow came up to visit and have a bite to eat with us, so at least Mum had lots of company, if even for just a short time. I've written elsewhere about making contact with Marjorie – it has been great fun catching up with her again after all those years

The dream cruise!

In mid-October of 2007, Joyce and I drove down to Southampton and met up with Mum and Sue at the railway station. After a spot of lunch in a *'Costa Coffee'* café just across the road, we transported the two ladies down to the docks, where they boarded the *Queen Mary 2* passenger liner, for a six-day voyage to New York! Once in 'the Big Apple', they were able to meet up with Tom Herlihy – as well as Lorraine & Phil. I believe a Broadway showing of *'Chicago'* was enjoyed by one and all. Mum and Sue then flew back to Manchester. Fortunately, Mum's health held up well for her dream trip, only to find, upon her return, that the dreaded cancer had hit her again. After tests at the Liverpool Women's Hospital, she was due to start radiotherapy treatment at Clatterbridge Hospital, probably sometime during February/March of 2008. It was only shortly before this was due, that her consultants decided that the best option was going to be surgery, with a planned date for the operation being February 26th.

Joyce and the girls

Having settled down into civilian life in 1967, we moved into Chapel House, Longmoor Road, Greatham, Hampshire. Lorraine was just coming up to school age at the time, so it was inevitable that she started at the local Greatham Primary School. Michelle was to follow in her footsteps a few years afterwards. Thus it was that, in November 1972, Joyce was able to 'start work', when she also joined Greatham Primary School – as a 'dinner lady'. I have a feeling that she also went on to work for a while at Blackmoor School (St Matthews in Drift Road) - and definitely for some time at a school down Chalet Hill in Bordon. Anyway, by the time that 1976 came around, she had moved up to a position as 'Assistant Cook' at Bordon County Junior School in Budds Lane, under the supervision of Jeanette Bruce, who became a firm friend.

(We still see Jeanette and her husband Ian occasionally, despite the fact that they took up residence in Spain for a number of years – and have now moved to Turkey. The reason we see them is twofold. Firstly, they still maintain a house in Liss, just behind where Joyce still works. Secondly, their son Allister and his wife Helen live in a bungalow just up the road to us. Unfortunately, Allister suffers from a very physical type of MS, which has almost left him wheelchair bound. But he has a strong character and determinedly drives his wheelchair into some impossible places!)

Around the same time, we finally became a 'two-car' family, with the purchase of an old *Austin Cambridge*. Prior to that, Joyce had bought a little moped, from *Motorcycle City* at North Camp, Aldershot, as transport – never the safest or most comfortable in cold and/or wet weather. Early in 1977 she had to attend a cookery course over at Winchester, so the luxury of four wheels became a vital necessity! I seem to remember that the weather was particularly bad while she was on that course – always the way, isn't it?

Joyce's 'career' in the school meals service finally came to an end in May 1988. At the time, Council-controlled jobs were being 'contracted out' and Joyce had just about had enough anyway. After all those years of bending over sinks, it must have taken a good while for her to straighten her back out! Later that year, without much real confidence that she could get such a post, she applied for a job as a solicitor's receptionist at a firm called *Burley & Geach*, located in Petersfield. We were all delighted when she got the post, but sadly it didn't last all that long as the firm decided to shed a few staff and Joyce's was a sort of 'last in, first out' position. Mind you, it wasn't too much of a wrench to leave, as the hours were 'full time' and her office didn't even have a window to look out through! However, the job did give her the chance to 'dress up' every day and also brought in a few extra bob. (It also gave her the contact address for Colyton in Devon, where we subsequently spent many happy hours!)

It must have been the following year (1989) that she took a temporary job at the *Forestry Commission* research station up at Alice Holt, on the way to Farnham, but that was only for a few weeks, leading up to Christmas. Early in 1990 she applied for another job, this time as a hairdressing assistant at the *'Just You'* salon in Liss, and she has been there ever since. In fact, apart from Audrey, who runs the salon, Joyce is the only other person who has stayed on, there has always been an almost constant changeover of staff. She works part-time only and enjoys the chance to meet different people every day – but she's now the oldest (and best-looking) 'junior' on record!

She certainly knocks spots off some of the young girls who have 'worked' there for short periods – they always find it much too taxing! Audrey is hoping that Joyce will stay on as long as possible, saying that when Joyce retires – she'll go too! (They are both still going strong as I bring this history up to date early in 2008!)

It wasn't deliberate, I swear, but we almost lost both of the girls on separate occasions! With Lorraine, it was down at the market in Portsmouth's Charlotte Street. She must have wandered off and, after the initial panic, we spotted her being carried aloft on a policeman's shoulders. With Michelle, it was down on Woolacombe Beach in North Devon.

Michelle and Lorraine

That was very scary, your mind considers all sorts of horrible mishaps, but thankfully it all ended up safely in the end.

Lorraine started her education at Greatham School on August 20th 1968 (by gum, that already seems a lifetime ago!). Michelle followed her there on April 26th 1971, I can still see the two of them in their little pink gingham dresses that were the school uniform then. Both of the girls were very much into reading and we encouraged them as much as possible. The house was always full of books by Enid Blyton, Nina Bawden, Arthur Ransome and such. They still like reading, but busy life schedules diminish the amount of time available. Early in 1974, Lorraine passed the 'eleven-plus' examination, it must have been the last year in which that exam was still in existence – long since abandoned in the interests of 'comprehensive education'.

With that, she went on to attend *Eggar's* Grammar School over in Alton, where she progressed at a very good rate. Never one to shirk her studies, she finally completed her 'A' Levels in the summer of 1981. I recall taking her to visit the universities at Reading and Hull and I think she also went by train to visit another one over in mid-Wales. But nobody could have been more pleased than me when she was accepted to study a Psychology degree at Liverpool University. I can't remember why, but it was October 1982 when she finally started up there – we took her up to see her settle in at a 'hall of residence' down in the Aigburth area. The room was nothing to write home about, pretty small and dingy looking, and I'm sure Joyce had a tear or two in her eye as we drove away!

Meanwhile, Michelle had also passed through Greatham School and gone on to secondary education at Petersfield, that was in September of 1977. She'll be the first to agree that she was never very strong on the academic side of life, and the gang of girls that she fell in with were certainly going to nothing to help things along in that particular direction! Mind you, she certainly tried to enjoy life to the full – I lost count of the number of occasions I sat in the car park at Liss railway station, awaiting her arrival on the last train from Petersfield. But finally, in August 1983, she arrived back from a holiday in Minorca to find me waiting at the airport with the good news that she had passed four 'O' Levels. A few tears – of joy – were shed on that occasion, especially as she had Sarah and Suzie alongside her when the news was announced!

In January of the following year, Michelle started on a Youth Training Scheme (YTS) at the council offices in Petersfield, I think it was something to do with the road repair system. She also went back into education for a while, at Southdown College down near Havant, but never really got fully into any further serious studying. In July of 1987 she started work as an Admin Assistant at Petersfield Job Centre and, on occasion, also at the one in the Forest Centre in Bordon. I often used to pop down there and see her during my lunch break.

She was finally tempted to try her hand as 'a rep' with *Martin Dawes*, a mobile phone company whose headquarters we often see nowadays, as they are based on the *Gemini* retail park at Warrington, not far away from where both my Mum and sister Sue now live. I think her job really was to 'sweet talk' clients into believing that 'the cheque is in the post', the idea being that nobody is really going to get very angry with a smartly-dressed attractive young lady! I can remember her having to drive through London on occasion, when she would phone me to check my map and tell her which way to go next! But even the 'glamour' of a company car and lots of travelling soon wore off and she later went back into the Civil Service, working at the Army Camp with me at Bordon.

Lorraine's three-year spell at university passed by in a flash. She spent a year 'in residence', then moved into a house with some other students down in Aigburth. When my Mum came back to Liverpool in 1983, I think Lorraine actually stayed with her for a while – getting paid to clean the stairs in the block of flats in Cambridge Road, Crosby! Anyway, with Mum up there, with Sue and Pam 'on the doorstep' and Lorraine not too far away, it gave Joyce and I plenty of opportunities to get up to Merseyside to see them all. Eventually, in the summer of 1985, Mum joined Joyce and myself at Lorraine's graduation ceremony at the Philharmonic Hall. It wasn't too long afterwards that Mum went off to Australia again, having married Bill Walker.

More weddings

While at Liverpool, Lorraine had met Steve Burgoyne, and they were married at St John's Church in Greatham in March 1987 – fairly unforgettable, as it snowed heavily for most of the day! Steve came from Worsley, on the southern fringe of Manchester, so it was inevitable that the couple set up home in that area. They had a couple of places in Swinton, before moving up to a village called Hoddlesden. That was on the side of the Pennines above a town called Darwen, not too far from Blackburn. Joyce and I visited quite often and got to know the area fairly well. As well as Blackburn, Bolton and Burnley weren't too far away, while there was great scope for walking, around some of the reservoirs that had been constructed to store water for the industrial towns of southern Lancashire. Another place that we loved when we visited it was Clitheroe, settled just below the Pendle Hills. On top of that, it was only a short distance to drive across the moors and into the Dales countryside of Yorkshire, with towns like Holmfirth, Settle and Skipton to visit.

I recall one particular occasion when we visited Hoddlesden along with Eileen & Mike. We four had been up to Barmouth for our usual Easter holiday – this was in 1993 – and we were invited to visit Lorraine & Steve over the following weekend. There was a pub in the village called *'The Ranken Arms'* and we all went there for lunch. I know that Mike and I had liver and bacon casserole with onions and it was absolutely delicious! There was another pub that I recall, near one of the reservoirs, where they served the most delicious pint of *Timothy Taylor's* best bitter, well worth the price!

In the meantime, Michelle had started going out with James Fitzpatrick, who was still serving in the Royal Navy at the time. If I remember correctly, towards the end of his service, he was involved in being on stand-by, ready to pick up British people from Sierra Leone, when there was the usual bout of civil war in that African country. James came to live with us for some time and, over one weekend, he and Steve Burgoyne fitted a new kitchen for us here at home, that must have been towards the end of 1990. Upon leaving 'the Andrew', James opted for a job with the Fire and Rescue Service up at Leicester, his hometown. Eventually, in July of 1991, he and Michelle set up home in Cosby, a village on the southern outskirts of Leicester, where they have been ever since.

Lorraine had taken a management job with *McDonalds* and, over a few years, ran many of their restaurants up in Lancashire, at such places as Bolton, Chorley and Rochdale, amongst others. I can remember that it often involved her working until late at night and we always worried about her having to drive home in the early hours. Eventually she moved away from the 'service' side of the business and somehow made a niche for herself on the training side, especially concerning the use of computers in the stores all around the country. Inevitably, she and Steve seemed to spend more time apart than together and their marriage ran into problems. I know they tried hard to make a go of things, particularly when they were both in Western Australia with us at the end of 1996. Lorraine had the benefit of a 'sabbatical' - a thirteen-week break from work as a reward for all her years with *McDonalds*. She went to Oz with 'our Sue' for around two weeks and then joined Joyce and myself in FNQ and Melbourne, before heading back to Perth, where Steve finally joined us.

Lorraine's career change meant that she was now spending more and more time in London. So, in December of 1997, she persuaded Steve to move down to East Finchley, where they bought a flat not too far from *McDonalds* headquarters. Sadly, things never did work out after that and, around May of 1998, Lorraine came down to visit us here in Greatham by herself, to announce that she and Steve were splitting up.

Happily, things seemed to be settled amicably and it wasn't too long before Lorraine introduced us to her new love, Phil Le Brun. Phil is an undoubted computer whiz kid and also works at *McDonalds'* East Finchley headquarters office – although he spends a lot of time flying around the world on projects!

As well as their busy lifestyle, both Lorraine and Phil have been eager to add to their educational achievements. In the early months of 2004, they were both awarded their 'MBAs' – it's supposed to stand for Masters of Business Administration, but in fact I'm pretty sure it should be *Masters of the Black Arts*! I do know that they both put in a huge amount of hard work into their projects, and may possibly be embarking on yet further studies in the future. Another plan on the cards, as I type this in, is a wedding in 2005! As they say in the trade, watch this space.

And now – grandparents!

When Michelle and James moved into their house in the Leicestershire village of Cosby in the summer of 1991, it wasn't too long afterwards that they were announcing the expectant arrival of a baby! Our first grandson, Thomas James, duly arrived on 22nd October 1992. It was the following year that the happy couple then got married, at the Register Office in Leicester! It's all done differently to the way it happened in our day! As the happy couple went off on honeymoon, young Tom came home with us to Greatham, while Lorraine also accompanied us, in order to look after him while Joyce and I were at work. I have constant memories of Tom, bouncing up and down in one of those devices that fits over a doorway frame – it was our method of tiring him out so that he would sleep well!

Calum Joseph Fitzpatrick joined the family in March 1995. I can't recall exactly when it happened, either before or after his arrival, but it certainly necessitated an extension to the house, giving an extra bedroom and a second living room downstairs. Calum appears to have taken after his Dad in his sporting abilities, being very good at physical activities. He liked playing football at first, but that proved a passing fad! But he has taken particularly well to karate and is becoming quite a star at that particular sport.

It took quite a long while for us all to realise that Tom was afflicted by a type of learning disability – and even longer for the educational authorities to sort out a proper learning environment. It was after he had started at play-school that the first signs of a problem were spotted. Unfortunately, the educational system in Leicestershire didn't – and still doesn't – have its own dedicated special-needs schools and Tom was allowed to pass into the normal educational system. He was certainly done no favours by the local school in Cosby – a great pity that, as it was right on the doorstep and seemed an ideal situation at first. He was eventually passed on to another school in the locality but, again, the facilities there were not up to the task. It wasn't until 2004, and after a long and testing battle by both Michelle and James, that Tom started attending a special school up near Belper, in Derbyshire. It came highly recommended, with a reputation as one of the best schools of its type. One major difficulty with that arrangement was that there was an hour's journey – or longer – at the beginning and end of every school day. However, Tom seemed to be getting on really well up there at first, but due to changes in the school staff, such as losing the excellent headmaster, the school soon deteriorated.

Once again, Michelle and James had a battle on their hands and, after much soul-searching, decided that the best school for Tom was another one near Nottingham. They were eventually able to get him started there after the summer holiday in 2005 and, as Christmas 2005 approaches now as I write, there are definite signs of progress. But we hate to get our hopes up too high, there have been so many setbacks in the past. There's no doubt that Tom is very bright, but needs to learn things in a different way to the standard methods used in mainstream schools. At long last, this now appears to be taking place. We all just hope that Tom can get some decent education in the next few years. After a couple of terms at his new school, Tom is certainly making good progress – and seemingly growing taller day by day! At the age of thirteen, he is almost six feet high, and towers over the rest of us!

Foreign affairs!

In mid-February 2005, Joyce and I were very excited at the prospects of a holiday in the Caribbean - a spot we'd only had a brief association with when we visited Nassau, Bahamas, way back in 1983. The purpose of our holiday was to 'be there' for Lorraine's wedding to Phil on February 22nd, which turned out to be a splendid affair, enjoyed by all who attended. It certainly was super to get away from England's grey skies at that time of year! The wedding took place on St Lucia, a beautiful little island, where Joyce and I spent two very happy weeks, it seemed almost like our own honeymoon, everything went so perfectly.

But the day after our return, we came down to earth with a bump, when Joyce had to go into the Royal Haslar hospital at Gosport for a knee operation! This had been a long-standing problem, which probably started back when Joyce fell on that knee when playing netball, and exacerbated by her falling off her bike after a 26-mile ride in June 2003. Fortunately, after 'keyhole' surgery, it was found that there was no permanent damage and, having 'washed out' the cartilage, the surgeon told Joyce that she was very good for her mileage! I can certainly testify to that! While Joyce was being operated on, I took advantage of taking a ferry trip between Gosport and Portsmouth!

It wasn't long after Joyce's operation that we went off on another of our annual Easter trips to Barmouth with Eileen and Mike. Thankfully, Joyce was able to do all the walks with us and even a bit of gentle climbing towards the end of the week, in the shape of the Precipe and Panorama walks. We had only been back home a few days when Michelle rang to say that Calum was being rushed into hospital with suspected appendicitis. It turned out to be an acute case and the little lad was operated on just in time. Joyce and I dashed up on a Thursday morning and spent a couple of days 'looking after' Tom, who was still on a half-term beak from school. It was nice to spend some quality time with him. As we left Cosby on the Sunday, it was hoped that Calum would be fit enough to go home the following day. Fortunately, he went on to make a good recovery.

With Phil having been a 'world traveller' on *British Airways* for many a long month, as part of his ongoing project work with *McDonalds*, both he and Lorraine had mulled over the prospect of moving to the States on a semi-permanent basis. Phil works very much under the head office in Chicago and, by early 2005, had spent almost as much time there as in Finchley. So it came about that, in June of that year, we set off up to Finchley to say *'Cheerio'* to them, as they were due to move to Wheaton, Illinois, on June 22nd. How long they will stay there depends largely on how well they

settle into the lifestyle and how successful they are in the working environment. Their present plan is to stay for maybe two or three years, but we shall have to wait and see. We also said farewell to Jake. After a long life of fifteen years, very old for a dog, he has developed a tumour in his leg. It had been planned that he should go to the States, but Lorraine eventually - and sadly - decided that it was fairer to have him put to sleep.

Lorraine and Phil's Carribean wedding

And that's the way it worked out. The Le Bruns went off to the States and, by all accounts, have settled in there nicely. As I write this, we are preparing to go and visit then for a couple of weeks, starting August 28th. In fact we won't be their first visitors, as we were beaten to the punch by Sue and Des! While they were away, this left Mum slightly out on a limb, so we took a trip up to Culcheth and brought her down to stay with us for a few days. I then took her back by myself and, on her 85th birthday, I had to take her to Warrington Hospital for pre-operative checks, as she will shortly having cataracts removed from both eyes.

Our visit to the Chicago area was an excellent one. The Le Brun residence is a splendid three-storey town-house, with good road access to the surrounding area. Wheaton turned out to be a far-western suburb of Chicago, with a good train service into the city – once you had reached the station that is! But Joyce and I have never minded walking and we took advantage of both 'shank's pony' and the *Metra* train system to get around to a variety of places. Not too long afterwards, after a couple of days up with the Fitzpatricks, Lorraine & Phil paid us a flying visit. They had been to the wedding of Helen & Demi, down at Cirencester, then dropped in on us for a couple of nights. As one may guess, we visited *Madhuban,* our favourite Indian restaurant, during their stay!

Since their move to Chicago, Lorraine and Phil have carried on with their travels on behalf of *McDonalds.* Lorraine was hoping to drop in on us early in 2006, during a European trip – but the next thing we know, she was sending us an e-mail from Mexico City! A trip to Germany was next on her agenda, followed by both L and P being sent down to Orlando, Florida, to attend a convention. I know they are planning to be in Sydney, Australia, later this year, that's summer 2006, where they are hoping to meet up with Sue and Geoff, over from New Zealand, as well as Pam and family. Sian has recently moved to Melbourne, so Pam and Kate will be flying across from WA to fit it all in.

On June 12th 2006, we finally had Lorraine able to fit us in, on a busy-schedule visit to the UK. She'd been in the Midlands and up to the north-east, then on a meeting at Finchley, before she caught a train down to Liss, where we picked her up. She had one whole day with us, during which we enjoyed a long walk over at Bentworth, before I had to drop her off at Heathrow for her return flight. She was looking forward to that Australian trip previously mentioned – and we have an invitation to visit Wheaton again sometime the following year. It hardly seemed any time at all before Lorraine was back over here again! This was prior to she and Phil meeting up with friends Sam & John and heading off to Croatia on holiday. She'd originally been planning to be here on business, but that got postponed and she decided to have three days with us instead. We managed to fit in another visit to *Madhuban* with Helen & Tim, plus a long walk over at Alresford, during some very warm and sunny weather. So hot on the last evening that we even had to have the fan on!

Just prior to Joyce's sixty-second birthday, we had the pleasure of another 'flying visit' from Lorraine, this time with a colleague from Chicago called Pam. They had been on business at Heathrow for a few days, then able to fit in a two-day visit to Hampshire over the weekend. We were able to get across to Winchester and Petersfield on the Saturday, dodging the showers, but Sunday turned out better and we had a nice walk along the seafront at Southsea, followed by a visit to Jane Austen's house over at Chawton.

Later that year, May 31ˢᵗ to be exact, Joyce and I flew across to New York, where we were later met by Lorraine & Phil for a holiday that was basically a whirlwind tour of the eastern seaboard of the United States, followed by a whiz through Canada! It was during this visit that we met Jasmine, their new puppy – which had given them the incentive to move to a house with a garden! This they duly did, shortly after we came home, and they are now living in Naperville, which is a few miles further away from Chicago than Wheaton. Then, on September 14ᵗʰ, it was *our* turn to pick *them* up, as they arrived in the UK for a two-week holiday. They were over here to attend a wedding in Wokingham, and we basically took them from Heathrow to their hotel just outside Bracknell. We had a pleasant afternoon with them, in warm sunshine, walking firstly around Windsor for a couple of hours and then around Wokingham itself. On the Sunday, after the wedding, they took a train from Reading down to Bodmin, where friends Sam & John picked them up, and all four of them then headed down to Suzy's bungalow in dear old Padstow.

It was only a short while later that L & P were in England again, this time for Sam & John's wedding in Dorset! This was just for a few days and they managed to spend a day with us during that time. We all went down to Emsworth for a few hours, then later enjoyed a *'Madhuban'* curry, along with Helen & Tim. With us due to visit them at their new home in Naperville for Christmas, we are probably currently seeing more of them now that when they were living in Finchley! That visit to Naperville eventually took place, based around Christmas and New Year, 2007 into 2008.

Back to the boys!

By the summer of 2005, Calum had joined a local 'Leadership' class in karate and has been awarded his 'green belt' – with a blue stripe! He's certainly doing well and is making good progress at his normal schooling too. Tom started at his new school after the summer break of 2005, but once again the 'authorities' are making a mess of things. He has enjoyed the school so far, with the staff seemingly able to handle him very well, and making good progress. One benefit has been that he has been having shorter travel times and his taxi not having to pick him up so early each morning.

So now that he has settled into this routine – and routine is absolutely essential for Tom's well-being – then of course 'they' now want to change things! It obviously all comes down to budgets with the LEA, there is no chance that any individual requirement will enter the equation. The plan is that, as from today, Monday October 31st, he will be back to sharing transport with another youngster – with all the inevitable routine change that this will bring. Michelle and James are resisting this change and we wish them all success in their battle against these so-called 'experts' – they seem to have been fighting these battles for far too long.

Thankfully, as I update this account at the beginning of May 2006, Tom seems to have settled down really well and making great strides forward. His biggest problem is being unable to transfer what he is thinking down onto paper in written form. But the main thing is that he is much happier nowadays, and sprouting upwards at a very fast rate too! I think he is taller than anyone else in the family now and seems likely to top six foot very soon!

At the beginning of July 2006, Joyce and I went up for one of our regular weekends at Cosby and, as had become the norm in previous years, we brought Tom back down to stay with us for a week. Not only did that give Tom the chance to have a holiday, but it gave Michelle a much-needed break from having Tom permanently at home that summer. One particularly good day we had was down at Portsmouth Dockyard, where we were able to take Tom aboard *HMS Warrior* and *HMS Victory*, have a tour of the harbour and see some of the modern ships, and see the wreck of the *Mary Rose*, flagship of King Henry VIII. But I think the highlight of Tom's day was in the 'Action Stations' building, with its simulators and games!

Final update

For quite a while, Michelle went to work as a cleaner, in the offices of a firm of printers. But she was also quite often having to clean the shop floor as well. Finally, during the latter half of 2007, she applied for the 'temporary' post of classroom assistant, helping out during school times, with a young boy who has severe leaning difficulties. There is no doubt that, with the experience she has had with Tom, she is eminently able – though not officially 'qualified' – to fit the task. As I mentioned, the post was 'temporary', on a short-term contract, but she is hoping that it leads to something longer lasting in the future.

288

Greatham, Hants, GU33 6AG

We moved into our 'new' (and so far, only!) house on the last day of October 1967. As detailed elsewhere, one main reason was that it was located right next door to my civilian supervising instructor at Bordon, George Armitage. This then had the great benefit that we were able to share the transport to and from work over the next twenty years or so. No doubt we saved ourselves a few quid over those years and, to use the modern parlance, did our bit to reduce pollution and help save the planet - although we never looked at it in quite that way at the time! Prior to moving in, I had been bringing bits and pieces, furniture, cutlery etc, down to SEME with me in the morning from Reading, then popping down to Chapel House at lunch break to drop them off. I'm pretty sure that I remember my Dad visiting Reading during that period and coming down to Greatham at one point, before we'd even laid the carpet. I'll never forget that carpet, we picked it up from the *Co-op* in Reading - it was mainly dark brown, with sort of orange sunbursts as the pattern.

A lot of the other fittings and furnishings were either sales items, second-hand or donations from family, friends and neighbours. There was one bedroom carpet that I think came from Pat and Roy Clark, one of those rubber-foam backed things with a striped pattern that eventually fell to bits on us! (I may be wrong, but the 'nursery rhyme' linoleum may still be under it today!) And I'm pretty sure too that we used an old iron-frame bedstead for a good number of years, it really was heavy and took some shifting! That came from Mrs Brunston, who lived at the top end of Queen's Cottages. It was certainly a case of 'beggars can't be choosers' in those days. We were still bringing bits and pieces down from Reading when I managed to write off our first car, on Guy Fawkes night, just a few days after we'd officially moved into Chapel House.

Joyce, at quite a young age!

One main reason for settling down as a civilian was to provide a steady base for the girls to get their education. Greatham School lies just a short walk away from the house and it was August 1968 when Lorraine started up there, with Gwen Brooker as the headmistress. We can still picture Lorraine in her pink gingham dress and this scene was to be repeated when Michelle followed her, starting her schooling in April 1971. In between those dates, Joyce had also volunteered to be 'Tawny Owl' for the local Brownie pack, which both of the girls joined. The pack operated from the Rectory, this when John Russell was the Rector. Rita Gerard was not only a teacher at Greatham, but she also acted as the 'Brown Owl'; while next door neighbour Susan Armitage took up the post of (I think!) 'Little Owl'.

Joyce starts work

Once we had the two girls settled into routine, Joyce was able to take a job, beginning as a 'dinner lady' at Greatham School in November the following year, that was 1972. The only other two names I can recall from those kitchen days are the two Maureens – Cross and Graham – who both still live in the village. Joyce obviously kept that job for a while, but then towards the end of 1976 she started working as a cook up at another school in Bordon. Eventually she went to work at the school in Budd's Lane, Bordon, virtually opposite the Army camp where I worked. Here, she worked alongside Jeanette Bruce and Shirley James, both of whom have kept in touch (just!) over the years. Both Jeanette and her husband Ian have long since retired. They now own a house down in Liss, as well as living for a large part of each year out in Spain.

I remember that we went to their daughter Sally's wedding many years ago – that was to the local professional at Blackmoor Golf Club, but sadly didn't last too long. By coincidence, son Allister Bruce has recently (2004) moved into a bungalow just up Longmoor Road. As I write, he is 'living with' his wife-to-be, Helen, their wedding is set for June 2005. Allister suffers from progressive MS, but makes the best of life

– we often stop for a chat as we walk past their place. Shirley's husband Mervyn – or 'Jesse' for obvious reasons – was another ex-REME guy who went on to work as an instructor at SEME. He also joined the TA and, at one time, was the ASM of 9 Field Workshop, the unit that I joined in 1979. *(You'll find a tale about Jesse in the Chapter on my TA service.)*

Joyce stayed in the school meal service right up until the end of May in 1988. It was at that time that the service began to be handed over to contractors and I think that Jeanette, Shirley and Joyce all decided at the same time that they didn't want to work for some outside firm with no real interest except to make money out of it. I used to drop in at Bordon County Junior School quite often during my lunch break, after all it was only 'across the road' from my job at SEME. So I appreciate just what effort those girls put in over the years on behalf of the children. As well as the preparation of the food, then the cooking of same, it then had to be served with a smile – after which came the really hard part of cleaning all those pots and pans, ovens, floors etc. It was pretty backbreaking at times I can tell you, and I think it took Joyce about four or five years before her back got used to the upright position again!

Next-door neighbours

Greatham lies just about four miles south of Bordon, so travelling in and out of work took only a short time, even allowing for a stop to pick up the morning paper. Before Joyce started working, I remember that George and I even used to dash home for a spot of lunch each day! That was fairly easily achieved, as the camp was only a ten-minute drive from home, and it was just nice to have a break in the middle of the day, away from the working environment. I can't remember for how long we carried on doing that, but I know that, with George being a diabetic, he needed to have meals at a regular time each day. Over the years, his health gradually deteriorated and he eventually had to give up work. At times he would lapse into a drowsy state and would require an instant input of something sweet to raise his sugar level. I remember that there was at least one occasion when I had to pop next door and give him an injection. George was an ex-Royal Engineer and had served in Egypt, most likely the Canal Zone, during the Second World War. I remember him once telling me a story about an underground cesspit, in the desert near Port Said, that had built up such a layer of gas that it finally exploded, shedding its load of 'whatever' all over the surrounding area! After he'd become a civilian instructor, he'd worked at the two apprentice schools at Harrogate and Chepstow, before moving to Bordon to take up his supervisory post.

I believe that George had been diagnosed with diabetes as long ago as his wartime service and, unfortunately, the type of insulin that he had used for many years afterwards had slowly but inevitably caused his kidneys to fail. He went on to have a transplant, followed by a second, before finally succumbing to it all in May 1988. George's widow Dorothy still lives next door with younger son Keith. Elder son Clive married Jacqueline and they now live outside of the village, along with two children, a boy and a girl. Daughter Susan got married to a chap called Peter – we even attended the wedding – but they split up a few years afterwards. I think Susan is married again now, to another George, and they live down near Gloucester somewhere.

I've mentioned elsewhere on what a great help George could be when it came to car repairs. Well, Clive Armitage really took a leaf out of his father's book and became something of an expert himself. So, at the first rattle of a toolbox out on the drive, it became customary for both George and Clive to soon have their overalls on and be stuck in to the latest repair. Gearboxes, clutches, even whole engines in the case of my old *Cortina* – they'd all get the treatment! My only complaint against Clive is the fact that when he got married and left home, the ladder that used to hang on the wall of next door's garage disappeared from sight! Very handy that ladder – I don't think the gutter gets cleaned out so often nowadays!

The village

When we first arrived in Greatham, it was pretty well served by local shops. Just up the road a way was a small grocery shop run by a couple by the name of Pooley. I can't recall his first name, but I know that his wife's name was Shirley. She was quite a good seamstress and altered the trousers for me when I bought a suit for Lorraine's wedding in 1987. Their marriage ended and he went off to Rhodesia, which is where I believe he originally came from. Shirley stayed in the house, *'Broadleigh'*, for a number of years afterwards, taking up with a guy named Jim Farrar, who was a photographer by profession. He actually ran his business from the premises for a while. I'm pretty sure that Shirley later married Jim and they now live elsewhere.

Down towards the bottom of the road, just past *'The Oaks'* caravan site, an elderly couple by the name of Pearcey (if that's the right spelling) ran a similar small shop, which has long since been converted for private use. When they were still there, it really was an old-fashioned place, I swear some of the medicine bottles had been there since around the time of the Boer War! When they sold up, the shop was taken over by the Angus family and, when they'd had enough, the Booths took over for a number of years. Dave Booth was friendly enough, but his wife Lilian was a bit of a mystery! She always seemed so miserable and I swear that she only ever smiled at those customers who regularly used the shop. If, like us, you shopped at a supermarket in Petersfield or elsewhere, and only 'topped up' with an occasional visit to the local shop, it took all of Lilian's time and effort to even serve you; and then it came with a tight grimace and total lack of charm! The Booths had two daughters, Angela and Karen, who must have been of similar age to our two I'm sure they appear on Brownie/Guide photos that we have tucked away. For a short while, the premises were converted for use by Albert Baker, a member of the *Mouth & Foot Painting Artists*, who became something of a local celebrity as a school governor. Nowadays, it is just a plain house and I think recent inhabitants have named it Longmoor House.

Around the corner from Longmoor Road, along what was then the main A325 road between Petersfield (to the south) and Farnham (to the north), lay two public houses. The first one, *'The Queen'*, was always a bit of a drab place and eventually closed down around 2002. But it re-opened in 2004 as *'The Greatham Inn'*, so at least the village still has a pub these days. The second hostelry used to be called *'The Woolmer Hotel'* and old photographs show it as quite a splendid looking place. Around the time of our arrival in the village, its name changed to *'The Silver Birch'*, and it was quite a thriving spot in those days. As mentioned elsewhere, I went there to work part-time as a barman for a couple of years, when money was pretty tight.

Like many village pubs in the latter 20th-century, business gradually reduced and the *Silver Birch* suffered too. There was a period when an Italian guy, Giovanni, ran a restaurant within the pub, but this probably lasted only a couple of years and, not long afterwards, the doors closed for the last time. Currently there is a large notice board outside the derelict place announcing the arrival of *'Silver Birch Mews'*, in other words a housing development. Plans are also 'in place' to build four houses on half of the car park adjacent to *'The Greatham Inn'*. *(As I peruse these words again in May 2007, both housing developments are under way at these two sites.)*

In between the two pubs was the Post Office, which was then attached to the 15th-century *'Welldigger's Cottage'*. Resident in 1967 was the Stamp family – very aptly named for the Post Office. *(In those days we still had a 'Village Bobby', who lived in an official police house round in Bakersfield – and went by the name of PC Penny – good name for a 'copper'!)* Stan Stamp was an ex-Navy guy who sported 'a full set' – naval term for a large beard. Poor Stan must have got into financial problems of some sort because, under the threat of investigation by the authorities, he shot himself on the premises, leaving wife Pat to bring up the family alone. This was followed by their departure and the business was taken over by a pair of Londoners named Sampson. As well as being the PO, the premises had also been a small grocery shop of sorts, and the Sampsons continued this for a number of years. When they departed from Greatham, the PO then moved up to its present position at the far end of the village and became the business of Joyce and John Clarke, again with a grocery-style shop and newsagents, which continues to this day. The Clarkes eventually sold out to Linda and Peter Stevens who, in turn, handed over to the present incumbents, Delma and Elwyn Evans, who came up from the Swansea area. The Stevens moved down to Bishop's Waltham, Joyce Clarke died a few years ago, but old John still lives in the village and we often bump into him when we are out walking. *(We later heard that John also died, at a nursing home in Liss, sometime during 2007.)*

When the PO closed down and the Sampsons left, the shop area then became *'The Game Centre'* for a few years. Today, one would immediately think that this meant a shop where you could buy computer games, but in fact the 'game' in question was the provision of such things as pheasant, partridge, rabbit etc. It was never intended to be a shopping outlet, being mainly used as a delivery centre for a firm based elsewhere. It eventually met the same fate as most of the other businesses already mentioned. So we are left now with only one 'shop' of any sort in Greatham, that being the present Post Office and Stores at the far northern end of the village, just opposite the roundabout.

This roundabout has been a fairly recent addition, being part of the Woolmer Road 'bypass' that now cuts Greatham off from the normal traffic flow. Back in the early 1990s, construction started on the A3 dual carriageway to by-pass the towns of Petersfield and Liphook. The old A3 used to run right through these towns and presented a nightmare during the heavy summer holiday traffic. The new road opened in July 1992 and the immediate effect upon us personally was the vast increase in background noise! Thank goodness someone provided the impetus for a general claim from most villagers for compensation. This provided enough cash for us to fully double-glaze the house to modern standards. It is now only when the doors and/ or windows are left open that the full effect of traffic noise can still be heard.

Back in 1992, I don't think that people in Greatham realised that they had been let down so badly by the 'planners' – and I use that term reservedly! All the traffic coming down from the Farnham/ Bordon area, to link up with the new road, came directly through Greatham. For those people living on the A325, it was a nightmare, they could hardly get their cars off the drive at busy periods. Thanks to the efforts of such people as Colonel Michael Digby, our local Councillor, Greatham eventually became fully by-passed by the Woolmer link, which gave us the roundabout previously mentioned. The small stretch of road that leads into Greatham is named *'Digby Way'*, in honour of Michael's campaigning. We also got a second roundabout at the southern end of the village, where the road goes off through Selborne to Alton.

Between the end of Longmoor Road and that second roundabout lie both the village Churches, one now an ancient ruin, the other being the most prominent building seen for miles. There is also the village school, the village hall and many other well-known buildings. All of these are well covered in the book that I had published late in 2003, *'A History of Greatham'*, so I will dwell on those no further! When we arrived in 1967, Greatham also had its own garage, virtually opposite *The Queen* and run by Ray Flack. He sold off the garage and adjoining land many years ago and there is now a small housing estate, *'Todmore'*, on the same site – quite an improvement really.

Friends and neighbours

Apart from the Armitages, when we first moved into Greatham we knew nobody else. I'm pretty sure that Joyce used to say hello to other mothers when she walked the girls to school when they were very young, but we never really had any friends amongst them. I guess it was when Joyce started playing netball for a team called *'The Jays'* that we began to make lifetime connections. That was in April 1972, so we had already been in Greatham for most of five years! Our closest friends are Helen and Tim Gould, who also arrived as newcomers to the village, from their original home in Essex. They set up home in Bracken Cottage, which is up towards the now only village shop, but later moved down to Snailing Lane, off the Selborne Road. Their only child, Rebecca, was born in 1977 and I know that Lorraine definitely used to 'baby-sit', though perhaps Michelle was too young at the time. *(Joyce suffered a nasty knee injury during her netball days, which still trouble her to this day – she eventually had 'clean out' keyhole surgery on it, but it still gives the occasional 'twinge'.)*

Also connected with the local netball scene was Sandra Berriman, although I think she was only involved in the refereeing side at the time. She and husband Tony owned the butcher's shop in Liss Forest and both Lorraine and Michelle went on to start their 'work experience' as Saturday-morning assistants in the same shop. In those years, we often used to walk down to West Liss, down into the main village of Liss, and then back through Liss Forest, it made a nice circular walk. Now, however, the traffic is just too busy. The Berrimans have both retired now, but still live in Liss Forest and we just occasionally bump into them. Jackie Marie was another netball player. I think she did play for *The Jays* for a period, but certainly played on well after the other girls called it a day, for another local team, Shottermill, of quite a high standard. Her husband Bill worked in the factory run by Tim Gould and Pete Williams, just behind the railway station in Alton, right up until 2003. It was around the same time that I went to work as a part-time driver for *Gould & Williams*, as Bill's retirement left them short-handed on the factory floor.

The Maries used to live up the road from us, but then built a house on land that belonged to Bill's father, up behind what is now the Post Office, in Pansy Lane. Jackie and Bill have three children, sons Steve and Neil and daughter Andrea. All three were much into sport, and used to play badminton against the rest of us 'oldies' for a few years. Neil still lives at home and I believe he now runs *Nursted Builders*, the firm he joined straight from school. Patrick – or Pat – and Shirley Redpath lived along the Petersfield Road, between the garage site and what used to be the PO in Stan Stamp's day. They have two children, Mark and Julie. Mark went into plumbing as a trade and has done many a fine job for us – we are currently waiting for him to fit a new central-heating boiler! Sadly, Pat and Shirley were involved in a horrific accident at the end of October 2000, when a tree fell onto their car up at Hindhead. Pat died shortly afterwards, while Shirley was left permanently crippled and is now confined to a wheelchair. She now lives with Julie and her family at Cowplain and is a great example to us all, on how to combat all that life can throw at one. We, along with Helen and Tim, go down to visit her when we can, and occasionally take her out on day-trips. *(Sadly, at the beginning of August 2005, Shirley was unable to fight off the effects of a chest infection, possibly pneumonia, and she died peacefully. The Church in Greatham was packed for her funeral.*

By coincidence, another 'Sandra and Tony' lived just up the road from the Redpaths, in the form of the Allan family. They have two sons, Nigel and Martin. Nigel followed Tony into the plumbing trade and I think he was once in partnership with Mark Redpath. Sandra went on to run the village play-school, located in the village hall, but an unfortunate situation with the Charities Commission put paid to that! *(It also created a very unhappy situation that involved many of us in the village, but I won't make a meal of it here!)* Sandra and Tony later moved down to Swanage, while Nigel and his family lived in their old house for a few months, before also heading off to pastures new.

Another couple that has lived in the village for quite some time are the Cawkells – I think that's how you spell it! – Chris and Dave. They used to live a few doors away from us up Longmoor Road, I think they have two sons and definitely have a daughter, Tara. She used to come and knock on the door to ask if our two could play with her. She was a tiny thing and I used to open the front door, look straight ahead and pretend there was no-one there! I also used to call her *'Ta-ra-de-bum-de-eh'*, I wonder if she remembers? Anyway, after being in dire financial straits at one time, Dave Cawkell finally made good. The family moved to Forge House on the Selborne Road for a few years, before settling now in a large place on Snailing Lane, not far from Helen and Tim. August 28 2006 brought an 'event to remember', when the Goulds' daughter Rebecca had a wedding party, held in a marquee on Tim's hallowed ground – the tennis court! Rebecca and David Eades had married around four weeks previously, at Lake Como, but the party was held basically as a reception – just minus the service!

Home improvements!

After living in the house for almost three years, I think the first main job that I tackled was the building of a porch, on the side of the house that has the front door. There was already a roof, supported by two metal posts, so my task was to build a brick base about halfway up and then to fill the remainder with windows. Having never done any building previously, it is remarkable that the brickwork still stands almost forty years later! I've written elsewhere of picking up a window-frame from a work colleague – and that is still there too. But the woodwork has been replaced a couple of times I think – and that includes the door.

The first wood I used was garnered from a gypsy-site up the old Longmoor Road towards Liphook, and soon started to rot from the inside! Paid help was on hand for the first rebuild in 1984 from chippy John Keep, who lived up near the old PO. Then he came back to do a similar renovation in 2001. John's first wife Joan died at a young age and he re-married and moved to Haslemere with his new wife Jo some years ago. But I have called on him a few times, when woodworking jobs have been required. All the internal doors in the house were re-hung by John, as fashions changed. Many years ago, in a fit of 'open-planning madness', I removed the banisters from the side of the stairs, only to have John rebuild them again a few years ago.

Our back garden when we moved in was hardly of any size at all. Fortunately, I was able to borrow some money against my mortgage and afford to buy a plot of land alongside that virtually trebled the size of the garden. It certainly paid off many years later, when two houses suddenly appeared in what had been a splendid garden next door! That garden once belonged to Bower Cottage, up the road. In 1967, the owners were a family called Maynard, who had a daughter Jill, around the same age as our two girls. Jill used to come and play in our garden. When the Maynards eventually moved, another family moved in, the husband of which was some sort of diplomat, if I recall correctly. There were two little girls, and I think I'm right in remembering their names as Pippa and Suki. They also played with our girls and, when they moved away to Runfold, near Farnham, we went there to visit them just the once.

Bower Cottage had originally been three separate cottages in a terrace. At one stage the property was bought by the same 'farmer' who had sold us the land in order to extend our garden. He hoped to develop the whole field behind the houses in Longmoor Road for housing and, as part of his 'cunning plan', knocked down the cottage nearest the road in an attempt to provide access. To our great pleasure, planning permission was never granted and the fields behind us remain pretty much the same now as they ever were. Over the years, both cattle and horses have roamed around, but in latter years it has been horses only. The latest collection has taken a liking to eating the shrubs so carefully nurtured by Joyce!

At the end of 1973, with Joyce having been at work for just over a year, we'd obviously put some money together, because we could then afford to have double-glazed sliding patio doors fitted! The original 'French doors' had been fitted 'inside out' and used to leak like mad whenever it rained! Over the following four years we had the rear windows of the house, in the lounge and two bedrooms, double-glazed in the same style and by the same firm. They had done some work for Jan at her house as far as I remember, were based in Reading and run by a guy named Manning. Eventually of course, all those old aluminium doors and windows were replaced by modern PVC-type, after the 'noise compensation' award mentioned earlier.

On an 'on-and-off' sort of basis, I spent most of 1976 in refurbishing the kitchen. I remember tiling most of it with orange tiles - quite the fashion at the time I suppose! (I think there are still a few left behind the washing machine!) The floor also had a makeover with dark and light vinyl tiles in a checkerboard pattern. It must have been that year too that I built the corner seating that remains with us to this day, despite Joyce's efforts to have me take it down! It still does the job of providing both seating and storage. Towards the end of 1990, Steve Burgoyne and James Fitzpatrick both assisted in re-vamping the kitchen by putting in new units. That left me then to replace those now outdated orange tiles for something more tasteful and which still survive today!

1978 brought a couple of minor improvements that have proved their worth over the following years! Bert May, a colleague from work, gave me an aluminium loft-ladder that remains in place today. Prior to that, access to the loft was by standing on a stepladder, then hauling ones self up by the elbows! Fitting a proper ladder then led to the loft floor being reinforced with lots of wood, most of provided by packing cases from SEME. The second addition was an electric shower, fitted over the bath. This had to be moved in 1980 when I had John Preston in to re-arrange the bathroom completely – the bath had originally been in front of the window! Since then, the

298

shower has been replaced by a more modern, power-assisted type – but I still like my bath every night!

Going back to our arrival in Chapel House in 1967, we were the proud owners of a telephone – when the number was still referred to in the term 'Blackmoor 265'! It just shows you how hard up we must have been in those days, because we couldn't afford to keep it. Any phone calls then had to be made from one of two phone-boxes in the village, one near to the school and the other outside the old PO. It is amazing to look back and find that we didn't replace the house phone until the beginning of 1979! I mean, who can make do without a phone nowadays?

Towards the end of 1989 we had a lad called Jamie Wells build us a couple of brick arches, one at either end of the side of the house. John Keep later fitted a heavy wooden door in the rear arch, as extra security and privacy. It was the same Jamie who had built a garden wall across the patio, between our place and New House. The fence had blown down in the 'great storm' of 1987 – and the wall itself fell down after more extreme winds in 1990! Jamie then came back and built a reinforced wall that, thankfully, still stands today.

Another story comes to mind, regarding the time when Uncle John (Hodgson) was close to death in hospital and Mum had decided to come over from Australia to see him. We had arranged to pick her up from Heathrow, I think it must have been on a Sunday. Anyway, the previous day, we were going to go up to Reading to visit Eileen & Mike. It had been raining 'cats and dogs' for a while and still pouring down on that Saturday morning, February 3rd 1990. Going down the hill into Selborne, we had to negotiate quite a flood of water across the road and, by the time we were heading out of the village on the other side, we thought it just too dangerous to go on, as the roads were awash. Instead of turning around, because we already knew that Selborne was flooded on 'our' side, I decided to take the turn through Hartley Mauditt and down into Oakhanger. Bad decision! We ran into a veritable wall of water, which came up over the car bonnet! I managed to reverse out of this swimming pool, but the car engine was coughing and spluttering like mad.

We limped back into Selborne and parked up outside the White House, which I knew belonged to a guy who worked at my Army Camp at Bordon. We scrounged a load of dry cloth from him and managed to dry out the engine to a certain extent. Backtracking, we then took the road directly from Selborne into Oakhanger, then up into Bordon towards the main road. The roads really were terrible and the police had cars out at various junctions, warning of the floods ahead in all directions. Thankfully, we managed to negotiate our way through lots of deep water, got onto the A325 about two hours after we'd originally left home, and headed south. When we got as far as *The Queen* public house, it was to find the bottom of Longmoor Road completely under water! Once again we took a chance and worked our way around the corner, up our road and onto the drive! My car was still suffering from a very damp engine and I couldn't trust it to make the trip to the airport next morning. In the end, our Cliff, accompanied by Des, came down to meet Mum and take her up north. Sadly, of course, John died a few days afterwards, but Mum was grateful to have had the chance to be with him at the end.

It was 1986 when we finally said farewell to the original central-heating boiler that was installed when the house was first built. So it must have been more than twenty years old by then, which is about par for the course. It was constructed from cast iron and must have weighed a ton. I remember having to dismantle part of it occasionally for cleaning purposes. The replacement boiler was a lot more efficient, being of copper construction, and that too has now reached the end of its useful life – or so we are told by the experts! *(Anyway, as mentioned above, it is due to be replaced this year (2005), hopefully just after the Easter holiday.)*

It was the heating system as such that provided us with the biggest disaster as far as the house goes. After our third visit to Australia over Christmas 1996, we returned to a deep-frozen England. Now we'd been warned of the cold conditions from TV reports and I'd phoned to ask Helen to put the heating on, prior to our return. This she (or Tim?) did, but unknown at the time was the fact that heating pipes in the loft had already frozen solid. Thus, as the house warmed up, the pipes burst and the whole front of the house was flooded - mainly our bedroom and the garage, but the kitchen was also pretty badly hit. Thanks to the house insurance, we soon had the assistance of an assessor, who did all that we asked of him. It took a few months I think, but we must have had everything back in good order by the summer of 1997.

Towards the end of 2000, builder Kevin Gillett arrived to start work on our front garden. We had planter the dreaded *leylandiae* many years previously and the two that we had finally let grow had now reached above rooftop height. Kevin had them removed for us, then built a new low brick wall around the area, as well as re-laying the concrete drive, which was literally falling to bits! For the next few months, Kevin gradually paved around the front and side of the house, before moving into the back garden and laying down some new paths and a patio at the far end. We also had a new fence erected and had the garden shed disguised by the addition of some trellis.

Medical matters

In mid-February 2005, Joyce and I were very excited at the prospects of a holiday in the Caribbean, a spot we'd only had a brief association with when we visited Nassau, Bahamas, way back in 1983. The purpose of our holiday was to 'be there' for Lorraine's wedding to Phil on February 22nd. The day after our return, Joyce had to go into the Royal Haslar hospital at Gosport for a knee operation! This had been a long-standing problem, which probably started back when Joyce fell on that knee when playing netball, and exacerbated by her falling off her bike after a 26-mile ride in June 2003. Fortunately, after 'keyhole' surgery, it was found that there was no permanent damage and, having 'washed out' the cartilage, the surgeon told Joyce that she was very good for her mileage! I can certainly testify to that!

It wasn't long after Joyce's operation that we went off on our annual Easter trip to Barmouth with Eileen and Mike. Thankfully, Joyce was able to do all the walks with us and even a bit of gentle climbing towards the end of the week, in the shape of the Precipe and Panorama walks. We had only been back home a few days when Michelle rang to say that Calum was being rushed into hospital with suspected appendicitis. It turned out to be an acute case of peritonitis and the little lad was operated on just in time. Joyce and I dashed up on a Thursday morning and spent a couple of days 'looking after' Tom, who was still on a half-term break from school. It was nice to spend some quality time with him. As we left Cosby on the Sunday, it was hoped that Calum would be fit enough to go home the following day.

During the following week we had the pleasure of seeing Sue and Geoff again, over from New Zealand and staying down at Nailsea for the duration of two months. They came up here for a couple of days – then on the following day, Lorraine and Phil came to drop Jake off for a couple of weeks! L & P's plans are to live and work in Chicago for two to three years, probably beginning in June 2005, and this was to be a sort of fact-finding mission to check out the final details. They stopped here overnight before I drove them to Heathrow, and we all enjoyed a meal at the *Madhuban* Indian Restaurant in Liss, along with Helen and Tim, Rebecca and David – this just after Joyce and I had enjoyed a similar evening meal there with Sue and Geoff!

Early in May, I woke up one night with dreadful pain in my back and had to call out the emergency doctor. He diagnosed a kidney stone – which brought back memories of a similar attack some forty years previously! I went to see my own doctor, Dale Egerton, who agreed that this was the problem and arranged for me to have an ultrasound scan. In the waiting period I took some pain-killers, which made me feel ten times worse, so quickly dispensed with them. I had the scan on May 17th and unfortunately it wasn't too clear to the medics what the problem was, so they said I'd cave to have a CT scan as a follow-up. This is the 'Computer Topography' scan that gives a three-dimensional view of your insides, especially good with soft tissue problems. *(About a month after that latest scan, I rang the Surgery and was told that everything appeared to be 'all clear', although I resisted the chance to have an appointment with the doctor – if there **had** been anything untoward, I'm hoping he would have called me!)*

More house news!

As mentioned earlier, we decided on having a new central heating system fitted. This had basically come about because the outside flue on the old (1986) boiler had began to leak, leaving dangerous icy patches outside the front door during the colder weather. We had it checked out and found that, because it was an old asbestos type, any replacement needed to be 'modern' and fulfil the latest building regulations, as well as costing us around £1,000! This led to the decision that it would be more economic to go 'the whole hog' and have a new boiler. Of course it is never that simple! Any new boiler would be of a type that would involve a new water cylinder, new piping, new header tank – it goes on and on. But realising that the 'old' boiler had almost reached the end of its estimated useful life, we decided on a complete replacement. Thus, on June 20th 2005, Mark Redpath arrived to start work - as originally planned some eighteen months previously!

I'm glad to report that since that new boiler installation, we have had piping hot water ever since – with me turning the boiler off well before its timed cessation. Hopefully we are saving money! Mind you, that'll make up for the repairs that were necessary in the kitchen! With the boiler on the floor replaced by a wall-mounted type, that left quite a big hole in the system! However, the 'old' flooring had long given cause for dissatisfaction (done by 'cowboys' after the flooding of early 1997), so it was a pleasure to refit the kitchen with laminated flooring in a tiled pattern. Thanks again go to John Keep, who also boxed in the new water pipes and made a fitted unit to fill 'the hole'. Another 'bonus' was that we over ordered on the flooring, so John is due back on August 25th to fit out the bathroom in the same style.

Sometime during April 2006, a chap rang the doorbell to chat about replacing the old wooden roofing fascia and soft-boards with new white UPVC fittings. I asked him to send a quote and mentioned it to Keith next door. We eventually decided to go ahead and have both houses done at the same time, as the cost was reduced as against having it done individually. June 22nd saw two guys turn up in their 'white van' and start the job. Inevitably, these jobs always lead on to other things, because they

302

reported that the 'slipped' tiles on the front of our house had been caused by rotten battens. By next morning, about a quarter of our roof area had been stripped back to reveal the ugly scene! They also found a couple of wasp nests and a hornet nest, so it was a good chance to clear it all out and try to 'make good', for a few years at least. There's always something!

We were quite pleased with the eventual outcome, which will prevent the necessity of ever having to paint again – not that I've had to do that too often anyway – but anything for an easy life! And on that score, it wasn't long afterwards that I asked the same firm if they could 'clad' the porch in the same white UPVC material. That duly happened so that, by the end of August 2006, the need for painting the porch had been greatly diminished – there's only that old window frame from Joe Price that will need the occasional touch up!

By the early months of 2007, the 'new' fence along the back of the garden was looking rather sad for itself. One of the reasons for this had been the presence of a regular supply of horses in the field behind us, with their constant nibbling at the new shoots of the trees and shrubs. In their nibbling, they also managed to push the fencing about, causing damage and eventual collapse in places. So, here at the moment, late April, we have old mate Kevin back with us, reconstructing the fencing - hopefully as a more permanent fixture!

And now – finally ....

All that appeared in this family history in the previous pages was completed during March 2008. No doubt I shall continue to maintain a 'diary of events', aided by the use of a computer, until the old fingers find it too difficult to type in at the keyboard. Thus, if anyone should wish to see 'what happened next' – they will need access to my old PC. It is not exactly 'steam driven', but pretty damn close! I am indebted to Lorraine and Phil who, as far back as February 1999, brought me down a 'spare computer'. It has been 'updated' a few times in the intervening years, giving me connections first to the Internet and e-mail facilities and, more recently, to 'Broadband'. I also owe a debt of thanks to old pal Ken Anderson, now living out in Spain, who has been greatly involved in the publication of all my books from the technical side of things. The exercise has proved immensely satisfying, not only with this particular effort, but also with my previous books, as mentioned in Chapter 16. As per the title – it has been 'A Happy Life', blessed by family and friends.

Myself, with Joyce and the girls, 1970s

Appendix A
Certificates (or copies) presently in my possession

Registration district: Shifnal, Salop (or Shropshire)
Parish Church: Shifnal
Nov 7 1847: Marriage of John Gripton to Mary Walker *(paternal great great-grandparents)*

Registration district: Shifnal, Counties of Salop and Stafford
Sub-district: Shifnal
Jan 26 1850: Birth of Joseph Gripton *(paternal great-grandfather)*

Registration district: Madeley, County of Salop
Sub-district: Dawley
Sept 30 1857: Birth of Elizabeth Chetter *(paternal great-grandmother)*

Registration district: Ludlow, Counties of Salop and Hereford
Sub-district: Ludlow
November 27 1870: Birth of **Eliza Griffiths** *(maternal great-grandmother)*

Registration district: West Derby & Toxteth Park
Parish Church: Walton-on-the-Hill, County of Lancaster
December 25 1872: Marriage of **James Hodgson** (over 21) to **Ellen Matthews** (20) (paternal great-grandparents)

Registration district: West Derby & Toxteth Park
Sub-district: Walton, County of Lancaster
Dec 3 1874: Birth of **Jane Hodgson** *(paternal grandmother)*

Registration district: Shifnal, Salop
Parish Church: Shifnal
Mar 5 1877: Marriage of Joseph Gripton **(27)** to Elizabeth Chetter *(paternal great-grandparents)*

Registration district: Wellington
Sub-district: Wombridge, County of Shropshire
Dec 16 1880: Birth of Joseph Gripton *(paternal grandfather)*

Registration district: West Derby
Sub-district: Kirkdale, County of Liverpool
Sept 13 1895: Birth of **Annie Hodgson** *(maternal grandmother)*

Registration District: Walton-on-the-Hill (St Mary's, Kirkdale)
Parish Church: Walton-on-the-Hill, County of Lancaster
April 20th 1902: Marriage of **Joseph Gripton** (21) to **Jane Hodgson** (27) *(paternal grandparents)*

Registration district: West Derby
Sub-district: Walton, County of Liverpool
Nov 09 1910: Birth of **Joseph Gripton** *(father)*

Registration district: West Derby
Sub-district: Walton, County of Liverpool
Aug 17 1920: Birth of Ruth Hodgson *(mother)*

Registration district: Liverpool North
Parish Church: Walton-on-the-Hill, County of Lancaster
Nov 11 1939: Marriage of **Joseph Gripton** (29) to **Ruth Hodgson** (19) *(parents)*

Registration district: Liverpool North
Sub-district: Walton Park
Aug 24 1940: Birth of **Peter Douglas Gripton** *(that's me folks!)*

Registration District: Reading
Sub-district: St Mary, County of Reading
February 3rd 1910: Birth of **Arthur Stanley Jones** *(Joyce's father)*

Registration District: Reading
Sub-district: St Giles, County of ReadingOct 24 1911: Birth of **Juliet Elizabeth Lailey** *(Joyce's mother)*

Registration district: Reading, Berks
Parish Church: St Giles, County of Reading
Aug 7 1933: Marriage of **Arthur Stanley Jones** (23) to **Juliet Elizabeth Lailey** (21) *(Joyce's parents)*

Registration district: Reading
Sub-district: St Giles
Jan 16 1945: Birth of Joyce Ann Jones *(my much younger wife!)*

Registration district: County Borough of Reading
Parish Church: St Giles
Aug 25 1962: Marriage of Peter Douglas Gripton **(22)** to Joyce Ann Jones **(17)** *(yes folks, it's all legal!)*

Appendix B
A potted family history since meeting Joyce

1961   Jan 28 – I meet Joyce at 'The Oxford' Ballroom', Reading
Aug 24 - 21st birthday - got engaged to Joyce up in Walton
Nov 05 - A son, Kevin, for June & Wack in Reading

1962   Aug 25 - Married to Joyce, at Saint Giles Church, Reading

1963   Jun 22 - Eileen and Mike married - also at Saint Giles Church, Reading
Jul 31 - Lorraine born in Wokingham hospital, Berks

1964   Jun 15 – 'Granny' Gripton dies up in Crosby, Liverpool
Jun 27 - A daughter, Karen, for June and Wack
Nov 23 - Jan and Roy married out in South Africa

1965   Aug 25 - A daughter, Colette, for Jan and Roy – born in S. Africa
Nov 17 - A son, Mark, to Eileen and Mike

1966   Feb 26 - Michelle born at The Grange, Liss, Hants

1967   Oct 10 - A daughter, Sarah, to Eileen and Mike

1968   Apr 02 - A second daughter, Lisa, to Jan and Roy

1970   Jul 14 - Another daughter, Suzanne, to Eileen and Mike

1971   Mar 28 - Mum Jones dies at home in 17 Queens Cottages, Reading

1972   Jun 17 - Stan and Doris marry at Reading Register Office
Jul 02 - Aunty Betty Gripton dies up in Liverpool

1974   Jul 15 - Dad Jones (Stan) dies at home of a heart attack

1975   Aug 02 - Sheila and Geoff married in Perth, Western Australia
Nov 08 - Sue and Des married in Brixton, at Lambeth Town Hall

1978   Aug 19 - Pam and Steve married at Southport, Lancs.

1979   Feb 15 - 'Nin' Hodgson dies up in Anfield, Liverpool
Jun 02 - Jacquie and Steve married in Germany
Oct 27 - A son, Craig, for Jacquie and Steve

1982   Nov 23 - A son, Thomas, for Sue and Des, born in Miami, Florida

1983	Apr 05 - Jack Whitley dies out in Perth, West Australia
1985	Apr 01 – A daughter, Sian, for Pam and Steve
	Sep 28 - Mum and Bill Walker married at Crosby Town Hall, Liverpool
1986	Jul 12 - Sonia and Kevin married at Tilehurst, Reading
1987	Mar 07 - Lorraine and Steve married at Saint John's Church, Greatham, Hants
	Jun 20 - Colette and Mark married at Radnage, High Wycombe
	Jul 11 - A daughter, Natasha, for Sonia and Kevin
	Aug 25 - Silver Wedding – Joyce and I have been married 25 years today
1988	Jun 22 - Eileen and Mike celebrate their Silver Wedding anniversary
	Dec 14 - Karen and Graham married up in Reading
1989	Jul 22 - Lisa and Martin married at Earley, Reading
	Nov 24 - Jan and Roy's 25th Anniversary
	Nov 27 - A daughter, Lisa, for Russell and Angela
	Dec 08 - Russ and Angela married out in Germany
1990	Feb 17 - Uncle John Hodgson dies in Walton Hospital
	Mar 29 - Uncle Bob Gripton also dies, in Liverpool
	May 29 - A girl, Rebecca, for Karen and Graham
	Aug 28 - Another girl, Abigail, for Sonia and Kevin
1991	Jun 08 - Another girl, Lucy, for Karen and Graham
	Aug 17 - Corinna and Mark married up in Reading
	Sep 06 – A son, Owen, for Colette and Mark
1992	Jul 11 - Sarah and Stephen married at Barkham, near Arborfield, Berks
	Sep 12 - Sue and Geoff married, over in New Zealand
	Oct 22 – A son, Thomas James, for Michelle and James
1993	Mar 20 - Michelle and James married up in Leicester
1994	Aug 02 - Another daughter, Imogen, for Colette and Mark
	Aug 20 - A daughter, Daisy, for Sarah and Stephen
	Oct 29 - Suzie and Nick married in Reading
	Nov 12 - Another girl, Kate, for Pam and Steve, out in Perth, WA
	Nov 15 - A son, Jacob, for Karen and Graham, in Reading
1995	Jan 16 - Joyce's 50th birthday
	Mar 06 - Aunty Dorothy Gripton dies, up on the Wirral
	Mar 24 - Another son, Calum Joseph, for Michelle and James
1996	Feb 22 - A second daughter, Brogan, for Sarah and Stephen
	Mar 13 - A daughter, Erin, for Corinna and Mark
	Apr 30 - A son, Samuel, for Susie and Nick

1997	Mar 26 - A son, Joshua, for Sarah and Stephen
1998	Jun 21 - Uncle John Gripton dies over on the Wirral, Cheshire
	Aug 20 - Another daughter, Neve, for Corinna and Mark
	Sep 09 - And now a daughter, Amber, to Susie and Nick
2000	Jan 20 - Dad Gripton passes away up in Liverpool
	Nov 04 - Another daughter, Fern, for Sue and Nick
2002	Dec 04 - Bill Walker dies out in Perth, WA
2004	Apr 06 - 'Our Sue' hits the big five-zero
	Jun 12 - Kevin's ex-wife Sonia dies, leaving two daughters behind
2005	Feb 22 – Lorraine and Phil married – on the beach in St Lucia
	Apr 25 – A son, Matthew, for Emma and Kevin, born in Guildford
	Aug 24 – Hit my 65th birthday – now an official OAP
2006	Aug 10 – A daughter, Amye, to Emma and Kevin
2007	Oct 20 – Sarah and Andy married, down at Lynton, N Devon
2008	Feb 11 – Another son, Rowan, for Emma and Kevin

Lightning Source UK Ltd.
Milton Keynes UK
UKOW02f0851160214

226534UK00008B/284/P